LSD, Marihuana, Yoga, and Hypnosis

Modern Applications of Psychology

under the editorship of

Joseph D. Matarazzo

UNIVERSITY OF OREGON MEDICAL SCHOOL

LSD, MARIHUANA, YOGA, AND HYPNOSIS

THEODORE XENOPHON BARBER

Medfield State Hospital, Harding, Massachusetts

ALDINE PUBLISHING COMPANY

Chicago

First published 1970 by
Aldine Publishing Company
529 South Wabash Avenue
Chicago, Illinois 60605

Library of Congress Catalog Card Number 73-115935
SBN 202-25004-1
Printed in the United States of America

To Catherine, Ted, Rania, and Elaine

This book is concerned with the psychological and physiological effects of yoga, hypnosis, major psychedelic drugs (LSD, mescaline, and psilocybin), and minor psychedelic drugs (marihuana, hashish, and other cannabis derivatives). These conditions have the following in common:

It is generally believed that psychedelic drugs, yoga, and hypnosis give rise to altered states of awareness or consciousness.

Psychedelics, yoga, and hypnosis are said to tap unused potentialities of man.

Psychedelics, yoga, and hypnosis have traditionally been viewed as part of abnormal psychology and as discontinuous from other known psychological phenomena.

Each of these conditions has aroused controversy and emotionalism.

Although yoga, hypnosis, and some psychedelic drugs such as peyote and cannabis have been known for many years, research on these topics is rather recent. In fact, practically all of the rigorous research in these areas has been carried out by individuals alive today.

The recent research shows that many common beliefs concerning psychedelics, yoga, and hypnosis are simply untrue.

This text presents a new approach to psychedelics, yoga, and hypnosis. It differs from most previous books in these areas in that it treats each topic as continuous with other known psychological phenomena and as a part of social psychology. The text also differs from most previous treatises in that it does not assume that psychedelics, yoga, and hypnosis can bring out unused mental or physical capacities in man, or can heighten awareness or give rise to enhanced creativity, or can produce altered states of consciousness, suspension of conventional reality-orientation, changes in body-image, or changes in perception.

These and other long-held assumptions are critically analyzed; they will be accepted if, and only if, they are clearly supported by empirical data.

In addition to questioning traditional assumptions, the hard-headed approach employed in the text involves the following:

The focus of the book is *not* on the subjects' unobservable internal states. The question at the forefront is *not* how to define the state of awareness or consciousness of the psychedelic subject, the yogi, or the hypnotic subject. Hypothetical constructs which refer to unobservable internal states — such as altered state of consciousness, samadhi, or hypnotic state — will be held in abeyance while we focus on observable phenomena. The question to be asked first is, What overt behaviors and verbal reports are clearly observable when psychedelic drug is taken, yoga is practiced, or hypnotic-induction procedures are administered? Instead of treating the phenomena traditionally associated with psychedelic drugs, yoga, or hypnosis as undifferentiated conglomerates, an attempt will be made to differentiate and treat separately each of the many phenomena associated with each of these areas of inquiry.

After specifying the observable overt behaviors and verbal reports that need to be explained, we will delineate observable antecedent variables that are present in psychedelic, yogic, or hypnotic situations and that might be functionally related to the observable behaviors.

Scientific research will be reviewed to determine which of the many antecedent variables present in these situations are important or necessary, and which are irrelevant, in producing the overt behaviors and verbal reports that are to be explained. From the available empirical data, an attempt will be made to assign *relative weights* to each of the major classes of antecedent variables that play a role in producing each of the behavioral phenomena.

Theory construction is viewed as follows: Satisfactory explanations of these complex areas of psychology will come about most proficiently, not by prematurely postulating general principles or broad-scope theories, but by clearly specifying each of the behaviors associated with psychedelic drugs, yoga, and hypnosis, analyzing empirically the validity of each supposed behavioral phenomenon, and patiently isolating empirically denotable antecedent variables that are instrumental in producing each validated phenomenon. If and when empirical research demonstrates that the consequent phenomena in each of these areas are functionally related to specifiable antecedent variables, we should be able to formulate general principles that can explain the antecedent-consequent relations. An integration of the general principles will, in turn, constitute an empirically-based theory in the area of inquiry.

It should be emphasized that the book is tied together by the common methodology and manner of analyzing complex phenomena which is found in each chapter. Each chapter questions long-held assumptions, critically analyzes the phenomena associated with the topic, holds in abeyance hypothetical constructs that have been traditionally used in theories of the phenomena, and analyzes the complex antecedent variables that may be causally related to the complex effects.

The major aim in writing this book is not simply to demonstrate the importance of psychedelics, yoga, and hypnosis, or simply to present substantive material pertaining to these topics. The main purpose of the book is to illustrate a way of thinking and a method of analysis toward so-called soft areas of psychology. If, after studying the text, the reader is able to think a little more critically and to accept fewer assumptions when he attempts to understand *other* psychological phenomena, this aim will have been accomplished.

The book is subdivided into two parts. Part A, concerned with psychedelic drugs and cannabis derivatives, includes Chapters I and II. Chapter I delineates 13 sets of phenomena (overt behaviors, verbal reports, and physiological changes) associated with LSD, mescaline, psilocybin, and other psychedelic drugs and attempts to relate these consequent phenomena to antecedent variables that are present in the drug situation. Chapter II approaches marihuana, hashish, and other cannabis derivatives in the same way and, in addition, critically analyzes a series of long-accepted notions pertaining to these drugs. Part B, which discusses yoga and various hypnotic phenomena and presents a theory of hypnotism, includes Chapters III-VII. Chapter III (written in collaboration with former yogi Abdulhusein S. Dalal) shows that many popular concepts concerning yoga and yogic feats are fallacious. Chapter IV critically evaluates the contention that suggestions given under hypnosis can produce sensory alterations (e.g., color-blindness, deafness, hallucinations), can affect cutaneous functions (e.g., produce blisters, remove warts, mitigate ichthyosis), or can produce a wide variety of other physiological effects. Chapter V critically reviews the empirical data pertaining to the effects of hypnosis on pain, and Chapter VI is concerned with the contention that hypnotic age-regression reinstates behaviors characteristic of childhood. Chapter VII functionally relates hypnotic behaviors to antecedent variables (procedural, subject, and experimenter variables) present in hypnotic situations and attempts to unify the empirically-determined antecedent-consequent relations under a parsimonious theoretical framework.

T.X.B.

Contents

Psychedelic Drugs and Cannabis Derivatives

CHAPTER I

LSD, Mescaline, Psilocybin, and other Psychedelic Drugs

CONTENTS

3

LSD, Mescaline, Psilocybin, and other Psychedelic Drugs

From 1943 to 1963 d-lysergic acid diethylamide (LSD) was dispensed primarily by physicians and scientists in clinical and experimental settings. During this period professional journals published more than 2000 studies concerning the pharmacological, psychological, and therapeutic effects of the drug. Around 1963 three interrelated events occured: the drug entered the black-market; more and more laymen began to use it illicitly in settings which were not supervised by professionals; and reports began to accumulate that the drug was producing psychotic-like reactions and chromosomal damage. These recent events, widely publicized in newspapers and magazines, have led to emotionalism and confusion concerning the effects of LSD. The confusion appears to be widespread among laymen; it is also present to a degree among psychologists and physicians who are often called upon to present the facts concerning the drug to non-professional audiences.

The general types of phenomena associated with LSD will be specified in this chapter. Also, antecedent variables that are functionally related to the phenomena will be delineated. By specifying the antecedent variables, the consequent events, and the antecedent-consequent relations as objectively and dispassionately as possible, it is hoped that this chapter will be useful for behavioral scientists, especially when they are asked to discuss the drug with laymen, will help to mitigate the sensationalism and emotionally-tinged confusion that is now prevalent, and will help to prepare the ground for further research and for a general theory of psychedelic, psychotomimetic, or hallucinogenic drug effects.

5

Similarity of Action of LSD, Mescaline, Psilocybin, and Other Drugs

The effects of LSD are qualitatively similar to those produced by peyote or mescaline and by psilocybin (Hollister & Hartman, 1962; Unger, 1963). It also appears that several other drugs, such as dimethyltrypta- mine, give rise to comparable consequences. Before turning our atten- tion to LSD, let us briefly discuss the drugs which appear to exert similar effects.

PEYOTE, MESCALINE, AND PSILOCYBIN

Peyote is obtained from button-shaped growths on a cactus (Peyotl) that thrives in Southern Texas and Northern Mexico. In pre-Columbian times, the Aztecs and other Indians in Mexico ate the plant ceremo- nially. After 1870, the peyote cult spread to the United States, partic- ularly to the Plains, where nearly all Indian tribes began to use it (LaBarre, 1964). Toward the end of the nineteenth century, in- vestigators such as Weir Mitchell (1896) and Havelock Ellis (1898) wrote enthusiastically about the use of peyote to study mental function- ing and visual perception. In 1896 the active alkaloid—mescaline—was isolated from peyote, and in 1918 it was recognized that the molecular structure of mescaline (3, 4, 5-trimethoxy phenyl ethylamine) was re- lated to the structure of epinephrine.

Although a few investigators (Beringer, 1927; Fernberger, 1923; Klu- ver, 1928; Lewin, 1931) studied the psychological effects of mescaline during the 1920's, work in this area tended to subside during the 1930s and did not have an especially important impact in psychology or psy- chiatry. In fact, the early work with mescaline might have been forgotten if a new drug—LSD—had not been synthesized. However, after Hoffmann synthesized LSD in 1943 and after it was discovered that very small quantities of LSD produced effects very similar to those of mescaline, the interest of scientific investigators in psychotomimetic drugs such as mescaline and LSD increased dramatically. Also, more recently, it has been shown thay psilocybin (4-hydro-xy- N-dimethyltryptamine orthophosphate), which Hoffman isolated from the mushroom *Psilocybe mexicana,* produces effects that are similar to those of LSD and mescaline.

Subjects generally report that the subjective effects of LSD, mesca- line, and psilocybin are not only very similar but are practically in- distinguishable (Abramson, 1960; Isbell, 1959; Wolbach, Miner & Is- bell, 1962). Furthermore, subjects who become tolerant to one of these drugs (who require larger and larger doses to experience the characteristic drug effects) also become tolerant to the others (Balestrieri & Fontanari, 1959; Isbell, Wolbach, Wikler, & Miner, 1961). Although LSD, mescaline, and psilocybin appear to produce similar effects, there are a few differences in their modes of action. For instance, at apparently equivalent doses, LSD and mescaline exert noticeable somatic and psychological effects over a period of 8 to 12 hours whereas the action of psilocybin lasts only 3 to 4 hours. However, the important point that requires emphasis is that the similarities in the effects of LSD, mescaline, and psilocybin far outweigh the differences.

DET, DMT, DOM, AND OTHER COMPOUNDS

There is evidence to indicate that dimethyltryptamine (DMT) and diethyltryptamine (DET) produce short-lasting effects which resemble those of LSD (Rosenberg, Isbell, Miner, & Logan, 1964; Szara, Rockland, Rosenthal, & Handlon, 1966). It also appears that another compound—2, 5-dimethoxy-4-methyl-amphetamine (DOM)—at doses greater than 5 milligrams, produces effects (lasting about 8 hours) which resemble those produced by LSD, mescaline, or psilocybin (Hollister, Macnicol, & Gillespie, 1969; Snyder, Faillace, & Hollister, 1967; Snyder, Faillace, & Weingartner, 1968).[1]

Many other drugs that may have LSD-type effects have been reviewed by Farnsworth (1968), Hoffer and Osmond (1967), Hollister (1968), and Schultes (1969). These include, for example, ololiuqui (found in morning-glory seeds) and new drugs labeled as Ditran (*N*-ethyl-3-piperidyl cyclopentylphenyl glycolate) and Sernyl (l-[1-phenylcyclohexyl] piperidine monohydrochloride). However, it is not clear at present whether the latter set of drugs should be classified with the LSD-type drugs or should be placed in a separate class. For instance, although ololiuqui contains d-lysergic acid amide (LAD) and other alkaloids, it has not yet been determined unequivocally whether its effects are similar to those of LSD, mescaline, and psilocybin or whether it merely gives rise to drowsiness, fatigue, or apathy (Isbell & Gorodetzky, 1966).

Although similar effects are produced at appropriate dose levels by LSD, mescaline, psilocybin, DET, DMT, and other drugs, in this chapter the emphasis will be on LSD. I do not focus on LSD because it is more interesting or more important than the other drugs, but because there is a mass of research on this drug and very little on the others. By

---

1. It appears that DOM is the compound that has been recently labeled as STP by drug users. Other drugs that have been called STP by drug users appear to include Ditran, and a combination drug that includes LSD, DMT, psilocybin, and peyote (Ungerleider, 1968).

integrating the research on LSD we may be able to attain a general perspective that will be useful in understanding not only LSD but also many other drugs that produce similar effects.

Overview of Variables

It is my own opinion (Barber, 1969) that a useful integration of complex data in any area of psychology can be attained by proceeding as follows:

Delineate as precisely as possible both the phenomena associated with the area of inquiry and the antecedent variables that might be related to the phenomena.

Empirically relate the phenomena (consequent variables) to the antecedent variables. These functional relations between antecedent-consequent variables constitute the facts of the area of investigation.

Subsume the antecedent-consequent relations under general principles. Integrated sets of such general principles, which relate previously-established antecedent-consequent relations and which predict new, or not yet verified, relations, constitute the useful theories of psychology.

In order to integrate the available complex data concerning LSD and similarly-acting drugs, I will first specify the antecedent variables present in the drug situation which might play a role in eliciting the effects, and then attempt to delineate functional relations between each of the antecedent variables and each of the consequent effects. Also, I will begin to relate these antecedent-consequent relations under more general principles and thus begin to formulate a theory in this area of inquiry.

Let us first briefly summarize the antecedent variables and then the dependent variables or consequent effects.

OVERVIEW OF ANTECEDENT VARIABLES

LSD and other LSD-type drugs (e.g., mescaline or psilocybin) are always taken at a specific dose by a specific individual in a specific situation; consequently we can hypothesize that the effects that follow ingestion of these drugs will vary with the dose, with factors inherent in the person who takes them, and with factors imbedded in the situation. The phenomena or effects present in LSD-situations could thus vary with several sets of antecedent variables (Table 1, column 1) including the drug-dose, the situation, the subject's set, and the subject's personality characteristics. Each of these antecedent variables will be discussed in detail shortly.

OVERVIEW OF DEPENDENT VARIABLES
(CONSEQUENT EFFECTS)

Table 1, column 2, lists some of the major phenomena that are often observed after subjects have taken LSD or other similarly-acting drugs such as mescaline or psilocybin. These dependent variables, or consequent effects, include the following: a series of somatic-sympathetic effects; changes in "body-image"; a dreamy-detached feeling; reduced performance on intellectual and motor tasks; alterations in the way time

Table 1. Antecedent and Consequent Variables Associated with LSD-Type Situations

Antecedent Variables	*Dependent Variables (Consequent Effects)*	*Other Possible Consequent Effects*
A. *Drug* — chemical structure and dose	1. *Somatic-sympathetic effects* — e.g., pupillary dilation, physical weakness, dizziness	10. *Effects on chromosomes*
B. *Situation* — where the drug is administered, the way *S* is treated by *E* and by others, the emotional atmosphere, whether *S* is alone or in a group	2. *Changes in body-image* — e.g., body or limbs feel as if they have changed in size, shape, weight, or relative proportions	11. *Effects on embryo or fetus*
C. *Set* — *S*'s attitudes, expectancies. and motivations	3. *Dreamy-detached feelings*	12. *Effects on creativity*
D. *S's personality characteristics*	4. *Reduced intellectual-motor proficiency*	13. *Therapeutic effects*
	5. *Changes in time perception*	
	6. *Changes in visual perception*, e.g., enhancement of colors, distortions in appearance of objects, apparent undulations of objects	
	7. *Changes in audition, olfaction, gustation, and synesthesia*	
	8. *Heightened responsiveness to primary suggestions*	
	9. *Changes in moods and emotions* — varying from euphoria and ecstasy to dysphoria and psychotic-like reactions	

is experienced; changes in visual perception; changes in hearing, smell, or taste and synesthesia; enhancement of responsiveness to primary suggestions; and changes in moods and emotions. Several other effects, which have been attributed to LSD, are more controversial than the nine that have just been listed. These more debatable effects (Table 1, column 3) include damage to chromosomes, damage to the embryo or fetus, enhancement of creativity, and therapeutic effects.

Each of the 13 sets of effects or dependent variables will be discussed in detail later in this chapter. First, let us look closely at the antecedent variables involved in the LSD situation.

Antecedent Variables

Table 1, column 1, lists four sets of antecedent variables that are present in LSD situations. These antecedent variables are as follows: the drug (a specific chemical compound that is administered at a specific dose); the situation in which the drug is administered; the subject's set (his attitudes, expectancies, and motivations) with respect to the drug situation; and the subject's unique personality characteristics. Each of these four sets of antecedent variables will now be discussed in turn.

THE DRUG

The drug per se—the specific chemical molecule that is labeled LSD, mescaline, psilocybin, etc.—is probably the most important factor, but not the only relevant factor, in producing the phenomena listed in Table 1, column 2. This section briefly summarizes the chemistry of these drugs and discusses the important factor of drug-dose. In addition, this section reviews data pertaining to the relationship between observed effects and the presence of the drug in the body, and the attainment of tolerance for the drug.

Chemistry. Mescaline belongs to the large group of chemicals known as biogenic amines, many of which (e.g., epinephrine and norepinephrine) play important roles in the human body. LSD is a colorless, odorless, water-soluble, semisynthetic compound obtained by condensation of d-lysergic acid with diethylamine. An important component of its chemical structure is an indole ring— . The indole ring is also found in psilocybin, dimethyltryptamine (DMT), and diethyltryptamine (DET).

The complex chemistry and pharmacology of these compounds has been reviewed in detail by Metzner (1963). With respect to the chemistry of these compounds, three important considerations merit emphasis:

The indole ring is also found in serotonin (5-hydroxytryptamine), a chemical which appears to play an important role in the chemistry of the central nervous system, possibly as a transmitter of nerve impulses. It has been hypothesized that the psychological action of LSD is due to its serotonin antagonism (Wooley & Shaw, 1954). Although this hypothesis has not been confirmed (Cerletti & Rothlin, 1955), recent studies suggest that LSD may be linked with serotonin in complex ways that remain to be delineated (Aghajanian, Foote, & Sheard, 1968; Andén, Corrodi, Fuxe, & Hökfelt, 1968; Rosecrans, Lovell, & Freedman, 1967).

Small changes in the stereochemical configuration of LSD produce drastic changes in its psychological effects (Giarman, 1967; Rothlin, 1957). For instance, although *d*-lysergic acid diethylamide produces marked psychological effects, its mirror-image compound, *l*-lysergic acid diethylamide, is without any psychological action whatsoever.

The effects produced by these compounds appear to be closely related to their electron-donating activity. Snyder and Merrill (1965) showed that LSD, mescaline, psilocybin, and DMT are electron donators whereas structurally similar analogues, that do not exert noticeable psychological effects, have very little electron donating activity.

Dose. LSD is effective in very small quantities. One hundred to 350 micrograms of the drug (one microgram is a millionth part of a gram) generally elicit a wide range of psychological phenomena.[2] To produce comparable effects, psilocybin is given at much larger doses, around 30,000 micrograms, and mescaline is administered at still larger doses, around 350,000 to 500,000 micrograms.[3]

Three important points need to be underscored concerning the dose of the drugs:

A dose-response relation can be demonstrated when subjects are considered *individually.* The same person will tend to report more effects and more intense effects with increasingly higher doses of LSD (Abramson, Kornetsky, Jarvik, Kaufman, & Ferguson, 1955b; Isbell, Belleville, Fraser, Wikler, & Logan, 1956; Klee, Bertino, & Weintraub, 1961).

A dose-response relationship is very difficult to demonstrate when subjects are considered together *in a group* (Klee et al., 1961). Subjects

2. We shall henceforth refer to 100-350 micrograms of LSD as an average or moderate dose of the drug. Also, we shall at times refer to the dose of LSD in terms of micrograms per kilogram of body weight. Since a kilogram is equal to approximately 2.2 pounds, a subject weighing 165 pounds who receives 1 microgram per kilogram is receiving 75 micrograms of the drug.

3. These average doses apply only when the drug is taken orally. When the spinal route is used, only about 1/10th the oral dose is required and the effects begin almost immediately (S. Cohen, 1967b, p. 35).

differ in response to the same dose; also, two subjects may report similar effects even though one receives a high dose and the other a low dose. Different responses to the same dose may be due to differences among subjects in ability to detoxify and excrete the drug and/or to interindividual differences in personality characteristics or in attitudes and expectancies toward the situation.

At very high doses of the drug (e.g., 1000 or more micrograms of LSD), subjects tend to become confused and disoriented (Freedman, 1968; Reynolds & Peterson, 1966). However, the disorientation produced by very high doses is not unique to LSD-type drugs; many drugs will produce confusion and disorientation if taken at high doses (S. Cohen, 1967b, p. 11).

The three points listed above were empirically documented in an important experiment by Klee et al. (1961) in which 12 subjects were given LSD in three sessions at doses of 1, 2, and 4 micrograms per kilogram of body weight and then were given LSD again in three additional sessions at doses of 4, 8, and 16 micrograms per kilogram. A latin-square design was used to counterbalance the doses in each of the three sessions. The experiment was double-blind in that neither the three medical observers nor the subjects knew which dose of LSD was being used. Although there was little agreement among the medical observers as to which of the subjects (seen in groups) had received the smaller or higher doses, there was perfect agreement for the dose received by any one subject over three sessions; that is, the observers were able to tell when any one subject had received 1, 2, or 4 micrograms per kilogram of LSD in the first three sessions or 4, 8, or 16 micrograms per kilogram in the last three sessions. For any one subject, the visual effects, some of the somatic-sympathetic effects, and intellectual impairment and confusion clearly increased with increasingly higher doses of LSD.

Although most of the phenomena listed in Table 1, column 2, are more obvious in individual subjects with higher doses, there are some exceptions. For instance, it appears that some of the somatic-sympathetic effects (e.g., trembling, sweating, and tachycardia) and some of the mood-emotional changes (e.g., euphoria or dysphoria and psychedelic experiences) are not significantly correlated with the drug dose (Abramson, Jarvik, Kaufman, Kornetsky, Levine, & Wagner, 1955a; Hoffer & Osmond, 1967, pp. 103-104). The failure to find a dose-response relationship here indirectly supports the hypothesis that some of the somatic-sympathetic effects and mood-emotional changes may be functionally related to extra-drug variables such as the situation, and the subject's set and personality.

Relation of effects to presence of LSD in the body. Until just a few years ago, investigators agreed that LSD rapidly disappeared from the body and that its effects were due to secondary biochemical events which it triggered. This consensus was based on experiments that showed a very short half-life of LSD in mouse blood and brain. In a more recent study (Aghajanian & Bing, 1964), LSD (2 micrograms per kilogram) was administered intravenously to 5 human subjects and its concentration in the plasma was determined serially over 8 hours. The drug disappeared slowly from the plasma, was still present in small amounts at 8 hours, and was present in the plasma in relatively large quantities during the period of peak effects. Also, there was a significant correlation between the rate of disappearance of LSD and the recovery of normal performance on an arithmetic test. Since the presence of the drug in the blood is probably closely related to its presence in the brain, it appears highly unlikely that, in the human, LSD triggers a reaction that outlasts its stay in the central nervous system.

Development of tolerance and cross-tolerance. In general, there is rapid development of tolerance for LSD; that is, after three or more days of repeated use, the previously effective dose no longer produces the same intensity of responses (Abramson, Jarvik, Gorin & Hirsch, 1956). Furthermore, after a week or more of daily use, administration of as much as four times the standard dose fails to restore the original intensity of the reactions (Isbell et al., 1956; Isbell, Rosenberg, Miner, & Logan, 1964). However, on discontinuation of LSD for a few days, tolerance is lost rapidly (Isbell et al., 1964). Although tolerance to LSD appears to develop rather quickly in man, Freedman, Appel, Hartman, and Molliver (1964) presented data indicating that there may be differences among species and that the patterns of tolerance may depend upon the interaction of several variables including the specific responses measured, the quantity of the drug administered, and the schedule of dosage.

When repeated administration of LSD has produced tolerance for most of the effects of the drug, the subjects are also tolerant to most of the effects of mescaline and psilocybin (Balestrieri & Fontanari, 1959; Isbell et al., 1961). This important *cross-tolerance* phenomenon suggests that these three drugs either impinge upon common metabolic processes, affect the same areas in the brain, or involve a chain of reactions that converge upon a final common pathway.[4]

4. The relatively rapid tolerance that develops for these drugs does not mean that they are addictive. At the present time there is no evidence that these drugs lead to addiction which, in addition to tolerance, involves a physiological dependence and a withdrawal illness when the drug is discontinued.

SITUATION

There appears to be a consensus among workers in this area that situational variables play an important role in determining the nature and magnitude of the effects associated with LSD-type drugs. The following are considered situational variables: the role that the experimenter or therapist assumes, including what he expects the drug reactions to be, what explicit or implicit suggestions he gives, and what types of responses he reinforces; whether the subject receives the drug in a clinical or experimental setting; whether the drug is administered to a group of individuals or to one subject alone; and what types of activities are required of the subject after he has taken the drug. It is rather surprising that very few experiments have been designed to assess the effects of these situational variables. In fact, there appear to be only two experiments that explicitly manipulated situational variables. The situational antecedent variable that was manipulated in both studies was *direct, explicit suggestions from the experimenter*. Let us briefly describe these studies.

In a double-blind experiment, Levis and Mehlman (1964) gave moderate doses of mescaline (about 350,000 micrograms) to 15 subjects and placebos to another 15 subjects. The subjects were divided into three groups, each group containing 5 mescaline and 5 placebo subjects. One of the three groups was not given suggestions as to what to expect. The other two groups received a list of written statements suggesting many of the effects of the drug. The suggestions given to one of these two groups were the reverse of those given to the other. For instance, subjects in one group were told that they would feel depressed but would not experience visual illusions, whereas subjects in the other group were told that they would not feel depressed but would experience visual illusions. In general, the suggestions did *not* exert a significant effect on the subjects' reports of their experiences. Regardless of the suggestions, subjects receiving mescaline, but not those receiving the placebo, reported visual illusions, visual hallucinations (with eyes closed), feelings of depression and uneasiness, and other effects. The suggestions significantly influenced only one of the dependent variables listed in Table 1, column 2, namely, changes in moods and emotions. Although subjects receiving mescaline reported more feelings of depression as compared to those receiving a placebo, mescaline subjects who received the suggestion that they would feel depressed reported this mood more often than mescaline subjects not receiving the suggestion. In brief, the study indicated that explicit suggestions can influence the subjects' mood (feelings of depression) during the drug session but the other effects of the drug are not so easily influenced by explicit suggestions.

Fogel and Hoffer (1962) studied the effects of hypnotic suggestions on the reaction to LSD. Only one subject was used in the investigation. The subject received 100 micrograms of LSD and reported visual effects, for instance, she stated that the face of one of the experiments seemed changed. At this point, she was hypnotized and given the suggestion that on opening her eyes everything would be normal. On awakening, the subject stated that, although the experimenter's face still appeared somewhat distorted, it now looked more normal than it did previously. However, the subject also stated that she still felt sensitive to touch. In addition, her pupils remained widely dilated. Although Fogel and Hoffer concluded that the hypnotic suggestions to be normal were effective in making the subject appear to be nearly normal, the results can also be interpreted as indicating that the reactions to LSD were affected only to a small degree by the hypnotic suggestions.

The studies described above appear to indicate that explicit suggestions from the experimenter may *not* play as potent a role in influencing the drug effects as has at times been assumed. There is also indirect evidence to indicate that many, if not most, of the LSD effects are elicited when explicit and implicit suggestions are minimized, for instance, when subjects do not know that they have received LSD. For example, Johnson (1968) administered 500 or more micrograms of LSD to one group of alcoholics and a combination of sodium amytal with methamphetamine (methedrine) to another group. The patients did not know that they were receiving LSD. Subjects receiving LSD (but not those receiving sodium amytal and methamphetamine) showed many, if not all, of the typical LSD effects; LSD produced significantly greater difficulty in thinking, gross disturbances in time sense, feelings of loss of control, changes in the meaning of self and environment, body-image changes, emotional disorganization, and visual perceptual distortions. Along similar lines, Milman (1967) presented a case of accidental LSD ingestion in a 5-year-old girl. Although the child was not aware that she had ingested a drug, she showed perceptual distortions, changes in moods and emotions, and impaired intellectual-motor proficiency.

The study by Levis and Mehlman, summarized above, indicated that a situational variable (explicit suggestions from the experimenter) can affect one of the consequent variables listed in Table 1, column 2 (changes in moods and emotions). Other studies also indicate that situational variables can influence the subjects' moods and emotions during the drug session. The available data suggest that: if experimenters are friendly and relaxed, subjects show little anxiety; if experimenters adopt an impersonal, hostile, or investigative attitude toward the drugged subjects, the subjects tend to manifest anxiety, hostility, or paranoid-like responses (Unger, 1963); LSD subjects tend to have a more positive experience (more feelings of love and elation) when a therapist is present during the session (Johnson, 1968); and subjects tend to be more anxious and depressed when the drug is given to them in individual sessions rather than together in a group (Slater, Morimoto, & Hyde, 1957).

In summary, the data indicate that one of the effects associated with LSD — changes in moods and emotions — can be influenced by situational variables such as suggestions from the experimenter, the attitudes of the experimenter, and whether the drug is given to subjects in a group or individually. Although various situational variables seem to influence the LSD subjects' moods and emotions, it has not as yet been demonstrated that situational variables significantly influence the other dependent variables listed in Table 1, column 2, such as the somatic-sympathetic effects, the body-image changes, the dreamy-detached feelings, or the visual perceptual effects.

SET

There appears to be a consensus among workers in this area that the effects observed during the drug session are also markedly influenced by several variables that are commonly subsumed under the term set. These set variables include, for example, the subjects' attitudes, expectancies, and motivations toward the drug situation. The available data indicate that the subject's set influences one of the dependent variables listed in Table 1, column 2, namely, changes in his moods and emotions, and may also exert a weaker influence on the other dependent variables.

Metzner, Litwin, and Weil (1965) presented data indicating that the subject's pre-experimental set plays a role in determining his moods and emotions during the drug session. They asked 82 subjects, prior to receiving 25,000 to 30,000 micrograms of psilocybin, "How apprehensive are you about taking the drug?" and "How good do you feel about taking the drug today?" Pre-experimental apprehension was significantly correlated with anxious mood during the session and with some of the somatic-sympathetic effects such as headache or nausea ($rs = .23$ to $.33$). Also, small but significant correlations around .30 were obtained between the subject's pre-experimental statement that he felt good about taking the drug and pleasant mood and feelings of empathy during the drug session.

A study by Abramson et al. (1955a) indicates that the nature and magnitude of the effects elicited by a relatively small dose of LSD are functionally related to subject's pre-experimental expectations. In this study, each subject received, in random order, a placebo, a small dose of LSD (25-75 micrograms), or a somewhat higher dose (around 100 micrograms). All subjects completed a questionnaire pertaining to the changes they experienced in somatic, visual, and cognitive functions. The number of responses checked by the subjects under the placebo condition was significantly correlated with the number checked under the small dose of LSD ($r = .66$) and also under the somewhat higher dose ($r = .60$). One cogent interpretation of these correlations is that at least one-third of the variance in response to a relatively small dose of LSD (25-100 micrograms) is independent of the drug per se and is related to factors which determine response to a placebo, such as subjects' expectancies as to what effects are likely to occur. It appears probable, however, that when higher doses of LSD are administered, the subjects' set accounts for a smaller proportion of the variance.

Subjects' motivations for taking the drug also appear to play a role in determining the types of moods and emotions that are elicited during the drug session. Motivations for taking the drug vary widely. A large proportion of American Indians ingest peyote at specified times in religious settings with the avowed purpose of attaining spiritual goals. Some American intellectuals have taken LSD with a similar aim, namely, to heighten inner experiences, to develop hidden personal resources, or to attain esthetic or religious-mystical experiences (Blum, 1964, p. 6). Other individuals have ingested the drug with friends, as part of an interesting and somewhat unusual social evening. More recently, some young Americans have taken LSD for kicks, or to confront an experience that has been advertised as somewhat dangerous and yet important, or to validate their membership in a subculture which espouses an ideology that values the drug experience (Welpton, 1968). It seems that these different motivations lead to somewhat different experiences during the drug session. Apparently, individuals who take LSD in an experimental setting manifest less euphoria than those who take the drug in a non-experimental social setting, and individuals who use LSD with the hope of attaining esthetic experiences or of developing hidden personal resources report the greatest number of religious-type experiences (Blum, 1964).

Although situational and set variables appear to play an important role in determining the subject's moods and emotions during the drug session, let us not make a mistake by overemphasizing the role of these variables in determining the other effects associated with LSD-type drugs such as alterations in visual perception. A recent important study by Ditman, Moss, Forgy, Zunin, Lynch, and Funk (1969) indicates that, *when the situation and subjects, set are held constant,* LSD-type drugs *but not other types of drugs* produce changes in visual perception, changes in body-image, and other effects listed in Table 1, column 2. In this study, one of the following 3 drugs were given in random order and under double-blind conditions to 99 alcoholics: 75 milligrams of methylphenidate (Ritalin) which is usually considered to be a mild stimulant; 75 milligrams of a tranquilizing drug—chlordiazepoxide (Librium); or 200 micrograms of LSD. All subjects were told that they were receiving LSD and were treated as if they had received LSD. The question at issue was, Would an intravenous injection of a substance *thought to be LSD* produce an LSD reaction, when "set and setting" remained identical for all subjects—even though the drug was not the expected LSD but either methylphenidate or chlordiazepoxide? On the day following the drug session, all subjects were given 156 items to sort which pertained to their drug experiences. LSD far outranked the other two drugs in eliciting visual distortions (e.g., "walls and floors moved and flowed," "colors seemed brighter"), visual illusions or hallucinations (e.g., "solid objects changed their shapes and even disappeared"), changes in "body-image" (e.g., "one side of my body felt different from the other"), other sensory and perceptual alterations (e.g., "music affected my mood much more intensely than usual"), and mystical or religious feelings ("I felt in contact with wonderful, unknown forces in the Universe").

PERSONALITY

Whether or not a subject becomes suspicious, hostile, and paranoid during the drug session appears to be functionally related to his pre-drug personality. In a study by Linton and Langs (1964), 30 subjects ingested 100 micrograms of LSD after they had completed a battery of personality instruments such as the Rorschach, Thematic Apperception Test (TAT), Minnesota Multiphasic Personality Inventory (MMPI), clinical interviews, and autobiographies. Individuals who were judged as guarded and overdefended on the basis of the personality measures showed the greatest number of somatic-sympathetic effects and the greatest degree of anxiety during the LSD session. Also, when pre-existing paranoid-like tendencies were detectable from the personality battery, these tendencies were expressed openly after ingestion of the drug (Langs & Barr, 1968).

Klee and Weintraub (1959) also presented data indicating that paranoid-like reactions during an LSD session can be predicted from

pre-experimental interviews which focus on current interpersonal relations. A paranoid-like response under LSD was found in mistrustful,
complaining, fearful persons, who often used projection as a defense.
Similarly, von Felsinger, Lasagna, and Beecher (1956) reported that the
few subjects who had hostile or paranoid-like reactions under LSD also
manifested "suspicious attitudes in interpersonal relations" during the
pre-drug interviews and on the Rorschach test.

A more recent study (McClothlin, Cohen, & McGlothlin, 1967)
presented evidence that the subjects' personality characteristics are related to the general "intensity" of the reactions elicited under LSD. In
this study, 24 subjects first completed a battery of personality tests
(TAT, Holtzman Ink-blots, MMPI, California F Scale, Morris'
Ways-to-Live, a scale measuring naturally-occurring hypnotic-like experiences, and several others). Subsequently, the subjects ingested 200
micrograms of LSD in a relatively standardized experimental situation,
and their reactions to the drug were assessed by their self-reports and by
observers ratings. Subject who reacted more intensely to the drug had
obtained significantly higher scores on the following personality measures: aesthetic sensitivity and imaginativeness; preference for a more
unstructured, spontaneous, and inward-turning life; and orientation toward ideas and intuition. Also, the subjects with more intense experiences tended to be less aggressive, competitive, and conforming, and
they reported that they had previously had a greater number of natural
hypnotic-like experiences. Subjects manifesting the least intense reactions to LSD, had obtained higher scores on measures of rigidity and
dogmatism and placed stronger emphasis on control.

Kornetsky and Humphries (1957) found a high correlation ($r = .94$)
between the psychasthenia scale of the MMPI and the subjective effects
reported by subjects who had received 50 micrograms of LSD. However, at a higher dose (100 micrograms) the correlation between the
psychasthenia scale and the subjective effects was not significantly
different from zero ($r = .14$). Since a high score on the psychasthenia
scale is usually interpreted as indicating unreasonable fears and over-
reaction to stimuli, these results, if replicated, would indicate the following: a personality dimension (psychasthenia) is related to subjects' response to a low dose of LSD (but not to a higher dose); the greatest
response to a low dose is found in subjects who characteristically manifest unreasonable fears and who overreact to stimulation.

In brief, the studies cited above, and also other studies (DiMascio,
Rinkel, & Leiberman, 1961) indicate that personality variables play a

role in determining both the overall intensity of the reaction to LSD and the degree to which the subject becomes anxious, hostile, or paranoid during the LSD session.[5]

Consequent Variables

To formulate an explanation or theory in this area, it is necessary to specify the effects to be explained and to relate each of the effects to antecedent variables present in the drug situation. Each of the consequent effects listed in the second column of Table 1 will now be specified concretely and related to the antecedent variables listed in Table 1, column 1.

SOMATIC-SYMPATHETIC EFFECTS

Beginning within an hour after ingestion of LSD (or mescaline or psilocybin) and extending for another hour or two, subjects experience a variety of interelated somatic effects that resemble those found when the sympathetic nervous system is stimulated (Barron, Jarvik & Bunnell, 1964; Salvatore & Hyde, 1956). Most subjects report that they feel physically weak, unsteady, or giddy, and some state that they feel dizzy or drowsy or as if they are about to pass out (Fichman, 1957; Linton & Langs, 1962; Malitz, Esecover, Wilkens, & Hoch, 1960). Restlessness and difficulties in breathing are quite often present. Subjects also typi-

---

5. It seems appropriate to mention at this point that many investigators have contended that so-called schizophrenic individuals are much less reactive to LSD than normals. However, this contention appears to be a simplification of the available data. If a distinction is made between acute and chronic schizophrenics, the data indicate the following:

Acute or nondeteriorated schizophrenics are clearly affected by the drug, at least as much as normals. After LSD or mescaline ingestion, acute schizophrenics typically show increased disorganization and an exaggeration of their psychotic symptoms (Hoch, 1955; Savage, 1955).

After taking LSD, some chronic schizophrenics show marked changes from their usual patterns of behavior and others show an intensification of their usual symptoms (Cholden, Kurland, & Savage, 1955). However, some chronic schizophrenics appear not to be noticeably affected by small or moderate doses of the drug; for example, they do not seem to show changes in moods and emotions or changes in visual perception. The apparent failure of some chronic schizophrenics to manifest some of the characteristic effects of the drug may be due to one or more of the following: They may fail to communicate the drug effects. As Fiddleman (1961, p. 151) has pointed out, "It may very well be that the schizophrenic is familiar with the strangeness involved in the experience under LSD and that it takes a dose massive enough to disrupt severely the sensory input/output relationship for the schizophrenic to be disturbed by the agent." Many chronic schizophrenics have been maintained on a long-term chlorpromazine treatment. Chlorpromazine appears to be an LSD antagonist; that is, when chlorpromazine is present in the body and a drug such as LSD or psilocybin is taken, the characteristic reaction to the LSD-type drug is markedly reduced (Isbell & Logan, 1957; Keeler, 1967).

cally state that they feel as if they are trembling (von Felsinger et al., 1956). Each of these drugs produces enlargement of the pupil (mydriasis) and enhancement of tendon reflexes such as the knee jerk. Body temperature and systolic and diastolic blood pressure are often elevated but changes in pulse and respiration are quite variable (Isbell et al., 1956; Isbell & Jasinski, 1969). Nausea is reported by a small number of subjects who have taken LSD or psilocybin and by a larger number who have taken peyote.

As mentioned previously in this chapter, some of the somatic-sympathetic effects are functionally related to situational variables and to the subject's set and personality. For instance, it appears that nausea is more likely to follow ingestion of LSD if the subject is anxious prior to taking the drug. Also, more of the somatic-sympathetic effects are reported by guarded and overdefended individuals.

Although situational, set, and personality variables play a role in determining the nature and magnitude of the somatic-sympathetic effects, it appears that the most potent factor in determining these effects is the dose of the drug. A subject reports more of these effects, and more intense effects, as the drug dose in increased (Klee et al., 1961). If, as seems likely, the somatic-sympathetic effects are primarily due to physiological changes produced in the body by the drug, and are influenced only to a limited extent by such variables as expectations, suggestions, anxiety, and personality, then studies which monitor autonomic and physiological variables may expect to find a close relationship between subjects' reports of somatic-sympathetic effects and physiological changes. A study by Feigen and Alles (1955) provided data which support this conjecture. These workers monitored skin temperature continuously in subjects who had received mescaline (300,000 micrograms). When the subjects reported that they felt cold, the objective measurements showed that the temperature of the skin had dropped markedly.

Most of the effects mentioned above appear to be due to stimulation of the sympathetic nervous system. (LSD also seems to produce sympathetic stimulation in animals as indicated by dilated pupils, tachycardia, elevated body temperature, piloerection and hyperglycemia.) Administration of LSD in humans also leads to other physiological changes which resemble those found during sympathetic stimulation or when a person is aroused, excited, or under stress. The latter changes include, for example, leucocytosis with a fall in circulating eosinophils, increase in blood sugar, reduction in blood potassium, slight elevation in 17-ketosteroids, a moderate increase in 17-hydroxycorticoids, and a mobilization of lipids with an increase in free fatty acids (Hollister, 1968).

LSD-type drugs usually fail to produce clear-cut changes on the electroencephalogram (EEG). However, when EEG changes are noted, they are generally of the type found during arousal, anxiety, or stress—that is, there is a progressive desynchronization with the waves becoming lower in amplitude and increased in frequency (Brazier, 1964; Hollister, 1968; Rodin & Luby, 1966; Shagass, 1967; Wikler, 1957). Along similar lines, LSD tends to produce a reduction in variability and energy content of the EEG of the type which typically accompanies states of excitation and arousal (Goldstein, Murphree, Sugerman, Pfeiffer, & Jenney, 1963). In fact, these EEG changes (desynchronization and reduction in variability and energy content) which are, at times, produced by LSD resemble those produced by stimulants such as amphetamines (S. Cohen, 1968; Hollister, 1968).[6]

CHANGES IN BODY-IMAGE

Next to the somatic-sympathetic effects, changes in the feeling of the body and limbs appear to be the most consistent effects of these drugs (Guttman, 1936; Linton & Langs, 1962). Practically all subjects state that their body or a limb feels strange or funny, or heavier or lighter than usual, or as if it has changed in size or shape (Malitz et al., 1960; Masters & Huston, 1966). Reports such as the following are characteristic: "left arm feels strange, more elastic," "arms and legs feel detached," "right arm feels numb, legs feel shorter," "arms feel longer" (Bercel, 1956). More bizarre feelings are also reported by some subjects, especially at higher drug doses; e.g., "I feel as if my body is melting into the background," "My body feels apart from my brain," "I feel like I am floating in space" (Bercel, 1956; Ditman et al., 1969).

Practically all subjects report changes in tactile sensibility (M. Jarvik, 1967a). The body surface or parts of the limb surfaces feel as if they have been mildly anesthetized, with the flesh becoming "rubbery" (Masters & Huston, 1966, p. 68). Most commonly, drugged subjects report feelings of numbness in the hands. The change in tactile sensitivity also appears to be related to a changed sensitivity to textures (S. Cohen, 1967b, p. 51). Objects touched or handled often seem altered, for instance, a pencil may feel too hard or too soft (Guttman, 1936).

The altered sensations from the body and limbs and the altered sense of touch are among the most consistent effects of LSD. For instance, Abramson et al. (1955a) emphasized that the most reliable reports dis-

6. The heightened activation or arousal associated with LSD may help explain the finding that subjects who have received this drug during the day or immediately before going to bed at night typically show an increase in restlessness or body motility during sleep and an increase in the percentage of dream time (Green, 1965; Muzio, Roffwarg, & Kaufman, 1966).

tinguishing 50 and 100 micrograms of LSD from a placebo included "peculiar feelings of limb," "lightness of limbs," and "sensitivity of skin." Although these changes, which have been labeled by many writers as body-image changes and by other writers as depersonalization, may be affected to a degree by situational, set, and personality variables, they appear to be due primarily to the drug per se and to be more prevalent at higher dose levels. Also, empirical studies tend to support the subjects' spontaneous verbal reports of alterations in sensations from body and limbs. For instance, Edwards and Cohen (1961) showed that tactile sensitivity, as indicated by two-point discrimination, is significantly impaired with LSD (125 micrograms). The same investigators also found a reduction in the ability to perceive warmth applied to the skin. Along similar lines, Liebert, Werner, and Wapner (1958) presented data indicating that, with a small dose of LSD (40 micrograms), there is an increase in the perceived size of one's head and in the length of one's arm.

DREAMY-DETACHED FEELINGS

Within an hour after ingesting LSD (or mescaline or psilocybin), subjects typically feel lightheaded, as if they have ingested two martinis (Bercel, 1956). The lightheaded feeling is often associated with or followed by a dreamy feeling of detachment, apartness, or awayness which may appear, to an objective observer, as passivity or reverie (Hollister, 1968, p. 118; Klee, 1963; Unger, 1963). These dreamy-detached feelings seem to be among the most characteristic effects of the drugs (Linton & Langs, 1962; Rodin & Luby, 1966). For instance, Abramson et al. (1955a) reported that dream-like feelings was one of the subjective questionnaire items that clearly differentiated a placebo from 50 and 100 micrograms of LSD.

The dreamy-detached feelings appear to be related to changes in cognitive functioning; concentrating or attending becomes less proficient, and a rapid flow of ideas is at times experienced. The latter changes in turn seem to be related to decrements in performance on intellectual-motor tasks which will be discussed in the next section.

Two points should be emphasized here:

Although the LSD subject tends to feel detached, passive, or indifferent, he nevertheless is aware of what he is doing and is fully oriented. With the exception of very large doses of LSD, the subject has insight into the experimental setting, is able to give oral or written reports of his ongoing experiences, and does not have amnesia afterwards.

The dreamy-detached feelings are rarely present continuously. On the contrary, an important aspect of these feelings is that they come and go in a wavelike fashion (S. Cohen, 1968).

The periodic or wavelike alterations characterize not only the dreamy-detached feelings but also many other of the effects listed in Table 1, column 2, for example, the variations in moods and emotions, and performance on intellectual and motor tasks. The wavelike variations that enter into the other effects will be discussed later in this chapter.

REDUCED INTELLECTUAL-MOTOR PROFICIENCY

As stated above, it appears that the dreamy-detached feelings are related to difficulties in attending and concentrating, and in controlling the flow of thoughts (Guttmann, 1936; Linton & Langs, 1962; Malitz et al., 1960). The latter difficulties in turn may be related to impaired performance on intellectual and motor tasks.

LSD gives rise to a dose-related decrement in performance on a variety of tasks. Although the decrement may not be noticeable at lower dose-levels, it can be consistently demonstrated at higher doses.[7] For instance, although impaired memory for paired associates may not be observed below 72 micrograms of LSD, it is rather consistently found at dose levels above 100 micrograms (Silverstein & Klee, 1958). This dose-related reduction in performance below base-line levels has been shown for abstract thinking, short-term memory, spatial relations, Porteus maze, interpretation of proverbs, manual reaction time to visual and auditory stimuli, dual pursuit test, mirror-image drawing, digit symbol substitution, digits forward and backward, simple addition, and serial subtraction (S. Cohen, 1968; Hollister, 1968; Jarvik, 1967a; Wikler, 1957). The impaired performance found with commonly-used doses of LSD is greater than that found with the commonly-used doses of other drugs such as chlorpromazine, meperidine, and secobarbital (Kornetsky, Humphries, and Evarts, 1957).

The reduced ability to perform intellectual and motor tasks is not necessarily obvious to the subjects. Some subjects, who report few effects of the drug, show marked decrements in task performance; other subjects who feel they are greatly affected may show only small impairment (Kornetsky et al., 1957). Also, the ability to perform typically varies in wavelike fashion; subjects at times reach almost normal levels

7. Although decrements in performance with high doses of LSD can be consistently demonstrated with subjects who have taken LSD a small number of times, no studies have attempted to determine if LSD produces similar decrements in subjects who have taken LSD many times.

and then, within a few minutes, manifest very low performance levels (Szara et al., 1966).

It has been hypothesized that the intellectual-motor impairment associated with LSD-type drugs is due to one or more of the following: anxiety; reduced motivation to perform the tasks; or reduced ability to attend and concentrate. However, anxiety does not seem to be a necessary factor because subjects who do not appear anxious show the decrements in performance. Although lack of motivation may play a role, it is probably not the most important factor. For instance, in one study (M. Jarvik, 1967a) 12 subjects who had received LSD were offered ten dollars to surpass their last placebo performances on an arithmetic test. None were able to do so although they all stated that they tried to perform maximally. It appears that the most important factor in producing the reduced proficiency is a difficulty in maintaining focus on the task. The distractability and the difficulty in shifting set can be inferred from subjects' reports that their concentration spans are shortened, their minds wander, and they are unable to control their thoughts (Hoffer & Osmond, 1967, p. 120). The distractibility becomes quite striking at high doses of the drug when subjects are generally unable to maintain sufficient attention and concentration to complete the tasks.

CHANGES IN TIME PERCEPTION

At low doses of LSD, mescaline, psilocybin, and other similarly-acting drugs, some subjects report alterations in the ways they experience time passing; at higher doses, most subjects report changes in their perceptions of time. Data presented by Kenna and Sedman (1964) are characteristic; with low doses of LSD, 8 of 29 subjects reported changes in the way they experienced time passing; with higher doses, 20 of 29 reported such changes. Although subjects who have taken LSD, mescaline, or psilocybin typically state that it seems to be passing more slowly than usual, a few state that it seems to be passing more quickly. Also, some subjects state that they have lost track of time or that they have a sense of timelessness (Beringer, 1927).

Studies which compared time estimations under a control condition and after the ingestion of LSD also indicate that the judgment of time is affected by the drug. Benda and Orsini (1959) reported that, as compared to the control estimates, subjects under LSD underestimated 10 and 30-second intervals. Boardman, Goldstone, and Lhamon (1957) found that although LSD did not significantly affect subject's estimation of one-second intervals, it increased the variability of their estimate. In another study (Aronson, Silverstein, & Klee, 1959) subjects were asked to estimate four different intervals (15, 60, 120, and 240 seconds) with and without LSD. Under the drug the subjects overestimated each of the intervals to a significant degree, indicating that LSD makes time appear to pass more slowly than usual.

The alterations in time perception may be due in part to decreased attention and increased indifference. They may also be related to the pyrogenetic action of LSD, since time is typically experienced as passing more slowly when body temperature is elevated (Fischer, Griffin, & Liss, 1962). Although the aforementioned factors may play a role, it appears likely that the changes in time perception are more closely related to the change in the number of events that claim the center of attention. Under the influence of LSD-type drugs, the number of events that fill a given unit of time is increased. When a time interval is filled with events or changes it seems to pass swiftly as it is experienced but, retrospectively, it seems longer than intervals with fewer changes.[8]

CHANGES IN VISUAL PERCEPTION

Changes in visual perception are among the most characteristic effects of LSD-type drugs (Guttman, 1936; Isbell et al., 1956). When a moderate dose has been ingested, almost all subjects report some changes in the perception of colors, or in the size or form of objects, persons, or their own body. For instance, one to two hours after receiving 100 micrograms of LSD, 15 of 16 subjects stated that shapes or colors were altered in some way (Fiddleman, 1961). The intensity of the changes in colors or in shapes of objects appears to be positively correlated with the subjects' normal visual imagery abilities; subjects who state that they can normally project visual images (visualizers) report more intense visual effects with LSD than subjects who normally possess weak visual imagery (non-visualizers) (Brown, 1968; Shryne & Brown, 1965).

Visual effects with eyes open. Within one or two hours after LSD ingestion, and usually continuing in an undulating manner for several hours, many subjects report that colors seem brighter or more saturated, intense, or vivid. At higher doses, subjects typically report that colored afterimages persist longer than usual and that they can see colors, colored patterns, or halos at the edges of objects or on the wall (Bercel, 1956; Masters & Huston, 1966; pp. 152–153). Simultaneous contrast also appears more pronounced; that is, contours or outlines of objects, especially edges, appear to become sharper or better defined (Kluver,

---

8. Changes in time perception are also found with other types of drugs. For instance, in a recent study (Ditman et al., 1969), subjects who had received either LSD or a mild stimulant (methylphenidate or Ritalin), but not those who had received a tranquilizer (chlordiazepoxide or Librium), characteristically checked the statement "Hours went by like seconds—or one second seemed to last forever."

1928). Depth relations change so that two-dimensional objects at times seem to be three-dimensional (Kieffer & Moritz, 1968). Distortions in perspective occur; corridors typically appear longer than usual and objects may seem to fluctuate in distance (Anderson & Rawnsley, 1954; Hoffer & Osmond, 1967, p. 112). A magnification of detail, which may be related to changes in contours, perspective, or simultaneous contrast, is also common (Rodin & Luby, 1966). The changes in depth and perspective are apparently also related to subjects' reports that they experience a distortion in their image when they look at themselves in a mirror (Masters & Huston, 1966, p. 83).

Other common visual effects include alterations in the size or shape of objects; for example, the features of another person may be perceived as distorted or at least changed in some way. Parts of one's own body may seem larger or smaller; for instance, a typical report is: "As I moved my hand toward me, it increased in size." At higher dose levels, subjects often report apparent movement or undulations of surfaces; the wall may seem to pulse or ripple in and out, or a piece of paper on which the subject is writing may seem to be making wave-like motion (Ditman et al., 1969; Hoffer & Osmond, 1967, pp. 113-114).

Experimental studies tend to corroborate the subjects' report of altered visual perception. Hartman and Hollister (1963) found that colored afterimages and the subjective colors elicited by flicker were increased by LSD, mescaline, and psilocybin. In the same study, the duration of aterimages was prolonged significantly by psilocybin but not by LSD or mescaline. Under double-blind conditions, Keeler (1965) showed that psilocybin significantly changed an objective measure of afterimage perception.

Edwards and Cohen (1961) reported that the Mueller-Lyer illusion is slightly enhanced under LSD. The same investigators demonstrated that constancy decreased when the standard object was 30 cm. away but not when it was 180 cm. It appears that LSD increases the displacement of the vertical produced by body tilt (Liebert, Wapner, & Werner, 1967). Also, LSD augments the variability in judging the size of test objects (Weckowicz, 1959).

Visual effects with eyes closed. When the eyes are closed, every normal individual observes phosphenes (luminescent colors and star-like objects) in his visual field. When subjects who have received a moderate or high dose of LSD, mescaline, or psilocybin close their eyes in a dark room, they typically report that the phosphenes are more vivid than those perceived normally and some subjects state that the luminescent colors, star-like lights, and patterns change into formed objects such as architectural structures, carpets, lattice work, diamonds, or other gem-like objects (S. Cohen, 1968; Ditman et al., 1969; Huxley, 1954).[9] Experiments by Knoll and coworkers seem to support the contention that LSD-type drugs augment the phosphene phenomenon. First, these investigators showed that phosphenes with clear forms can be evoked by stimulation of the brain from cranial electrodes with pulses ranging in frequency from 1 to 30 cycles per second (Knoll & Kugler, 1959). Then, in a second experiment (Knoll, Kugler, Hofer, & Lawder, 1963), they showed that, under LSD, mescaline, and psilocybin, a greater number of patterned phosphenes are elicited by the electrical stimulation and there is an increase in the vividness of the formed phosphenes.

Visual effects and the concept of hallucinations. The foregoing considerations can be summarized as follows: When moderate doses of LSD, mescaline, or psilocybin have been ingested and the subjects' eyes are open, the great majority of subjects report some alteration in visual perception such as changes in the color or form of objects; also, when the subjects' eyes are closed, they report perceptions of vivid colors, patterns and, at times, formed objects. These visual phenomena have been commonly subsumed under the word hallucination and the drugs have been labeled as hallucinogens. Is the term hallucination applicable?

The term hallucination is ambiguous; one writer will use it to refer to one set of events, while another writer uses it to refer to a somewhat different set. To specify the referents for this term, we need to consider a series of events that can vary along three dimensions: the complexity of the phenomena perceived, which can vary from simple lights, colors, or patterns to complex formed persons or objects; whether the subjects' eyes are closed or open when he perceives the phenomena, and the degree to which the subject believes that the things perceived have an independent existence—are 'out there.' If the term hallucination is used strictly to refer to the extreme end of each of the three dimensions, it can be stated definitively that these drugs very rarely produce hallucinations. That is, subjects who have ingested the drug rarely report, when their eyes are open, that they perceived formed persons or objects which they believe are out there (S. Cohen, 1967a). Although complex formed objects are at times perceived, this almost always occurs only when the subjects' eyes are closed. Also, whenever formed objects are perceived (either with eyes opened or closed), the subjects are practically always aware that the visual effects are due to the drug and are not out there.

---

9. In most instances, the drugged subjects continue to see these visions when they open their eyes in the dark room. However, when the light is turned on, practically all subjects state that the visual phenomena have become very faint or have disappeared (Pahnke & Richards 1966).

Furthermore, as Cohen (1967b, p. 52) has pointed out, LSD subjects report perceptions of formed objects which they seem to believe are existential realities only in very rare instances in which there seems to be disturbances in thinking and feeling.

On the other hand, if the term hallucination is to be used loosely to refer to the perception with eyes open of lines, patterns, or colors which the subject knows are not really out there, or to refer to the perception of more complex formed objects with eyes closed, then hallucinations can be said to be quite common with these drugs.

Physiological changes underlying the visual phenomena. Snyder and Reivich (1966) have shown that LSD becomes highly concentrated in the visual system. These investigators gave high doses of LSD to squirrel monkeys and used a sensitive and specific fluorometric method to determine the amount of unchanged LSD in the brain. As compared to its concentration in the cortex, cerebellum, and midbrain, the concentration of LSD in the iris was 18 times as high and its concentration in the optic chiasma and lateral geniculate was 2 to 6 times as high.

The visual phenomena that follow ingestion of LSD, mescaline, and psilocybin appear to be correlated with physiological changes that occur throughout the entire visual system, extending from the pupil, lens, and retina on through the lateral geniculates and the occipital cortex. We will trace some of these physiological alterations and discuss the changes that occur in various structures within the eyeball, the possible relations between the LSD visual phenomena and entoptic phenomena, and the relation of the visual phenomena to physiological changes in higher levels of the visual system.

Pupil. LSD, mescaline, and psilocybin produce an enlarged pupil (mydriasis). Since dilation of the pupil allows more light to stimulate the retina, reduces the depth of focus, and maximizes the effects of spherical, chromatic, and other aberrations, it may play a role in producing some of the visual effects which are associated with these drugs. For instance, it may be related to the LSD subject's report that his vision is blurred, he finds it difficult to focus his eyes, and he has a feeling that there is too much light. The enlarged pupil, by maximizing chromatic aberration, may also be functionally related to reports, which are proffered by some LSD subjects, that they perceive a rainbow effect—a series of rainbow-like colors at the edges of objects. Although the mydriasis produced by LSD-type drugs may give rise to blurring, difficulty in focusing and, possibly, the rainbow effect, it does not appear to be an important factor in producing the visual distortions and illusions which are commonly associated with these drugs. In a pertinent experiment (Bertino, Klee, Collier, & Weintraub, 1960), subjects first received a sympathetic-blocking agent (dibenzyline) and then ingested LSD. Although dibenzyline blocked the mydriasis produced by LSD, the subjects still manifested visual distortions and illusions.

Lens. LSD affects the ciliary muscle, producing partial cyclo-plegia — partial paralysis of the accommodation mechanism (Payne, 1965). (Accommodation is affected by the contraction of the ciliary muscle, resulting in relaxation of the lens zonules and an increase in the lens thickness.) The change in ciliary muscle and lens function, and the associated partial failure of accommodation, may play a role in produc-ing the distortions of spatial perception. For example, these changes may be related to the reports given by some subjects under LSD that objects seem larger or smaller than normal (Heaton, 1968, pp. 138-139).

Intra-ocular pressure. LSD tends to produce a significant rise in intra-ocular pressure (which is apparently correlated with a rise in sys-tolic and diastolic blood pressure) (Holliday & Sigurdson, 1965). Since phosphenes may be due, in part, to pressure on the retina by the fluids of the eyeball (Ladd-Franklin, 1927), the elevated intra-ocular pressure found with LSD may be functionally related to the subject's report that the luminescent dots and colored patterns (phosphenes) which he per-ceives with closed eyes are more vivid than normal. The elevated in-tra-ocular pressure may also be related to the rainbow effect reported by some LSD subjects, since, to the trained ophthalmologist, a patient's report of colored halos around lights or objects arouses the suspicion of raised pressure in the eyeball (Adler, 1962, p. 8).

Retina. Several studies suggest that LSD may exert a direct effect on the retina which is independent of its effects on higher levels of the visual system.

Burian, Fleming, and Featherstone (1958) presented subthreshold light flashes every four seconds to rabbits which were immobilized in a light-tight box. Under LSD the subthreshold stimuli produced an in-creased voltage of the electroretinogram.

Krill, Weiland, and Ostfeld (1960), working with humans, showed that the beta wave of the electroretinogram increased in amplitude with LSD. This was subsequently confirmed by Rodin and Luby (1966). Krill, Alpert, and Ostfeld (1963) also presented data indicating that the effect on the beta wave may be due to a direct action of LSD on retinal functions (*not* due to centrifugal influences on the retina from higher centers). Two subjects with total optic nerve atrophy but with function-ing retina in at least one eye were exposed to LSD. The beta wave amplitude increased in the same way as with normal-sighted subjects.

Edwards and Cohen (1966) used a complex procedure to ascertain whether the locus of misperception of size with LSD was peripheral or in higher levels of the visual system. They compared size misperception when two stimuli were presented either independently to the two eyes or simultaneously to both eyes. Edwards and Cohen reasoned that if the misperception occurs at the retinal level, the two situations should produce the same degree of misperception, that is, higher levels of the visual system should simply receive information from the retina which was already distorted. Since the two situations produced an equal degree of misperception of size, Edwards and Cohen concluded that the locus of the effect was peripheral, presumably retinal, rather than at higher levels of the visual system.

Several other studies have also been concerned with the effects of LSD on retinal functions. However, it is debatable whether these studies demonstrated a direct effect of the drug on the retina. The problem here is that it is very difficult to show that effects observed in the retina originate there and are not due to centrifugal action from higher levels of the central nervous sytem. Let us look briefly at the relevant studies.

Apter and Pfeiffer (1957) observed spontaneous retinal potentials in anesthetized cats 10 minutes after intraperitoneal injection of LSD (100 micrograms). Two sets of data indicated that the potentials originated in the retina and were not due to the action of centrifugal fibers: one, the spontaneous action potentials were first picked up in the retina and then in the optic nerve; also, when the optic nerve was severed while the spontaneous potentials were being recorded, the spikes in the occipital cortex and those in the proximal stump of the optic nerve disappeared while those in the distal stump of the optic nerve and retina persisted. However, Short (1958) failed to confirm the results of Apter and Pfeiffer. In a brief report, he stated that no significant changes were noted in the cat electroretinogram over a three hour period following intraperitoneal or intracarotid injections of LSD over a wide dose range.

Jacobson and Gestring (1959), also working with cats, found that large doses of LSD (more than 50 micrograms per kilogram of body weight) produced spontaneous retinal potentials in 40 per cent of the animals. However, contrary to the findings of Apter and Pfeiffer, these spontaneous retinal potentials were abolished by section of the optic nerve. To explain these results, Jacobson and Gestring hypothesized the existence of an inhibitory center at a higher level of the nervous sytem which affects the electrical activity of the retina through centrifugal fibers.

In summary, although retinal activity is altered by LSD, it is questionable whether the visual illusions and distortions associated with this drug can be attributed simply to its effect on the retina. In fact, the evidence at present indicates that reciprocal interactions and feedback mechanisms integrate all levels of the visual system and that retinal activity is closely integrated with activity at higher levels. Consequently, it appears likely that the visual phenomena associated with LSD are due to its effects on the visual system qua system and not simply due to its effects on one anatomical area such as the retina. These considerations will be further amplified below, after we discuss the relations between entoptic phenomena and the visual effects that are produced by LSD-type drugs.

Entoptic phenomena. Every normal individual is able to see some structures within his own eyeball. These entoptic phenomena (visual phenomena that have their seat within the eye) include, for example, the 'floaters' or muscae volitantes—small, hazy specks, spots, or hairlike objects that drift across the field of vision with movements of the eyes. (If the reader is not aware of these floaters, they can be brought into view by staring at a bright, uniform background). These 'spots before the eyes' are due to floating impurities, such as red blood cells, in the vitreous humor which cast shadows on the retina and are seen as hovering in space (White & Levatin, 1962).

Under special circumstances individuals can also perceive other structures within their eyeballs, such as the capillaries in the superficial layers of the retina and the corpuscles moving within the capillaries (Best & Taylor, 1950, pp. 1136-1137; Purkinje, 1918). Also, "a white surface viewed through a pinhole held near the primary focal point produces a shadow of the iris on the retina. The irregularities in the margin are clearly visible and changes in the size of the pupil can be observed directly. . . This method of viewing also makes visible spots and folds in the cornea, star figures and incipient cataracts in the lens, and opacities in the vitreous body. . ." (Fry, 1959, p. 669). There is also suggestive evidence that, under special conditions of viewing, we may at times be able to perceive the layers of rods and cones in our own eyeball (Horowitz, 1964; Marshall, 1935).

Marshall (1937) hypothesized that mescaline (and presumably LSD or psilocybin) reduces "the threshold of the visual centres for the perception of low intensities of light-energy so that, with closed eyes or in the dark such almost infinitesimal [entoptic] stimuli . . . are in some measure perceived." Similarly, Kluver (1942) hypothesized that the following three types of forms, which are characteristically perceived by mescaline subjects when their eyes are closed, may be due to an enhanced sensitivity to entoptic phenomena: spiral-like forms; tunnel or funnel-like forms (or cones, vessels, or alleys); and grating or lattice-type forms (or fretworks, honeycombs, chessboards, or cobwebs). It appears possible that entoptic observation of the superficial retinal blood vessels could give rise to the spiral-like forms; the cells in these vessels, or spots on the cornea or lens, could produce the dot-like apparitions or star-like objects; and entoptic observation of the regular arrangement of the rods and cones could give rise to the grating or lattice-type forms.

Clearly, further studies are needed in which ability to perceive entoptic phenomena is tested with and without LSD-type drugs. Verification of the hypothesis that the drugs lower the threshold for perception of entoptic phenomena would be a major breakthrough in understanding the mechanisms underlying at least some of the visual effects of the drugs.

Higher levels of the visual system. Although alterations in retinal activity, phosphenes, and structures within the eyeball that give rise to entoptic phenomena appear to play a role in producing the visual effects associated with LSD, mescaline, and psilocybin, there is reason to believe that higher levels of the visual system are also involved. For instance, the phosphene phenomenon cannot be attributed simply to retinal activity. Higher levels of the visual system are also implicated because the phosphenes observed with eyes closed can be seen in precisely the same way with either eye (LaBarre, 1964, p. 142), and the shape of electrically-induced phosphenes is not affected by movements of the eyeball (Knoll et al., 1963). (If electrically-produced phosphenes were due simply to retinal activity, variations in their shape would be expected with eyeball movements because such movements change the position of the retinal elements in the electrical field.)

Also, as pointed out earlier in this chapter, Jacobson and Gestring (1959) could explain their findings concerning retinal activity with LSD only by positing a higher center that exerts an inhibitory effect on the functioning of the retina. The effects of higher centers are also evident in data presented by Krill et al. (1963). These investigators found that blind individuals who perceive some visual phenomena in normal life, such as spots, flickers of lights, or colors, report that LSD increases the frequency and intensity of such visual events. Since the retina in these blind individuals was not functioning, it appears that a normal retina is not necessary for the occurrence of at least some of the LSD-induced visual effects and that higher levels of the visual system must play an important role.[10] It appears likely that at least some of the visual pheno-

10. Although much more experimental data are available pertaining to the effects of LSD on higher levels of the visual system, most of the data cannot be clearly interpreted. Let us look at two examples:

LSD produces an increase in the tonic activity level of the optic tract and the lateral geniculate body in unanesthetized, unrestrained cats in both light and dark (Schwartz & Cheney, 1965). It is not clear, however, whether this increased resting activity is due to impulses originating in the retina or to centrifugal impulses originating at higher levels of the nervous system.

mena associated with these drugs are related to the simple noncolored forms commonly obtained by stimulation of Area 17 of the cortex, to the complex and colored visual effects that are at times elicited by stimulation of the temporal lobe, and to the simple and also complex visual effects that can be elicited by stimulation of other areas of the visual system such as the optic radiations, optic tract, optic chiasm, or optic nerve (Penfield, 1958; Weinberger & Grant, 1940).

Krill et al. (1963) concluded that the concept of "localization" may not be a useful term in attempting to understand the visual phenomena elicited by LSD-type drugs. My own conclusions agree with this conclusion and also with the statement that, "Perceptual disturbances produced by LSD obviously involve more than the neural machinery comprising the classical visual pathways. Insofar as activation of a considerable proportion of the neuraxis from mesencephalon to forebrain occurs as a consequence of a particular visual stimulus, it is well to keep in mind the involvement of diffusely organized nonspecific projection systems in the overt manifestations of the drug" (Purpura, 1967).

AUDITION, OLFACTION, GUSTATION, AND SYNTHESIA

Audition. Some subjects under LSD, mescaline, or psilocybin state either that familiar sounds have acquired unusual qualities or that music is especially beautiful and overpowering (Guttman, 1936). However, many subjects do not give reports of this type; at various dose levels of the drugs, a substantial number of subjects report that sounds are not perceived in an especially different way.

At the present time it is not clear whether LSD-type drugs exert a direct effect on audition. Changes in hearing reported by a small proportion of subjects could be due to their focusing on sounds that they had previously neglected or to their attending to certain elements of complex sounds. There is evidence to indicate that the latter type of focusing and attending may be more closely related to situational variables and to the subject's set rather than to the effects of the drug per se. This evidence comes from a recent study (Ditman et al., 1969) in which the subjects received either LSD, a tranquilizer (Librium), or a mild stimulant (Ritalin) and all subjects were told that they were receiving LSD and were treated as if they had received LSD. The group that had received the

Large doses of LSD reduce the postsynaptic response to photic stimulation in the lateral geniculate nucleus of the cat (Bishop, Field, Hennessy, & Smith, 1958; Evarts, 1957). However, this result may be irrelevant in explaining the visual phenomena associated with LSD because brom-lysergide, which does not produce any visual phenomena, also depresses synaptic transmission in the lateral geniculate nucleus (Jacobsen, 1963, p. 491).

tranquilizer checked the following statement as often as the LSD group: *I felt the beauty and meaning of music as never before.*

Olfaction and Gustation. The foregoing considerations with respect to audition also apply to olfaction and gustation. In most subjects, these senses are not noticeably affected by LSD-type drugs (Guttmann, 1936). However, a small proportion of subjects who have taken LSD, mescaline, or psilocybin report either that food tastes better (or worse), their sense of smell is more acute, or they are aware of odors not sensed by an objective observer (Ditman et al., 1969). It is not clear to what extent reports of this type are due to changes in focusing or in attending which may be produced by such variables as expectancy and suggestion. Further studies are needed in which effects on audition, gustation, and olfaction are carefully evaluated in drugged subjects who do not expect a change in these modalities. Investigations along these lines are especially important in order to determine how general are the effects of LSD-type drugs on the central nervous system.

Synesthesia. Very few subjects who have taken an LSD-type drug spontaneously proffer reports that stimulation of one sense modality is perceived as a sensation in a different modality (synesthesia), e.g., "I saw music" (Ditman et al., 1969). However, such reports are quite often obtained when the experimenter attempts to elicit them. For instance, in one study (Klee, 1963) the experimenter clapped his hands in the air while the subjects, who had received a high dose of LSD, were observing visual patterns with their eyes closed; the subjects typically reported that they saw flashes of colors in time with the clapping. In another study (Guttmann, 1936) mescaline subjects were exposed to music while they were perceiving lines and patterns with their eyes closed; the subjects typically reported that the lines moved and changed colors in harmony with the music. Similarly, a third study (Hartman & Hollister, 1963) showed that, as compared to non-drug controls, drugged subjects exposed to pure tones reported significantly more colors and patterns elicited by the tones. It remains to be determined, however, to what extent this type of synesthesia can be directly attributed to the LSD-type drug and to what extent it is due to situational, set, and personality variables.

HEIGHTENED RESPONSIVENESS TO PRIMARY SUGGESTIONS

In an earlier section of this chapter, we considered suggestions as antecedent or independent variables that might influence the phenomena elicited in LSD situations. In the present section, responses to suggestions will be treated as dependent variables that may be affected by administration of the drug.

Many workers in this area have contended that LSD-type drugs augment suggestibility. An important problem that arises in testing this contention is that the term suggestibility refers to at least two relatively distinct phenomena:

One type of suggestibility is denoted by responses to direct, explicit suggestions such as suggestions that the subject's body is swaying forward, he cannot bend his arm, or he cannot remember what occurred. When direct suggestions of this type are administered, it is quite clear to the subject exactly what responses are expected and desired from him. This kind of suggestibility has been labeled as *primary suggestibility* and also as the *type of suggestibility that has been traditionally associated with the word hypnosis* (Barber, 1965).

Another type of suggestibility, which seems to resemble what is commonly termed *gullibility,* is denoted by responses which are elicited indirectly; for instance, the subject is asked if he sees a certain form on a Rorschach card and is rated as suggestible if he answers affirmatively. In these instances, it is not necessarily clear to the subject that the experimenter expects or desires a specified response.

Although the second type of suggestibility has not as yet been assessed in LSD-type situations, the first type of suggestibility has been tested in two experiments. Middlefell (1967) found that, as compared to a condition in which subjects received a placebo, 75 micrograms of LSD significantly enhanced responses to direct suggestions of body sway in neurotics (but not in schizophrenics or depressives). Sjoberg (1965) showed that commonly-used doses of LSD and mescaline, but not psilocybin, raised responses to direct suggestions of hand lowering, arm rigidity, age-regression, hallucination of a voice, etc. LSD and mescaline produced gains of 1.5 to 2.0 points on a 17-point suggestibility scale. A formal hypnotic induction procedure also raised scores on the same scale by about the same degree (1.8 points). (Other studies, Barber, 1969, indicate that task-motivation instructions, to try to perform maximally, produce a similar increment in response to direct suggestion). In brief, it appears that primary suggestibility or the type commonly associated with hypnosis is enhanced by LSD-type drugs. Whether or not these drugs also augment the second type of suggestibility, which is related to gullibility, remains to be determined.

CHANGES IN MOODS AND EMOTIONS

In general, the behaviors observed in LSD situations are functionally related to the drug dose and to extra-drug variables (the situation and the subject's set and personality). However, some of the effects are more closely related to the dose of the drug than to the extra-drug variables; these include, for example, some of the somatic-sympathetic effects such as pupillary dilation, alterations in body-image, dreamy-detached feelings, reduced intellectual-motor proficiency, and changes in visual perception. Other effects observed in LSD situations appear to be more closely related to the extra-drug variables than to the dose of the drug; these include the changes in moods and emotions discussed here.

Whether or not and to what degree subjects experience changes in moods and emotional reactions in the drug situation appears to depend primarily on their interpretation of the other effects that are occurring and this interpretation in turn appears to depend primarily on such variables as the situation and the subject's set and personality (Schachter, 1966). As Becker (1967) has pointed out, LSD and related drugs produce a variety of effects, and subjects do not attend to, interpret, and react to the effects in the same way.

The mood-emotional reactions observed after ingestion of LSD, mescaline, or psilocybin vary from subject to subject and also within the same subject during the course of the drug session. With respect to inter-subject variability we can distringuish four types of reactions:

A few LSD subjects manifest very little change in mood. These minimal responses are found primarily in individuals with highly investigative sets, for example, scientists who take the drug in order to observe its effects and who are in familiar surroundings with scientific colleagues.

Many subjects become happy, talkative, and jocular after taking an LSD-type drug (S. Cohen, 1968; Ditman & Bailey, 1967; Guttmann, 1936). In some cases, the feeling of happiness becomes quite intense and gives rise to bliss, exaltation, and ecstasy. These ecstatic-transcendental reactions will be discussed in detail below.

The perceptual alterations and the unusual body sensations appear to make a substantial number of LSD subjects jittery and anxious (S. Cohen, 1967b). Some of the anxious subjects withdraw psychologically from the situation and appear depressed while others become suspicious of the experimenter and the experimental setting. In rare instances, the accumulating tension may culminate in panic or a psychotic-like reaction.

Quite frequently, moods and emotions are labile during the drug session, shifting from euphoria (relaxed, happy, and sociable) to dysphoria (jittery, tense, and fearful) and back again to euphoria in a wavelike fashion (Katz, Waskow, & Olsson, 1968).

We can place these four types of mood-emotional reactions that are observed with LSD-type drugs in broader context by underscoring three important points:

The number of times the subject has previously received the drug tends to influence his mood and emotional reactions. The first drug experience usually arouses more anxiety than later ones.

Mood during the session is related to mood immediately prior to the session. If the subject is anxious, apprehensive, or depressed prior to taking the drug, his mood will most likely be intensified after he takes it. If the subject is relaxed and in a pleasant mood prior to the session, he will most likely have pleasant experiences during the drug session (Metzner et al., 1965).

Moods and emotions vary widely not only in the same subject during the course of one drug session but also from person to person and from situation to situation. As Smart, Storm, Baker, and Solursh (1967, p. 24) have pointed out, when the drug is ingested in a group setting it may result in greater talkativeness and animation (for which the group setting provides a ready opportunity) and may be interpreted as elation by the subject as well as by others. Anxiety is more likely in a strange setting, with unfamiliar people, where some nervousness may be already present, and where the subject is told little or nothing in advance about the procedure.

As stated above, LSD-type drugs at times give rise to extreme emotional reactions. One type of extreme reaction can be labeled as an *ecstatic-transcendental reaction* and the other can be labeled as a *panic or psychotic-like reaction*.

Ecstatic-transcendental reactions. After taking an LSD-type drug, a substantial number of subjects become cheerful and talkative, have a sense of well-being, and tend to compare the effects of the drug with their previous experience of slight drunkenness with alcohol. The euphoric feelings at times become intense and are described by subjects as joy, bliss, serenity, or enchanted contentment. Some subjects undergoing this type of "peak" experience (Maslow, 1962) also pass through a stage in which their thoughts and ideas seem to be of great importance, new ideas become more readily accepted, and there is a feeling of achieving profound insights into themselves, life, or reality (Freedman, 1968; Guttmann, 1936). (Whether or not subjects who feel that they have achieved deep insights have actually done so is by no means clear from the data available at present.)

Given a set for religious or mystical experiences, the subject may interpret his feelings of joy, novelty, and boundlessness in religious-mystical terms. However, Masters and Huston (1966) reported that only 5 per cent of their subjects (11 of 206) had an "illumination" experience which the subjects regarded as religious. Working with 55 subjects, Solursh and Rae (1966) found that one subject who received a small dose of LSD (150 micrograms) and another who received a very large dose (1400 micrograms) both approximated the "psychedelic" experience. Johnson (1968) reported that 500 micrograms of LSD gave rise to "transcendental" experiences in only 3 of 48 alcoholics (6 per cent). Although the terms 'illumination,' 'psychedelic' experience, and 'transcendental' experience are not clearly defined and are used in somewhat different ways by different investigators, it is clear that these terms refer to something that is quite uncommon (found in less than 6 per cent of the subjects). After completing an investigation that aimed to produce psychedelic experiences, McCabe (1968, p. 107) concluded that "The drug dosage is only one of many variables which determine the extent of psychedelic reactivity, not the least of which are the therapist's personality, skills, and ability to induce trust and confidence in the patient, as well as the patient's expectations, fears, and personality organization in general." Along similar lines, Pahnke (1967) concluded that the elicitation of psychedelic reactions are "largely dependent upon extra-drug variables . . . mystical experiences are the hardest [to produce], certainly not automatic, even under optimal conditions."

Pahnke came to the above conclusion after carrying out an important investigation (1963) in which an attempt was made to maximize all of the extra-drug variables that might be related to psychedelic reactions. To maximize the possibility of eliciting mystical experiences, only theological students were used as subjects. To maximize the subjects' set, several preparatory meetings were held in which the theological students were indoctrinated with respect to the religious potentials of the drug. To maximize situational variables, the experiment was conducted during a Good Friday service in a protestant chapel, and the subjects were together in groups, with an experienced guide assigned to each group. Using a double-blind procedure, 20 subjects were given 30,000 micrograms of psilocybin and 20 were given an active placebo (nicotinic acid which produces feelings of warmth and tingling of the skin). After receiving the drug or placebo, each subject participated in a two and one-half hour Good Friday service which included organ music, solos, readings, prayers, and personal meditation. Soon after the drug session, each subject wrote an account of his experiences and completed a 147-item questionnaire measuring phenomena of mysticism (a sense of cosmic oneness, transcendence of time and space, deeply felt positive mood, sense of sacredness, feeling of insight and illumination, etc.) A follow-up interview was also held at six months. The psilocybin group

scored significantly higher than the placebo group on each of the measures of mystical or transcendental experiences, and these differences
between the groups were still present at the 6-month follow-up. In this
experiment in which variables such as expectancy, trust, confidence, and
group support were maximized, eight of the ten psilocybin subjects had a
few of the experiences that are associated with mysticism, and three or
four of the ten had moderately marked experiences (passing from 60 per
cent to 70 per cent of the 147-items which measured the phenomena of
mysticism).

As stated previously in this chapter, LSD-type drugs almost always
affect moods and emotions, but these effects are usually not extreme.
That is, in most LSD situations, only a small proportion of subjects
manifest either the ecstatic-transcendental reaction or the second type of
extreme mood-emotional reaction—the panic or psychotic-like reaction.

Panic and psychotic-like reactions. In some instances, bewilderment
and anxiety is produced by the unusual phenomena that occur after drug
ingestion (i.e., by the unusual changes in body-image, the
dreamy-detached feelings, and the visual distortions and illusions). An
anxious reaction is the most common type of 'bad trip.' When an anxious reaction occurs in an experienced user of the drug it is usually due
to the high dose he has received. At low or moderate doses, an anxiety
reaction is more likely in the person who has not previously used the
drug (Smith & Rose, 1968). Personality variables also seem to play a
role in determing whether the subject will become anxious. As Fiddleman (1961, p. 152) concluded from a study using the MMPI, "What
appears to be a crucial factor involved here is not so much the type of
controls or defenses one typically employs, but rather the ability to
tolerate ambiguity, to be able to accept the strangeness which seems to
be the result of the physiological and sensory effects of the drug. Those
who are able to tolerate this change will tend to have a less frightening
and disrupting experience with LSD . . . ".

In a small number of subjects the anxiety increases in intensity and
the reaction can be appropriately labeled as panic. These individuals feel
that they have lost control over bodily processes, thoughts, and emotions. Becker (1967) has analyzed this type of reaction as follows: "[The
subject may decide] that he has lost his grip on reality, his control of
himself, and has in fact 'gone crazy.' [He may also decide] that the
change is irreversible or, at least, that things are not going to be changed
back very easily. The drug experience, perhaps originally intended as a
momentary entertainment, now looms as a momentous event which will
disrupt one's life posibly permanently. Faced with this conclusion, the
person develops a full-blown anxiety attack, but it is an anxiety caused

by his reaction to the drug experience rather that a direct consequence of the drug use itself."

Prior to 1963, untoward reactions lasting more than 24 hours were quite rare. The LSD-type drugs were almost exclusively dispensed by physicians in clinical or experimental settings, and care was taken to exclude subjects who were judged to be seriously maladjusted or disturbed. Although some subjects became depressed, anxious, or panicky during the drug session, these reactions almost always subsided either when the physician reassured the subject that his experiences were similar to those that others had with the drug or when the physician administered a tranquilizing drug such as chlorpromazine.[11] For instance, in studies extending over a period of 15 years with 300 patients and 100 volunteers, Malitz (1966) did not observe any untoward reactions which endured beyond the experimental session. Malitz pointed out that "The contrast between the relative safety of hallucinogens administered under carefully planned hospital conditions and the tragic accidents which have occurred through their unsupervised and unrestricted use is strikingly dramatic." As of 1963, Leuner had treated 110 neurotic patients (including suicidal cases and depressions) without serious problems—"no suicides, no psychoses, no untoward emotional explosions, no arrests" (Caldwell, 1968, p 106). Working with 206 subjects, Masters and Houston (1966) similarly reported that "No subjects ever experienced a post-session psychotic reaction, much less attempted suicide." Hollister (1968) reported that about 1 per cent of experimental subjects who had received LSD or psilocybin showed aggressive outbursts, panic, or dissociative reactions. Freedman (1968) summarized his wide experience by asserting that, when a skilled therapist is present, about 1 per cent or less of LSD sessions may be unexpectedly traumatic. Others who have used LSD in psychotherapy report that LSD is about as safe as other drugs (Geert-Jorgensen. Hertz, Knudsen, & Kristensen, 1964; Levine & Ludwig, 1964; Ling & Buckman, 1963; McCabe, 1968, p. 150).

In 1960, S. Cohen published an important survey pertaining to the untoward reactions produced by these drugs. He compiled the results obtained by 44 investigators who had published experimental or clinical studies pertaining to LSD or mescaline. These investigators had administered the drugs on about 25,000 occasions to 5,000 individuals at

11. Chlorpromazine is almost always effective in quieting the anxious or panicky LSD subject. However, in rare instances, chlorpromazine did not reduce the anxiety or panic and, in a very small number of instances, its administration enhanced the panic reaction (Schwartz, 1967). A recent study (Halasz, Formanik, & Marrazzi, 1969) suggests the possibility that the *dose* of chlorpromazine may be an important factor in determining how it will affect anxiety or panic associated with LSD.

doses ranging from 250 to 1500 micrograms of LSD and from 200,000 to 1,200,000 micrograms of mescaline. From these data Cohen estimated the rates of major complications as follows:

	Experimental subjects	Patients in therapy
Attempted suicide	0/1000	1.2/1000
Completed suicide	0/1000	0.4/1000
Psychotic reactions enduring for more than 24 hours	0.8/1000	1.8/1000

It should be noted that the suicides among the patients occurred many months after their last LSD session and that the suicide rate among patients in therapy who are not given LSD may be higher than the rate among the LSD patients. S. Cohen (1966, p. 186) concluded from these and other data gathered subsequently that "in the hands of experts these agents are relatively safe" but the drugs "should not be lightly or frivolously consumed."

Around 1963 a dramatic change occurred in the use of these drugs. LSD became a household word and was widely adopted by youth, especially college students. Kleber (1967) has delineated several factors that converged to produce this change. Prestigeful authors (Huxley, 1954; Watts, 1962) wrote uncritically about the marvelous effects of these drugs. Leary and Alpert received wide publicity when they campaigned for the drugs and raised a furor, first at Harvard, then in Mexico, and then throughout the United States. To a substantial proportion of the educated youth it appeared that Timothy Leary was a martyr who was persecuted by the establishment. About the same time there was an increasing preoccupation with personal and social dissatisfaction, especially among the youth, as well as increasing academic and competitive pressures. Also, there was a correlated increase in interest in existentialism and Eastern philosophies. Interrelated with the above was the growth of the "hippie" movement which adopted black-market LSD and marihuana as elements in a culture that glorified the use of drugs.

During recent years, a substantial number of individuals, who have been taking black-market preparations of LSD and other drugs, have been seen at psychiatric clinics or emergency rooms at urban hospitals. Most of these individuals were self-referred (Robbins, Robbins, Frosch, & Stern, 1967). After taking the illicit preparation in unsupervised settings, they were overwhelmed by some aspect of their experience, and came to the hospital in an anxious condition. Reassurance from a sympathetic physician or 50 milligrams of chlorpromazine were usually sufficient to abate the anxiety within 24 to 48 hours. A representative report (Ungerleider, Fisher, & Fuller, 1966) pertains to 70 individuals who came to the emergency room of a Los Angeles hospital ostensibly in association with black-market LSD complications. The presenting symptoms included confusion, anxiety, depression, or hallucinations. Forty-five of the 70 were relieved of their confusion and anxiety without being admitted to the hospital and the other 25 were hospitalized.

During recent years, illicit preparations containing LSD and other drugs have also been associated with attempted suicide, successful suicide, homicidal threats, successful homicide, antisocial or psychopathic behavior, psychosis, and grand-mal seizures (S. Cohen & Ditman, 1963; Schwarz, 1968; Smart & Bateman, 1967; Fisher & Ungerleider, 1967; Keeler & Reifler, 1967). In the case of homicide (Knudsen, 1964), a 25-year-old woman murdered her boy friend two days after the last of five LSD sessions. This woman had been previously diagnosed as a psychopathic personality, had been hospitalized in a mental institution several times, and had been indulging very heavily for about five years in drugs, alcohol, and promiscuous sex.

Cohen and Ditman (1963) presented the case of a 10-year-old boy who accidentally swallowed a sugar cube impregnated with LSD. A severe reaction occurred with visual distortions, illusions, and anxiety. Although the reaction generally subsided after three days, it seems that the child continued at certain times to experience visual illusions, with concomitant anxiety, during the following three months. Along similar lines, Milman (1967) presented the case of a 5-year-old girl who unknowingly ingested an LSD sugar cube. The child cried, screamed, seemed disoriented, and was taken to a hospital. After 4 or 5 hours of hospitalization with intermittent napping the child became relatively calm, unfrightened, and responsive. However, her verbalizations seemed to indicate that she was experiencing body-image distortions. A series of electroencephalograms were taken during and after her stay in the hospital (one day, 5 days, 2 months, 5 months, and 9 months after ingestion of the LSD); with the exception of the final EEG record, each record showed dysrythmia with high voltage slow wave activity and was judged to be abnormal.[12] Milman concluded from these data that LSD may produce more prolonged reactions in children than in adults, possibly because the growing cells in the central nervous system of a child are more susceptible to toxic products than the neural cells of an adult. This conclusion may be incorrect. If adults ingest LSD accidentally, without knowing what they are ingesting, they might also respond in the same way as the child in Milman's study.

Another type of seemingly untoward effect is the flash-back, the spontaneous recurrence of some of the LSD effects days, weeks, or months after the last ingestion of the drug. At times, these flash-backs appear to constitute a recall of the memorable drug experience caused by encountering a cue present at the time of the original experience. At

12. Milman also concluded that the child's IQ (derived from Ammon's Quick Test) was depressed soon after LSD ingestion and did not return to normal until about five months afterwards. This conclusion is unwarranted. A statistical analysis of the IQ scores shows that they do not differ significantly immediately after and five months after the ingestion of LSD (Schmitt, 1968).

other times, the spontaneous recurrence seems to constitute an appreciation of the visual illusions, transient feelings of depersonalization, and introspective moments of everyday life (Hollister, 1968, p. 15). There is evidence to indicate that these recurrences are related to high frequency of LSD use and typically occur when the individual is under stress (Pahnke & Richards, 1966; Smart & Bateman, 1967). Since there is no evidence whatsoever that LSD is retained in the organism more than 24 to 48 hours, and very little if any evidence that LSD sets off a chain of biochemical reactions that continue long after LSD is no longer present in the body, it appears that these flash-backs are most likely due to situational and psychological factors present at the time they occur.

The panic reactions and the psychotic-like reactions observed during recent years in hospital emergency rooms can be placed in broader context by noting the following:

The great majority of individuals who manifest adverse reactions have a history of psychopathology (Hensala, Epstein, & Blacker, 1967; Ungerleider, 1968; Welpton, 1968). Ungerleider et al. (1966) were able to trace the histories of most of the individuals who were admitted to a Los Angeles hospital with an LSD-associated psychotic-like reaction. Of those who were traced back, 67 per cent had previously been psychiatric inpatients or outpatients. Frosch, Robbins, and Stern (1965) studied 12 patients intensively who were admitted to Bellevue in association with LSD complications; 7 of these "clearly had long standing schizophrenia," 3 were judged as borderline psychotics with schizoid personalities, and the remaining 2 were diagnosed as having a long-standing personality disorder.

Blumenfield and Glickman (1967) presented data pertaining to 25 individuals with LSD complications who were seen at the emergency room at Kings County Hospital in Brooklyn. The great majority of these individuals (72 per cent) had been under psychiatric care prior to their LSD experience. The pre-drug personality was judged to be psychotic in 60 per cent and borderline psychotic in 20 per cent. Forty per cent had police records, 88 per cent had been using other drugs, and 40 per cent had a history of heroin use. Blumenfield and Glickman drew the following conclusions: "It appears that the use of LSD is spreading to some members of lower socioeconomic groups. Many of these users are high school dropouts with histories of antisocial behavior and criminal offenses as well as previous experience with other habituating and addicting drugs including heroin. . . When these individuals take LSD and are later brought or present themselves to our psychiatric emergency room, most are found to be in need of long-term hospitalization. This need for hospitalization does not appear to be solely or even to the largest extent to represent a toxic effect of drug ingestion but rather the interaction of chronic psychiatric conflicts with current environmental pressures."

Hensala et al. (1967) noted that individuals who were hospitalized with psychotic-like reactions, supposedly in association with LSD ingestion, had been using a wide variety of drugs indiscriminately. In fact, the data presented by Hensala et al. strongly indicated "not that LSD use is producing a new type of hospital patient, but rather that a group already using drugs in the community has added a new agent to its list." Along similar lines, Cohen and Ditman (1963) referred to the problem of *multihabituation* — "the misuse of a variety of sedatives, narcotics, stimulants, and hallucinogens taken in series by borderline individuals."

In many of the cases mentioned above, it is questionable whether pure LSD was ingested. The illicit drug was from an unknown source, in unknown amounts, and of unknown purity (Kleber, 1967). Also, during recent years, methamphetamine or methedrine ('speed') and other inexpensive drugs have at times been added to LSD (Carey, 1968, p. 119; S. Cohen, 1969, p. 24). Since methamphetamine typically produces tachycardia and muscle tremor and often produces anxiety, its combination with LSD can easily lead to a panic reaction (Smith & Rose, 1968). Furthermore, some present-day drug abusers intentionally combine LSD with marihuana, hashish, amphetamines, or barbiturates (Ditman, 1968). Also, there are suggestive data that illicit preparations of LSD at times contain unidentified ergot compounds (Hoffer & Osmond, 1967, p. 98). In brief, we do not know whether untoward reactions or psychotic-like reactions that were attributed to black-market LSD were primarily due to this drug or to other drugs that were taken in combination with or separately from LSD.

It appears that some of the individuals who have been experimenting with LSD have done so with the hope of ameliorating or curing personality disturbances. Relevant here is a careful study conducted by Glickman and Blumenfield (1967) with 15 individuals who were hospitalized in association with LSD ingestion. All 15 began taking LSD during life crises which they felt inadequate to handle and which were related to longstanding difficulties in social and sexual adjustment. Glickman and Blumenfield deduced from the clinical material that these individuals took LSD with the hope that it would help them overcome their problems. However, when their hope was not fulfilled, they projected upon LSD the cause of their further problems. Additional studies are needed to determine how often unstable individuals, who have taken LSD, unjustifiably place the blame for their problems on LSD.

It needs to be understood that the great majority of individuals who manifest psychotic-like reactions after ingesting illicit LSD or a drug presumed to be LSD were having serious problems before taking the drug. As Glickman and Blumenfield (1967) and other investigators have concluded, it appears likely that, in most of these cases, "the psychoses, suicides, and homicides which have been reported as LSD reactions" would have occurred without LSD ingestion. However, LSD may have served a catalytic function—it may have speeded up a psychopathological process. As S. Cohen and Ditman (1963) stated, "It is possible that [in predisposed individuals] LSD disrupts psychic homeostatic mechanisms and permits reinforcement of latent delusional or paranoid ideas."

Although untoward reactions usually appear to involve an interaction between LSD and schizoid trends or unsteady reality testing, a small number of individuals who apparently were functioning adequately before taking the drug have had serious adverse reactions after taking it (Ungerleider, Fisher, Fuller, & Caldwell, 1968). Individuals who appear to be in relatively good mental health can become emotionally shaken when they discover that their usual sense of mastery has been suspended by the drug; fighting to overcome the drug effect, some of these individuals may manifest fear or panic, impaired judgment, suicidal ideation, and possibly psychotic-like reactions. Although careful attention to selection of subjects, drug dosage, and experimental setting can minimize the risks, it appears that there is no guarantee that a person will not have a 'bad trip' with LSD (Schwartz, 1968; Smart & Bateman, 1967). This same conclusion also holds for a wide variety of other drugs; many drugs, for example, morphine, are relatively safe in carefully supervised medical settings; however, outside of carefully supervised situations they can lead to serious complications.

EFFECTS ON CHROMOSOMES

A quite different type of untoward effect that might be produced by LSD has been widely publicized in recent years. During 1967 and 1968 a series of papers appeared in *Science, Nature,* and other prestigious professional journals concerning the effects of LSD on chromosomes. These studies can be divided into three sets which will be discussed in turn: effects on chromosomes of white blood cells in vitro; effects on chromosomes of white blood cells in vivo; and effects on meiotic chromosomes.

Effects on leucocytes in vitro. M. Cohen, Marinello, and Back (1967) reported that the moderate amounts of LSD placed in tissue culture of leucocytes resulted in breakage of chromosomes during mitosis in 10-20 percent of the cells, and the breakage rate with LSD was more than double the rate with control cultures. Subsequently, L. Jarvik and Kato (1968; Kato & L. Jarvik, 1969) found the rates of chromosomal abnormalities to be 5 percent in control leucocyte cultures and 10 percent in leucocyte cultures exposed either to aspirin or to LSD.

Effects on leucocytes in vivo. Irwin and Egozcue (1967) took blood samples from eight individuals who had been using LSD and other drugs, and from nine non-user controls. Six of the eight drug users as compared to one of the nine controls showed a significant degree of chromosomal abnormalities. In a more extended study with a larger number of subjects, the same authors (Egozcue, Irwin, & Maruffo, 1968) found a mean chromosome breakage rate of 19 per cent among LSD users, as compared to 9 per cent for controls; however, there was much overlap in the distributions and the number of chromosome breaks was not correlated with the total dosage of LSD. Another study (M. Cohen, Hirschhorn, & Frosch, 1967) also found a significantly greater number of chromosome breaks in individuals who had been taking a wide variety of drugs, including LSD, than in non-drug users (controls).

The control groups in these studies were comprised of individuals who did not use drugs. The appropriate control group, however, would consist of individuals who have not taken LSD but have taken the wide variety of other drugs used by the experimental group. Two recent studies (Nielsen, Friedrich, Jacobsen, & Tsuboi, 1968; Nielsen, Friedrich & Tsuboi, 1968) showed that the nature of the comparison group is very important. Patients who had been treated with LSD and those who had been treated with other drugs such as chlorpromazine did not differ significantly in the number of chromosomal gaps and breaks. However, as compared to patients who were not on drugs, the LSD patients showed a significantly greater number of chromosomal gaps and breaks.

Several studies appear to contradict those summarized above. Bender and Sankar (1968) failed to detect chromosomal damage in leucocytes of schizophrenic children who had received daily LSD doses of 100–150 micrograms for 5.5 to 35 months. A subsequent follow-up of these children carried out by the same investigators (Sankar, Rozsa, & Geisler, 1969) reported similar results. However, these results are ambiguous because the life cycle of the circulating leucocyte may not exceed two years, and the schizophrenic children were studied 20–48 months after exposure to LSD (Irwin & Egozcue, 1968). In another recent study (Hungerford, Taylor, Shagass, LaBadie, Balaban, & Paton, 1968) leucocytes were cultured from a series of patients prior to and after receiving three doses of LSD (usually 200 micrograms per dose). Although there was a small increase in chromosomal aberrations immediately after the last dose, these aberrations were no longer present one month afterwards. Loughman, Sargent, and Israelstam (1967) found that, as compared to non-user controls, eight individuals who had been exposed to recent heavy doses of LSD did not show a significant increase in chromosomal abnormalities. Similarly, another investigation (Sparkes, Melnyk, & Bozzetti, 1968) failed to find significant chromosome damage in eight individuals who had taken 12 to 100 doses of LSD (at 250 micrograms or more per dose). In the latter investigation, the most recent dose of LSD was taken about one to three months prior to assessment of chromosome damage. In another study (Abuzzahab, Yunis, Schiele, & Marrazzi, 1969), chromosomes of lymphocytes from peripheral blood were studied prior to and after administration of LSD in the treatment of alcoholics. The doses of LSD ranged from 65 to 300 micrograms. No chromosome abnormalities were found. Abuzzahab et al. cogently criticized previous studies in this area which reported chromosome abnormalities with LSD for failure to measure chromosome aberrations *prior to* LSD exposure. Comparable results were presented in a recent report by Judd, Brandkamp, and McGlothlin (1969). The latter investigators performed chromosome analyses on three groups of subjects: nine heavy users of LSD who were continuing to use the drug; eight heavy users of LSD who had ceased using the drug at least 15 months prior to the study; and eight drug-free control subjects. No significant differences in chromosome breakage rates were found among the three groups and no temporal factor was found relating to LSD ingestion to chromosome damage. The mean breakage rates for all three groups was 1.8 or less. Tjio, Pahnke, and Kurland (1968) have also apparently failed to find chromosome damage in LSD users.

In brief, it appears that some studies but not others have found a significant degree of chromosomal aberrations in individuals who had apparently ingested LSD over a period of months or years. The contradictory results may be due, in part, to differences in the amount of time intervening between the subject's last dose of LSD and the assessment of chromosome damage. In fact, the study by Hungerford et al. (1968) indicates that, if the assessment is made within one month after the subject' last exposure to LSD, some increase in chromosomal aberrations may be expected; however, if the assessment is made more that one month after exposure to LSD, it is unlikely that the chromosomal aberrations will still be present. However, this is not the complete story; as Smart and Bateman (1968) have pointed out, elevated rates of chromosomal abnormalities have been found six months after the last dose of LSD (Irwin & Egozcue, 1967), seven to eight months after the last dose (M. Cohen, Hirschhorn, & Frosch, 1967), and also one year after the last dose (Egozcue et al., 1968). Clearly, much more research is needed to determine the relationship between chromosomal abnormalities and the time elapsed since the subject took LSD.

Another problem here is that there is little agreement across studies about the control or base-level of chromosomal abnormalities (Smart & Bateman, 1968). For instance, Bender and Sankar (1968) found an abnormality rate of 2 per cent in their controls, whereas Irwin and Egozcue (1967) reported that their controls showed an abnormality rate of 12 per cent. Smart and Bateman (1968) have cogently commented that, "The wide range of accepted basal rates of abnormality must lead to reduced confidence in the conclusions about the effects of LSD."

It should also be noted that the chromosomal effects that were observed in the above studies were not necessarily due to LSD. With few exceptions, the subjects were taking a wide variety of other drugs in addition to LSD and the effects could have been produced by one or more of the other drugs. In addition, some of the LSD users in these studies were apparently members of the hippie subculture which seems to have a high incidence of malnutrition and venereal diseases; the latter factors may contribute to chromosome abnormalities.

It is also noteworthy that the types of chromosomal breaks attributed to LSD can also be produced by common viruses and by many common chemicals. Apparently, chromosomal breaks can be produced, in vitro, by sugar, salt, and artificial sweeteners (cyclamates) and, in vivo in at least some animals, by injection of cortisone or Vitamin A, by injection of some antibiotics, hormones, or salicylates, and by vitamin deficiencies (Stone, Lamson, Chang, & Pickering, 1969; Wilson & Warkany, 1965).

Effects on meiotic chromosomes. In a recent study (Browning, 1968), massive doses of LSD (4000 micrograms per gram) were injected into the abdomen of *Drosophila* males. Of the original 75 males, only 15 (20 per cent) survived and only 10 (13 per cent) were fertile. The surviving fruitflies showed a significant increase in recessive lethal mutations in the X chromosomes. Using non-lethal doses of LSD, Grace, Carlson, and Goodman (1968) found no mutations or chromosome breaks in premeiotic, meiotic, or postmeiotic sperm of *Drosophila* males. Tobin and Tobin (1969) also failed to find any mutagenic effects in fruitflies exposed to non-lethal doses of LSD. Vann (1969) showed that there is a threshold dose-response for the mutagenic action of LSD in *Drosophila;* recessive lethal mutations are produced by very high concentrations of LSD (2000 micrograms per milliliter) but not by lower concentrations (100 micrograms per milliliter).

Skakkebaek, Philip, and Rafaelsen (1968) showed that very high doses of LSD (1000 micrograms per kilogram) produce a significant increase in abnormalities of meiotic chromosomes in mice. M. Cohen and Mukherjee (1968) injected 25 micrograms per kilogram of LSD into 10 male mice. (The dose is 6-8 times the typical dose taken by human LSD users). As compared to the meiotic cells of control animals, there was a significant increase in chromosome damage among the mice treated with LSD (3.4 against 0.3 breaks per 100 cells). The chromosome damage reached a maximum between 2-7 days after injection with a subsequent decline and return to control levels after 3 weeks.

In brief, it appears that very high or toxic doses of LSD injected into fruitflies and high doses of the drug injected into mice cause damage to the sex chromosomes. However, it appears that nontoxic doses of the drug do not produce deleterious chromosomal effects in the sex cells of fruitflies and it remains to be determined whether low doses of the drug damage the sex cells of mice.

EFFECTS ON EMBRYO OR FETUS

A series of recent studies suggest the possibility that ingestion of LSD during pregnancy may harm the embryo or fetus. Before turning to the effects of LSD on the pregnant human female, let us summarize the studies conducted with animals.

High doses of LSD (30 times the typical human dose) given intraperitoneally to pregnant mice on gestation days 6, 7, 8, or 9 caused a highly significant increase in the incidence of lens abnormalities in the fetuses (Hanaway, 1969). Along similar lines, Auerbach and Rugowski (1967) injected moderate doses of LSD intraperitoneally into pregnant mice. When the injection was made on the day of pregnancy when fetal malformations are most likely to occur in this species (day 7), 57 per cent of the offspring showed gross abnormalities such as brain and facial defects. A control group of mice showed abnormalities in 10 per cent of the offspring. When the injection was made later than day 7 of pregnancy, the abnormalities in the offspring of the LSD-treated mice did not exceed those in a control group. However, another study (DiPaolo, Givelber, & Erwin, 1968) which generally followed the procedures of the Auerbach and Rugowski study, but used smaller doses of LSD (0.5-30 micrograms), found that fetuses from mice injected with LSD on day 7 of pregnancy did not differ from the fetuses of control mice.

Geber (1967) injected small doses of LSD subcutaneously into pregnant hamsters on the eighth day of gestation. The resorption rate (8-14 per cent) and the fetal mortality rate (7-17 per cent) was higher than in a control group of pregnant hamsters (1-2 per cent). Also, the surviving fetuses showed body edema, localized hemorrhages, and malformations in the brain, spinal cord, liver, and body viscera. However, DiPaolo et al. (1968) presented contradictory results. Syrian hamsters were injected intraperitoneally with 10–300 micrograms of LSD on days 6, 7, or 8 of pregnancy. The LSD-treated animals did not differ from control animals in fetal mortality, resorptions, or malformations.

Alexander, Miles, Gold, and Alexander (1967) injected LSD (5 micrograms per kilogram) into rats during the fourth day of pregnancy. The rats either aborted or produced abnormal offspring with stunting of development. When LSD was injected into rats after the fourth day of pregnancy, the offspring were normal. Control rats that did not receive the drug also produced healthy litters. However, Warkany and Takacs (1968) presented contradictory results. They injected 1 to 100 micrograms of LSD into 34 rats during the fourth or fifth day of pregnancy. The LSD-treated rats did not differ from control rats in the percentage of resorptions and fetal abnormalities. To account for the conflicting results in the Alexander et al. experiment and in their experiment, Warkany and Takacs noted that the preparation of LSD and the stocks of rats were different in the two experiments. However, in a subsequent study, Uyeno (1969) used the same stock of rats that had been used previously by Alexander et al. and failed to confirm their results. Uyeno found that reproductive success was not significantly different when gravid rats were injected on the fourth day of pregnancy with saline or with LSD (5 micrograms per kilogram).

Fabro and Sieber (1968) found no abnormalities in the fetuses of rabbits which were given daily doses of LSD (up to 100 micrograms per kilogram) on the critical days of pregnancy (days 7–9).

In brief, fetal abnormalities were produced in some experiments but not in others when LSD was injected into mice, hamsters, and rats at an appropriate early day of pregnancy. In the single experiment with rabbits, such abnormalities were not produced. It appears that whether or not abnormalities are produced may depend upon such variables as the dose of LSD, differences among species, differences among various stocks of the same species, the exact day of pregnancy on which the drug is injected, and the type of LSD preparation. It should be noted, however, that a variety of agents, e.g., various vitamins and hormones, can produce stillbirths and abnormal offspring if they are injected directly into the abdominal cavity of pregnant rodents early in pregnancy and that viruses, X-rays, noise, and hypoxia are also potent inducers of developmental malformations in pregnant mice (Wilson & Warkany, 1965).

Although LSD injections produce deleterious effects during pregnancy in some species, it is not clear whether LSD taken in usual doses orally by pregnant human females also results in abortions or fetal abnormalities. M. Cohen, Hirschhorn, Verbo, Frosch, and Groeschel

(1968) found that, as compared to matched controls, nine children (ranging in age from 2 months to 5.5 years) who had been exposed to LSD *in utero* showed significantly elevated frequencies of leucocytal chromosomal damage. Although the mothers of these nine children had taken LSD during their pregnancies, and although the children showed chromosomal damage, each child was healthy and none manifested noticeable birth defects.

Although many women have taken LSD during pregnancy, only a few cases have been reported of early abortion (Jacobson & Magyar, 1968) or of birth defects in the offspring (Carakushansky, Neu, & Gardner, 1969; Hecht, Beals, Lees, Jolly, & Roberts, 1968; Zellweger, McDonald, & Abbo, 1967). Of course, the latter cases do not answer the important question because around 2 per cent of all human pregnancies result in some congenital defect (Sato & Pergament, 1968; Smith & Rose, 1968). As with certain other diseases and drugs, however, the effects of LSD on human pregnancies may not become apparent until many years after birth. Two comments are relevant:

Although it has not as yet been shown that LSD damages the sex cells of humans or leads to stillbirths or defective offspring, the data from other species strongly suggest that it would be wise for women not to take LSD unless they are certain that they are not pregnant (Houston, 1969; Idänpään-Heikkilä & Schoolar, 1969). (The same proviso may very well apply to *any* drug; it appears wise for women not to take any drug that they can avoid if they might possibly be pregnant.)

A substantial number of North American Indians have been using peyote for several generations. (At the present time there are about 225,000 Indian members of the Native American Church which uses peyote as an integral part of the ritual.) I have been unable to find any published reports which might indicate that peyote has given rise to abortions or defective offspring among the users. It thus appears possible that if LSD is shown to produce abnormalities in human offspring, it might simply be replaced by peyote or mescaline.

EFFECTS ON CREATIVITY

Several studies have attempted to confirm the hypothesis that LSD-type drugs enhance creativity.

In one study (Zegans, Pollard, & Brown, 1967), graduate students were given either a placebo or a small dose of LSD (0.5 micrograms per kilogram). Overall, the LSD subjects and the placebo controls did not differ significantly in performance on a battery of creativity tests which included remote associations, originality of word associations, and creation of original designs from tiles.

In another study (McGlothlin, Cohen, & McGlothlin, 1967) 72 volunteer graduate students were divided into three groups. The experimental group received 200 micrograms of LSD; one comparison group received a very small dose of LSD (25 micrograms); and another comparison group received 20 milligrams of amphetamine. In each of the three groups, the subjects received the specified drug dose three times under double-blind conditions. A battery of creativity tests was administered prior to the first drug session and then two weeks and six months after the last drug session. The battery included four tests of divergent thinking, three art scales, and tests of artistic performance, imagination, originality, and remote associations. The three groups did not differ significantly on the creativity tests at either the two weeks or the six months assessment. However, at the six-months interview, 25 per cent of the subjects in the 200 microgram LSD group, 9 per cent in the amphetamine group, and 0 per cent in the 25 microgram LSD group, stated that the drug experience had resulted in increased creativity in their work. Also, subjects in the 200 microgram LSD group stated that they had purchased significantly more musical records, had attended significantly more musical events, and had a greater appreciation of music. In brief, although LSD did not enhance performance on creativity tests, it appeared to augment musical appreciation and to produce a subjective feeling of enhanced creativity.

In another study (Berlin, Guthrie, Weider, Goodell, & Wolff, 1955) four graphic artists made drawings while under the influence of LSD or mescaline. Afterwards, a panel of fellow artists compared the drawings made under the drug with samples of the artist's usual work. The panel reported that the drug impaired the technical execution of lines and the employment of color, and that, since the impaired technical execution resulted in lines and colors that were less controlled and more free, the drawings seemed to be more imaginative and to have greater esthetic value.

Another investigation (Harman, McKim, Mogar, Fadiman, & Stolaroff, 1966) was conducted with 27 subjects who met four criteria: the subjects had not been previously exposed to psychedelic drugs; they were in occupations which required creative problem solving (e.g., engineering, physics, mathematics, art, and architecture); they were psychologically normal; and they were motivated to discover, verify, and apply problem solutions. The subjects were asked to bring unsolved professional problems to the drug session. The independent variables included the following: each subject received 200,000 micrograms of mescaline in a group session (with 3 or 4 other subjects); each subject was told to turn off his analytic faculties, to relax, and to stop using cognitive perceptual processes in familiar ways in order to heighten the likelihood of discovering new ways; and each subject spent three hours quietly listening to music. After the initial preparatory period which extended over more than three hours, a battery of creativity tests was administered (Fluency Scale from the Purdue Creativity Test, Miller Object Visualization, and Witkin Embedded Figures Test). Subsequently, each subject spent three or four hours working on his chosen professional problem. Overall, the mescaline subjects showed significant improvement on the tests of creativity. Also, they stated that their abilities were heightened. Furthermore, 75 per cent of the subjects subsequently reported that the solutions to professional problems which they obtained under mescaline were of practical value and acceptable to their clients. (The acceptable solutions included, for example, an engineering improvement to a magnetic tape-recorder, a commercial building design, and a mathematical theorem.) Although the data strongly indicated that creativity was enhanced in this study, they did not demonstrate that the enhancement was due to the administration of mescaline. Many variables were confounded with the administration of mescaline. An additional study is needed which includes a necessary control group. The control subjects should *not* receive mescaline (or any other LSD-type drug) but should be selected as meeting the same four criteria as the drug group and should be treated in the same way as the drug group (e.g., they should be told to turn off their analytic faculties and given a quiet period of preparation while listening to music). It appears possible that Harman et al. have hit upon methods for enhancing creative performance that are independent of the use of LSD-type drugs.

In brief, the hypothesis that psychedelic drugs enhance creativity has not been clearly confirmed or disconfirmed. Although it appears unlikely that these drugs raise performance on creativity tests in graduate students, they may have an effect on artists or other individuals who are highly concerned about their creativity. The carefully controlled study in this area remains to be done. Further studies should take the following into consideration: In most of the previous investigations, creativity was assessed while the subject was still under the influence of the drug. Since intellectual performance and hand-eye coordination is less proficient under the drug, these studies may not have been fair tests of the creativity hypothesis. Further research should either attempt to partial out the effects of impaired intellectual-motor performance, or should assess creativity after the drug is excreted from the body (as in the McGlothlin et al. study), or should aim to determine if the drugs enhance creativity through alterations of old interests and the production of new ones (Hoffer & Osmond, 1967, p. 127).

THERAPEUTIC EFFECTS

LSD has been used in the therapy of neurosis and other non-psychotic psychiatric conditions. LSD has also been used in the therapy of prisoners, of alcoholics, and of patients with terminal cancer pain. Let us evaluate the usefulness of LSD in treating each of these different types of patients. We will begin with its use with non-psychotic psychiatric patients.

Therapy of neurosis and other non-psychotic psychiatric conditions. LSD has been reported to be useful in the treatment of neurosis, sociopathic disorders, and sexual perversions. Levine and Ludwig (1964) noted that much of the enthusiasm for the therapeutic use of LSD stems from its "purported ability to accelerate the process of psychotherapy by facilitating abreaction and the emergence of previously repressed material, increasing the transference reaction, stimulating the production of fantasy material, intensifying affectivity, diminishing excessive intellectualization, dissolving the patient's customary defenses, and thereby allowing him to face his problems more honestly." Unfortunately, the enthusiastic claims are usually based upon uncontrolled and unreplicable studies. Also, in most of the studies in this area either the dependent variables (the end results or aims of therapy) were vague or, if clear-cut criteria for improvement were specified and patients met the criteria, it was impossible to ascertain which of the many variables in the therapy situation were effective in producing the improvement.

A number of psychiatrists in Europe, and a few in the United States, have practiced *psycholytic therapy* which involves the administration of low doses of LSD over a rather long period of time to patients undergoing psychoanalysis. These practitioners almost always claim excellent results. This claim cannot be evaluated at the present time. No study has as yet been published which compared the results obtained with patients assigned at random to psycholytic therapy and to the same type of psychoanalytic therapy which did not include the use of LSD.

A substantially larger number of psychiatrists have practiced *psychedelic therapy* in which one or more high doses of LSD are given to the patient with the aim of producing a 'cosmic experience.' The psychedelic session is preceded by several interviews in which the patient's problems are discussed, a patient-therapist relationship is established, and strong expectancies concerning the LSD session are developed. As Cole and Katz (1964) have pointed out, psychedelic therapy appears to combine drug therapy, brief psychotherapy, aspects of Freudian insight-oriented psychotherapy, mystico-religious exhortation, strong suggestions, pressure on the patient to confront his problems head on, and one or more prolonged 8–10 hour session during which the patient experiences the LSD effects and discusses his problems, needs, and past experiences in a prolonged and intensive manner. This complex mixture of variables appears to help at least some patients. However, we do not know which of the many variables subsumed under the term psychedelic therapy are effective in producing the improvement. In an attempt to ascertain the effective variables, Smart et al. (1967) analyzed 20 studies that used psycholytic or psychedelic therapy with non-psychotic psychiatric patients. With few exceptions, the studies did not include a control group. In the few studies that included a control group, the patients were not assigned at random to experimental and control treatments. Also, objective measures of improvement were not used, the judgment that the patient had improved was made either by the therapist or by the patient himself (not by an objective or 'blind' observer), and there was no long-term follow-up. In no case could it be determined whether the percentage rated as improved or markedly improved differed from that found in a group undergoing the same type of therapy without LSD.

However, there are at least two investigations in which LSD therapy with neurotics was compared with standard therapy and the patients were assigned at random to the treatments. In the first investigation (Robinson, Davies, Sack, & Morrissey, 1963) 87 neurotic in-patients were randomly assigned to one of the following three treatments: eight weeks of standard psychotherapy; eight weeks of standard psychotherapy plus cyclonal and methedrine given at weekly intervals; and eight weeks of standard psychotherapy plus LSD (50 micrograms initially and increasing weekly by 25 micrograms). Ratings made by a 'blind' psychiatrist before and after the eight week therapy, showed no significant differences among the three treatments in the degree of patient improvement.

In the second investigation (McCabe, 1968) 85 neurotic in-patients were assigned at random to one of the following three treatments: a standard treatment for neurotics employed at the hospital which heavily emphasized group therapy; psychedelic therapy which included one session with a low dose of LSD (50 micrograms); and psychedelic therapy which included one session with a relatively high dose of LSD (350 micrograms). Under the standard treatment the patients participated in 20 hours of group therapy. Before receiving LSD, the patients assigned to the psychedelic groups were exposed to 20 hours of psychedelic therapy which included many not-clearly-specified therapeutic procedures plus intensive indoctrination concerning the benefits of LSD. After completing the 20 hours of psychedelic therapy, the latter patients participated in one lengthy (10-12 hours) individual session in which they took LSD and were treated in an unspecified way by the therapist and a nurse who were constantly present. Prior to and after each of the three treatments the patients completed the Minnesota Multiphasic Personality Inventory, the Eysenck Personality Inventory, and the Shostrom Personal Orientation Inventory. Analyses of the inventories indicated that the two psychedelic treatments had a significantly greater effect than the standard treatment in facilitating self-actualization and in reducing anxiety, worry, depression, and social withdrawal. In general, the psychedelic group that had received the one high dose of LSD did not differ on the inventories from the psychedelic group that had received the low dose. In brief, this study indicated that psychedelic therapy tends to be somewhat more effective with neurotics than standard hospital therapy, at least as indicated by the patient's responses to inventories. Which of the many variables included in psychedelic therapy were effective and which irrelevant in producing the ostensible therapeutic effects cannot be determined from this study. However, another recent investigation (Ditman et al., 1969) suggests the possibility that the use of LSD may be irrelevant; that is, the same effects might have been obtained if the psychedelic therapy had been conducted in the same intensive way but another drug (e.g., a mild stimulant such as methylphenidate) had been substituted for LSD.

In summary, although the enthusiastic claim made by practitioners of psycholytic therapy or psychedelic therapy with neurotic patients have not yet been clearly supported by empirical data, there is suggestive evidence that some of the many variables subsumed under the term psychedelic therapy (e.g., intensive attention given to the patient) may be helpful, at times, in the treatment of certain types of neurotic patients (Shagass & Bittle, 1967).

Therapy of prisoners. In an investigation carried out by a team of investigators from Harvard (Leary, 1968), prison inmates were given psilocybin about four times in doses of 20,000 to 70,000 micrograms. Each drug session included a group of prisoners and one or two Harvard investigators who also ingested the drug. A brief follow-up indicated that the prisoners who had participated in the drug sessions stayed out on parole longer than the other prisoners. However, as S. Cohen (1967b) pointed out, the psilocybin group enjoyed a special status both while in prison and also during parole. While in prison, the psilocybin group developed close relations with the investigators and received a special pre-parole course of instructions. During parole, the psilocybin group received special assistance in obtaining loans, employment, and housing and spent many hours in friendly interaction with and receiving advice from their friends at Harvard. Furthermore, a longer follow-up (four years after the beginning of the experiment) showed that the rate of return to prison was not significantly different in the psilocybin group and the control group (Robbins et al., 1967, p. 992). What can we conclude from this study? At best, it appears that convicts who receive psilocybin together with many other special benefits may tend to stay out on parole a little longer than convicts who receive neither psilocybin or any other benefits. Of course, no conclusions can be drawn with respect to the role played by psilocybin until another study is carried out in which a control group of prison inmates receives the special assistance but does not receive the drug.

Therapy of alcoholism. Nine studies that were published prior to 1964 reported that psychedelic therapy with alcoholics produced dramatic improvement. However, a recent review (Smart et al., 1967) pointed out that none of these investigations included objective measures of change or a follow-up and eight of the nine did not include a control group. Furthermore, in the one which included a control group, the controls were not selected at random and were treated entirely differently from the LSD group.

More recent investigations included a control group. Smart et al. (1967) randomly assigned 30 alcoholic patients at the Toronto Clinic to one of three treatments: the standard treatment used at the clinic for alcoholics; the standard treatment plus one session in which the patient received a very high dose of LSD (800 micrograms); and the standard treatment plus one session in which the patient received an active placebo (ephedrine). The three treatment groups did not differ significantly in abstinence or amount of drinking at a 6-month and also at a 2-year evaluation. The LSD treatment reduced the amount of drinking in this investigation to the same degree as in earlier investigations, but the reduction was no greater than that produced by ephedrine or by the standard treatment alone. (Specifically, about 80 per cent of the patients showed a reduction in alcohol intake in each of the three treatments.) Similarly, Hollister, Shelton, and Krieger (1969) found that dextroamphetamine was generally as effective as LSD in reducing drinking in 72 alcoholics, and Bowen, Soskin, and Chotlos (1968) found that alcoholics treated with a combination of LSD and Human Relations Training were approximately equal in adjustment status after one year to alcoholics treated through Human Relations Training alone.

In another investigation (Van Dusen, Wilson, Miners, & Hook, 1967), 56 female alcoholics were given LSD in one, two, or three drug sessions. The LSD dose in each session averaged 400 micrograms and ranged from 100 to 800 micrograms, depending on the amount needed to elicit an LSD reaction in the patient. At 6, 12, and 18 month assessments, no significant differences were found in abstinence or amount of drinking between the LSD patients and a control group of female alcoholics who were treated at the same facility without LSD. Also, there were no significant differences in results obtained with patients receiving LSD in one, two, or three sessions.

Johnson (1968) randomly assigned 95 patients at an alcoholic clinic to one of four treatments: routine treatment used at the clinic for alcoholism; routine treatment plus one session in which the patient received 300 to 600 micrograms of LSD without his therapist being present; a treatment which was the same as the second treatment but the patient's therapist was present; and a treatment which was the same as the third treatment but the patient received sodium amytal and methedrine instead of LSD. The study was single-blind—the patients did not know what type of drug they had received. Each of the four treatments was associated with improvement at a one-year follow-up, but there were no significant differences among them.

In another study (Ludwig, Levine, Stark, & Lazar, 1968) 176 alcoholic in-patients were randomly assigned to one of four treatments: conventional therapy used at the hospital with alcoholics; conventional therapy plus one session in which the patient received LSD (3 micrograms per kilogram); a treatment which was the same as the second treatment except that the LSD was given together with psychotherapy; and a treatment which was the same as the second except that the LSD was given together with hypnosis and psychotherapy. At a three-year evaluation, none of the LSD treatments produced greater benefit than was realized by the conventional therapy without LSD.

Some positive results were presented in a recent preliminary report (Kurland, Unger, Savage, Olsson, & Pahnke, 1968). Of 101 alcoholics followed for six months, 67 had received a high dose of LSD (450 micrograms) in one psychedelic session and 34 had received a small dose (50 micrograms) in one session. At the 6-month evaluation, a significantly greater reduction in alcohol intake was found in the patients who had received the high dose. Also, among the alcoholics who had received the high dose, those who had marked psychedelic reactions during the drug session showed a significantly greater reduction in alcohol intake than those who had minimal reactions. The authors explained the differences in results between their study and other studies which yielded negative results as due to differences in the way the LSD sessions were conducted. They stressed that the critical factor was the amount and quality of the psychotherapy given during the LSD session.

However, since a striking drop-off in sobriety is often found six months after the treatment of alcoholics, evaluation of this study must be suspended until longer follow-up results are available.

Therapy of terminal cancer pain. LSD may be useful in reducing pain and suffering among terminally ill patients. Kast and Collins (1964) gave either 100 micrograms of LSD or one of two analgesic drugs (Dilaudid or Demerol) to 50 terminal cancer patients who were suffering from pain. LSD showed a more protracted and effective action than the other two drugs; it was superior in reducing reports of pain, especially during and after the third hour. In subsequent studies which did not utilize control groups, Kast (1966, 1967) again reported that 100 micrograms of LSD was effective in reducing distress and lifting mood and outlook in terminally ill patients.

Although LSD seemed to be effective in these investigations, it was surprising that some patients refused a second administration of the drug, many were indifferent to repeated administration, and only a few asked for it again. Further research is clearly needed to confirm the findings of Kast and to determine more precisely the effects of the drug on terminally ill patients.

Present and Future Status of LSD-Type Drugs

During recent years there has been a marked decline in research on LSD. It appears likely that the decline will continue into the immediate future. However, after the present furor has abated, we may expect a revival of research with LSD, with LSD-type drugs such as mescaline, psilocybin, and dimethyltryptamine, and with plants that appear to possess LSD-type activity. The latter plants include, for example, various species of *Datura* which has a long history of use in the religious or magical rites of various preliterate cultures; *Amanita muscaria* (fly agaric) which has been used for its LSD-type effects among preliterate tribes in Siberia; various species of the jungle tree *Virola* that grows around the Amazon; the dried seed of *Myristica fragrans* (nutmeg) and also the seeds of *Peganum harmala* (Farnsworth, 1968; Schultes, 1969). Before we discuss the indications for future research in more detail, let us look at the present legal status of these drugs and at the present research.

LEGALITY

The Federal Drug Abuse Control Amendments of 1965 made the manufacturing, processing, distribution, or sale of hallucinogens (LSD and similarly acting drugs) punishable by up to one year in jail and a $1000 fine. Although the sale of these drugs was made illegal, no penalty was included for their possession. However, additional amendments were passed in 1968 which made possession of the drugs a misdemeanor (except when prescribed by a licensed physician).

Attempts to legally supress the LSD-type drugs appear to have no more chance of succeeding by themselves than attempts to prohibit the sale of alcohol and narcotics. However, the furor during recent years with respect to psychotic effects and chromosome damage attributed to LSD has apparently had an effect in reducing the use of this drug. Although the use of black-market LSD has ostensibly declined among the youth, it appears that other drugs, some of which produce LSD-type effects, have been substituted.

What is needed at the present time is a broad-scope public health education campaign about these drugs. Their properties need to be demythologized by providing factual information and by avoiding emotional appeals which are rejected by most youth and which may serve to increase drug use (Fort, 1968). However, public health information requires a basis of facts. To gather such facts concerning possible dangers and benefits, additional scientific research is needed. Let us now glance at the research picture.

PRESENT RESEARCH

With passage of the federal law prohibiting the manufacture of LSD, the legal manufacturer of the drug (Sandoz) placed the entire legitimate supply in the hands of the National Institute of Mental Health. LSD-type drugs were subsequently treated by the National Institute of Mental Health and the United States Food and Drug Administration in the same way as other experimental drugs which are legally distributed only to qualified investigators who administer them in the course of an approved program of research. Thus, in practice, LSD-type drugs are legally available only to researchers working under a government grant or for a State or Federal agency.

A joint Federal Drug Administration-Public Health Service Psychotomimetic Agents Advisory Committee was established in the Fall of 1967 to expedite the processing of research applications pertaining to these drugs. To conduct research in this area, an investigator must obtain a research grant either from the National Institute of Mental Health or from another governmental agency and must file an investigational new drug application (IND) with the Federal Drug Administration. Around 1966 and 1967 at least 35 new projects were approved (Caldwell, 1968, p. 115).

Until very recently, qualified investigators did not find it too difficult to carry out research in this area. Kurland (1967) emphasized that "It isn't too difficult to do research in this area if you submit a protocol. . . If you have studies that you want to pursue, I'm pretty sure that if they meet the judgment of your scientific peers, they will be approved. Whether it will be funded is another matter, because there are priorities in these matters. One must be aware that there are only certain amounts of money available to go into programs." However, following the 1967–68 reports that LSD produced chromosomal damage and fetal malformations, it became very difficult to carry out experimental research with this drug on human subjects. Although experiments with animals and observational studies of individuals who use illicit LSD are being carried out, it will probably remain difficult to conduct experimental LSD studies with human subjects until such time as the question of possible chromosomal damage and fetal malformations is fully resolved.

FUTURE RESEARCH

Even if all research with LSD were to be outlawed, other drugs are already available which seem to exert very similar effects and still others will be isolated. Consequently, it appears likely that LSD-type drugs will continue to play a role in experimental psychiatry and psychology for many years to come. They will be used as tools to manipulate and study changes in body image, time perception, and normal and abnormal cognitive processes. They will be used in the study of visual processes such as space and color phenomena, normal and abnormal visual perception, simultaneous and successive contrast, entoptic phenomena, illusions, pseudo-hallucinations, hallucinations, synesthesia, and the relation of peripheral to central factors in vision (Kluver, 1928). Although indiscriminate use of LSD-type drugs in therapy is contraindicated, they may find an adjunctive role in treating selected behavioral disorders and in alleviating pain or improving the mood of chronically ill patients.

The more urgent need, however, is for broad-scale intensive research to accomplish the following four aims:

It is necessary to delineate more precisely the differences and similarities among the drugs which have been mentioned in this review—LSD, psilocybin, mescaline, dimethyltryptamine, DOM, Sernyl, Ditran, etc. It appears that each of these drugs may give rise to some or many of the effects listed in Table 1, column 2 (page 9). However, there are also indications that the effects produced by one drug are not identical to those produced by another and that the drugs are acting on different parts of the central nervous system.

It is necessary to delineate more precisely the relative importance of each of the antecedent variables listed in Table 1, column 1—drug-dose, situation, set, and personality. For example, studies which focus on set could be conducted along the following lines. The effects produced by an

LSD-type drug could be compared with those of an active placebo which the subjects are led to believe is an LSD-type drug. Such *active placebos* might include, for example, epinephrine (which produces some of the somatic-sympathetic effects that are found with LSD-type drugs but does not appear to produce the other effects) and nicotinic acid (which produces feelings of warmth and tingling of the skin). Studies along these lines could test the hypothesis that subjects who react euphorically, or mystically, or anxiously to the LSD-type drug also react in a similar way to an active placebo.

The interactive effects of drug-dose, situation, set, personality, and other antecedent variables need to be specified. To delineate interactive effects, it is necessary to use factorial experimental designs. (Although many studies have been performed with LSD-type drugs, none have used a factorial design.)

It is imperative to determine the long-term chronic effects of these drugs.

Toward a Theoretical Formulation

Several writers have formulated general principles that might encompass most or all of the effects of LSD-type drugs. For example, Fiddleman (1961, p. 17) proposed that "LSD appears to be a stressor whose main effects tend to be the establishment of a situation which is unique and which has no referent in most individual's experience." Similarly, von Felsinger et al. (1956, p. 424) write that "primary drug changes can constitute a stressful situation for particular individuals and they may react with vigorous restitutive activity. The complete drug reaction may then be best explained in terms of the individual's defense system or his characteristic reaction to stress or threat in general."

Other writers have proposed that LSD-type drugs have an inhibitory effect on sensory threshholds, or on perceptual processes, or on the activity of the brain. For instance, Leary, Litwin, and Metzner (1963) propose that these drugs produce a "diminution or suspension of the normal processes of perceptual selection and inhibition." S. Cohen (1967b, pp. 238–239) has presented a related formulation; he writes that "LSD may temporarily and selectively disinhibit the brain's inhibitory activity" and that the drug-produced disinhibition may allow "a more primal, fantasy, dreamlike condition" to emerge in which "the boundaries of the self are diffused, and the learned, imposed meanings of objects are altered to a point where objects have no significance except for themselves. Colors become, by loss of inhibitory influence, more saturated and brilliant, and the viewed object is seen in its primary form unencumbered by utilitarian values."

Other writers (e.g., Huxley, 1954; M. Jarvik, 1967b, p. 216) have postulated that LSD-type drugs either heighten the intensity and emotional significance of perceptions or give rise to novel experiences which alert the subject to notice things that he would not otherwise notice and to see the old and familiar in a new light.

Although each of the foregoing propositions may have a degree of validity, it is doubtful that these or any other broad principles which can be formulated at the present time adequately cover the complex effects of LSD-type drugs. It is the present author's opinion that research in this area will proceed more effectively, not by prematurely postulating general principles, but by clearly specifying each of the many effects associated with the drugs and proceeding to isolate antecedent variables that are instrumental in producing the effects. If research demonstrates that the many complex effects are related to a small number of antecedent variables, we may be able to formulate a few general principles to account for the effects. However, since very few functional relations between antecedent and consequent variables have been established, it appears too early to attempt to formulate a parsimonious theory.

Previous reviews in this area tended to treat the phenomena associated with LSD-type drugs as an undifferentiated conglomerate. Also, although many previous reviews listed drug-dose, situation, set, and personality among the important antecedent variables related to the phenomena, little attempt was made to assign relative weights to these antecedents. The present chapter differs from earlier reviews in that an attempt has been made to differentiate and to treat separately each of the many phenomena that are associated with these drugs, and to assign relative weights to each of the major classes of antecedent variables (Table 1, column 1) that play a role in producing each of the major consequent effects (Table 1, column 2). This analysis appears to indicate that some effects are more closely related to the dose of the drug than to the extra-drug variables (situation, set, and personality) whereas other effects are more closely related to the extra-drug variables than to the drug-dose.

The effects that appear to be closely related to the drug dose include most of the somatic-sympathetic effects, changes in body-image, dreamy-detached feelings, reduced intellectual-motor proficiency, and changes in visual perception. It appears that whether and to what degree subjects experience these effects is closely dependent on how much of the drug they receive. However, the extra-drug variables play a role in determining how much emphasis the subject places on these effects, how much attention he pays to them, and to what degree he elaborates upon and discusses them.

The effects that appear to be closely related to the extra-drug variables of situation, set, and personality include some of the somatic-sympathetic effects (such as nervousness, trembling, and difficulty in breathing) and changes in moods and emotions (ranging from euphoria to dysphoria or from psychedelic reactions to psychotic-like reactions). Although variations in drug-dose may produce some variations in mood, the type of moods and emotions that will be manifested appears to be closely dependent upon the situation and the subject's set and personality.

References

Abramson, H. A. Lysergic acid diethylamide (LSD-25): XXX. The questionnaire technique with notes on its use. *J. Psychol.,* 1960, *49,* 57-65.

Abramson, H. A., Jarvik, M. E., Gorin, M.H. and Hirsch, M. W., Lysergic acid diethylamide (LSD-25): XVII. Tolerance development and its relationship to a theory of psychosis. *J. Psychol.,* 1956, *41,* 81-105.

Abramson, H. A., Jarvik, M. E., Kaufman, M. R., Kornetsky, C., Levine, A., and Wagner, M. Lysergic acid diethylamide (LSD-25): I. Physiological and perceptual responses. *J. Psychol.,* 1955, *39,* 3-60.(a)

Abramson, H. A., Kornetsky, C., Jarvik, M. E., Kaufman, M. R., and Ferguson, M. W. Lysergic acid diethylamide (LSD-25): XI. Content analysis of clinical reactions. *J. Psychol.,* 1955, *40,* 53-60. (b)

Abuzzahab, F. F., Yunis, J. J., Schiele, B. S., and Marrazzi, A. S. A controlled study of the effects of LSD-25 on human chromosomes. In J. Wortis (Ed.) *Recent advances in biological psychiatry,* Vol. II. New York: Plenum Press, 1969.

Adler, F. H. *Textbook of ophthalmology* (7th ed.). Philadelphia: W. B. Saunders, 1962.

Aghajanian, G. K., and Bing, O. H. L. Persistence of lysergic acid diethylamide in the plasma of human subjects. *Clin. Pharmacol. Ther.,* 1964, *5,* 611-614.

Aghajanian, G. K., Foote, W. E., and Sheard, M. H. Lysergic acid diethylamide: Sensitive neuronal units in the midbrain raphe. *Science,* 1968, *161,* 706-708.

Alexander, G. J., Miles, B. E., Gold, G. M., and Alexander, R. B. LSD: Injection early in pregnancy produces abnormalities in offspring of rats. *Science,* 1967, *157,* 459-460.

Andén, N. E., Corrodi, H., Fuxe, K., and Hökfelt, T. Evidence for a central 5-hydroxytryptamine receptor stimulation by lysergic acid diethylamide. *Brit. J. Pharmacol.,* 1968, *34,* 1-7.

Anderson, E. W., and Rawnsley, K. Clinical studies of lysergic acid diethylamide. *Mont. Psychiat. Neurol.,* 1954, *128,* 38-55.

Apter, J. T., and Pfeiffer, C. C. The effects of the hallucinogenic drugs LSD-25 and mescaline on the electroretinogram. *Ann. N. Y. Acad. Sci.,* 1957, *66,* Art. 3, 508-514.

Aronson, H., Silverstein, A. B., and Klee, G. D. The influence of lysergic acid diethylamide (LSD-25) on subjective time. *Arch. Gen. Psychiat.,* 1959, *1,* 469-472.

Auerbach, R., and Rugowski, J. A. Lysergic and diethylamide: Effect on embryos. *Science,* 1967, *157,* 1325-1326.

Balestrieri, A., and Fontanari, D. Acquired and crossed tolerance to mescaline, LSD-25, and BOL-148. *Arch. Gen. Psychiat.*, 1959, *1*, 279-282.

Barber, T. X. Measuring "hypnotic-like" suggestibility with and without "hypnotic induction"; psychometric properties, norms, and variables influencing response to the Barber Suggestibility Scale (BSS). *Psychol. Rep.*, 1965, *16*, 809-844.

Barber, T. X. *Hypnosis: A scientific approach.* New York: Van Nostrand Reinhold, 1969.

Barron, F., Jarvik, M. E., and Bunnell, S., Jr. Hallucinogenic drugs. *Sci. Amer.*, 1964, *210*, No. 4, 29-37.

Becker, H. S. History, culture and subjective experience: An exploration of the social bases of drug-induced experiences. *J. Health Soc. Beh.*, 1967, *8*, 163-176.

Benda, P., and Orsini, F. Experimental study of time estimation under LSD. *Presse Med.*, 1959, *67*, 1000.

Bender, L., and Sankar, D. V. S. Chromosome damage not found in leukocytes of children treated with LSD-25. *Science*, 1968, *159*, 749.

Bercel, N. A., Travis, L. E., Olinger, L. B., and Dreikurs, E. Model psychoses induced by LSD-25 in normals: I. Psycho-physiological investigations with special reference to the mechanism of the paranoid reaction. *Arch. Neurol. Psychiat.*, 1956, *75*, 588-611.

Beringer, K. Der *Meskalinrausch.* Berlin: Springer, 1927.

Berlin, L., Guthrie, T., Weider, A., Goodell, H., and Wolff, H. G. Studies in human cerebral function: The effects of mescaline and lysergic acid on cerebral processes pertinent to creative activity. *J. Nerv. Ment. Dis.*, 1955, *122*, 487-491.

Bertino, J. R., Klee, G. D., Collier, D., and Weintraub, W. Clinical studies with dibenzyline and lysergic acid diethylamide. *J. Clin. Exp., Psychopath.*, 1960, *21*, 293-299.

Best, C. H., and Taylor, N. B. *The physiological basis of medical practice.* Baltimore: Williams & Wilkins, 1950.

Bishop, P. O., Field, G., Hennessy, B. L., and Smith, J. R. Action of d-lysergic acid diethylamide on lateral geniculate synapses. *J. Neurophysiol.*, 1958, *21*, 529-549.

Blum, R. *Utopiates.* New York: Atherton Press, 1964.

Blumenfield, M., and Glickman, L. Ten months experience with LSD users admitted to county psychiatric receiving hospital. *N. Y. State J. Med.*, 1967, *67*, 1849-1853.

Boardman, W. K., Goldstone, S., and Lhamon, W. T. Effects of lysergic acid diethylamide (LSD) on the time sense of normals: A preliminary report. *Arch. Neurol. Psychiat.*, 1957, *78*, 321-324.

Bowen, W. T., Soskin, R. A., and Chotlos, J. W. LSD as a variable in the hospital treatment of alcoholism: A follow-up study. Paper presented at Annual Meeting of VA Cooperative Studies in Psychiatry, Houston, 1968.

Brazier, M. A. B. The effects of drugs on the electroencephalogram of man. *Clin. Pharmacol. Ther.*, 1964, *5*, 102-116.

Brown, B. B. Subjective and EEG responses to LSD in visualizer and non-visualizer subjects. *EEG Clin. Neurophysiol.*, 1968, *25*, 372-379.

Browning, L. S. Lysergic acid diethylamide: Mutagenic effects in Drosophila. *Science*, 1968, *161*, 1022-1023.

Burian, H. M., Fleming, W. J., and Featherstone, R. M. Electroretinographic effects of LSD-25, Brom-LSD and LSM (lysergic acid morpholide). *Fed. Proc.,* 1958, *17,* 355.

Caldwell, W. V. *LSD psychotherapy.* New York: Grove Press, 1968.

Carakushansky, G., Neu, R. L., and Gardner, L. I. Lysergide and cannabis as possible teratogens in man. *Lancet,* 1969, *1,* 150-151.

Carey, J. T. *The college drug scene.* Englewood Cliffs, N. J.: Prentice-Hall, 1968.

Cerletti, A., and Rothlin, E. Role of 5-hydroxytryptamine in mental disease and its antagonism to lysergic acid derivatives. *Nature,* 1955, *176,* 785-786.

Cholden, L. S., Kurland, A., and Savage, C. Clinical reactions and tolerance to LSD in chronic schizophrenia. *J. Nerv. Ment. Dis.,* 1955, *122,* 211-221.

Cohen, M. M., Hirschhorn, K., and Frosch, W. A. In vivo and in vitro chromosomal damage by LSD-25. *New Eng. J. Med.,* 1967, *277,* 1043-1049.

Cohen, M. M., Hirschhorn, K., Verbo, S., Frosch, W. A., and Groeschel, M. M. The effect of LSD-25 on the chromosomes of children exposed in utero. *Pediat. Res.,* 1968, *2,* 486-492.

Cohen, M. M., Marinello, M. J., and Back, N. Chromosomal damage in human leukocytes induced by lysergic acid diethylamide. *Science,* 1967, *155,* 1417-1419.

Cohen, M. M., and Mukherjee, A. B. Meiotic chromosome damage induced by LSD-25. *Nature,* 1968, *219,* 1072-1074.

Cohen, S. Lysergic acid diethylamide: Side effects and complications. *J. Nerv. Ment. Dis.* 1960, *130,* 30-40.

Cohen, S. A classification of LSD complications. *Psychosomatics,* 1966, *7,* 182-186.

Cohen, S. Psychotomimetic agents. *Ann. Rev. Pharmacol.,* 1967, *7,* 301-318. (a)

Cohen, S. *The beyond within: The LSD story.* (2nd ed.) New York: Atheneum, 1967. (b)

Cohen, S. A quarter century of research with LSD. In J. T. Ungerleider (Ed.) *The problem and prospects of LSD.* Springfield, Ill.: C. C. Thomas, 1968. Pp. 22-44.

Cohen, S. *The drug dilemma.* New York: McGraw-Hill, 1969.

Cohen, S., and Ditman, K. S. Prolonged adverse reactions to lysergic acid diethylamide. *Arch. Gen. Psychiat.,* 1963, *8,* 475-480.

Cole, J. O., and Katz, M. M. The psychotomimetic drugs: An overview. *J. Amer. Med. Ass.,* 1964, *187,* 758-761.

DiMascio, A., Rinkel, M., and Leiberman, J. Personality and psychotomimetic drugs. *Proc. Third World Cong. Psychiat.,* 1961, *2,* 933-936.

DiPaolo, J. A., Givelber, H. M., and Erwin, H. Evaluation of teratogenicity of lysergic acid diethylamide. *Nature,* 1968, *220,* 490-491.

Ditman, K. S. The value of LSD in psychotherapy. In J. T. Ungerleider (Ed.) *The problems and prospects of LSD.* Springfield, Ill.: C. C. Thomas, 1968, Pp. 45-60.

Ditman, K. S., and Bailey, J. J. Evaluating LSD as a psychotherapeutic agent. In H. A. Abramson (Ed.) *The use of LSD in psychotherapy and alcoholism.* Indianapolis: Bobbs-Merrill, 1967, Pp. 74-80.

Ditman, K. S., Moss, T., Forgy, E. W., Zunin, L. M., Lynch, R. D., and Funk, W. A. Dimensions of the LSD, methylphenidate, and chlordiazepoxide experiences. *Psychopharmacologia,* 1969, *14,* 1-11.

Edwards, A. E., and Cohen, S. Visual illusion, tactile sensibility and reaction time under LSD-25. *Psychopharmacologia,* 1961, *2,* 297-303.

Edwards, A. E., and Cohen, S. Interaction of LSD and quantity of encoded visual data upon size estimation. *J. Psychopharmacol.,* 1966, *1,* 96-100.

Egozcue, J., Irwin, S., and Maruffo, C. A. Chromosomal damage in LSD users. *J. Amer. Med. Ass.,* 1968, *204,* 214-218.

Ellis, H. Mescal: A new artificial paradise. *Contemp. Rev.,* 1898, *73,* 130-141.

Evarts, E. V. A review of the neurophysiological effects of lysergic acid diethylamide (LSD) and other psychotomimetic agents. *Ann. N. Y. Acad. Sci.,* 1957, *66* (Art. 3), 479-495.

Fabro, S., and Sieber, S. M. Is lysergide a teratogen? *Lancet,* 1968, *1,* 639.

Farnsworth, N. R. Hallucinogenic plants. *Science,* 1968, *162,* 1086-1092.

Feigen, G. A., and Alles, G. A. Physiological concomitants of mescaline intoxication. *J. Clin. Exp. Psychopath.,* 1955, *16,* 167-178.

Fernberger, S. W. Observations on taking peyote (Anhalonium lewinii). *Amer. J. Psychol.,* 1923, *34,* 267-270.

Fichman, L. L. Psychological effects of Lysergic Acid Diethylamide as reflected in psychological test changes. Unpublished doctoral dissertation, Univ. of Calif. L. A., 1957.

Fiddleman, P. B. The prediction of behavior under lysergic acid diethylamide (LSD). Unpublished doctoral dissertation, Univ. of North Carolina, 1961.

Fischer, R., Griffin, E., and Liss, L. Biological aspects of time in relation to (model) psychoses. *Ann. N. Y. Acad. Sci.,* 1962, *96* (Art. 1), 44-65.

Fisher, D. D., and Ungerleider, J. T. Grand mal seizures following ingestion of LSD. *Calif. Med.,* 1967, *106,* 210-211.

Fogel, S., and Hoffer, A. The use of hypnosis to interrupt and to reproduce an LSD-25 experience. *J. Clin. Exp. Psychopath.,* 1962, *23,* 11-16.

Fort, J. LSD and the mind-altering drug (M.A.D.) world. In J. T. Ungerleider (Ed.) *The problems and prospects of LSD.* Springfield, Ill.: C. C. Thomas, 1968. Pp. 3-21.

Freedman, D. X. On the use and abuse of LSD. *Arch. Gen. Psychiat.,* 1968, *18,* 330-347.

Freedman, D. X., Appel, J. B., Hartman, F. R., and Molliver, M. E. Tolerance to behavioral effects of LSD-25 in rat. *J. Pharmacol. Exp. Therap.,* 1964, *143,* 309-313.

Frosch, W. A., Robbins, E. S., and Stern, M. Untoward reactions to lysergic acid diethylamide (LSD) resulting in hospitalization. *New Eng. J. Med.,* 1965, *273,* 1235-1239.

Fry, G. A. The image-forming mechanisms of the eye. In J. Field (Ed.) *Handbook of physiology. Section I. Neurophysiology,* Vol. 1, 1959, Pp. 647-670.

Geber, W. F. Congenital malformations induced by mescaline, lysergic acid diethylamide, and bromolysergic acid in the hamster. *Science,* 1967, *158,* 265-267.

Geert-Jörgensen, E., Hertz, M., Knudsen, K., and Kristensen, K. LSD-treatment: Experience gained within a three-year period. *Acta Psychiat. Scand.,* 1964, *40* (Suppl. 180), 373-382.

Giarman, N. J. The pharmacology of LSD. In R. C. De Bold & R. C. Leaf (Eds.) *LSD, man, and society,* Middletown, Conn.: Wesleyan Univ. Press, 1967, Pp. 143-158.

Glickman, L. and Blumenfield, M. Psychological determinants of "LSD reactions." *J. Nerv. Ment. Dis.*, 1967, *145*, 79-83.

Goldstein, L., Murphree, H. B., Sugerman, A. A., Pfeiffer, C. C., and Jenney, E. H. Quantitative electoencephalographic analysis of naturally occurring (schizophrenic) and drug-induced psychotic states in human males. *Clin. Pharmacol. Ther.*, 1963, *4*, 10-21.

Grace, D., Carlson, E. A., and Goodman, P. Drosophila melanogaster treated with LSD: Absence of mutation and chromosome breakage. *Science*, 1968, *161*, 694-696.

Green, W. J. The effect of LSD on the sleep-dream cycle. *J. Nerv. Ment. Dis.*, 1965, *140*, 417-426.

Guttmann, E. Artificial psychoses produced by mescaline. *J. Ment. Sci.*, 1936, *82*, 203-221.

Halasz, M. F. Formanek, J., and Marrazzi, A. S. Hallucinogen-tranquilizer interaction: Its nature. *Science*, 1969, *164*, 569-571.

Hanaway, J. K. Lysergic acid diethylamide: Effects on developing mouse lens. *Science*, 1969, *164*, 574-575.

Harman, W. W., McKim, R. H., Mogar, R. E., Fadiman, J., and Stolaroff, M. J. Psychedelic agents in creative problem-solving: A pilot study. *Psychol. Rep.*, 1966, *19*, 211-217.

Hartman, A. M., and Hollister, L. E. Effect of mescaline, lysergic acid diethylamide and psilocybin on color perception. *Psychopharmacologia*, 1963, *4*, 441-451.

Heaton, J. M. *The eye: Phenomenology and psychology of function and disorder.* Philadelphia: J. B. Lippincott, 1968.

Hecht, F., Beals, R. K. Lees, M. H., Jolly, H., and Roberts, P. Lysergic-acid-diethylamide and cannabis as possible teratogens in man. *Lancet*, 1968, *2*, 1087.

Hensala, J. D., Epstein, L. J., and Blacker, K. H. LSD and psychiatric inpatients. *Arch. Gen. Psychiat.*, 1967, *16*, 554-559.

Hoch, P. H. Experimental psychiatry. *Amer. J. Psychiat.*, 1955, *111*, 787-791.

Hoffer, A., and Osmand, H. *The hallucinogens.* New York: Academic Press, 1967.

Holliday, A. R., and Sigurdson, T. The effects of lysergic acid diethylamide II: Intraocular pressure. *Proc. West. Pharmacol. Soc.*, 1965, *8*, 51-54.

Hollister, L. E. *Chemical psychoses: LSD and related drugs.* Springfield, Ill.: C. C. Thomas, 1969.

Hollister, L. E., and Hartman, A. M. Mescaline, lysergic diethylamide and psilocybin: Comparison of clinical syndromes, effects on color perception and biochemical measures. *Comp. Psychiat.*, 1962, *3*, 235-241.

Hollister, L. E., Macnicol, M. F., and Gillespie, H. K. An hallucinogenic amphetamine analog (DOM) in man. *Psychopharmacologia*, 1969, *14*, 62-73.

Hollister, L. E., Shelton, J., and Krieger, G. A controlled comparison of lysergic acid diethylamide (LSD) and dextroamphetamine in alcoholics. *Amer. J. Psychiat.*, 1969, *125*, 1352-1357.

Horowitz, M. J. The imagery of visual hallucinations. *J. Nerv. Ment. Dis.*, 1964, *138*, 513-523.

Houston, R. K. Review of the evidence and qualifications regarding the effects of hallucinogenic drugs on chromosomes and embryos. *Amer. J. Psychiat.,* 1969, *126,* 251-254.

Hungerford, D. A., Taylor, K. M., Shagass, C., LaBadie, G. U., Balaban, G. B., and Paton, G. R. Cytogenetic effects of LSD-25 therapy in man. *J. Amer. Med. Ass.,* 1968, *206,* 2287-2296.

Huxley, A. *The doors of perception.* New York: Harper, 1954.

Idänpään-Heikkilä, J. E. and Schoolar, J. C. LSD: Autoradiographic study on the placental transfer and tissue distribution in mice. *Science,* 1969, *164,* 1295-1297.

Irwin, S., and Egozcue, J. Chromosomal abnormalities in leukocytes from LSD-25 users. *Science,* 1967, *157,* 313-314.

Irwin, S., and Egozcue, J. Chromosome damage in leukocytes of children treated with LSD-25. *Science,* 1968, *159,* 749.

Isbell, H. Comparison of the reactions induced by psilocybin and LSD-25 in man. *Psychopharmacologia,* 1959, *1,* 29-38.

Isbell, H., Belleville, R. E., Fraser, H. F., Wikler, A., and Logan, C. R. Studies on lysergic acid diethylamide (LSD-25): I. Effects in former morphine addicts and development of tolerance during chronic intoxication. *Arch. Neurol. Psychiat.,* 1956, *76,* 468-478.

Isbell, H., and Gorodetzky C. W. Effect of alkaloids of ololiuqui in man. *Psychopharmacologia,* 1966, *8,* 331-339.

Isbell, H., and Jasinski, D. R. A comparison of LSD-25 with $(-)$- Δ^9-*trans*-tetrahydrocannabinol (THC) and attempted cross tolerance between LSD and THC. *Psychopharmacologia,* 1969, *14,* 115-123.

Isbell, H., and Logan, C. R. Studies on the diethylamide of lysergic acid (LSD-25). *Arch. Neurol. Psychiat.,* 1957, *77,* 350-358.

Isbell, H., Rosenberg, D. E., Miner, E. J., and Logan, C. R. Tolerance and cross tolerance to scopolamine, N-ethyl-3-piperidyl-benzylate (JB-318) and LSD-25. In P. B. Bradley, F. Flügel, and P. Hoch (Eds.) *Neuropsychopharmacology,* Vol. 3. Amsterdam: Elsevier, 1964.

Isbell, H., Wolbach, A. B., Wikler, A., and Miner, E. J. Cross-tolerance between LSD and psilocybin. *Psychopharmacologia,* 1961, *2,* 147-151.

Jacobsen, E. The clinical pharmacology of the hallucinogens. *Clin. Pharmacol. Ther.,* 1963, *4,* 480-503.

Jacobson, C. B., and Magyar, V. L. Genetic evaluation of LSD. *Clin. Proc. Child. Hosp. D. C.,* 1968, *24,* 153-161.

Jacobson, J. H., and Gestring, G. F. Spontaneous retinal electrical potentials. *Arch. Ophthal.,* 1959, *62,* 599-603.

Jarvik, L. F., and Kato, T. Is lysergide a teratogen? *Lancet,* 1968, *1,* 250.

Jarvik, M. E. The behavioral effects of psychotogens. In R. C. DeBold and R. C. Leaf (Eds.) *LSD, man, and society.* Middletown, Conn.: Wesleyan Univ. Press, 1967, Pp. 186-206. (a)

Jarvik, M. E. Third discussion. In R. C. DeBold and R. C. Leaf (Eds.) *LSD, man and society.* Middletown, Conn.: Wesleyan Univ. Press, 1967. P. 212. (b)

Johnson, F. G. LSD in the treatment of alcoholism. Paper presented at Annual Meeting of American Psychiatric Association, Boston, June, 1968.

Judd, L. L. Brandkamp, W. W., and McGlothlin, W. H. Comparison of chromosomal patterns obtained from groups of continued users, former users, and nonusers of LSD-25. *Amer. J. Psychiat.,* 1969, *126,* 626-633.

Kast, E. LSD and the dying patient. *Chicago Med. Sch. Quart.,* 1966, *26,* 80-87.

Kast, E. Attenuation of anticipation: A therapeutic use of lysergic acid diethylamide. *Psychiat. Quart.,* 1967, *41,* 646-657.

Kast, E., and Collins, V. J. A study of lysergic acid diethylamide as an analgesic agent. *Anesth. Analg.,* 1964, *43,* 285-291.

Kato, T., and Jarvik, L. F. LSD-25 and genetic damage. *Dis. Nerv. Syst.,* 1969, *30,* 42-46.

Katz, M. M., Waskow, I. E., and Olsson, J. Characterizing the psychological state produced by LSD. *J. Abnorm. Psychol.,* 1968, *73,* 1-14.

Keeler, M. H. The effects of psilocybin on a test of after-image perception. *Psychopharmacologia,* 1965, *8,* 131-139.

Keeler, M. H. Chlorpromazine antagonism of psilocybin effect. *Int. J. Neuropsychiat.,* 1967, *3,* 66-71.

Keeler, M. H., and Reifler, C. B. Suicide during an LSD reaction. *Amer. J. Psychiat.,* 1967, *123,* 884-885.

Kenna, J. C., and Sedman, G. The subjective experience of time during lysergic acid diethylamide (LSD-25) intoxication. *Psychopharmacologia,* 1964, *5,* 280-288.

Kieffer, S. N., and Moritz, T. B. Psychedelic drugs. *Penn. Med.,* 1968, *71,* 57-67.

Kleber, H. D. Prolonged adverse reactions from unsupervised use of hallucinogenic drugs. *J. Nerv. Ment. Dis.,* 1967, *144,* 308-319.

Klee, G. D. Lysergic acid diethylamide (LSD-25) and ego functions. *Arch. Gen. Psychiat.,* 1963, *8,* 461-474.

Klee, G. D., Bertino, J., Weintraub, W., and Callaway, E. The influence of varying dosage on the effects of lysergic acid diethylamide (LSD-25) in humans. *J. Nerv. Ment. Dis.,* 1961, *132,* 404-409.

Klee, G. D., and Weintraub, W. Paranoid reactions following lysergic acid diethylamide (LSD-25). In P. B. Bradley, P. Demicker, and C. Radouco-Thomas (Eds.) *Neuro-psychopharmacology,* Amsterdam: Elsevier, 1959. Pp. 457-460.

Kluver, H. *Mescal: The "divine" plant and its psychological effects.* London: Paul, Trench, Trubner, & Co., 1928.

Kluver, H. Mechanisms of hallucinations. In Q. McNemar and M. A. Merrill (Eds.) *Studies in personality.* New York: McGraw-Hill, 1942, Chap. 10.

Knoll, M., and Kugler, J. Subjective light-pattern spectroscopy in the electroencephalographic frequency range. *Nature,* 1959, *184,* 1823.

Knoll, M. Kugler, J., Höfer, O., and Lawder, S. D. Effects of chemical stimulation of electrically-induced phosphenes on their bandwidth, shape, number and intensity. *Confin. Neurol.,* 1963, *23,* 201-226.

Knudsen, K. Homicide after treatment with lysergic acid diethylamide. *Acta Psychiat. Scan.,* 1964, *40* (suppl. 180), 389-395.

Kornetsky, C., and Humphries, O. Relationship between effects of a number of centrally acting drugs and personality. *Arch. Neurol. Psychiat.,* 1957, *77,* 325-327.

Kornetsky, C., Humphries, O., and Evarts, E. V. Comparison of psychological effects of certain centrally acting drugs in man. *Arch. Neurol. Psychiat.,* 1957, *77,* 318-324.

Krill, A. E., Alpert, H. J., and Ostfeld, A. M. Effects of a hallucinogenic agent in totally blind subjects. *Arch. Ophthal.,* 1963, *69,* 180-185.

Krill, A. E., Wieland, A. M., and Ostfeld, A. M. The effects of two hallucinogenic agents on human retinal function. *Arch. Ophthal.,* 1960, *64,* 724-733.

Kurland, A. A. The therapeutic potential of LSD in medicine. In R. C. DeBold and R. C. Leaf (Eds.) *LSD, man and society.* Middletown, Conn.: Wesleyan Univ. Press, 1967, Pp. 20-35.

Kurland, A. A., Unger, S., Savage, C., Olsson, J., and Pahnke, W. N. Psychedelic therapy utilizing LSD in the treatment of the alcoholic patient: a progress report. Paper presented at Annual Meeting of the American Psychiatric Association, Boston, May, 1968.

LaBarre, W. *The peyote cult.* (New Enlarged Edition) Hamden, Conn.: Shoe String Press, 1964.

Ladd-Franklin, C. Visible radiation from excited nerve fiber: the reddish blue arcs and the reddish blue glow of the retina. *Science,* 1927, *66,* 239-241.

Langs, R. J., and Barr, H. L. Lysergic acid diethylamide (LSD-25) and schizophrenic reactions. *J. Nerv. Ment. Dis.,* 1968, *147,* 163-172.

Leary, T. *High priest.* Cleveland: World Publishing Co., 1968.

Leary, T., Litwin, G. H., and Metzner, R. Reactions to psilocybin administered in a supportive environment. *J. Nerv. Ment. Dis.,* 1963, *137,* 561-573.

Levine, J., and Ludwig, A. M. The LSD controversy. *Comp. Psychiat.,* 1964, *5,* 314-321.

Levis, D. J., and Mehlman, B. Suggestion and mescaline sulphate. *J. Neuropsychiat.,* 1964, *5,* 197-200.

Lewin, L. *Phantastica, narcotic and stimulating drugs.* London: Routledge & Kegan Paul, 1931.

Liebert, R. S., Wapner, S., and Werner, H. Studies in the effects of lysergic acid diethylamide (LSD-25). Visual perception of verticality in schizophrenic and normal adults. *Arch. Neurol. Psychiat.,* 1957, *77,* 193-201.

Liebert, R. S., Werner, H., and Wapner, S. Studies in the effect of lysergic acid diethylamide (LSD-25). *Arch. Neurol. Psychiat.,* 1958, *79,* 580-584.

Ling, T. M., and Buckman, J. *Lysergic acid (LSD-25) and Ritalin in the treatment of neurosis.* London: Lambarde Press, 1963.

Linton, H. B., and Langs, R. J. Subjective reactions to lysergic acid diethylamide (LSD-25) measured by a questionnaire. *Arch. Gen. Psychiat.,* 1962, *6,* 352-368.

Linton, H. B., and Langs, R. J. Empirical dimensions of LSD-25 reactions. *Arch. Gen. Psychiat.,* 1964, *10.* 469-485.

Loughman, W. D., Sargent, T. W., and Israelstam, D. M. Leukocytes of humans exposed to lysergic acid diethylamids: Lack of chromosomal damage. *Science,* 1967, *158,* 508-510.

Ludwig, A., Levine, J., Stark, L., and Lazar, R. A clinical study of LSD treatment in alcoholism. Paper presented at Annual Meeting of American Psychiatric Association, Boston, May, 1968.

Malitz, S. The role of mescaline and d-lysergic acid in psychiatric treatment. *Dis. Nerv. Syst.,* 1966, *27,* 43-47.

Malitz, S., Esecover, H., Wilkens, B., and Hoch, P. H. Some observations on psilocybin, a new hallucinogen, in volunteer subjects. *Comp. Psych.,* 1960, *1,* 8-17.

Marshall, C. R. Entopic phenomena associated with the retina. *Brit. J. Ophthalm.,* 1935, *19,* 177-201.

Marshall, C. R. An enquiry into the causes of mescal vision. *J. Neuropath. Psychopath.,* 1937, *17,* 289-304.

Maslow, A. H. Lessons from the peak-experiences. *J. Hum. Psychol.,* 1962, *2,* 9-18.

Master, R. E. L., and Houston, J. *The varieties of psychedelic experience.* New York: Holt, Rinehart, & Winston, 1966.

McCabe, O. L. An empirical investigation of the effects of chemically (LSD-25)-induced "psychedelic experiences" on selected measures of personality, and their implications for therapeutic counseling theory and practice. Unpublished doctoral dissertation, Catholic Univ., 1968.

McGlothlin, W., Cohen, S., and McGlothlin, M. S. Long lasting effects of LSD on normals. *Arch. Gen. Psychiat.,* 1967, *17,* 521-532.

Metzner, R. The pharmacology of psychedelic drugs. I. Chemical and biochemical aspects. *Psyched. Rev.,* 1963, *1,* 69-115.

Metzner, R., Litwin, G., and Weil, G. M. The relation of expectation and mood to psilocybin reactions: A questionnaire study. *Psyched. Rev.,* 1965, *5,* 3-39.

Middlefell, R. The effects of LSD on body sway suggestibility in a group of hospital patients. *Brit. J. Psychiat.,* 1967, *113,* 277-280.

Milman, D. H. An untoward reaction to accidental ingestion of LSD in a 5-year-old girl. *J. Amer. Med. Ass.,* 1967, *201,* 821-824.

Mitchell, S. W. Remarks on the effects of Anhelonium lewinii (the mescal button). *Brit. Med. J.,* 1896, *2,* 1625-1629.

Muzio, J. N., Roffwarg, H. P., and Kaufman, E. Alterations in the nocturnal sleep cycle resulting from LSD. *EEG Clin. Neuro-physiol.,* 1966, *21,* 313-324.

Nielsen, J., Friedrich, U., Jacobsen, E., and Tsuboi, T. Lysergide and chromosome abnormalities. *Brit. Med. J.,* 1968, *2,* 801-803.

Nielsen, J., Friedrich, U., and Tsuboi, T. Chromosome abnormalities and psychotropic drugs. *Nature, 1968, 218,* 488-489.

Pahnke, W. N. Drugs and mysticism; An analysis of the relationship between psychedelic drugs and the mystical consciousness. Unpublished doctoral dissertation, Harvard Univ., 1963.

Pahnke, W. N. LSD and religious experience. In R. C. DeBold and R. C. Leaf (Eds.) *LSD, man and society.* Middletown, Conn.: Wesleyan Univ. Press, 1967. Pp. 60-84.

Pahnke, W. N., and Richards, W. A. Implications of LSD and experimental mysticism. *J. Relig. Health,* 1966, *5,* 175-208.

Payne, J. W. LSD-25 and accommodative convergence ratios. *Arch. Ophthal.,* 1965, *74,* 81-85.

Penfield, W. *The excitable cortex in conscious man.* Springfield, Ill.: C. C. Thomas, 1958.

Purkinje, J. E. *Opera omnia.* Prague: Society of Czech Physicians, 1918.

Purpura, D. P. Neurophysiological actions of LSD. In R. C. DeBold and R. C. Leaf (Eds.) *LSD, man and society.* Middletown, Conn.: Wesleyan Univ. Press, 1967. Pp. 158-185.

Reynolds, H. H., and Peterson, G. K. Psychophysiological effects of a large non-experimental dose of LSD-25. *Psychol. Rep.,* 1966, *19,* 287-290.

Robbins, E., Robbins, L., Frosch, W. A., and Stern, M. Implications of untoward reactions to hallucinogens. *Bull. N. Y. Acad. Sci.,* 1967, *43,* 985-999.

Robinson, J. T., Davies, L. S., Sack, E. L. N. S., and Morrissey, J. D. A controlled trial of abreaction with lysergic acid diethylamide (LSD-25). *Brit. J. Psychiat.,* 1963, *109,* 46-53.

Rodin, E., and Luby, E. Effects of LSD-25 on the EEG and photic evoked responses. *Arch. Gen. Psychiat.,* 1966, *14,* 435-441.

Rosecrans, J. A., Lovell, R. A., and Freedman, D. X. Effects of lysergic acid diethylamide on the metabolism of brain 5-hydroxytryptamine. *Bioch. Pharmacol.,* 1967, *16,* 2011-2021.

Rosenberg, D. E., Isbell, H., Miner, E. J., and Logan, C. R. The effects of N, N,-dimethyltryptamine in human subjects tolerant to lysergic acid diethylamide. *Psychopharmacologia,* 1964, *5,* 217-227.

Rothlin, E. Lysergic acid diethylamide and related substances. *Ann. N. Y. Acad. Sci.,* 1957, *66* (Art. 3), 668-676.

Salvatore, S., and Hyde, R. W. Progression of effects of lysergic acid diethylamide (LSD). *Arch. Neurol. Psychiat.,* 1956, *76,* 50-59.

Sankar, D. V. S., Rozsa, P. W., and Geisler, A. Chromosome breakage in children treated with LSD-25 and UML-491. *Comp. Psychiat.,* 1969, *10,* 406-410.

Sato, H., and Pergament, E. Is lysergide a teratogen? *Lancet,* 1968, *1,* 639-640.

Savage, C. Variations in ego feeling induced by d-lysergic acid diethylamide (LSD-25). *Psychoanal. Rev.,* 1955, *42,* 1-16.

Schachter, S. The interaction of cognitive and physiological determinants of emotional state. In C. D. Spielberger (Ed.) *Anxiety and behavior.* New York: Academic Press, 1966. Pp. 193-224.

Schmitt, J. A. Psychometric reaction to Milman's report. *J. Amer. Med. Ass.,* 1968, *203,* 166.

Schultes, R. E. Hallucinogens of plant origin. *Science,* 1969, *163,* 245-254.

Schwartz, A. S. and Cheney, C. Effect of LSD on the tonic activity of the visual pathways of the cat. *Life Sci.,* 1965, *4,* 771-778.

Schwartz, C. J. Paradoxical response to chlorpromazine after LSD. *Psychosomatics,* 1967, *8,* 210-211.

Schwartz, C. J. The complications of LSD: A review of the literature. *J. Nerv. Ment. Dis.,* 1968, *146,* 174-186.

Shagass, C. Effects of LSD on somatosensory and visual evoked responses and on the EEG in man. *Recent Adv. Biol. Psychiat.,* 1967, *9,* 209-227.

Shagass, C., and Bittle, R. M. Therapeutic effects of LSD: A follow-up study. *J. Nerv. Ment. Dis.,* 1967, *144,* 471-478.

Short, W. B., Jr. The effects of drugs on the electroretinogram of the cat. *J. Pharmacol. Exp. Ther.,* 1958, *122,* 68A.

Shryne, J. E., Jr., and Brown, B. B. Effect of LSD on responses to colored photic stimuli as related to visual imagery ability in man. *Proc. West. Pharmacol. Soc.,* 1965, *8,* 42-46.

Silverstein, A. B., and Klee, G. D. Effects of lysergic acid diethylamide (LSD-25) on intellectual functions. *Arch. Neurol. Psychiat.,* 1958, *80,* 477-480.

Sjoberg, B. M., Jr. The effects of lysergic acid diethylamide (LSD-25), mescaline, psilocybin and a combination of three drugs on primary suggestibility. Unpublished doctoral dissertation, Stanford Univ., 1965.

Skakkebaek, N. E., Philip, J., and Rafaelsen, O. J. LSD in mice; abnormalities in meiotic chromosomes. *Science,* 1968, *160,* 1247-1248.

Slater, P. E., Morimoto, K., and Hyde, R. W. The effect of group administration upon symptom formation under LSD. *J. Nerv. Ment. Dis.*, 1957, *125*, 312-315.

Smart, R. G., and Batemen, K. Unfavorable reactions to LSD: A review and analysis of the available case reports. *Canad. Med. Ass. J.*, 1967, *97*, 1214-1221.

Smart, R. G., and Bateman, K. The chromosomal and teratogenic effects of lysergic acid diethylamide: A review of the current literature. *Canad. Med. Ass. J.*, 1968, *99*, 805-810.

Smart, R. G., Storm, T., Baker, E. F. W., and Solursh, L. *Lysergic acid diethylamide (LSD) in the treatment of alcoholism.* Toronto: Univ. of Toronto Press, 1967.

Smith, D. E., and Rose, A. J. The use and abuse of LSD in Haight-Ashbury. *Clin. Pediat.*, 1968, *7*, 317-322.

Snyder, S. H., Faillace, L., and Hollister, L. 2.5-dimethoxy-4-methyl-amphetamine (STP): A new hallucinogenic drug. *Science*, 1967, *158*, 669-670.

Snyder, S. H., Faillace, L. A., and Weingartner, H. DOM (STP) a new hallucinogenic drug, and DOET: Effects in normal subjects. *Amer. J. Psychiat.*, 1968, *125*, 357-364.

Snyder, S. H., and Merrill, C. G. A relationship between the hallucinogenic activity of drugs and their electronic configuration. *Proc. Nat. Acad. Sci.*, 1965, *54*, 258-266.

Snyder, S. H., and Reivich, M. Regional localization of lysergic acid diethylamide in monkey brain. *Nature*, 1966, *209*, 1093-1095.

Solursh, L. P., and Rae, J. M. LSD, suggestion and hypnosis. *Int. J. Neuropsychiat.*, 1966, *2*, 60-64.

Sparkes, R. S., Melnyk, J., and Bozzetti, L. P. Chromosomal effect in vivo of exposure to lysergic acid diethylamide. *Science*, 1968, 160, 1343-1345.

Stone, D., Lamson, E., Chang, Y. S., and Pickering, K. W. Cytogenic effects of cyclamates in human cells in vitro. *Science, 1969, 164,* 568-569.

Szara, S., Rockland, L. H., Rosenthal, D., and Handlon, J. H. Psychological effects and metabolism of N, N-diethyl-tryptamine in man. *Arch. Gen. Psychiat.*, 1966, *15*, 320-329.

Tjio, J., Pahnke, W., and Kurland, A. Pre- and post-LSD chromosomal aberrations: A comparative study. Paper presented at American College of Neuropsychopharmacology, 1968.

Tobin, Jean M., and Tobin, J. M. Mutagenic effects of LSD-25 in *Drosophila melanogaster. Dis. Nerv. Syst.*, 1969, *30*, No. 2 Suppl., 47-52.

Unger, S. M. Mescaline, LSD, psilocybin, and personality change. *Psychiatry*, 1963, *26*, 111-125.

Ungerleider, J. T. The acute side effects from LSD. In J. T. Ungerleider (Ed.) *The problems and prospects of LSD*. Springfield, Ill.: C. C. Thomas, 1968. Pp. 61-68.

Ungerleider, J. T., Fisher, D. D., and Fuller, M. The dangers of LSD. *J. Amer. Med. Ass.*, 1966, *197*, 389-392.

Ungerleider, J. T., Fisher, D. D., Fuller, M., and Caldwell, A. The "bad trip"—the etiology of the adverse LSD reaction. *Amer. J. Psychiat.*, 1968, *124*, 1483-1490.

Uyeno, E. T. Current research in the evaluation of hallucinogens. Paper presented at the Western Psychological Assoc., Vancouver, June, 1969.

Van Dusen, W., Wilson, W., Miners, W., and Hook, H. Treatment of alcoholism with lysergide. *Quart. J. Stud. Alcohol.*, 1967, *28*, 295-304.

Vann, E. Lethal mutation rate in *Drosophila* exposed to LSD-25 by injection and ingestion. *Nature*, 1969, *223*, 95-96.

von Felsinger, J. M., Lasagna, L., and Beecher, H. K. The response of normal men to lysergic acid derivatives (di- and mono-ethyl amides). *J. Clin. Exp. Psychopath.*, 1956, *17*, 414-428.

Warkany, J., and Takacs, E. Lysergic acid diethylamide (LSD): No teratogenicity in rats. *Science*, 1968, *159*, 731-732.

Watts, A. W. *The joyous cosmology*. New York: Random House, 1962.

Weckowicz, T. E. The effect of lysergic acid diethylamide (L.S.D.) on size constancy. *Canad. Psychiat., Ass. J.*, 1959, *4*, 255-259.

Weinberger, L. M., and Grant, F. C. Visual hallucinations and their neuro-optical correlates. *Ophthal. Rev.*, 1940, *23*, 166-199.

Welpton, D. F. Psychodynamics of chronic lysergic acid diethylamide use. *J. Nerv. Ment. Dis.*, 1968, *147*, 377-385.

White, H. E., and Levatin, P. "Floaters" in the eye. *Sci. Amer.* 1962, *206*, No. 6, 119-127.

Wikler, A. *The relation of psychiatry to pharmacology*. Baltimore: Williams & Wilkins, 1957.

Wilson, J. G., and Warkany, J. *Teratology: Principles and techniques*. Chicago: Univ. Chicago Press, 1965.

Wolbach, A. B., Miner, E. J., and Isbell, H. Comparison of psilocin with psilocybin, mescaline and LSD-25. *Psychopharmacologia*, 1962, *3*, 219-223.

Woolley, D. W., and Shaw, E. A. A biochemical and pharmacological suggestion about certain mental disorders. *Proc. Nat. Acad. Sci.*, 1954, *40*, 228-231.

Zegans, L. S., Pollard, J. C., and Brown, D. The effects of LSD-25 on creativity and tolerance to regression. *Arch. Gen. Psychiat.*, 1967, *16*, 740-749.

Zellweger, H., McDonald, J. S., and Abbo, G. Is lysergic acid diethylamide a teratogen? *Lancet*, 1967, *2*, 1066-1068.

CHAPTER 2

Marihuana, Hashish, and Other Cannabis Derivatives

CONTENTS

Marihuana, Hashish, and
Other Cannabis Derivatives

During recent years the consumption of marihuana has increased tremendously in the United States. This upsurge in use has raised important psychological, medical, social, and legal questions: What are the effects of marihuana? Is it harmful? Will the use of marihuana and other forms of cannabis, such as hashish, continue to increase? Will strong pressures exist in the near future to modify or repeal the severe laws against the use of marihuana? What are the arguments for and against its legalization?

Use of Cannabis Throughout the World

The female of the common hemp plant, *Cannabis sativa,* produces a resin (cannabis) which has intoxicating properties. From this plant are derived a variety of preparations that have received different names in various parts of the world (Taylor, 1968). A low-potency preparation (with little resin content), derived from the flowering tops, leaves, and stems of the uncultivated female plant, is known as *bhang* in India, *kif* in Morocco, *dagga* in South Africa, *maconha* in parts of South America, and *marihuana* or *marijuana* in Mexico and the United States.[1] In India, a more potent preparation, *ganja,* is derived from the specially cultivated and harvested grades of the female plant. When the pure resin of the plant is used, the preparation is very potent and is known as *charas* in India and as *hashish* in various other parts of the world. Although

1. American users refer to marihuana as 'pot', 'grass', 'tea', or 'weed' and to the marihuana cigarette as a 'joint', 'reefer', 'stick', or 'roach'.

79

bhang is often taken in the form of a drink, the other preparations are usually smoked either in the form of cigarettes or by means of a water-pipe.

Writers often state that cannabis was used in China as an intoxicant about 5000 years ago. Although this contention cannot be satisfactorily documented, there is little doubt that the properties of cannabis were known in a variety of cultures prior to the time of Christ (Blum, 1969). In fact, around 430 B.C., Herodotus documented the use of cannabis for inebriating purposes among the Scythians (Rosevear, 1967).

Cannabis has been consumed for more than a thousand years in India, primarily as an intoxicant but also, at times, as an aid in meditation (Bloomquist, 1968). By the 10th century A.D. cannabis was also well-known throughout the Moslem world. The evil reputation of cannabis apparently began around the 11th century when it became associated with members of a Moslem sect who carried out secret assassinations of opponents.[2] It appears probable that the Western world became acquainted with cannabis from the Moslems during the Crusades (1096-1270 A.D.). However, it did not find widespread use in Europe until around 1800.

During the present century, cannabis preparations such as marihuana, and especially hashish, have been widely used in India, North Africa, and the Middle East. In many parts of India, moderate use of the drug is neither prohibited by law nor socially condemned. However, there are wide caste differences in usage. For instance, when both cannabis and alcohol are available, the non-aggressive Brahmins prefer cannabis whereas the agressive Rajputs prefer alcohol (Carstairs, 1954).[3] Laborers in India seem to use cannabis in somewhat the same way beer is used by laborers in the United States. Chopra and Chopra (1939, p. 25) write that "A common practice among labourers . . . is to have a few pulls at a ganja pipe or to drink a glass of bhang towards the evening. This produces a sense of well-being, relieves fatigue, stimulates the appetite, and induces a feeling of mild stimulation which enables the worker to bear the strain and perhaps the monotony of his daily routine of life more cheerfully. The low cost and easy availability of these drugs are important factors in their use by the working classes . . ." Cannabis has also been used in India by some religious sects in the belief that it

---

2. The terms *assassin* and *hashish* may derive from Hashishin or Hasan who was the leader of this sect (Blum, 1969).

3. There are also other indications that cultural values may play an important role in determining the extent of cannabis consumption. For instance, although opium and cannabis were equally available in pre-Communist China, the use of opium was much more prevalent than the use of cannabis.

helps the user to free his mind from worldly distractions and to concentrate on the Supreme Being (Chopra & Chopra, 1957b). Another group of individuals in India have used small doses of cannabis for 20 to 30 years without apparent harm and have lived to a ripe old age. These individuals began using the drug for some minor ailment (such as mild joint pains) and, since it seemed to relieve the ailment without causing harm, it was taken daily for many years (Chopra & Chopra, 1957b).

Cannabis preparations are also used by laborers and peasants in North Africa and various other parts of the world. The users typically claim that cannabis produces a happy mood and a feeling of heightened efficiency, e.g., "It makes me feel better, stronger, happier, or bigger" (Boroffka, 1966). Although moderate use of the drug is socially accepted (but not necessarily legally accepted) in India, North Africa, the Middle East, and various other parts of the world (in the same way as moderate use of alcohol is socially accepted in the United States), excessive use of cannabis is generally viewed as indicative of serious personality problems (McGlothlin, 1967).

Use of Marihuana in the United States

The more potent forms of cannabis, such as hashish, have rarely been used in the United States. Beginning around 1920, the least potent form of cannabis (marihuana) was used by a small number of Americans, especially by musicians and by underprivileged Negroes and Puerto Ricans in New York and other urban centers. Within recent years, marihuana has had a tremendous increase in popularity in American urban and suburban centers, especially among the youth. In fact, a survey of selected high schools and colleges in metropolitan centers indicated that the number of marihuana users more than doubled during the year 1968 (Blum, 1969, Vol. 1). Although representative surveys have not been conducted, it is estimated that during 1968 marihuana had been tried at least once by most college and high school students in the metropolitan centers and possibly 30% of the students were using it on a more or less regular basis (Blum, 1969; Krippner, 1968; Weil, Zinberg, & Nelsen, 1968). The use of marihuana was so widespread in some schools that turning on could be viewed as a puberty rite for entry into the adolescent subculture (Ungerleider & Bowen, 1969). In addition, it was estimated that about 75% of the American soldiers in Viet Nam were smoking marihuana (Oursler, 1968, p. 147; Stearn, 1969, p. 193).

Blum (1969, Vol. 2, p. 362) commented as follows on the drastic increase in marihuana use:

What is happening now, in 1968-1969, is what has been happening over the last fifteen years, ever since the "drug movement" (or craze) began with the introduction of mescaline (Huxley, 1954) and of LSD into the intellectual, artistic, and professional communities and spread to the student population in metropolitan centers. What we see now is a rapidly increasing tempo. While it took approximately ten years, by our estimate, for experimentation and use to shift from the older intellectual-artistic groups to graduate students, it took only an estimated five years to catch on among undergraduates, only two or three years to move to a significant number of high school students, and, then, within no more than two years, to move to upper elementary grades—although we have no sound data as yet on the numbers involved in elementary schools.

Many factors seem to underlie the recent increase in marihuana consumption among Americans. Some of these factors appear to be interrelated with broad social-cultural movements that brought about a permissive society, the generation gap, and the revolt of the youth. The new generation had been constantly exposed to television, w. s relatively highly educated, and had lived in the era of the Cold War and in a period of rapid social changes. Specific factors that converged to bring about a feeling of alienation among a substantial segment of the youth apparently included the prevalence of international and domestic violence, the Viet Nam War, the militarization of American society, race injustice, and poverty in the midst of affluence. For some youthful activists, the use of marihuana became a visible sign of dissent against the status quo alongside other signs such as demonstrations and certain styles of dress (Brotmen, Silverman, & Suffet, 1969).

Before marihuana was widely adopted, the United States had already become a drug-taking culture. Alcohol, tranquilizers, nicotine, caffeine, amphetamines, barbiturates, aspirin, and many other drugs were used in large quantities and had become an integral part of the American way of life. When chemicals are widely used in a culture to produce relaxation, to alter mood, or to produce well-being, it is not especially difficult for some of the members of the culture to adopt another substance, such as marihuana, which is also thought to produce desirable psychological effects.

As Brotman et al. (1969) have pointed out, the increasing use of marihuana can also be viewed as part of "the growing emphasis on the cultivation of aesthetic and mildly hedonistic sensibilities. The recent decades have brought a hastening fall of the Puritan ethic and the rise of a new ethic aimed at achieving pleasure in leisure activities and in other areas of life . . . Seen from this point of view, the use of drugs to produce pleasure and sensory stimulation is, under the impetus of the new ethic, an exploration of areas of behavior formerly rigidly proscribed."

Furthermore, the publicity given to LSD-type experiences during the late 1950s and early 1960s by such writers as Aldous Huxley, Allan Watts, and Timothy Leary helped to increase not only the use of LSD but also the use of marihuana (which was thought to produce some LSD-type experiences). Later, during 1967 and 1968, there was a decline in the use of LSD (apparently as a result of the widely-circulated reports that it produced chromosome damage) but there was an increase in the use of marihuana (which was apparently viewed as a safe drug)(Goode, 1969c; Oursler, 1968).

During the early 1960s, marihuana became an integral part of the hippie subculture which developed in American metropolitan areas (Allen & West, 1968). Within a few years, marihuana was adopted by a much larger group of young Americans who were becoming part of a counter-culture—a subculture that was radically disaffiliated from the mainstream assumptions of American society (Roszak, 1969). The underlying ideology among these groups seemed to emphasize both humanism (including tolerance, social equality, and encounter with one's fellow men) and also personal spontaneity or genuineness, experimentation, and the value of immediate pleasure and personal experience (Keniston, 1968; Simmons & Winograd, 1966). Others tried it out of boredom, or curiosity, or to go along with their friends (Blum, 1969, Vol. 2, p. 10). Once having tried marihuana, many individuals continued to use it socially in order to relieve tensions, or to feel good, or to seek an LSD-type experience (Keeler, 1968b).

In the United States at the present time, the use of marihuana is primarily a social phenomenon that involves primary groups of intimates. As Goode (1969b) has pointed out, marihuana is characteristically smoked by small groups of friends and intimates, a value consesus obtains within these social groups, and the use of marihuana helps to maintain cohesion of the groups.

Although the use of marihuana is primarily a social or group phenomenon, nevertheless, a recent study (Mankin, Hogan, Conway, & Fox, 1969) indicates that present-day American college students who use marihuana differ in personality characteristics from those who do not use it. The subjects were 148 male undergraduates at Johns Hopkins and Lehigh Universities. (Since the subjects were recruited at the campus student union and in an introductory psychology class, it is not clear to what extent the sample is representative of the students at the two universities.) Under anonymous conditions, the students completed a biographical questionnaire and the California Psychological Inventory (CPI). Of the total sample, 40 per cent stated that they had smoked or were still smoking marihuana (users), 30 per cent had never smoked marihuana (non-users), and 30 per cent stated that they had not and never would smoke marihuana (adamant non-users). The users differed from the others in that they tended to major in the humanities and the social sciences. Users, non-users, and adamant non-users did not differ significantly with regard to academic achievement. The users differed from the others on 10 of the 19 scales of the CPI. For instance, the users obtained significantly higher scores on the following CPI scales: Social Presence, Flexibility, Empathy, and Achievement via Independence. The adamant non-users obtained significantly higher scores on such scales as Responsibility, Self-Control, and Achievement via Conformance. The non-users generally fell between the users and the adamant non-users on each of the personality scales.

During recent years, the consumption of marihuana has also apparently increased among lower-class youths. Blumer (1967) has presented a report concerning the use of drugs, especially marihuana, among underprivileged youths (chiefly Negroes and Mexicans) in Oakland, California. The project was originally designed by Blumer to reduce the use of drugs in this population. However, the project workers were unable to change the youth's opinion of drugs. Blumer (1967) states that "The real reasons for the lack of success were the strong collective belief held by the youths that their use of drugs was not harmful and their ability to put up effective arguments, based usually on personal experience and observations, against claims of such harm" (p. 3).

Having failed to make a dent in the use of marihuana, Blumer (1967) and associates proceeded to study the social context of drug use among the underprivileged youth. The major conclusions, from an intensive investigation with more than 200 youthful drug users, were as follows:

Among these underprivileged youths, the use of drugs did not seem to be a disguised form of venting hostility toward society. On the contrary, the use of drugs was dependent on such factors as "access to drugs, acceptance by drug-using associates, kinds of images youngsters have of drugs, and the runs of experience that affect their interpretation of drugs" (p. 59). Furthermore, consumption of marihuana was an integral part of the adolescent subculture; it carried peer sanctions and was supported by a body of justifying beliefs.

The use of marihuana and other drugs could not be viewed as an effort to escape from reality. On the contrary, since the youths were growing up in a subculture that valued the use of drugs, and since they aspired to acceptance and recognition from their peers, they began to use drugs "as a positive effort to get into the major stream of reality as they saw it" (p. 59).

The youths were held to the continued use of marihuana and other drugs by the very fact of their association with one another. It appeared likely that as they began to marry, to acquire jobs, and to form new associates, they would break out of the fixed circle which held them to drug use.

Two recent studies indicate that the illegality of marihuana is not especially effective in preventing its use. In a study with 189 subjects (consisting largely of professional adults), McGlothlin and West (1968) found the following: Of those who had used marihuana more than 10 times, 88 per cent stated that they would use it in the future if it remained illegal and 90 per cent stated they would use it if it were legalized. Of those who had used marihuana less than 10 times, 60 per cent stated that they would use it in the future if it remained illegal and 68 per cent stated they would use it if it were legalized. Of those who had never used marihuana, 35 per cent stated that they might use it in the future if it remained illegal and 45 per cent stated that they might use it if it were legalized. King (1969) obtained similar results in a study with 518 college undergraduates: With respect to those students who had used marihuana, 88 per cent stated that they would probably continue to use it if it remained illegal and 90 per cent stated they would probably continue to use it if it were legalized. With respect to those who had never used marihuana, 31 per cent stated that there was a good chance they would use it in the future if it remained illegal and 40 per cent stated there was a good chance they would use it if it were legalized.

Effects of Marihuana

Let us delineate four important points with regard to the effects of marihuana as it is characteristically used in the United States:

Users typically state that they smoke marihuana in order to feel good, to relax, or to increase sociability (McGlothlin & West, 1968).

The subjective effects of marihuana are usually experienced as mild. As Blumer (1967, p. 84) has emphasized, the effects are generally so mild that "many youngsters had to be 'trained' to recognize the effects before they could experience pleasure, and regular users often quit for periods of time because of their inability to recognize when they were 'high'."

The nature and intensity of the effects appear to depend upon the technique used for inhalation, the number of cigarettes smoked, and the potency of the preparation. Samples of marihuana differ in potency, depending on the relative proportion of material from the flowering tops, leaves, seeds, and stems of the cannabis plant, the conditions under which the plants were grown, the method of harvesting, and the variety of cannabis (Korte & Sieper, 1965; Weil et al., 1968).

It appears likely that the effects are dependent not only on the grade and dose of the marihuana but also on such extra-drug variables as the situation, the subject's set (for example, his expectations and motivations for taking the drug), and the subject's personality. Although these extra-drug variables probably affect the nature of the marihuana experience, unfortunately, *no experimental studies have as yet been reported which delineated the main effects and the interactive effects of drug dose, situation, set, and personality.* Studies are clearly needed which experimentally manipulate situational variables, which assess the subject's set and his personality characteristics, and which use various dose-levels of marihuana.

In fact, very few rigorous studies have been conducted on the effects of marihuana as it is typically used in the United States. Although there are numerous reports which proffer unsubstantiated opinions about marihuana, only three investigations have been published, as of late 1969, which more of less meet minimal standards for scientific research. One of these investigations was published by the Mayor's Committee in 1944, a second was reported by Weil and associates in 1968, and the third was presented by Crancer and associates in 1969.

INVESTIGATION BY THE MAYOR'S COMMITTEE

During the late 1930's, marihuana was viewed as a social problem in the city of New York. Since reliable data concerning its use and consequences were not available, mayor Fiorello LaGuardia, in collaboration with the New York Academy of Sciences, appointed a committee (of physicians, psychiatrists, clinical psychologists, sociologists, and pharmacologists) to conduct both a survey pertaining to the use of marihuana in the city and an experimental study to determine its effects. The committee published a documented report in 1944. This report (Mayor's Committee, 1944) still remains the most comprehensive study of marihuana that is available.

The survey was carried out by trained personnel, four men and two women, from the Narcotic Division of the New York Police Department, who reported directly to the committee. These trained investigators lived in the environment in which marihuana was used and became acquainted with a large number of users. The report implies that the users were not aware of the official status of their companions, but this implication is not documented. After summarizing the data obtained in this way, by the method of participant observation, the committee came to the following conclusions:

Marihuana use was heaviest in Harlem and mid-town Manhattan. The great majority of users were Negroes and Puerto Ricans who were in their twenties and unemployed.

Almost all of the users felt that marihuana made them feel better and that it was not harmful in any way. In most instances, the behavior of the marihuana user was of a sociable and friendly nature. Cases of agressiveness were extremely rare.

Users could voluntarily stop smoking marihuana. When marihuana was not available, the users did not show signs of frustration. Also, withdrawal symptoms were not observed and there was no evidence of an acquired tolerance for the drug.

Although some users of marihuana were involved in criminal activities, it appeared that their activities were independent of the use of marihuana.

No convincing evidence was found to support the contention that marihuana smoking led to the use of hard narcotics such as heroin.

The Mayor's Committee also conducted a series of experimental studies with 72 inmates at the House of Detention for Women and at the prisons at Riker's and Hart Islands. Two-thirds of these subjects were experienced users of marihuana. The drug was administered orally and also in the form of marihuana cigarettes. The cigarettes usually contained either 2 cc. of the extract from the cannabis plant (a dose which appeared to be of the same order of magnitude as that usually taken by marihuana users) or 5 cc. of the plant (a dose which was clearly much higher than that usually taken by users). Although a placebo was also used in these studies, the subjects could earily tell that the placebos did not contain marihuana. (Since double-blind procedures were not possible, the data should, of course, be interpreted with caution.) The committee presented the following results:

When marihuana was smoked, the effects began almost immediately and lasted about three to five hours. Irrespective of dose and mode of administration, practically all subjects described feelings of lightness, heaviness, or pressure in the head, often accompanied by dizziness. Also common were heaviness in the limbs, unsteadiness, feelings of thirst or dryness in the throat, dilation of the pupils, and increase in pulse rate.

Almost all of the experienced users of marihuana manifested a euphoric state which usually ended in a feeling of drowsiness. The majority of inexperienced users also became high. However, in the inexperienced users, anxiety often alternated with the euphoria. The committee was of the opinion that the anxiety among the inexperienced users was due to uncertainty regarding the possibile effects of the drug and to disagreeable sensations that were present.

The duration and intensity of the effects tended to increase with higher doses. However, some subjects who received a moderate dose manifested effects that were reported by other subjects only at a high dose.

Six of the 72 subjects became anxious and disoriented during the marihuana session but returned to normal about three hours after the termination of the session. Two additional subjects showed psychotic-like behavior one to two weeks after they had participated in the marihuana sessions; the committee considered their behavior to be a manifestation of a prison psychosis and not directly related to their having taken marihuana. Another subject, an epileptic who had seizures about once a month, showed a confusional state which began soon after he had smoked a high dose of marihuana and which persisted for six days. With respect to this individual, the committee wrote as follows: "Epileptics are subject to such attacks, epileptic or epileptic equivalents, which may be brought on by any number of upsetting circumstances. In this case marihuana is the only known factor which precipitated the attack."

Additional effects of marihuana were also specified by the committee. With 2 cc marihuana, the

> subject experiences some reduction in drive, less objectivity in evaluating situations, less aggression, more self-confidence and a generally more favorable attitude toward himself . . . As the drug relaxes the subject, the restraints which he normally imposes on himself are loosened and he talks more freely than he does in his undrugged state. Things which under ordinary circumstances he would not speak about are now given expression. Metaphysical problems which in the undrugged state he would be unwilling to discuss, sexual ideas he would ordinarily hesitate to mention, jokes without point, are all part of the oral stream released by the marihuana . . . Physically the subject reports pleasant sensations of "drifting" and "floating" and he allows himself to become enveloped in a pleasant lassitude. After the administration of larger doses of marihuana (5cc.) the pleasurable sensations appear to be outweighed by concomitant feelings of anxiety and, in some cases, of physical distress, much as nausea (p. 131).

During the marihuana sessions the subjects were also tested on a series of mental and psychomotor tasks such as the Army Alpha Intelligence Test, Digit Symbol Substitution, Kohs Block Designs, and simple and complex reactions time. The effects of marihuana on intellectual-motor performance was found to be a function of three variables: the complexity of the task, the dose of marihuana, and the subject's previous experience with marihuana. The results in general were as follows:

The effects of marihuana were closely related to the complexity of the functions tested. Simpler functions, such as speed of tapping and simple reaction time, were only slightly affected by the high dose (5 cc.) and negligibly if at all affected by the moderate dose (2 cc.). However, both the high and the moderate dose of marihuana produced decrements in performance on the more complicated tasks such as complex reaction time and intelligence tests (on which there was a loss in both speed and accuracy).

In general, decrements in performance were greater at the high dose of marihuana.

The detrimental effects on the complex tasks were clearer in subjects who had not previously used marihuana. Experienced users showed very little if any decrement.

Although marihuana tended to produce a reduction in proficiency on complex tasks, it did not affect musical ability, estimation of short time intervals, extimation of small linear distances, auditory acuity, and grip strength.[4]

WEIL INVESTIGATION

In an investigation presented by Weil, Zinberg, and Nelsen (1968) and Weil and Zinberg (1969) an attempt was made to determine the effects of marihuana at doses commonly used in the United States, a double-blind placebo control was employed, and a clear distinction was made between the effects produced on inexperienced subjects and on chronic users.

The inexperienced subjects were nine college men, ages 21 to 26, who smoked cigarettes but had never tried marihuana. These subjects first participated in a practice session in which they were taught the proper way to inhale marihuana. (The practice in proper inhalation was conducted with ordinary tobacco cigarettes.) The subjects were then tested in three counterbalanced experimental sessions at each of which they smoked two cigarettes (reefers). The reefers were of three kinds: high-dose (1 gram of marihuana in each); low-dose (0.25 grams of marihuana plus tobacco); and a placebo reefer which was derived from parts of the male cannabis plant that do *not* contain the active chemical.

The experienced subjects were eight male college students who had been smoking marihuana regularly. These experienced subjects participated in only one session at which they smoked only the high-dose reefers.

4. A more recent study (Clark & Nakashima, 1968), with individuals who had not previously used marihuana, also found that performance on memory tasks and on complex reaction time tasks was generally impaired after oral ingestion of marihuana (at doses equivalent to the 2-5 cc. doses used in the study by the Mayor's Committee).

The results were as follows:

In general, the effects were at a maximum 15 minutes after the two marihuana reefers were smoked, were diminished after one hour, and were gone after three hours. No delayed or persistent effects beyond three hours were reported or observed. No adverse reactions—e.g., anxiety or panic—were noted in any of the subjects.

In both the experienced and the inexperienced subjects, the two marihuana cigarettes typically produced an increase in pulse rate and, at higher doses, hyperemia of the conjunctiva (dilation of the small blood vessels of the eyes, so that the white of the eye appeared red). Also, time perception tended to change; for example, as compared to estimates of time under the placebo condition, three of the nine inexperienced subjects under the low-dose marihuana and four of the nine under the high-dose judged time periods as being longer (a 5-minute period was estimated as 10 minutes).

Despite previous reports to the contrary, marihuana did not produce pupillary dilation and did not affect blood sugar levels in either the inexperienced or the experienced subjects.

After smoking the high-dose marihuana, the experienced users performed normally on psychomotor tasks (e.g., pursuit rotor and Digit Symbol Substitution). In contrast, after smoking marihuana, the inexperienced subjects were not able to perform as well as normally on the psychomotor tasks. These decrements in psychomotor performance were dose related; the inexperienced subjects showed a larger drop in proficiency at the higher dose.

After smoking marihuana, all of the experienced users reported that they were high. During the time they were high, the experienced subjects manifested *subtle* difficulties in speaking which may have been due to some difficulty in remembering from moment to moment the logical thread of what was being said. Also, as compared to pre-marihuana verbalizations, verbal samples taken during the marihuana high were rated by 'blind' judges as including more vivid imagery, a shift in time orientation from past or future to the present, increased free associative quality, and decreased awareness of a listener. However, during the marihuana high, the experienced subjects did not show any consistent changes on a self-rating mood scale which measured such factors as uneasiness, alertness, dreaminess, cheerfulness, and confidence.

In marked contrast with the experienced users, all of the inexperienced subjects reported minimum subjective effects after smoking marihuana. Although some inexperienced subjects stated that "things seemed to take longer", they were not confused, did not report distortions in visual or auditory perception, and, with one exception, did not report that they were euphoric or high. Only one inexperienced subject stated that he was high and this subject had previously expressed a desire to become high with marihuana.

The latter set of results are generally in line with Becker's (1953) analysis of the factors involved in becoming euphoric or high with marihuana. According to Becker, to attain a high, it is necessary for the individual to have a series of experiences in which he (a) learns to smoke marihuana in a way which will insure a sufficient dose, (b) learns to recognize the effects and associate them with the drug, and (c) learns to enjoy or at least not be anxious about the sensations which he perceives. Whether or not a pharmacological sensitivity to marihuana also occurs with repeated exposure remains to be determined.

CRANCER INVESTIGATION

It is commonly believed that individuals under marihuana are not able to perform normally on complex psychomotor tasks such as automobile driving. Consequently, it has been claimed that an increase in the use of marihuana will lead to an increase in the number of driving accidents. To determine the effects of marihuana on driving performance, Crancer, Dille, Delay, Wallace, and Haykin (1969) recently conducted a study as follows:

The subjects were 36 licensed drivers who were experienced marihuana users and familiar with the effects of alcohol. Driving performance was tested by a driving simulator consisting of a console mock-up of a car containing all the equipment relevant to driving. The car unit faced a screen on which a test film was projected. The test film gave the subject a driver's-eye view of the road as it led him through normal and emergency driving situations. Previous studies (Crancer, 1968; Wallace & Crancer, 1969) had indicated that the driving simulator test is significantly correlated with the performer's actual number of driving accidents (as judged by his previous five-year driving record) whereas the behind-the-wheel road test (used in driver licensing examinations) is not correlated with the performer's actual driving accidents.[5]

A Latin square design was used to test each subject on the driving simulator under three conditions: (a) *Marihuana high.* The subjects consumed two marihuana cigarettes totalling 1.7 grams. This dose of marihuana was sufficient to elicit subjective reports from the subjects that they were high. (b) *Alcohol intoxication.* Subjects consumed alcohol in amounts sufficient to give a reading of 0.10 per cent blood alcohol

5. It appears that the driving simulator test rather than the road test is a more valid index of actual driving performance because the former, but not the latter, exposes the subject to a series of hazardous driving situations.

concentration on the Breathalyzer. (c) *Control* (without marihuana or alcohol).

The dependent variables were: speedometer errors, steering errors, brake errors, accelerator errors, signal errors, and total errors. Scores on each dependent variable were obtained three times during each experimental session: Period A, one-half hour after smoking marihuana, taking alcohol, or the beginning of the control period; Period B, two hours after taking marihuana, etc.; and Period C, three and a half hours after taking marihuana, etc.

Analysis of variance for total errors showed no significant differences in simulated driving scores for subjects experiencing a marihuana high and the same subjects under the control condition. However, total errors were significantly increased (by 15%) under alcohol intoxication as compared to the control condition.

Separate analyses were performed on each of the dependent variables. As compared to the control condition, alcohol significantly increased accelerator errors in Periods A and B, signal errors in Periods A, B, and C, braking errors in Periods B and C, and speedometer errors in Period A. For the comparison of marihuana versus control a significant difference was found only for speedometer errors in Period A. (The increase in speedometer errors in Period A under marihuana does not mean that the subjects were driving at inappropriate speeds but that they spend less time monitoring the speedometer.) In general, these results appear to be consistent with those presented earlier indicating that *experienced* marihuana users manifest either a very small reduction in psychomotor proficiency under the drug (Mayor's Committee, 1944) or no reduction in proficiency (Weil et al., 1968).

Crancer et al. (1969) also carried out two supplementary studies, with a small number of subjects, which *suggest* that experienced marihuana users may be able to drive competently even at rather high doses of the drug, and individuals who have not previously used marihuana may be able to drive competently when they first take the drug. In the first supplementary study, four subjects (who had participated in the experiment described above) were retested on the driving simulator after they had smoked approximately three times the amount of marihuana used in the main experiment. Under this high dose, none of these experienced marihuana users showed a significant change in driving proficiency. In the second supplementary study, four individuals who had not previously used marihuana (inexperienced subjects) smoked sufficient marihuana to produce an increase in pulse rate and subjective reports that they were high; after the marihuana high was attained, the four subjects were tested on the driving simulator. As compared to their

control performance, each of these inexperienced subjects under marihuana showed no significant change in their driving scores.

In brief, the Crancer studies suggest (but do not conclusively demonstrate) that the effects of marihuana smoking on driving performance
may be much smaller than has been commonly assumed, and the marked
increase in marihuana use in the United States which has occurred
during recent years may not significantly increase the rate of driving
accidents. Further studies are urgently needed to determine to what
extent the Crancer results can be generalized to actual driving performance. Further studies are also needed to ascertain whether individuals
under marihuana must exert special efforts to attend and to concentrate
in order to drive proficiently, or are able to drive proficiently without
making a special effort to do so.

LSD-TYPE EFFECTS OF MARIHUANA AND HASHISH

As stated in Chapter 1, LSD-type drugs commonly produce a
dreamy-detached feeling, changes in time perception, and changes in
mood (either or both anxiety and euphoria). The effects of marihuana
tend to resemble these LSD-type effects; a substantial number of subjects who have smoked one to four marihuana cigarettes state that they
feel dizzy, detached, or as if they are in a dreamlike state; they feel that
time is passing slowly; and they feel either or both anxious and happy.

As stated in Chapter 1, LDS-type drugs also commonly give rise to
changes in body-image, changes in the quality of sounds, and alterations
in visual perception. A small number of individuals who have smoked
one to four marihuana cigarettes seem to experience effects of this type;
for instance, they may state that their limbs feel light, sounds have taken
on unusual qualities, they see colors and patterns on the wall, or they
perceive rooms or objects as changed in perspective or shape (Keeler,
1968a). Furthermore, a few marihuana users have reported flash-backs
or recurrences of marihuana effects long after the drug was no longer
present in their body (Keeler, 1967; Keeler, Reifler, & Liptzin, 1968), in
the same way as some LSD users report flash-backs or recurrences of
LSD effects.

Although *some* LSD-type effects are produced by marihuana as it is
commonly used in the United States, *more* LSD-type effects of greater
intensity are apparently produced by the pure resin of the cannabis plant
as it is commonly used in large dosages in North Africa, India, and other
parts of the world. (In fact, as compared to the grade of marihuana
commonly used in the United States, the pure resin from the plant,
hashish or charas, appears to be five to eight times more potent by
weight.) A series of reports (Ames, 1958; Bouquet, 1950-51; Chopra &

Chopra, 1957a; de Farias, 1955; Dontas & Zis, 1929; Fraenkel & Jöel, 1927; Louria, 1968; Martin, 1969; Miras, 1965; Murphy, 1966; Persaud & Ellington, 1967, 1968; Soueif, 1967) suggests that high potency extracts of cannabis (especially when taken over a long period of time) tend to give rise to the following effects which tend to resemble those associated with LSD-type drugs (compare Table 1, in Chapter 1):

Some of the *somatic-sympathetic* effects of cannabis are similar to those produced by LSD-type drugs, for example, both types of drugs, at times, produce an increase in tendon reflexes (Dontas & Zis, 1929). However, other effects of cannabis, for example, increase in pulse rate and dilation of the small blood vessels in the eyes, are not the same as those produced by LSD-type drugs (Ames, 1958; Chopra & Chopra, 1957a; Miras, 1965).

The *body-image changes* which are reported with high-potency cannabis preparations seem to resemble those produced by LSD-type drugs. These include a change in the feeling of body coherence (Fraenkel & Jöel, 1927), numbness in the extremities (Ames, 1958; Dontas & Zix, 1929), sensations of lightness in the limbs, or feelings that the limbs or head have lengthened or shortened (Ames, 1958).

Hashish and the other potent cannabis preparations tend to produce a *dreamy-detached feeling* (Bouquet, 1950-51), or a tranquilized feeling (Chopra & Chopra, 1957a), or a feeling of fluctuating between dreaming and waking (Ames, 1958; Fraenkel & Jöel, 1927). Although these dreamy-detached feelings appear to resemble similar feelings produced by LSD-type drugs, cannabis preparations (unlike LSD) often lead to drowsiness and deep sleep (Chopra & Chopra, 1957a; de Farias, 1955).

The *reduced intellectual-motor proficiency,* which is found both with potent cannabis preparations and with LSD-type drugs, may be interrelated with the dreamy-detached feelings and with difficulties in thinking and attending (Ames, 1958; Murphy, 1966).

Changes in time perception, with time typically seeming to pass more slowly, are found both with cannabis and with LSD-type drugs (Ames, 1958; Bouquet, 1950-51; Fraenkel & Jöel, 1927; Murphy, 1966; Soueif, 1967).

Hashish and other potent cannabis derivatives may at times produce *changes in visual perception* which tend to resemble those produced by LSD-type drugs (Ames, 1958; Murphy, 1966). These visual changes may include the following: objects or parts of one's own body seem further away, the shape and colors of objects are changed, and patterns are seen on the bare wall (Bouquet, 1950-51); also, rooms appear wider, floors seem to slope, colors become brighter and more luminous, and objects change in appearance (Fraenkel & Jöel, 1927; Soueif, 1967).

Hashish and other potent forms of cannabis may at times produce *changes in audition,* for example, music may seem more beautiful (Bouquet, 1950-51). At times, potent cannabis preparations also appear to give rise to *synesthesia* and to *changes in smell and taste* (Chopra & Chopra, 1957a).

It has been claimed that hashish produces *heightened responsiveness to primary suggestions* (Bouquet, 1950-51).

Both cannabis and LSD produce *changes in moods and emotions*—usually toward euphoria but at times toward anxiety and panic (Ames, 1958; Bouquet, 1950-51; Chopra & Chopra, 1957a; Fraenkel & Jöel, 1927; Louria, 1968; Murphy, 1966).

When the concentrated resin of cannabis is injected intraperitoneally into pregnant rats (but not pregnant mice), it may produce *fetal malformations* in the same way as LSD injections (Martin, 1969; Persuad & Ellington, 1967, 1968). However, many other substances injected into pregnant rats can also produce fetal malformations; these include insulin, penicillin, streptomycin, cortisone, and aspirin (Editorial, 1969).

In brief, the studies cited above suggest that high doses of hashish, and other preparations which contain relatively large amounts of the cannabis resin, may produce a set of effects which tend to resemble those produced by average doses of LSD (around 200 micrograms). It should be noted, however, that although LSD is a single chemical compound, hashish and other forms of cannabis include a wide variety of chemical compounds, most of which are pharmacologically inactive. The question that now arises is: Does the pharmacologically active chemical compound (or compounds) in cannabis produce effects which resemble those of LSD? A series of recent studies which bear on this question are discussed next.

EFFECTS OF TETRAHYDROCANNABINOL (THC)

The resin of the female cannabis plant contains a series of chemical compounds that have been labeled as cannabinols, cannabidiols, and tetrahydrocannabinols. It appears likely that the latter group of compounds—the tetrahydrocannabinols—are the most active in producing psychological effects (Isbell, Gorodetzsky, Jasinski, Claussen, Spulak, & Korte, 1967). One of the tetrahydrocannabinols was recently isolated from hashish in the form of Δ ^{9}-trans-tetrahydrocannabinol or THC. THC is now available in small quantities for research purposes.

Isbell and associates (Isbell, 1967; Isbell et al., 1967) administered THC at various doses both orally and also by smoking to 40 experienced marihuana users formerly addicted to opiates and who were serving sentences for violation of the United States Narcotic Laws. The results can be summarized as follows:

THC consistently elevated the pulse rate. Dilation of the small blood vessels of the eye was produced by the higher doses. However, regard-less of the dose or the route of administration, THC did not produce significant changes in pupillary size, respiratory rate, systolic or diastolic blood pressure, or threshold for elicitation of the knee jerk.

At the lowest dose (120 micrograms per kilogram orally or 50 micrograms per kilogram by smoking) all subjects recognized the effects as similar to those of marihuana. All subjects reported alterations in mood, usually stating that they felt happy, silly, and relaxed.

At a higher dose (240 micrograms per kilogram orally or 100 micrograms per kilogram by smoking) the subjects reported alterations in visual and auditory perception (e.g., "colors are brighter" and "hearing is keener"), the body felt lighter, and time seem extended.

With a still higher dose (300-480 micrograms per kilogram orally or 200-250 micrograms per kilogram by smoking) all of the above effects were more pronounced and, in addition, most subjects reported changes in body image, visual illusions, feelings of unreality, and hallucinations.

Since the effects obtained at the high dose of THC seemed to resemble those produced by LSD, Isbell and associates next proceeded to make a direct comparison between THC and LSD.

The subsequent experiment (Isbell & Jasinski, 1969) was conducted with ten individuals who had been previously addicted to narcotics and who were also experienced marihuana users. At weekly intervals, the subjects received, in random order, a placebo, 0.5 micrograms per kilogram and 1.5 micrograms per kilogram of LSD intramuscularly, and 75 micrograms per kilogram and 225 micrograms per kilogram of THC by smoking. Neither the subjects nor the experimenters were told what drugs were being used on any particular day. (However, since one does not smoke LSD, it is questionable to what extent the double-blind procedures prevented subjects or experimenters from guessing the nature of the drugs.) Seven times during each of the test days, physiological measures such as pulse and blood pressure were taken and the subjects completed a questionnaire containing 63 items pertaining to their drug experiences. The results of this second experiment were as follows:

At the high dose of THC most of the subjects reported marked changes in body-image, illusions, delusions, and hallucinations. Most of the subjects retained insight and ascribed these effects to the drug. However, two subjects "lost insight, did not realize the effects were due to the drug and, even after they had recovered, had difficulty in accepting the fact that their psychotic experiences were due to a drug and more particularly that they were due to a drug isolated from marihuana."[6]

6. The quotation pertaining to the two individuals who lost insight is from a personal communication by D. R. Jasinksi to the present writer (May 29, 1969).

These two individuals, who lost insight with the high dose of THC, dropped out of the study, so that only eight subjects completed the experiment.

In general, THC and LSD could not be clearly distinguished on the subjective reports scale. Both drugs produced alterations in mood, changes in body image, visual distortions and, with higher doses, hallucinations. However, LSD was about 150 times as potent by weight as THC; for example, 75 micrograms per kilogram of THC were required to elicit the psychotomimetic subjective effects that were produced by 0.5 micrograms per kilogram of LSD. Although the two drugs generally produced quite similar subjective effects, certain items on the subjective scales distinguished the two drugs. For instance, some of the items that were higher under THC than LSD were, "I couldn't get mad at anyone right now," "My eyes itch and burn," and "My appetite is increased." Some of the items that were higher under LSD than THC were, "I feel anxious and upset," "Some parts of my body are tingling," and "I notice my hand shakes when I try to write."

LSD and THC produced different autonomic effects. LSD (but not THC) raised body temperature, systolic blood pressure, and pupil size, and lowered the threshold for the knee jerk. THC produced a greater increase in heart rate than LSD. In addition, THC (but not LSD) produced dilation of the small blood vessels in the eyes and a slight drooping of the upper eyelids.

In further study, the same authors (Isbell & Jasinski, 1969) showed that subjects who have become tolerant to the effects of LSD are not also cross-tolerant to THC. In this study ten subjects were given LSD by daily injection of 0.5 milligrams per kilogram and increasing to 1.5 milligrams per kilogram over a period of ten days. At the end of ten days the subjects manifested tolerance, that is, they showed very little response to LSD. On the eleventh day, the subjects received 225 milligrams per kilogram of THC; they showed the normal response to THC indicating that cross-tolerance had not also developed to this drug.

In brief, the Isbell studies indicate that THC can produce subjective effects which resemble those that characterize LSD (body image changes, changes in time perception, mood changes, feelings of unreality, visual distortions and illusions, and hallucinations), provided that the ratio of the THC dose to the LSD dose is about 150 to one. However, there are also indications that some differences exist between the subjective effects of THC and LSD, although the nature of these differences has not as yet been clearly elucidated.

Despite the overlap in the subjective effects, THC and LSD can be clearly distinguished by their autonomic effects. Because of the differences in the autonomic effects and the lack of cross-tolerance between the two drugs, it appears that THC and LSD may affect somewhat different processes within the central nervous system.

Several factors suggest caution in drawing general conclusions from the Isbell studies. First of all, the subjects were formerly addicted to opiates and may be unrepresentative of the general population. Secondly, the subjects were experienced users of marihuana and the results may not apply to non-users. Thirdly, although an attempt was made to use double-blind controls in these studies, it is questionable whether these controls were successful. Clearly, further studies are needed to determine more conclusively the similarities and differences in the subjective effects of various doses of LSD and THC.

Cannabis as a Social Problem

It has been claimed that cannabis leads to antisocial or criminal behavior, gives rise to psychological dependence if not to physical dependence, is a stepping-stone to the use of heroin and other narcotics, produces psychosis or mental illness, ruins physical health, and reduces the users motivation to achieve (Bouquet, 1950-51; Gomila & Lambou, 1938; Wolff, 1949). It is impossible, at the present time, to state unequivocally whether these claims have some degree of validity; we simply do not have scientific data pertaining to these contentions. Although definite answers cannot be given now, it is nevertheless incumbent upon us to attempt to derive the most probable answers from the available data. Tentative answers are urgently needed because marihuana use has drastically increased in the United States during recent years, there is every indication that its use will continue to increase in the near future, and policy decisions must be made now by government officials, educators, and parents. Let us summarize, as objectively as possible, the preliminary data that are now available.

ANTISOCIAL AND CRIMINAL ACTIVITY

Several earlier reports contend that marihuana and other forms of cannabis give rise to antisocial or criminal behavior because they impair judgment, weaken social restraint, and release inhibitions (Gaskill, 1945; Wolff, 1949). This contention is not clearly supported by the data. Although the act of acquiring marihuana is legally defined as a crime, no causal link has been demonstrated between the use of marihuana and the performance of other types of illegal behaviors. Andrade (1964) carried out a 10-year clinical study of individuals in Brazil who were accused of committing crimes under the influence of marihuana. In each case it was concluded that the crime was neither directly nor indirectly related to the use of marihuana; that is, in each instance, it appeared that the crime was due to situational and personality factors and would have been committed if the person had not used marihuana. Three investigations (Freedman & Rockmore, 1946; Marcovitz & Myers, 1944; Siler, 1933), which surveyed the use of marihuana among American soldiers, found that users were either of low intelligence or had psychopathic tendencies, and had begun to engage in antisocial activities before they started to use marihuana. As stated earlier in this chapter, the Mayor's Committee (1944) also concluded that there was no evidence that use of marihuana gave rise to antisocial or criminal behavior. Similarly, the recent British Government (1968) study could find no evidence that the increase in the consumption of cannabis in Britain is causing aggressive antisocial behavior or crimes. It also appears that the crime rate has not increased in areas of the United States where marihuana use has increased tremendously in recent years (Simmons, 1967). After an extensive survey of cannabis use in India, Chopra and Chopra (1957a) concluded that the drug reduces crime, writing that, "The result of continued and excessive use of these drugs in our experience in India is to make the individual timid rather than to lead him to commit violent crimes."

Although earlier studies indicated that a higher proportion of criminals than non-criminals used marihuana, this does not support the contention that marihuana leads to crime. The use of marihuana by a disproportionate number of criminals can be explained by the fact that until very recently the smoking of marihuana in the United States was much more prevalent among the lower classes of the population (that tend to have high crime rates) rather than among the educated or upper classes (that tend to have low crime rates).

Although very few, if any, recent writers claim that cannabis use is directly related to antisocial or criminal activity, some writers argue that there is an indirect relationship. For instance, Collier (1965) has stated that marihuana and other forms of cannabis produce a lethargic condition and the user loses his ability to earn an adequate living; consequently, the user may be driven to criminal activity in order to earn a living and to get more cannabis. However, other writers employ similar arguments to support the contention that cannabis reduces criminal activity; Watt (1965), in agreement with Chopra and Chopra as quoted above, suggests that the lethargy associated with continued use of cannabis stultifies the executive capacity for committing crimes.[7]

---

7. The arguments concerning the effects of cannabis on sexual activity are also contradictory. Although some authors argue that the use of cannabis leads to sexual excesses, others (e.g., Chopra & Chopra, 1957a, p. 21) note that "saintly people [in India] who wish

Although far more probing studies are needed in this area, we may tentatively conclude at present, in agreement with Nowlis (1969, p. 100), that it has not as yet been demonstrated that the use of cannabis is a direct cause of antisocial or criminal activity.

PHYSICAL AND PSYCHOLOGICAL DEPENDENCE

Many laymen seem to believe that marihuana and other cannabis derivatives produce addiction or physical dependence in the same way as heroin and other narcotics. This belief if fallacious; marihuana and other forms of cannabis do not produce addiction as defined by tolerance, physical dependence, and a withdrawal syndrome (Chopra & Chopra, 1957a). There is no evidence that users become physiologically tolerant to the effects of cannabis so that they have to increase the dose in order to obtain the desired effects. There is no evidence that cannabis produc- es a change in the user's physiological processes so that he requires continued administration of the drug in order to function properly. Also, when cannabis users stop taking the drug, they do not show an absti- nence syndrome or clear-cut withdrawal symptoms.

Although physical dependence of the type found with heroin and other opiates is not produced by cannabis, it can nevertheless be argued that cannabis users may become psychologically dependent on the drug. That is, some cannabis users may learn to rely on the drug for a feeling of well-being and they may desire or crave the drug in order to have this feeling. This appears to be true, at least for some individuals; some users appear to desire cannabis as much as others desire tobacco or alcohol. Chopra and Chopra (1957a) write of such persons that "Having once started the use of the drug for some ailment or other, they could not feel normal without it. Life seemed brighter to them under the influence of the drug and their surroundings became more congenial and pleas- ant . . .". In brief, although many users of marihuana and other forms of cannabis do not become especially bothered when it is unavailable (they can 'take it or leave it'), other users become psychologically dependent on its euphoriant or intoxicating properties to such an extent that life seems dismal without it.

However, as McGlothlin (1967) has cogently argued, psychological dependence on a substance is not necessarily harmful in itself, since

---

to renounce worldly pleasures use cannabis for suppressing sexual desires". Apparently, cultural factors play an important role in determining the effects of cannabis on sexual behavior. In a recent study of 200 youthful marihuana users in the United States, 44 per cent said that marihuana increased their sexual *desire,* and 68 per cent said that it increased their sexual *enjoyment* (Goode, 1969a).

many forms of acceptable behavior (e.g., coffee drinking) can be included under this category. In addition, McGlothlin (1967) has pointed out that "The assessment of the harmfulness of psychic dependence must be based on the consequences of the behavior rather than its existence." Unfortunately, the long-term consequences of cannabis use are not definitely known at the present time.

One point, however, needs to be underscored with respect to psychological dependence on cannabis: the evidence at present strongly indicates that psychological dependence on the drug is usually found in individuals who are judged by clinical psychologists and psychiatrists as maladjusted or as having psychopathological tendencies. In a report on the use of kif (a form of cannabis) in Morocco, Benabud (1957, p. 8) noted that the importance of predisposing psychopathological tendencies justifies the well-known saying that "You are a kif addict long before you smoke your first pipe.". Chopra and Chopra (1939) concluded that psychological dependence on cannabis in India was present in individuals with psychic disorders or with faulty personality or mental make-up. Of the 1238 chronic users observed, nearly half had long-standing neurotic problems. Insomnia was commonly claimed by users to be an important reason why they started to use and continued to use the drug. Other users had hysterical symptoms or were hypochondriacs or gave a history of psychosomatic ailments. Interestingly enough, many of these individuals claimed improvement in their neurotic symptoms after they began to use cannabis. Somewhat along similar lines, Freedman and Rockmore (1946, Part 1) noted that a substantial proportion of marihuana users in the American army claimed that they began to use and continued to use the weed because it relieved their headaches.

A STEPPING-STONE TO HEROIN

A number of earlier writers claimed that cannabis users often stepped-up to heroin and other hard narcotics "in a search for greater thrills". Unequivocal data that support this claim are not available at present. Although many heroin addicts have previously used cannabis (and alcohol and tobacco), it does not follow that cannabis (or alcohol ot tobacco) was causally related to the use of heroin. It is clear, however, that the great majority of cannabis users do not progress to heroin (Nowlis, 1969, p. 100). Also, it is claimed that in areas of the United States where marihuana use and the number of marihuana arrests have dramatically increased in recent years, the use of narcotics such as heroin and arrests for such use have either not increased or have shown a decline (Sim-

mons, 1967; Mandel, 1967; McGlothlin, 1967).[8] Recent studies of marihuana users in the United States indicate that the drug subculture based
upon marihuana that has developed among the youth includes strong
prohibitions against heroin and other narcotics (Blumer, 1967, p. 73). In
fact, subcultural norms appear to be the most important factors in
determining whether or not a marihuana user will or will not step-up to
hard narcotics such as heroin. Recent studies, summarized by Goode
(1969b), strongly indicate that marihuana smokers will use other drugs
such as LSD which their subculture approves but will almost certainly
not use drugs such as heroin when these are disapproved by their friends
and intimates.

Although the evidence does not support the contention that use of
marihuana is directly related to the use of heroin, it is possible that use
of the two drugs may be indirectly related. For instance, individuals who
are members of a marihuana subculture which does not have strong
prohibitions against heroin may be more prone than others to try a wide
variety of drugs including heroin. Furthermore, given the present laws,
users of marihuana may find 'hard' narcotics more available than
non-users and there is probably a correlation between the availability of
narcotics and their use.

If brief, there does not appear to be a direct relationship between the
use of marihuana and the use of narcotics. However, there may be a
complex indirect relationship between the use of the two types of drugs
and intensive studies are needed to probe into the nature of this possible
relationship.

MENTAL ILLNESS

Earlier observations from North Africa indicated that cannabis users
had a disproportionately high rate of admissions to mental hospitals.
Although some writers concluded from these observations that cannabis
causes mental illness, an alternative possibility was never excluded;
namely, that cannabis was used primarily by urban slum dwellers in
North Africa, and individuals from this group have a disproportionate
high rate of admissions to mental hospitals irrespective of whether or not
they use cannabis.

Several studies carried out in the United States suggest that marihuana is not directly related to mental illness. Siler (1933) was unable to

8. Although these data do not support the stepping-stone hypothesis, they also do not
conclusively disconfirm it. It is possible that heroin use may be declining in the total
population while at the same time it is increasing in that segment of the population that
uses marihuana.

find cases of psychosis due to marihuana smoking in a sample of several hundred American soldiers. Freedman and Rockmore (1946) also failed to uncover any history of mental hospitalization in a sample of 300 soldiers who had been smoking marihuana for an average of seven years. Furthermore, it appears that areas in the United States that have recently had a marked increase in the use of marihuana have not had a noticeable increase in the rate of mental illness (Simmons, 1967).

Although marihuana and other forms of cannabis have not been shown to lead directly to mental illness, there is a possibility that, among individuals who have serious problems in adjustment, marihuana may serve as one among many possible precipitants to a mental breakdown. Blum (1969, Vol. 1, p. 77) has noted that "The evidence for drug as demon is slim; the evidence for people in trouble using drugs so that they exaggerate their difficulties — in spite of what can be their immediate intent of assuaging their troubles — is considerable.". Along similar lines, Nowlis (1969), p. 100) concluded, from a review of the literature, that "Although high dosage levels of potent forms of cannabis may produce toxic psychotic episodes lasting from a few hours to a few days, most evidence indicates that true psychoses of appreciable duration occur only in predisposed individuals".

Four points are relevant here:

Every population includes a group of unstable individuals who have a high probability of experiencing a psychotic breakdown at some point in their lives. It is inadvisable for these individuals to use marihuana — or other drugs such as alcohol, amphetamines, or barbiturates (Ausubel, 1964).

It is by no means clear, at the present time, how we can prevent unstable individuals from using drugs.

Although marihuana smoking may, at times, shift the precarious balance in unstable individuals toward mental illness, we do not know when or how this occurs.

It appears that marihuana smoking does not always noticeably affect the mental health of unstable individuals and there are some indications that it may, at times, help them to maintain their precarious stability. However, we do not know when, how, or under what conditions these effects occur.

PHYSICAL HEALTH

Chopra and Chopra (1957a, p. 19) noted that more than half of the cannabis users in India "had a healthy look and did not show any apparent untoward effects produced by the habit". However, they also pointed out that, in nearly half of the users, "The general bodily nutrition suffers, because the money which should be spent for the purpose of procuring wholesome and nutritious food is used to buy the drug.".

In an earlier study in India, Chopra and Chopra (1939) noted that no moderate users of cannabis claimed any health problems, whereas most heavy users indicated that there was some impairment in their health. Of those who used high doses of potent preparations such as charas (hashish), 72 per cent showed conjunctivitis, and most had respiratory ailments such as sore throat, pharyngitis, bronchitis, or asthma.

It should be noted that heavy users of cannabis in India, and also in other parts of the world such as North Africa, consume at least two to six grams of charas or hashish per day, which is apparently equivalent to smoking at least 20 to 60 marihuana cigarettes (McGlothlin & West, 1968). Although heavy use of potent preparations is associated with problems in physical health, McGlothlin and West (1968) have also pointed out that "Moderate use of the less potent cannabis preparations in the East is not considered to be a health problem; and, in fact, bhang (the Indian equivalent of marihuana) is not even considered to fall within the definition of cannabis by Indian authorities and so *is excluded* from U.N. treaty control.".

In brief, the evidence at present fails to demonstrate that moderate use of cannabis produces health problems. However, it appears that heavy use of potent cannabis preparations is directly related to conjunctivitis and respiratory ailments and may also be indirectly related, through a neglect of proper nutrition, to a general deterioration in physical health.

AMOTIVATIONAL SYNDROME

Countries such as India and Morocco have Skid Rows comprised of hashish users who neglect hygiene and personal habits and who lack ambition. Earlier studies often noted that cannabis users tended to be rather unproductive, passive, or unmotivated individuals and that prolonged use of the drug tended to reinforce this amotivational syndrome (McGlothlin, 1967). Some of the earlier authors viewed the amotivational syndrome as a direct result of the use of cannabis; for instance, Lewin (1931, p. 12) claimed that "Moroccans who were in the service of Europeans proved serviceable and reliable until they smoked kif.". However, it is not clear whether use of cannabis is causally related to the loss of ambition, whether individuals who were never ambitious or who have lost or are losing their motivation and drive are likely to abuse cannabis, or whether serious involvement with any drug (cannabis, alcohol, or whatever) simply tends to be inconsistent with serious involvement with work and achievement.

Prohibition or Legalization of Marihuana

At the present time, American law carries very serious penalties against the use of marihuana. Its use or sale is a grave crime, a felony, under Federal law. In fact, present Federal laws impose a 2- to 40-year sentence for possession of marihuana. State laws are often even more severe (Fort, 1969). Should these severe penalties be reduced or eliminated? Let us summarize the arguments that can be formulated for and against retention of the present laws.

The arguments for maintaining penalties against marihuana include the following:

If legal controls are removed, the consumption of marihuana would increase. Easy availability results in the greater use of drugs as indicated by the high rate of narcotic addiction among physicians, pharmacists, dentists, and nurses (Pescor, 1943). In fact, legalization of marihuana will encourage use among the young and the psychologically disturbed, just those individuals who should not be using it.

If the penalties against marihuana are removed, the consumption of more potent forms of cannabis such as hashish and THC would also increase, and the extent of abuse would be much greater than is presently the case with marihuana.

If marihuana is legalized, its production and distribution might be taken over by 'big business.' Advertising campaigns might be conducted, the television screen might show beautiful women extolling its blissful benefits, door-to-door salesmen might compete for sales, grocery stores might offer extra 'stamps' for purchasing it, and it might be sold to elementary school children and to patients in mental hospitals.

The long-term effects of marihuana have not been carefully explored. In India, North Africa, and the Middle East, where potent forms of cannabis are used, many observers have warned against its effects on mental and physical health. Until definite data are available pertaining to long-term effects, we should not allow cannabis preparations to be more widely used than they are at present.

Increased marihuana consumption will tend to increase the number of automobile accidents. The recent study by Crancer et al. (1969), which failed to show that marihuana materially reduces performance on the *driving simulator test,* cannot be viewed as conclusive. Since marihuana, at least at higher doses, tends to produce changes in the sense of time, a slowing of reflexes, and visual distortions, it appears likely that in at least some individuals it will produce some reduction in driving proficiency.

The use of marihuana may not lead *directly* to the use of hard narcotics such as heroin. However, a culture which does not discourage the use of marihuana may also find it more difficult to discourage the use of heroin.

Although the use of marihuana may not by itself produce a reduction in drive and motivation, its continual use may reinforce an amotivational syndrome that is already present.

Those favoring either a marked reduction or a total removal of penalties for the use of marihuana can present the following arguments and recommendations:

Many of the contentions against the use of marihuana are due to a confusion between its effects and those of more potent extracts of the cannabis plant such as hashish and THC. No one is urging the legalization of hashish and THC. The argument pertains only to marihuana which is used at present in the United States to produce a mild euphoria, to relax or to relieve tensions, and to increase sociability (McGlothlin & West, 1968). Present-day users of marihuana find that it provides a safe and enjoyable release – a pleasing sense of relaxation and calm (Oursler, 1968, pp. 42-43).

In the same way as other 'crimes without victims', marihuana smoking is a private activity and does not harm anyone else. To enforce the marihuana laws, we must police the private lives of citizens; this cannot be done without invading their privacy (Fort, 1969). Legislatures should not interfere with the rights of citizens to determine such personal matters as whether or not they will smoke marihuana.

The present severe laws are not especially effective in preventing the use of marihuana (Bloomer, 1967). In fact, two recent studies (King, 1969; McGlothlin & West, 1968) indicate the following: With few exceptions, individuals who now use marihuana will continue to use it regardless of whether or not it is legalized; and, of those individuals who do not use marihuana, it appears that only a small proportion, probably no more than 10 per cent, are deterred from using it *because* it is illegal. Furthermore, it appears likely that persons who are now deterred from using marihuana because of the legal penalties will use it moderately if at all when it is legalized, whereas individuals who use it excessively will do so regardless of its legal status (McGlothlin, 1967, p. 201). The laws against marihuana do not prevent its abuse any more than the prohibition laws in the 1920s prevented the abuse of alcohol.

Any discussion about preventing the use of marihuana is more or less academic because a substantial proportion of American youth is using it now and there is every indication that its use will continue to increase. Since the use of marihuana is a social fact, the question at issue is not, How can we prevent its use?, but, How can we prevent its misuse or abuse?

There are marked inconsistencies in the present drug laws. Marihuana is strictly prohibited (is treated as a narcotic, which it is not) whereas alcohol is promoted with all of the power of advertising (McGlothlin, 1967). However, the recent British Government (1968) report noted that "in terms of *physical* harmfulness, cannabis is very much less dangerous than opiates, amphetamines and barbiturates, and also less dangerous than alcohol".

The present laws against the use of marihuana are selectively enforced. This inconsistent enforcement produces a disrespect for the law.

The penalties against the use of marihuana force otherwise law-abiding persons to engage in what is legally defined as a major crime. Individuals who are otherwise good citizens must dodge their own police and government agents and suffer social stigma, arrest, and other harm from society for indulging in moderate use of a drug (marihuana) that is no more harmful (and possibly less harmful) than alcohol or nicotine (Simmons, 1967). Furthermore, the present severe laws are helping to produce a youth subculture that is hostile to the laws and the law-enforcers, is alienated from the predominant culture, and is reinforced in its beliefs that the prevailing social norms are hypocritical (Fort, 1969).

Since the present laws are not preventing the use or abuse of marihuana to any important degree and since the laws are creating more problems than they solve, it appears that the laws against the use of marihuana will have to be repealed, sooner or later, in the same way and for very similar reasons as the laws against the use of alcohol was repealed in the 1930s. However, important problems must be solved long before the use of marihuana is legalized. As the British Government (1968) report pointed out,

> Safeguards against adulteration would have to be investigated and standards of inspection would have to be agreed; sources of supply would have to be considered; importation from countries where the supply was still illegal would present a particularly difficult problem; it might be necessary to devise a licensing system for manufacturing synthetics; much thought would have to be given to the mode of distribution; an attempt would have to be made to define permitted limits of intoxication and methods of detection; and special measures to protect minors would have to be incorporated into any such new law (p. 18).

Also, long before the laws are repealed, the following steps should be taken: Extensive research programs should be funded by the United States government to determine precisely the short-term and long-term consequences of marihuana use; educational programs should be instituted in the communities to present the scientific data that are available about the drug; schools should hire trained counselors able to discuss drug use with students in an open, frank, and non-patronizing manner (Ungerleider & Bowen, 1969); mental health programs should be instituted to aid those individuals who abuse marihuana or other drugs such as LSD, alcohol, nicotine, amphetamines, and barbiturates. Inadequate individuals who use drugs to help themselves adjust constitute a major social problem and the attention of mental health workers and other agents of society should be focused on them. Finally, if and when the use of marihuana is legalized, several additional steps should be taken: Legal penalties should be continued with respect to hashish, THC, and other potent forms of cannabis; marihuana should be sold only by licensed dealers and no advertising should be permitted; strick legal penalties should be imposed for any agressive or antisocial behavior that might be committed by individuals using marihuana (in the same way as penalties are imposed for improper behavior committed by the person using alcohol).

References

Allen, J. R., and West, L. J. Flight from violence: Hippies and the Green Rebellion. *Amer. J. Psychiat.*, 1968, *125*, 364-370.

Ames, F. A clinical and metabolic study of acute intoxication with Cannabis sativa and its role in the model psychoses. *J. Ment. Sci.*, 1958, *104*, 972-999.

Andrade, O. M. The criminogenic action of cannabis (marihuana) and narcotics. *Bull. Narcot. Drugs*, 1964, *16*, 23-28.

Ausubel, D. P. *Drug addiction: Physiological, psychological and sociological aspects*. New York: Random House, 1964.

Becker, H. S. Becoming a marihuana user. *Amer. J. Sociol.*, 1953, *59*, 235-242.

Benabud, A. Psychopathological aspects of the Cannabis situation in Morocco: Statistical data for 1956. *Bull. Narcot. Drugs*, 1957, *9*, 1-16.

Bloomquist, E. R. *Marijuana*. Beverly Hills, Calif.: Glencoe Press, 1968.

Blum, R. H. and associates. *I. Society and drugs, II. Students and drugs*. San Francisco: Jossey-Bass, 1969.

Blumer, H. *The world of youthful drug use*. Berkeley: School of Criminology, Univ. of California, 1967. (Mimeo)

Boroffka, A. Mental illness and Indian hemp in Lagos. *East Afr. Med. J.*, 1966, *43*, 377-384.

Bouquet, R. J. Cannabis. *Bull. Narcot. Drugs*, 1950, *2*, 14-30; 1951, *3*, 22-45.

British Government, Home Secretary. Advisory Committee on Drug Dependence. *Cannabis report.* London: Her Majesty's Stationery Office, 1968.

Brotman, R., Silverman, I., and Suffet, F. Drug use among affluent high school youth. In E. Goode (Ed.) *Marijuana.* New York: Atherton Press, 1969. Pp. 128-135.

Carstairs, G. M. Bhang and alcohol: Cultural factors in the choice of intoxicants. *Quart. J. Studies Alcohol.,* 1954, *15,* 220-237.

Chopra, R. N., and Chopra, G. S. The present position of hemp drugs. Addiction in India. *Indian Med. Res. Memoir,* 1939, No. 31, 1-119.

Chopra, I. C., and Chopra, R. N. The use of cannabis drugs in India. *Bull. Narcot. Drugs,* 1957, *9,* No. 1, 4-29. (a)

Chopra, R. N., and Chopra., I. C. Treatment of drug addiction. Experience in India. *Bull. Narcot. Drugs,* 1957, *9,* No. 4, 21-33. (b)

Clark, L. D., and Nakashima, E. N. Experimental studies of marihuana. *Amer. J. Psychiat.,* 1968, *125,* 379-384.

Collier, H. O. J. Discussion. In G. E. Wolstenholme and J. Knight (Eds.) *Hashish: Its chemistry and pharmacology.* Boston: Little, Brown, 1965. P. 14.

Crancer, A., Jr., *Predicting driving performance with a driver simulator test.* Olympia, Wash.: Washington State Dept. of Motor Vehicles, 1968.

Crancer, A., Jr., Dille, J. M., Delay, J. C., Wallace, J. E., and Haykin, M. D. Comparison of the effects of marihuana and alcohol on simulated driving performance. *Science,* 1969, *164,* 851-854.

de Farias, R. C. Use of Maconha (*Cannabis sativa* L.) in Brazil. *Bull. Narcot. Drugs,* 1955, *7,* 5-19.

Dontas, S., and Zis, P. Recherches expérimentales sur l'action du Haschich. *Arch. Intern. Pharmacodynam. Therap.,* 1929, *35,* 30-57.

Editorial. Cannabis—yet another teratogen? *Brit. Med. J.,* 1969, *1,* 797.

Fort, J. Pot: A rational approach. *Playboy,* 1969, *16,* No. 10, 131, 154, 216, 218, 220, 222, 225-228.

Fraenkel, F., and Jöel, E. Beiträge zu einter experimentellen Psychopathologie: der Haschischrausch. *Zeitsch. Ges. Neurol. Psychiat.,* 1927, *111,* 84-106.

Freedman, H. L., and Rockmore, M. J. Marihuana: A factor in personality evaluation and army maladjustment. *J. Clin. Psychopath.,* 1946, *7,* 765-782; *8,* 221-236.

Gaskill, H. S. Marijuana, an intoxicant. *Amer. J. Psychiat.,* 1945, *102,* 202-204.

Gomila, F. R., and Lambou, M. C. G. Present status of the marihuana vice in the United States. In R. P. Walton *Marihuana: America's new drug problem.* Philadelphia: J. B. Lippincott, 1938.

Goode, E. Marijuana and the politics of reality. *J. Health Soc. Beh.,* 1969, *10,* 83-94. (a)

Goode, E. Multiple drug use among marijuana smokers. *Social Probl.,* 1969, *17,* 48-64. (b)

Goode, E. The connection between marijuana and heroin. In E. Goode (Ed.) *Marijuana.* New York: Atherton Press, 1969. Pp. 61-65. (c)

Huxley, A. *The doors of perception.* New York: Harper, 1954.

Isbell, H. Studies on tetrahydrocannabinol I. Method of assay in human subjects and results with crude extracts, purified tetrahydrocannabinols and synthetic compounds. Lexington, Kentucky: Univ. of Kentucky Medical Center, 1967.

Isbell, H., Gorodetzsky, C. W., Jasinski, D., Claussen, U., Spulak, F. V., and Korte, F. Effects of (-)- Δ⁹-trans-tetrahydrocannabinol in man. *Psychopharmacologica,* 1967, *11,* 184-188.

Isbell, H., and Jasinski, D. R. A comparison of LSD-25 with (-)- Δ⁹-trans-tetrahydrocannabinol (THC) and attempted cross tolerance between LSD and THC. *Psychopharmacologia,* 1969, 14, 115-123.

Keeler, M. H. Adverse reaction to marihuana. *Amer. J. Psychiat.,* 1967, *124,* 674-677.

Keeler, M. H. Marihuana induced hallucinations. *Dis. Nerv. Syst.,* 1968, *29,* 314-315. (a)

Keeler, M. H. Motivation for marihuana use: A correlate of adverse reaction. *Amer. J. Psychiat.,* 1968, *125,* 386-390. (b)

Keeler, M. H., Reifler, C. B., and Liptzin, M. B. Spontaneous recurrence of marihuana effect. *Amer. J. Psychiat.,* 1968, *125,* 384-386.

Keniston, K. Heads and seekers: Drugs on campus, counter-cultures, and American society. *Amer. Schol.,* 1968, *38,* 97-112.

King, F. W. Attitudinal and behavioral determinants of drug use. Paper presented at Annual Meeting of American College Health Assoc., Oklahoma City, April 23, 1969.

Korte, F., and Sieper, H. Recent results of hashish analysis. In G. E. W. Wolstenholme and J. Knight (Eds.) *Hashish: Its chemistry and pharmacology.* Boston: Little, Brown, 1965. Pp. 15-30.

Krippner, S. Marijuana and Viet Nam: Twin dilemmas for American youth. Paper presented at Annual Meeting of Brooklyn Psychological Assoc., Nov. 16, 1968.

Lewin, L. *Phantastica, narcotic and stimulating drugs.* London: Routledge & Kegan Paul, 1931.

Louria, D. B. *The drug scene.* New York: McGraw-Hill, 1968.

Mandel, J. Myths and realities of marihuana pushing. In J. L. Simmons (Ed.) *Marihuana: Myths and realities.* North Hollywood, Calif.: Brandon House, 1967. Pp. 58-110.

Mankin, D., Hogan, R., Conway, J., and Fox, S. Personality correlates of undergraduate marihuana use. Paper presented at Annual Meeting of Eastern Psychol. Assoc., Philadelphia, April 10, 1969.

Marcovitz, E., and Myers, H. J. The marihuana addict in the army. *War Med.,* 1944, *6,* 382-391.

Martin, P. A. Cannabis and chromosomes. *Lancet,* 1969, *1,* 370.

Mayor's Committee. *The marihuana problem in the City of New York.* Lancaster, Pennsylvania: Jacques Cattell Press, 1944.

McGlothlin, W. H. Toward a rational view of marihuana. In J. L. Simmons (Ed.) *Marihuana: Myths and realities.* North Hollywood, Calif.: Brandon House, 1967. Pp. 163-214.

McGlothlin, W. H., and West, L. J. The marihuana problem: An overview. *Amer. J. Psychiat.,* 1968, *125,* 370-378.

Miras, C. J. Some aspects of cannabis action. In G. E. W. Wolstenholme and J. Knight (Eds.) *Hashish: Its chemistry and pharmacology.* Boston: Little, Brown, 1965. P. 37-47.

Murphy, H. B. M. The cannabis habit. *Addictions,* 1966, *13,* 3-25.

Nowlis, H. H. *Drugs on the college campus.* Garden City, N.Y.: Doubleday, 1969.

Oursler, W. *Marihuana*. New York: Paul S. Eriksson, 1968.

Persaud, T. V. N., and Ellington, A. C. Cannabis in early pregnancy. *Lancet,* 1967, *2,* 1306.

Persaud, T. V. N., and Ellington, A. C. Teratogenic activity of cannabis resin. *Lancet,* 1968, *2,* 406-407.

Pescor, M. J. A statistical analysis of the clinical records of hospitalized drug addicts. *Publ. Health Reports,* 1943, No. 143 Supplement.

Rosevear, J. *Pot: A handbook of marijuana*. New Hyde Park, N. Y.: University Books, 1967.

Roszak, T. *The making of a counter culture*. Garden City, N. Y.: Doubleday, 1969.

Siler, J. F. Marijuana smoking in Panama. *Milit. Surg.,* 1933, *73,* 269-280.

Simmons, J. L. The current marihuana scene. In J. L. Simmons (Ed.) *Marihuana: Myths and realities*. North Hollywood, Calif.: Brandon House, 1967. Pp. 7-14.

Simmons, J. L., and Winograd, B. *It's Happening: A portrait of the youth scene today*. Santa Barbara, Calif.: Marc-Laird Publications, 1966.

Soueif, M. I. Hashish consumption in Egypt, with special reference to psychosocial aspects. *Bull. Narcot. Drugs,* 1967, *19,* 1-12.

Stearn, J. *The seekers: Drugs and the new generation*. Garden City, N. Y.: Doubleday, 1969.

Taylor, N. The pleasant assassin: The story of marihuana. In D. Solomon (Ed.) *The marihuana papers*. New York: New American Library, 1968. Pp. 31-47.

Ungerleider, J. T., and Bowen, H. L. Drug abuse and the schools. *Amer. J. Psychiat.,* 1969, *125,* 1691-1697.

Wallace, J. E., and Crancer, A., Jr. *Licensing examinations and their relation to subsequent driving record*. Olympia, Wash.: Washington State Dept. of Motor Vehicles, 1969.

Watt, J. M., Discussion. In G. E. W. Wolstenholme and J. Knight (Eds.) *Hashish: Its chemistry and pharamacology*. Boston: Little, Brown, 1965. P. 13.

Weil, A. T., and Zinberg, N. E. Acute effects of marihuana on speech. *Nature,* 1969, *222,* 434-437.

Weil, A. T., Zinberg, N. E., and Nelsen, J. M. Clinical and psychological effects of marihuana in Man. *Science,* 1968, *162,* 1234-1242.

Wolff, P. O. *Marihuana in Latin America: The threat it constitutes*. Washington, D.C.: Linacre Press, 1949.

Yoga, Hypnotic Phenomena,
and a
Theory of Hypnotism

Yoga and Hypnotism

CONTENTS

THREE

Yoga and Hypnotism

BY ABDULHUSEIN S. DALAL AND
THEODORE X. BARBER

Both yoga and hypnosis are said to involve altered states of consciousness or trance states (Behanan, 1937; Das, 1963; Williams, 1948).
Also, both yoga and hypnosis have been popularly associated with
unusual phenomena. The yogi is thought to be able to control various
autonomic functions, to walk across burning coals, to be buried alive,
and to lie on nails. Similarly, the hypnotic subject is said to be able to
hold a heavy weight on his abdomen while lying stretched in midair with
supports only at his head and ankles. Also, it is commonly believed that
suggestions given to a deeply hypnotized subject produce insensitivity to
pain, hallucinations, regression to childhood, amnesia, deafness, blindness, colorblindness, and many other unusual phenomena. This chapter
will critically analyze the altered states of consciousness or trance states
said to be involved in yoga and in hypnosis, and also the phenomena
supposedly manifested by yogis and by hypnotic subjects. The discussion is based on recent empirical research in hypnotism (Barber,
1969; Barber, Dalal & Calverley, 1968; Dalal, 1966), A. S. Dalal's
studies in yoga covering nearly two decades and including seven years
devoted exclusively to the practice of yoga at Sri Aurobindo Ashram in
Pondicherry, India, and a review of all available empirical studies pertaining to the so-called yogic feats that have been published during the
past two decades.

The Terms Yoga and Yogi

Before we proceed to the main discussion, it is necessary to clarify the
terms *yoga* and *yogi*. Two main usages of the term *yoga* may be distinguished:

117

Strictly speaking, yoga refers to a system of beliefs and practices whose goal is to attain a union of the individual self with Supreme Reality or the Universal Self. In this sense there are several systems of yoga (Das, 1963; Wood, 1959; Woods, 1927). Each has an ethical-religious discipline at its core and each sees the trance state of samadhi as the final step in attaining union with Supreme Reality. However, each system of yoga emphasizes somewhat different processes for the attainment of samadhi and union. For instance, the eight-fold system of Raja Yoga, taught by Patanjali, includes self-control (yama), religious observances (niyama), physical postures (asana), regulation of the breath (pranayama), suppression of the flow of external sense impressions (pratyahara), concentration or fixed attention on an object (dharana), meditation or contemplation of an object for a long period of time (dhyana) and, finally, a state of absorption or trance in which the person is no longer conscious of his concentration (samadhi).

In its popular usage, especially current in the West, the term *yoga* has come to be associated more or less exclusively with the physical postures (asana) and the regulation of breathing (pranayama). This popular usage is not found in Indian philosophy. An individual who merely practices the postures and the breathing exercises (as some do for health or therapeutic purposes), without a concomitant consecration to a spiritual discipline and to the goals of yoga, is simply practicing a few yogic exercises; he is *not* practicing yoga in the strict sense.

The term *yogi* has a strict meaning, a more popular meaning, and also a fallacious meaning. Strictly speaking, a yogi is a person who has ostensibly attained the goal of yoga, namely, samadhi and a yoking with or union with Supreme Reality. In more popular usage, the term *yogi* refers to a person who practices a system of yoga regardless of whether or not he has attained samadhi or union. In its fallacious sense, the term *yogi* refers to an individual who labels himself as a yogi but who has *not* seriously practiced any system of yoga. The so-called yogic feats discussed in this chapter are not performed by yogis in the strict sense of the term, although they are performed by some who have not attained samadhi and by self-styled yogis.

Hypnotic and Yogic Trance

Both hypnosis and yoga are said to involve a state of trance. The hypnotic trance state has been traditionallly regarded as giving rise to hypnotic phenomena such as analgesia, hallucination, and amnesia. However, the yogic trance state of samadhi, contrary to popular belief, has not been regarded in the Indian tradition as necessarily related to so-called yogic phenomena such as voluntary control over autonomic functions, fire-walking, or lying-on-nails. Though the latter phenomena have been popularly subsumed under the term *yoga,* the Indian spiritual tradition has always looked down upon the pursuit of such unusual capacities as worldly and vainglorious. Since yoga aims at freedom from the 'world-illusion' through the achievement of samadhi, the attainment of unusual psychophysiological capacities and the attainment of samadhi tend to be mutually exclusive goals. The confusion between these two disparate goals appears to be due to the following:

Certain practices such as physical postures (asana) and breathing excercises (pranayama) have been associated with both goals. However, those who seek to develop unusual psychophysiological capacities take to a highly intensive and almost exclusive practice of such exercises, whereas those who aspire to attain samadhi follow highly variable systems of yoga which may, but often do not, include such exercises. In fact, at the Ashram where Dalal lived and practiced yoga, hardly anyone among the nearly one thousand practitioners of yoga was seriously concerned with the exercises pertaining to physical postures and breath regulation, although a few performed them for purposes of physical health.

Another reason for the widespread misconception of yoga as the ability to perform unusual feats lies in the fact that the general public in the West and also in India typically comes in contact only with self-styled yogis who demonstrate such feats, whereas yogis who seek to attain samadhi tend to lead inconspicuous lives. In fact, judging from Dalal's experiences, a very large number of those who claim to possess unusual yogic capacities have not practiced any form of yoga. Their public demonstrations of yogic powers often involve deception and they typically use the term *yoga* as a cloak for mendicancy — e.g., for promoting the sale of quack medicines and talismans.

PROBLEMS IN DENOTING HYPNOTIC
AND YOGIC TRANCE

Attempts to denote the hypnotic trance state objectively have not been sucessful (Chapter IV). Over a period of many years researchers have sought a physiological index that would differentiate the hypnotic trance state from the waking state but have failed to find one (Barber, 1961; Crasilneck & Hall, 1959; Gorton, 1949; Levitt & Brady, 1963). In the absence of a physiological index, the hypnotic trance state is usually inferred from hypersuggestibility; that is, from a high level of response to suggestions of analgesia, hallucination, age-regression, amnesia, and the like. However, the latter criterion gives rise to circular reasoning:

The hypnotic trance state is inferred from the high level of response to suggestions and, vice versa, the hypnotic trance state is used to account for the high level of response to suggestions from which it is inferred (Barber, 1964a; Chaves, 1968). Some investigators maintain that the hypnotic trance state can be denoted in terms of certain subtle but objective signs such as passivity, disinclination to talk, and fixed facial expression (Erickson, Hershman & Secter, 1961; Gill & Brenman, 1959). However, these signs are also unsatisfactory because they are functionally related to explicit or implicit suggestions to sit quietly for a period of time with eyes closed and to become relaxed, drowsy, sleepy, and passive (Barber, 1969; Barber & Calverley, 1969). Thus, when the hypnotic trance state is inferred from passivity, disinclination to talk, fixed facial expression, and other signs of this type, the state is judged to be present because the subject is responsive to suggestions and the inferred state is used circularly to account for the subject's responsiveness to suggestions.

There are practical difficulties to denoting the yogic trance state of samadhi. In the first place, the state appears to be extremely rare. Secondly, a yogi who has ostensibly attained samadhi is not likely to condescend to cooperate in a scientific investigation because in the eyes of such a yogi the work of the scientist is trivial and futile, if not presumptuous and sacrilegious.[1]

VERBAL REPORTS OF STATES
TREATED AS DEPENDENT VARIABLES

Since we do not have any clear-cut physiological indices of the hypnotic trance state, and since criteria based on overt responses to suggestions are entangled in circular reasoning, it appears that the least equivocal criterion for inferring the presence of a hypnotic trance state is the subject's report that he has experienced it. Similar considerations appear to apply to the yogic trance state of samadhi. Consequently, it appears that the appropriate scientific or empirical approach to the hynotic and yogic trance states consists in specifying the conditions under which *reports* of having experienced them are elicited and in delineating the contents of these states as they are *reported* by subjects.

1. Although A. S. Dalal is convinced from personal experiences that those yogis who believe they have attained samadhi are not likely to agree to serve as subjects in scientific experiments, it is certainly possible to enlist the cooperation of some practitioners of yoga who have not attained samadhi. However, researchers should be careful to ascertain what yogis mean by samadhi when they use this term to describe their experiences, because in several Indian vernaculars the term is employed rather loosely and is practically interchangeable with the term *dhyana* (meditation or contemplation).

The chief experiences reported to be associated with the hypnotic trance state are feelings of relaxation, feelings of unreality, feelings of automaticity and compulsion, alterations in body image, and certain unusual sensations (Barber & Calverley, 1969; Field, 1965; Ludwig & Levine, 1965). Recent studies which aimed to delineate the conditions under which reports of having been in hypnotic trance are elicited indicate that such reports are functionally related in a complex way to many denotable antecedent variables. These effective antecedents include the subject's preconceptions of what the hypnotic trance state is like, his pre-experimental expectations concerning whether and to what degree he will be hynotized, the degree to which he responds to suggestions and has new experiences during the hypnotic session, and cues transmitted by the experimenter to suggest that the subject was or was not hypnotized (Barber, 1969; Barber & Calverley, 1969; Barber, Dalal, & Calverley, 1968). Futhermore subjects' reports pertaining to their having experienced hypnotic trance are also partly dependent on subtle situational variables such as the wording of the questions used to elicit their reports (Barber, Dalal & Calverley, 1968). Consequently it appears that subjects may differ in their reports pertaining to whether or not they experienced hypnotic trance even though they had very similar experiences during the hypnotic session.

The samadhi experience is couched in complex and abstract terms, though it is said to be more concrete and real than sense experience. The state has been described as a triune experience of supreme Truth-Consciousness-Bliss (sat-chit-ananda) pertaining to an altogether different realm of experience and therefore impossible to describe except by metaphors and paradoxes. However, the most important element of the samadhi experience is thought to lie in the merger of personal consciousness with the Universal Self. The Universal Self, in turn, is conceived paradoxically as both immanent in all forms of existence and as transcending the manifest universe.

Some or all of the previous mentioned variables relating to subjects' reports of having been hypnotized (which have their obvious correlates in yoga) may play a role in the reported experience of samadhi. But for reasons already stated, researchers have not as yet found means to test empirically the hypothesis that reports of samadhi are functionally related to such factors as preconceptions, preexpectations, and suggestions from the spiritual guide (guru). Nor does it appear feasible to investigate empirically the role of numerous variables that are thought to be associated with the attainment of samadhi such as practices for self-control including sexual abstinence, physical postures, regulation of the breath, and various forms of concentration and meditation including long-continued fixation on an object and continual repetition of a sacred incantation.

However, several topics that have recently been approached empirically may shed some light on the reported experience of samadhi. One relevant topic has been labeled by Maslow as *peak-experiences*. According to Maslow, a substantial number of normal individuals in Western civilization report that they have had experiences as follows: "These moments were of pure, positive happiness when all doubts, all fears, all inhibitions, all tensions, all weaknesses, were left behind. Now self-consciousness was lost. All separateness and distance from the world disappeared . . . Perhaps most important of all, however, was the report in these experiences of the feeling that they had really seen the ultimate truth, the essence of things, the secret of life, as if veils had been pulled aside" (Maslow, 1962). Intensive studies with individuals who report these kinds of experiences can be conducted scientifically. Since there is considerable similarity in the reported contents of peak-experiences and of the samadhi experience, reliable data concerning one of these experiences should contribute to understanding of the other.

Another research area that seems to be related to samadhi has been labeled by Deikman (1963, 1966) as *experimentally-induced contemplative meditation*. Deikman instructs his subjects along the following lines.

> This experiment will explore the possibilities of seeing and experiencing when you cease thinking altogether and concentrate your attention on only one thing: the blue vase on the table in front of you. Look at the vase intently, focus all your interest on it, try to perceive the vase as directly as possible but without studying it or analyzing it. Have your entire mind concentrated on the vase, at the same time remain open to the experience—let whatever happens happen. All thinking must come to a stop so that your mind becomes quiet. Do not let yourself be distracted by thoughts, sounds, or body sensations—keep them out so that you can concentrate all your attention on the vase (Deikman, 1966).

Some experimental subjects who were given these instructions stated that they experienced striking changes in perception of the self and of objects and Deikman hypothesized that analogues of mystical experiences could also be achieved. These exploratory studies lead to the interesting possibility of studying experimentally some aspects of the samadhi experience. Further studies along these lines could also employ other forms of contemplative meditation besides perceptual concentration and could investigate other reported aspects of *ex-*

perimentally-induced contemplative meditation besides unusual perceptions (Maupin, 1965).

Finally, we might also point out that intensive studies of the psychedelic experience, reported by some individuals who have received LSD, mescaline, psilocybin, and similar drugs, may also further our understanding of samadhi (Chapter I).

Having discussed the trance states said to be involved in both hypnosis and yoga, let us turn to an analysis of the abservable phenomena that are supposedly exhibited by hypnotic subjects and by yogis or self-styled yogis.

Hypnotic Phenomena and So-called Yogic Phenomena

A striking similarity between the phenomena attributed to hypnosis and to yoga, as revealed by empirical studies, is that many of the phenomena are not what they at fist appear to be. Recent work has underscored this fact with regard to many of the phenomena traditionally subsumed under the label *hypnosis*. For instance, *hypnotic amnesia* is essentially different from amnesia as it is commonly understood. In hypnotic amnesia, the forgotten material is recognized more quickly than neutral control material, exerts the same objective effects (such as practice effects or retroactive inhibition effects) as material that is clearly remembered, and is readily verbalized by the subject when he is given explicit or implicit permission to do so (Barber, 1962b; Barber & Calverley, 1966; Graham & Patton, 1968; Patten, 1932; Sturrock, 1966; Thorne, 1967; Williamsen, Johnson & Eriksen, 1965). Similarly, the hypnotic deaf subject differs from the deaf person in that he is responsive to auditory stimulation. For instance, "hypnotic deafness" does not prevent the stuttering that is normally produced by delayed auditory feedback (Chapter IV also, Barber & Calverley, 1964b; Kline, Guze & Haggerty, 1954; Kramer & Tucker, 1967; Sutcliffe, 1961). To cite yet another instance, it has been popularly believed that in hypnotic age-regression the subject goes back psychophysiologically to the suggested age, relives the previous events, and manifests behavior appropriate to the suggested age. However, data presented in Chapter VI of this text demonstrate that there are important discrepancies between the behaviors of the hypnotically-regressed subject and the behaviors expected at the suggested age (Barber, 1962a; Barber, 1969). Similarly, data reviewed in detail elsewhere (Barber, 1961, 1963, 1964b, 1964c, 1965b, 1969) show that there are crucial differences between hypnotically-suggested and non-suggested or naturally-occurring analgesia, dreaming, hallucination, blindness, and color-blindness (Chapters IV and V).

Empirical investigations of so-called yogic phenomena also show them to be different from what they are naively conceived to be. Thus in the voluntary stoppage of the heart claimed by a few yogis or self-styled yogis, no voluntary control over the heart musculature is directly involved and the heart does *not* stop. At best, a few individuals in India have demonstrated an ability to slow the heart by utilizing methods "involving retention of the breath and considerable muscular tension in the abdomen and thorax, with closed glottis" (Wenger & Bagchi, 1961). At times, these maneuvers retard venous return to the heart, the cardiac sounds cannot be detected with a stethoscope, and the palpable radial pulse seems to disappear. However, electrocardiographic and plethys-mographic records show definitely that the heart is in continuous action (Wenger & Bagchi, 1961; Wenger, Bagchi & Anand, 1961).[2]

The feat of fire-walking also takes on a somewhat different appearance in the light of the following observations:

> In south India and in other locations it [fire-walking] seems to be a common practice in connection with religious or other celebrations. We are informed, however, that the coals are well covered with ashes and that the "walk" is more like a "run". Moreover, the participants are not yogis; they are the young men of the villages. And, since they have seldom or never worn shoes, the epidermis of the soles of their feet is reported to us as being $1/8''$ to $1/4''$ in thickness. There may be fire-walkers with tender feet, but we have not seen or heard about them in India (Wenger & Bagchi, 1961).

Apparently, no case of fire-walking by a yogi has as yet been documented whereas numerous non-yogis have rather easily performed the feat. Among the latter is a British university student who walked in bare feet with perfect safety across a 12 foot trench with a surface temperature of 800° C. (Brown, 1938; Ingalls, 1939). Price (1937) discussed this demonstration as follows:

> There was not the slightest trace of blistering . . . each foot was in contact with the embers for not more than about a third of a second. This time factor (plus *confidence* and a steady, deliberate placing of the feet) is the secret of fire-walking. The low thermal conductivity of the wood ash may be a contributory factor. We received no evidence that "faith" or a specially induced mental state played any part in the performance.

2. Wenger and Bagchi (1961) pointed out a possible artifact in an earlier study by Brosse (1946) whose published EKG records of an Indian subject showed a gradual reduction in heart potentials to near zero. They noted that "during breath retention there is a deviation in position of the heart so that potentials in lead I are decreased, but those in lead III are increased. Dr. Brosse's record of 'heart control' involved lead I only. Had she measured any other lead her conclusions concerning voluntary control of the heart probably would have been as negative as are ours."

The fire walking-feat has also been performed before competent observers in the United States by Coe (1957), a chemist living in Florida. With eight steps he crossed bare-footed a 14-foot pit of red-hot coals without suffering pain or forming blisters. After reviewing the literature of physics and chemistry to discover possible principles that might be involved, he proffered the following hypothesis:

> First there is natural moisture present on the surface of the skin. Under intense heat the skin sweats, and the moisture, which enters the spheroidal state, is converted to vapor which occupies 22.4 molar volumes of the original moisture. This is why a microscopically thin layer of moisture can be a protection . . . The hotter the object the longer the spheroidal state is maintained, and the greater the protection afforded by the cushion of vapor (Coe, 1957).

Whether or not Coe's hypothesis accounts for the phenomenon can be determined in further research.

Writers such as Behanan (1937) state that, by intensive practice of certain types of yogic exercises, voluntary control can be acquired over the diaphragm, the anal sphincters, the recti abdominis muscles, and the muscles involved in vomiting. Careful research is needed to validate these claims. At the present time the contentions are based on hearsay evidence; they have not as yet been documented scientifically. Wenger and Bagchi (1961), who have carried out the most extensive scientific investigation in this area, were unable to find anyone in India who could demonstrate unequivocal *voluntary* control over the anal or urethral sphincters, although they did find "those who employ a catheter or other form of tube and, with its help, are able to draw up water into the bladder or lower bowel." Wenger and Bagchi found one person in India who could regurgitate voluntarily. However, this person stated that he did not have any special training; he had discovered accidently that he could vomit at will and used it occasionally as a cleansing device.

Wenger and Bagchi also found a yogi who could produce perspiration on his forehead within one and a half to 10 minutes after he began concentrating. They placed this feat in context as follows:

> This man had spent parts of two winters in caves in the Himalayas. During such periods, usually alone and unclad except for an animal skin, much of his time was spent in meditation . . . The cold distracted him, and his teacher advised him to concentrate on *warmth* and to visualize himself in extremely high temperature situations . . . He reported gradual sucess *after about six months of practice*. Later he found that in a moderate climate the same practices produced not only increased sensations of warmth but perspiration.

Wenger and Bagchi also found one subject who was able to defecate at will. They stated that "He employed a particular position and movement of the tongue to aid in this control. Again the control had only been gained after long practice. In all of these forms of control it seems reasonable to assume that conditioning had occurred." Exactly what the hypothesized conditioning involved, however, is not clear and requires careful study (Katkin & Murray, 1968; Kimble, 1961; Razran, 1961).

A few yogis or self-styled yogis have supposedly buried themselves alive (Rao, *et al.,* 1958). A well-publicized case of a yogi who buried himself for 62 hours was documented by Vakil (1950), who pointed out that the feat did not demonstrate that the yogi was able to survive with little or no oxygen for the following reasons: The oxygen requirement of a man lying perfectly still is about 2.5 cubic feet of air per hour. Therefore, the oxygen content of the cubicle in which the yogi was entombed, measuring 5.5' x 4.5' x 8', was sufficient to support a person substantially more than 62 hours.

A common belief is that yogis are able to lie on a bed of nails and to thrust metal spikes into their flesh. However, Dalal, during his seven years' training in yoga, did not hear of any practitioner of yoga who claimed to be able to perform such feats. Rather, they are performed by a small number of fakirs and dervishes (religious mendicants) who are often confused with yogis. Although Wenger and Bagchi (1961) found no individuals in India "who stuck needles into their bodies," they found one person who lay on beds of nails. Wenger and Bagchi noted that "For the latter the task was easy. By practice he had learned to relax the muscles of the back, and the nails were close together and not very sharp." It should also be noted that the apparent analgesia or the stoicism may at times be due to the fact that some of these individuals who lie on nails are addicted to hashish or opium (Rawcliffe, 1959). When the nails are not blunt and when no drugs are taken, the performance demonstrates a not too unusual ability to tolerate a certain amount of pain. The French author, Heuzé, who demonstrated the feat of sticking hatpins through his flesh, insisted that such performances can be learned by most individuals who possess average patience and fortitude (Heuzé, 1926).

The feats discussed above are not an integral part of training in yoga. There is evidence to indicate, however, that the breathing and postural exercises, which are part of some but not all systems of yoga, may be accompanied by significant autonomic changes and may give rise to enduring changes in autonomic balance with possible beneficial effects on mental and physical health (Wenger & Bagchi, 1961). These possible changes in autonomic system functioning which may be produced by some yogic exercises, and also be related exercises such as those involved in "autogenic training" (Gorton, 1959; Schultz & Luthe, 1959), appear to offer rewarding possibilities for further empirical investigations.

Research Methodology

Critiques of research in hypnosis (Barber, 1962c, 1967, 1969) indicate that much of the early experimentation in this area was vitiated by faulty methodology. Several of the criticisms that have been delineated with respect to hypnotic research are equally applicable to research pertaining to yoga or to so-called yogic feats.

Perhaps the most common fallacy in both areas is the assumption that special factors have to be invoked in order to explain the observed phenomena. For instance, it has been commonly assumed that the hypnotic phenomenon termed the *human-plank feat* (in which the subject lies stretched in midair with only his head and feet resting on supports) involves a special factor which comes into play during the hypnotic trance. However, empirical evidence demonstrates that this feat can be performed by at least 80 per cent of unselected control subjects who are firmly told to make their body rigid and to keep it rigid (Barber, 1969; Collins, 1961). Again, it has been commonly supposed that hypnotic hallucinations are a rare phenomena that can be elicited only in a deep hypnotic trance. No well-defined criteria of what constitutes a hypnotic hallucination have been specified, so that in practice the phenomenon is said to be elicited when the subject testifies that he sees or hears something which is not actually present. However, experimental studies show that a considerable number (at least one-third) of unselected control subjects also testify that they see objects and hear sounds that are not present when suggestions intended to produce hallucinations are given to them in a non-hypnotic setting (Barber & Calverley, 1964a; Bowers, 1967; Spanos & Barber, 1968). Along related lines, no systematic attempts have been made to ascertain to what extent the so-called yogic feats can be elicited from untrained individuals. Evidence cited previously in connection with fire-walking and burial-alive suggests that some of these feats require a certain amount of courage, but no special training.

A related methodological error common to hypnosis and yoga is the failure to employ a control for the assumed independent variable. For instance, hypnotic blindness is said to produce alterations in physiological processes related to vision such as elimination of the EEG alpha block response which normally follows visual stimulation. However, experimental studies with controls indicate that the same effect can be demonstrated in non-hypnotic subjects (Chapter IV). A study demonstrating a similar effect on alpha blocking due apparently to yogic meditation (Anand, Chhina & Singh, 1961) is vitiated by the same failure to employ a control for the assumed independent variable. In fact, it appears that, with a few possible exceptions, sudies on yogis lack scientific validity due to failure to employ necessary controls and are useful only for suggesting lines of future inquiry.

Still another methodological pitfall is the use of the same subjects under the experimental and control conditions. Several studies in hypnotism suggest that under these circumstances subjects are apt to respond differently under the experimental (hypnotic) and control treatments because they think they are expected to or should perform differently under each treatment (Barber, 1962c, 1967, 1969; Orne, 1959; Pattie, 1935; Wolberg, 1948). The same problem is present in studies in yoga. For instance, using himself as a subject, Behanan (1937) compared the effects obtained when certain yogic breathing exercises were practiced alone and when they were combined with a 20-minute period of concentration. The differences in results under the two conditions could not be unequivocally viewed as treatment effects; they could have been produced by Behanan's divergent expectations concerning the results that would be obtained under the two treatments. In brief, since subjects participating in studies on hypnosis or on yoga typically except divergent results under the experimental and control conditions, it is advisable to assign one group of subjects to the experimental condition and a different group to the control condition. Of course, such an independent-groups experimental design is maximally efficient when the subjects allocated randomly to each group are matched on relevant variables such as on base-level response to a suggestibility scale.

Finally, research in hypnosis as well as in yoga tends to be characterized by inadequately-defined terms. The ambiguity of terms such as *amnesia* and *hallucination* in the field of hypnosis has been pointed out above. Similarly, various writers on yoga assign different connotations to terms such as *meditation*. The contradictory findings pertaining to EEG correlates of meditation reported by Anand *et al.* (1961), Das and Gastaut (1955), and Wenger and Bagchi (1961) may be due to disparate techniques of meditation involved in the three investigations.

Overview

Yogi samadhi and hypnotic trance have been popularly regarded as states of consciousness in which an individual has access to unique experiences and unusual capacities. However, empirical studies appear to indicate the following: attempts to denote these states of consciousness independently of the subject's verbal report have not proved successful; a critical scrutiny of the observable phenomena that are popularly associated with the term *hypnosis* (e.g., hallucination, age-regression, amnesia, and the human-plank feat) and with the term *yoga* (e.g., fire-walking, burial-alive, lying-on-nails, and voluntary control over various autonomic functions) tends to divest them of the mystery with which they have been enveloped; some of the assumptions regarding the factors effective in producing the phenomena have failed to be validated by empirical studies; and several conclusions drawn from the past studies of the phenomena are invalidated by methodological errors.

It may be fruitful for present-day researchers to direct greater attention to the experiences that are associated with yogic samadhi and with hypnotic trance. However, since the experiences are inferred from the subjects' verbal reports, the findings of such studies will necessarily apply to the *verbal reports* rather than to the experiences per se. Such caution and scepticism are demanded by the fact that reports of having had certain types of experiences during the hypnotic session depend on numerous factors such as on cues given by the hypnotist concerning what he believes the subject experienced (Barber, 1969; Orne, 1959). This important finding in hypnosis was made possible by questioning traditional assumptions regarding the hypnotic state. It is necessary to pose similar questions with regard to experiences subsumed under the term *samadhi* in order to ascertain if factors similar to those affecting the subjects' reports in hypnosis also operate here.

With regard to the explanation of observable phenomena, a beginning has been made in hypnosis in that a series of antecedent variables underlying hypnotic hypersuggestibility has been delineated (Barber, 1965a, 1969). In yoga, the few studies carried out so far suggest that some yogic exercises may be accompanied by significant changes in the autonomic nervous system and may give rise to enduring changes in autonomic balance. Further studies are needed to isolate the independent variables in yogic exercises which are effective in producing autonomic changes. Investigations of this type may prove to be at least as fruitful as those which isolate the variables involved in performing the so-called yogic feats.

References

Anand, B. K., and Chhina, G. S., and Singh, B. Some aspects of electroencephalographic studies in yogis. *EEG Clin. Neurophysiol.*, 1961, *13*, 452-456.

Barber, T. X. Physiological effects of "hypnosis". *Psychol. Bull.*, 1961, *58*, 390-419. (See also Chapter IV in this text.)

Barber, T. X. Hypnotic age regression: A critical review. *Psychosom. Med.*, 1962, *24*, 286-299. (a) (Chapter VI)

Barber, T. X. Toward a theory of hypnosis: Posthypnotic behavior. *Arch. Gen. Psychiat.*, 1962, *7*, 321-342. (b)

Barber, T. X. Experimental controls and the phenomena of "hypnosis": A critique of hypnotic research methodology. *J. Nerv. Ment. Dis.*, 1962, *134*, 493-505. (c)

Barber, T. X. The effects of "hypnosis" on pain: A critical review of experimental and clinical findings. *Psychosom. Med.*, 1963, *25*, 303-333. (See also Chapter V in this text.)

Barber, T. X. "Hypnosis" as a causal variable in present-day psychology: A critical analysis. *Psychol. Rep.*, 1964, *14*, 839-842. (a)

Barber, T. X. , Hypnotic "colorblindness", "blindness", and "deafness". *Dis. Nerv. Syst.*, 1964, *25*, 529-537. (b)

Barber, T. X. Toward a theory of "hypnotic" behavior: Positive visual and auditory hallucinations. *Psychol. Rec.*, 1964, *14*, 197-210. (c)

Barber, T. X. Experimental analysis of "hypnotic" behavior. A review of recent empirical findings. *J. Abnorm. Psychol.*, 1965, *70*, 132-154. (a)

Barber, T. X. Physiological effects of "hynotic suggestions": A critical review of recent research (1960-64). *Psychol. Bull.*, 1965, *63*, 201-222. (b) (See also Chapter IV in this text.)

Barber, T. X. "Hypnotic" phenomena: A critique of experimental methods. In J. E. Gordon (Ed.) *Handbook of clinical and experimental hypnosis.* New York: Macmillan, 1967. Pp. 444-480.

Barber, T. X. *Hypnosis: A scientific approach,* New York: Van Nostrand Reinhold, 1969.

Barber, T. X., and Calverley , D. S. An experimental study of "hypnotic" (auditory and visual) hallucinations. *J. Abnorm. Soc. Psychol.*, 1964, *68*, 13-20. (a)

Barber, T. X. and Calverley, D. S. Experimental studies in "hypnotic" behavior: Suggested deafness evaluated by delayed auditory feedback. *Brit. J. Psychol.*, 1964, *55*, 439-466. (b)

Barber, T. X. and Calverley, D. S. Toward a theory of "hypnotic" behavior: Experimental analyses of suggested amnesia. *J. Abnorm. Psychol.*, 1966, *71*, 95-107.

Barber, T. X. and Calverley, D. S. Multidimensional analysis of "hypnotic" behavior. *J. Abnorm. Psychol.*, 1969, *74*, 209-220.

Barber, T. X., Dalal, A. S., and Calverley, D. S. The subjective reports of hypnotic subjects. *Amer. J. Clin. Hyp.*, 1968, *11*, 74-88.

Behanan, K. T. Yoga: A scientific evaluation. New York: Dover, 1937.

Bowers, K. S. The effect of demands for honesty on reports of visual and auditory hallucinations, *Int. J. Clin. Exp. Hyp.*, 1967, *15*, 31-36.

Brosse, T. A psycho-physiological study. *Main Curr. Mod. Thought*, 1964, *4*, 77-84.

Brown, B. G. A report on three experimental fire-walks by Ahmed Hussain and others. *Univ. London Couns. Psychic. Inv.*, 1938, Bull. 4.

Chaves, J. F. Hypnosis reconceptualized: An overview of Barber's theoretical and empirical work. *Psychol. Rep.*, 1968, *22*, 587-608.

Coe, M. R., Jr. Fire-walking and related behaviors. *Psychol. Rec.,* 1957, *7,* 101-110.

Collins, J. K. Muscular endurance in normal and hypnotic states: A study of suggested catalepsy. Honor's thesis, Department of Psychology, University of Sydney, 1961.

Crasilneck, H. B. and Hall, J. A. Physiological changes associated with hypnosis: A review of the literature since 1948. *Int. J. Clin. Exp. Hypn.,* 1959, *7,* 9-50.

Dalal, A. S. An empirical approach to hypnosis: An overview of Barber's work. *Arch. Gen. Psychiat.,* 1966, *15,* 151-157.

Das, J. P. Yoga and hypnosis. *Int. J. Clin. Exp. Hypn.,* 1963, *11,* 31-37.

Das, N. N. and Gastaut, H. Variations de l'activité' électrique du cerveau du coeur et des muscles squelettiques au cours de la méditation et de'l'extase' yogique. *EEG Clin. Neurophysiol.,* Suppl., 1955, *6,* 211-219.

Deikman, A. J. Experimental meditation. *J. Nerv. Ment. Dis.,* 1963, *136,* 329-343.

Deikman, A. J. Implications of experimentally induced contemplative meditation. *J. Nerv. Ment. Dis.,* 1966, *142,* 101-116.

Erickson, M. H., Hershman, S., and Secter, I. I. *The practical applications of medical and dental hypnosis.* New York: Julian Press, 1961.

Field, P. B. An inventory scale of hypnotic depth. *Int. J. Clin. Exp. Hypn.,* 1965, *13,* 238-249.

Gill, M. M. and Brenman, M. *Hypnosis and related states.* New York: International Universities Press, 1939. Pp. 38-39.

Gorton, B. E. The physiology of hypnosis. *Psychiat. Quart.,* 1949, *23,* 317-343 and 457-485.

Gorton, B. E. Autogenic training. *Amer. J. Clin. Hypn.,* 1959, *2,* 31-41.

Graham, K. R. and Patton, A. Retroactive inhibition, hypnosis, and hypnotic amnesia. *Int. J. Clin. Exp. Hypn.* 1968, *16,* 68-74.

Heuzé, P. *Fakirs, fumistes et cie.* Paris, 1926.

Ingalls, A. G. Fire-walking. *Sci. Amer.,* 1939, *163,* 135-138.

Katkin, E. S. and Murray, E. N. Instrumental conditioning of autonomically mediated behavior: Theoretical and methodological issues. *Psychol. Bull.,* 1968, *70,* 52-68.

Kimble, G. A. *Hilgard and Marquis' conditioning and learning.* (2nd ed.,) New York: Appleton-Century-Crofts, 1961.

Kline, M. V., Guze, H., and Haggerty, A. D. An experimental study of the nature of hypnotic deafness: Effects of delayed speech feedback. J. Clin. Exp. *Hypn.,* 1954, *2,* 145-156.

Kramer, E. and Tucker, G. R. Hypnotically suggested deafness and delayed auditory feedback. *Int. J. Clin. Exp. Hypn.,* 1967, *15* 37-43.

Levitt, E. E. and Brady, J. P. Psychophysiology of hypnosis. In J. M. Schneck (Ed.) *Hypnosis in modern medicine.* (3rd ed.) Springfield, Ill.: Charles C. Thomas, 1963. Pp. 314-362.

Ludwig, A. M. and Levine, J. Alterations in consciousness produced by hypnosis. *J. Nerv. Ment. Dis.,* 1965, *140,* 146-153.

Maslow, A. H. Lessons from the peak experiences. *J. Hum. Psychol.,* 1962, *2,* 9-18.

Maupin, E. W. Individual differences in response to a Zen meditation exercise. *J. Cons. Psychol.,* 1965, *29,* 139-145.

Orne, M. T. The nature of hypnosis: Artifact and essence. *J. Abnorm. Soc. Psychol,* 1959, *58,* 277-299.

Patten E. F. Does post-hypnotic amnesia apply to practice effects? *J. Gen Psychol,* 1932, *7,* 196-201.

Pattie, F. A. A report on attempts to produce uniocular blindness by hypnotic suggestion. *Brit. J. Med. Psychol.,* 1935, *15,* 230-241.

Price, H. Kuda Bux. *Spectator,* 1937, *158,* 808.

Rao, H. V. G., Krishnaswamy, N., Narasimhaiya, R. L., Hoenig, J., and Govindaswamy, M. V. Some experiments on "yogi" in controlled states. *J. All-India Inst. Ment. Health,* 1958, *1,* 99-106.

Rawcliffe, D. H. *Illusions and delusions of the supernatural and the occult.* New York: Dover, 1959.

Razran, G. The observable unconscious and the inferable conscious in current Soviet phychophysiology: Interoceptive conditioning, semantic conditioning, and the orienting reflex. *Psychol. Rev.,* 1961, *68,* 81-147.

Schultz, J. H, and Luthe, W. *Autogenic training.* New York: Grune & Stratton, 1959.

Spanos, N. P. and Barber, T. X. "Hypnotic" experiences as inferred from subjective reports: Auditory and visual hallucinations. *J. Exp. Res. Pers.,* 1968, *3,* 136-150.

Sturrock, J. B. Objective assessment of hypnotic amnesia. Paper presented at Eastern Psychological Association, Annual Meeting, New York, April 15, 1966.

Sutcliffe, J. P. "Credulous" and "skeptical" views of hypnotic phenomena: Experiments in esthesia, hallucination, and delusion. *J. Abnorm. Soc. Psychol.,* 1961, *62,* 189-200.

Thorne, D. E. Memory as related to hypnotic suggestion, procedure, and susceptibility. Unpublished doctoral dissertation, University of Utah, 1967.

Vakil, R. J. Remarkable feat of endurance by a yogi priest. *Lancet,* 1950, *2,* 871.

Wenger, M. A. and Bagchi, B. K. Studies of autonomic functions in practitioners of Yoga in India. *Behav. Sci.,* 1961, *6,* 312-323.

Wenger, M. A., Bagchi, B. K., and Anand, B. K. Experiments in India on "voluntary" control of the heart and pulse. *Circulation,* 1961, *24,* 1319-1325.

Williams, G. W. Hypnosis in perspective. In L. M. LeCron (Ed.) *Experimental hypnosis.* New York: Macmillan, 1948. Pp. 4-21.

Williamsen, J. A., Johnson, H. J., and Eriksen, C. W. Some characteristics of posthypnotic amnesia. *J. Abnorm. Psychol.,* 1965, *70,* 123-131.

Wolberg, L. R. *Medical Hypnosis.* Vol. I. New York: Grune & Stratton, 1948. P. 49.

Wood, E. *Yoga.* Baltimore: Penguin Books, 1959.

Woods, J. H. *The Yoga-system of Patanjali.* Cambridge: Harvard University Press, 1927.

CHAPTER 4

Physiological Effects of
Hypnosis and Suggestions

CONTENTS

133

FOUR

Physiological Effects of
Hypnosis and Suggestions

This chapter reviews investigations pertaining to the effects of hypnosis and suggestions on physiological functions. Two questions will be at the forefront of discussion: What physiological functions can be influenced by suggestions given under hypnotic and waking experimental treatments? Of the many independent variables subsumed under the labels *hypnosis* and *waking,* which are effective and which irrelevant to producing the physiological effects observed?

HYPNOTIC EXPERIMENTAL TREATMENTS
AND THE PRESUMED HYPNOTIC TRANCE STATE

In general, the investigations summarized in this chapter compared results obtained under two experimental treatments: a hypnotic treatment, and a waking treatment. The hypnotic experimental treatment, but not the waking treatment, typically incorporated one set of variables that was subsumed under the term *hypnotic-induction procedure* and a second set of confounded variables. The hypnotic-induction variables characteristically included: instructions designed to produce positive motivation to respond to suggestions, suggestions of relaxation and drowsiness, suggestions of entering deep trance or a hypnotic state, and suggestions that it is easy to respond to further suggestions (Barber, 1965a; Barber & Calverley, 1964f, 1965a). The variables confounded with the hypnotic experimental treatment typically included: preselection of subjects as meeting criteria for high suggestibility or hypnotizability, preliminary practice sessions in which subjects were trained to respond to a wide variety of suggestions, assumption by the subject of an eyes-closed

135

recumbent or semisupine position during the experimental session, and administration of direct or indirect suggestions intended to elicit particular physiological manifestations.

Although the hypnotic experimental treatment, but not the waking treatment, typically included the four hypnotic-induction variables and the four confounded variables listed above, researchers tended to overlook some of these variables when they interpreted their results. In many instances, the effects noted under the hypnotic experimental treatment were simply attributed to a presumed altered state of consciousness on the part of the subject, namely, a hypnotic state or a trance state, even though no attempt was made to exclude the possibility that the effects could have been produced by any one or a combination of the eight variables mentioned above regardless of the presence or absence of hypnotic trance. Pertinent here are recent experiments (Barber, 1964c, 1965b; Barber & Calverley, 1962, 1963b, 1963c, 1964c, 1964g, 1965a; Barber, Karacan, & Calverley, 1964; Parker & Barber, 1964) which indicate that subjects who have been exposed only to the first of the above experimental vaiables, namely, motivational instructions, show surprisingly high levels of response to suggestions of thirst hallucination, body immobility, selective amnesia, enhanced strength and endurance, enhanced learning proficiency, and so on. Whether or not subjects who have received only motivational instructions are in a hypnotic state remains to be demonstrated. This raises a crucial question: By what criteria can it be stated that a subject is in hypnosis or in hypnotic trance? To denote the presence of hypnosis or trance, researchers in this area generally use one or both of the following criteria:

The subject is said to be in hypnotic trance if he manifests a high level of response to test-suggestions of the type included in the scales devised by Davis and Husband (1931), Friedlander and Sarbin (1938), and Weitzenhoffer and Hilgard (1959), for example, test-suggestions of limb or body rigidity, hallucination, and amnesia. However, when the supposed causal variable (hypnotic trance) is inferred from the dependent variable (response to test-suggestions), it is difficult to avoid the tautology that subjects respond to test-suggestions because they are in trance and we know that they are in trance because they respond to test-suggestions.

In other instances, the presence of hypnotic trance is denoted by such criteria as rigid facial expression, lack of spontaneity and initiative, disinclination to talk, lack of humor, literal-mindedness, etc. (Erickson, Hershman, & Secter, 1961, pp. 55-58; Gill & Brenman, 1959, pp. 38-39; Pattie, 1956, p. 21; Weitzenhoffer, 1957, pp. 211-212). However, the same investigators who use these characteristics to denote trance also do not hesitate to state that such characteristics can be removed, by explicitly suggesting to the subject that he no longer show them, and many subjects will continue to remain in hypnotic trance and, furthermore, some hypnotized subjects never manifest such characteristics (Erickson, 1962; Gill & Brenman, 1959, p. 36; Pattie, 1956, p. 21). By what criteria is it stated that subjects who do not manifest such characteristics are in hypnosis or trance? Because they manifest a high level of response to test-suggestions. And why are they responsive to suggestions? Because they are in trance.

Even if researchers agreed as to what they meant by and how they were to denote hypnosis or hypnotic trance, and even if they could avoid circular reasoning when employing this construct, it would still remain to be demonstrated that the physiological effects which will be described below are due primarily to the presence of a trance state within the subject and not due to one or more of the external manipulable variables that are part of or are confounded with the hypnotic experimental treatment (Barber, 1964a).

In brief, hypnotic experimental treatments, as opposed to waking treatments, incorporate many variables. In the discussion which follows we shall ask continuously: Which of the multitude of variables included in or confounded with the hypnotic experimental treatment were effective and which irrelevant to producing the physiological effect observed?

Sensory-Perceptual Processes

COLOR-BLINDNESS

To induce color-blindness in six trained hypnotic subjects, Erickson (1939) employed a complex procedure which included the following: gradual induction of a profound somnambulistic hypnotic trance; slow, gradual induction of total blindness; awakening of the subject in the blind condition so that he would experience distress and anxiety; induction of a second trance condition; explanations to the subject that vision would be restored but that a certain color or colors would not be detectable; suggestions of amnesia for the critical color or colors; administration of the Ishihara during suggested (green, red, red-green, and total) color-blindness; administration of the Ishihara without suggested color-blindness in the waking state and in the simple trance state. The results of this involved experiment (which included 13 separate administrations of the Ishihara to each subject) appeared to be as follows: all subjects had normal color vision during the waking state and in the simple trance state; during suggested color-blindness, the numerals on some of the Ishihara cards were read in the manner characteristic of the green, red, red-green, or total color-blind. Erickson concluded that the hypnotic procedure was effective in inducing "consistent deficiencies in color vision comparable in degree and character with those found in actual color blindness." However, Grether (1940) criticized this conclusion noting that (a) red-green color-blindness does not exist in nature (this is a generic term referring to symptoms common to red-blindness and green-blindness); and (b) the deficiencies in color vision found among persons with actual red-blindness, green-blindness, or total color-blindness are quite different from those which Erickson attempted to induce. Harriman (1942) repeated part of Erickson's procedure, suggesting amnesia for red and then for green to 10 deeply hypnotized subjects; although these subjects responded to the Ishihara in a manner similar to Erickson's subjects, Harriman concluded, in accordance with Grether's critique, that the alterations induced "resemble attitudinal changes more closely than they resemble profound changes in sensory content." However, no attempt was made to determine if the lengthy and involved hypnotic procedure employed in the investigation was actually necessary to induce such visual anomalies.

Barber and Deeley (1961) hypothesized that normal subjects, instructed to remain inattentive to red or green, give similar responses to the Ishihara as hypnotic color-blind subjects. As a preliminary test of color vision, the American Optical Company Pseudo-Isochromatic Plates were administered to ten normal subjects. Each subject was then presented with the Ishihara plates and instructed as follows: "Now look at these cards. As I present each card, try as hard as you possibly can to pay no attention to the red. Look carefully at the rest of the card, but ignore the red; just don't let yourself see it." After completing this task the Ishihara cards were presented again and similar instructions were given to "try as hard as you possibly can to pay no attention to the green." Finally, the subject was instructed to report what he naturally saw on the Ishihara plates. The results were as follows: (a) The responses to the Pseudo-Isochromatic Plates and to the final administration of the Ishihara indicated normal color vision in all subjects. (b) When instructed to pay no attention to red and then to green, 92 of 320 (29 per cent) of the total responses of the ten normal subjects were similar to the responses expected from persons with natural red-blindness or green-blindness. Of the 320 responses given to the Ishihara by Harriman's ten deeply hypnotized subjects during suggested red-blindness and green-blindness, 85 (or 27 per cent) were similar to the responses expected from the red-blind or green-blind. In brief, the Barber and Deeley experiment showed that normal persons who have been instructed to concentrate away from red or green give similar responses on the Ishihara as deeply hypnotized subjects who have been given elaborate suggestions to induce color-blindness.

The findings of Barber and Deeley were confirmed by Rock and Shipley (1961) in an experiment with eight subjects. The latter investigators administered the Ishihara six times to each subject individually under a waking treatment. On the first four trials the subject was asked to respond as if he were green, red, red-green, and totally color-blind. On the fifth trial he was asked to give his normal responses. On the sixth trial he was asked to report all of the numerals that he could detect on the Ishihara cards. On the first four trials the subjects read many of the Ishihara cards in the manner expected from congenitally color-blind individuals. (These unselected awake subjects gave approximately as many color-blind responses as were given by the highly selected deeply hypnotized subjects participating in Erickson's, 1939, experiment.) The fifth trial showed that all subjects possessed normal color vision. The sixth trial showed that seven of the eight subjects had no difficulty in detecting all of the numerals seen by color-blind individuals. Rock and Shipley concluded that since "color anomalies can be induced simply by asking the subject to do so, hypnotically-induced color blindness as a deep sensory alternation still needs to be proven."

Bravin (1959) had previously reported comparable findings. In preliminary sessions his subjects were tested for normality of color vision, and were shown how color-blind individuals perceive red and green as various shades of the same color by exhibiting one card of the Ishihara under colored lights. Thirty subjects, selected as capable of deep trance, were then randomly assigned to three hypnotic treatment groups with ten to each group. After the administration of a hypnotic-induction procedure plus 40 minutes of additional suggestions intended to deepen the hypnotic trance, subjects in one group were given suggestions of red-green color blindness to be executed after awakening, subjects in the second group were instructed to role play color blindness after awakening, and subjects in the third group were tested in the hypnotic trance state without suggestions of color blindness. An additional group of ten unselected waking subjects were simply instructed to role play color blindness. Subjects in the hypnotic color-blind group, the hypnotic role-play group, and the waking role-play group gave some responses to the Pseudo-Isochromatic test which resembled those expected from persons with red-green blindness. The waking role-play group gave more color-blind responses (p<.10) than either the hypnotic color-blind or the hypnotic role-play groups.

In summary, the experimental evidence strongly indicates that some responses resembling those expected from congenitally color-blind individuals can be elicited either by suggesting color blindness to selected subjects under a hypnotic experimental treatment (Erickson, 1939; Harriman, 1942) or by simply instructing unselected subjects under a waking treatment to try to ignore red and green or to try to respond as if color-blind (Barber & Deeley, 1961; Bravin, 1959; Rock & Shipley, 1961).

BLINDNESS

Are suggestions of total blindness effective in altering physiological processes related to vision? Hernandez-Peon and Donoso (1959) presented a neurophysiological experiment which, although not a direct study of suggested blindness, nevertheless promises to contribute to our understanding of this phenomenon. Electrodes were deeply implanted in the occipital lobes of five patients who had undergone trephination for diagnostic explorations. With the occipital electrodes in place, the room was darkened and the patient was stimulated by electronic lamp flashes at the rate of 1/millisecond. In each case the electrographic recording showed an evoked potential simultaneous with the photic stimulation. Subsequently, when two of the patients, whom the experimenters judged to be especially suggestible, were given repeated verbal suggestions that the light intensity was greater than that actually applied, the electrographic recordings indicated an enhancement of the photically evoked potentials; when given the suggestion that the intensity of the light had diminished, while it actually remained constant, the recordings showed a diminution of the evoked potentials. However, in related experiments the same investigators demonstrated that the magnitude of the photically evoked potentials was consistently reduced whenever the attention of the subject was distracted, e.g., when instructed to solve a difficult arithmetic problem mentally or when asked to recall an interesting experience. From these experiments and from a series of related studies by other workers summarized in the paper, the authors suggested that during " 'voluntary attention' as well as by suggestion, transmission of photic impulses is modified at the retina by centrifugal influences. These influences, acting during wakefulness, are probably related to organized activity of the reticular formation of the brain stem under the control of the cortex" (p. 394).

Beck and co-workers (Beck, 1963; Beck, Dustman, & Beier, 1964) presented ostensibly contradictory results. They used 18 subjects, selected as manifesting high hypnotic suggestibility, to study the effects of hypnotic suggestions on the evoked electrocortical potentials that follow a brief flash of light. Under a control condition, the evoked potential responses to a flashing light (1/second) were led off the occipital area, amplified, and then averaged by electronic computer. The evoked responses were also recorded in the same way under a counterbalanced hypnotic treatment which included suggestions that the flashing light was bright and then dim. Contrary to the expectations of the experimenters, the suggestions given under the hypnotic treatment failed to affect the potentials; although the subjects testified that the light appeared bright and then dim, there was no significant increase in the averaged evoked potentials to the light flashes during suggested brightness nor was there observable diminution during suggested dimness.

Underwood (1960) set out to ascertain whether hypnotic blindness for a specified object produces objective consequences that are similar to those produced by actual blindness. He used two optical illusions in which a pattern of lines distorts a superimposed figure. Twelve highly trained hypnotic subjects were exposed to a hypnotic-induction procedure and, when they appeared to be in hypnotic trance, were shown the figures superimposed on the patterns and given the suggestion that the patterns were absent. If the suggestions produced objective effects similar to those found when the patterns are actually absent, the subjects should perceive the figures as undistorted. Although nine of the 12 hypnotized subjects claimed that they could not see the patterns, they responded as if they could see them; all subjects reported the degree of distortion which is normally produced by the patterns on each optical illusion.

In earlier studies, Dorcus (1937), Lundholm and Lowenbach (1942), and other workers had noted that the pupillary reaction to light stimulation is not altered during hypnotic blindness. However, since pupillary constriction to light is found during some types of organic blindness (e.g., bilateral destruction of the occipital visual areas — Madow, 1958), this response is not a satisfactory index of blindness and workers in this area have generally focused on an ostensibly more satisfactory response — alpha blocking on the electroencephalogram (EEG).

Alpha blocking to photic stimulation appears to be a totally involuntary response which is almost always present in normal persons and never present in the blind. A series of investigations has demonstrated that when the room is darkened and the eyes are closed, most normal persons typically show an alpha rhythm on the EEG (consisting of waves with a frequency of eight to 13 cycles per second and an amplitude of about 50 microvolts); a light flashed into the closed eyes of these individuals is almost always effective in causing alpha block or alpha desynchronization (i.e., in replacing the alpha rhythm with small fast waves) within 0.4 second (Jasper & Carmichael, 1935); and persons with total blindness of neurological origin do not show alpha blocking under these conditions (Callahan & Redlich, 1946).

Lundholm and Lowenbach (1942), Barker and Burgwin (1948), and Ford and Yeager (1948) found that hypnotic suggestions of blindness did *not* prevent alpha blocking when the subjects opened their eyes in an illuminated room. However, these experiments are based on a methodological error: In normal persons the act of opening the eyes *per se*—whether in darkness or in an illuminated room—almost invariably results in alpha desynchronization (Loomis, Harvey & Hobart, 1936; Yeager & Larsen, 1957). To determine if hypnotic suggestions of blindness are effective in preventing the alpha desynchronization which normally occurs after visual stimulation, it is therefore necessary for the subject either to keep his eyes continuously open or continuously closed during the experiment. These conditions were present in three investigations. Loomis et al. (1936) demonstrated that when total blindness was suggested to an excellent hypnotic subject whose eyes were kept open continuously with adhesive tape, the alpha rhythm did *not* show desynchronization during photic stimulation. This was repeated 16 times with the same results; whether the room was illuminated or darkened made no difference whatsoever—the alpha rhythm was continuously present until the subject was told that he could once again see. In a subsequent experiment, Schwarz, Bickford, and Rasmussen (1955) found that after suggestions of blindness seven of 11 hypnotic subjects (with eyes taped open) showed occasional alpha waves when the room was illuminated. In another study, Yeager and Larsen (1957) instructed five subjects to keep their eyes continuously closed during the experiment. Hypnotic and post-hypnotic suggestions were given that the subject would not be aware of the light stimulation. In the majority of trials no alpha blocking occurred when light fell upon the closed eyes.

The above studies indicate that suggestions of blindness given under a hypnotic experimental treatment are at times effective in eliminating an involuntary physiological response which normally follows visual stimulation, namely, alpha blocking on the EEG. However, a similar effect can be demonstrated in subjects who have not been given an hypnotic-induction and who do not appear to be in the trance state. Loomis et al. (1936) found that when a uniformly illuminated bowl was placed over the eyes of a normal person who was instructed not to focus on any specific part of the light pattern, the alpha waves appeared fairly regularly. Along similar lines, Gerard (1951) stated: "With a little practice I can look directly at a 100-watt light . . . and, by deliberately paying no attention to it, I can have my alpha waves remain perfectly intact; then with no change except what I can describe in no other way than as directing my attention to the light, have them immediately disappear" (p. 94). Jasper and Cruikshank (1937) published similar findings. In brief, although some hypnotized subjects, who have been given suggestions of blindness, continue to show an occipital alpha rhythm part of the time or all of the time when stimulated by light, a similar effect can be demonstrated in normal persons who are instructed to pay no attention to visual stimuli.

In another study, Schwarz et al. (1955) found that five hypnotized subjects who had been given suggestions of blindness did not show eye movements when urged to look at an object. The restriction of eye movements was indicated both by electromyographic eye leads and by the marked suppression of lambda waves on the EEG. These investigators suggested that the restriction of eye movements during hypnotic blindness is an attempt to shut off all alerting stimuli that might interfere with the successful accomplishment of the suggestion. Along similar lines, Barber (1958b) presented evidence indicating that seven excellent hypnotic subjects deliberately refused to look at an object which they had been told that they could not see; observation of eye movements indicated that they typically focused on all parts of the room *except* where the object was situated. When interviewed after the experiment, most of the subjects readily admitted that they purposely refused to carry out the active process of turning the head and focusing the eyes on the object, e.g., "I was almost carefully not looking at it," "I kept looking around it or not on it."

In an earlier study, Pattie (1935) gave five good hypnotic subjects the suggestion that they were blind in one eye. Four responded to a series of visual tests (stereoscope, perimetry, filters, Flees' box, plotting the blind spot, ophthalmological examination) with normal vision in both eyes; however, one subject responded to all tests as if she were actually blind in one eye. In a second experiment the 'blind' subject was given a more complicated filter test; the results indicated that the 'blind' eye was not impaired to the slightest degree and Pattie concluded that the former tests were thus invalidated. When questioned in a subsequent hypnotic session, the subject revealed, after much resistance, that she had given a convincing demonstration of uniocular blindness because of the following: During the stereoscopic test the two images were separated a second after exposure and this gave her the necessary knowledge to fake the test; she had practiced determining the blind spot at home after the experimenter had first attempted to plot it; on the Flees' box with crossed images she saw there were mirrors in there and figured somehow that the one on the left was supposed to be seen with the right eye, etc.

The above studies appear to indicate that the good hypnotic subject, who has been given suggestions of blindness, purposely attempts to inhibit responses to visual stimuli. This suggests the following hypothesis which can be easily confirmed or disproved: The responses to photic stimulation which characterize deeply hypnotized subjects who have been given suggestions of blindness can be duplicated by normal persons who are asked to remain inattentive and unresponsive to visual stimuli.

VISUAL THRESHOLDS

Kliman and Goldberg (1962) measured visual word-recognition thresholds, first under a base-line condition and then under counter-balanced hypnotic and waking experimental treatments. There was no overall difference in the ease of recognition of the tachistoscopically presented words under the hypnotic and waking treatments. However, words originally difficult to perceive (words with high base-line thresholds) were perceived more easily under the hypnotic treatment; and, under the waking treatment, there was a tendency toward reduction in thresholds for words originally easy to perceive (words with low base-line thresholds).

In a series of subsequent studies, Zamansky and collaborators (Scharf & Zamansky, 1963; Zamansky & Brightbill, 1964; Zamansky, Scharf, & Brightbill, 1964) presented evidence indicating that the degree of reduction in word-recognition thresholds obtained under both hypnotic and waking experimental treatments is highly correlated with the initial threshold level. Subjects with low initial thresholds showed little or no reduction in thresholds under any of the experimental treatments. Subjects with high initial thresholds tended to show reduced thresholds under all experimental treatments. (The treatments included hypnosis with suggestions that the words would be perceived easily and quickly; a waking treatment with monetary reward for improved performance; a waking treatment in which the subjects were told, incorrectly, that the apparatus was being temporarily modified so as to facilitate their identification of the words; and a waking treatment with no special incentives.)

MYOPIA (NEARSIGHTEDNESS)

Kelley (1958, 1961) attempted to improve visual acuity in 14 myopic subjects by suggestions given with and without a preceding hypnotic-induction procedure. Seven subjects who could not be hypnotized constituted the waking-suggestions group, and one deep-trance subject and six light-trance subjects constituted the hypnotic group. Subjects participated in from one to three experimental sessions. The following types of indirect suggestions were used to improve visual acuity: With the subject's eyes closed, the experimenter described pleasant scenes in detail and then suggested to the subject that he should keep the frame of mind developed in the imagining situation as he opened his eyes. It was suggested that the subject would look at the visual figures on the chart with an attitude of relaxed interest and effortlessness, without making any particular effort to see. It was suggested that the subject would feel as if he were looking over great distances when he looked at the chart. Although each type of suggestion was effective with some subjects, the suggestions to imagine pleasant scenes were the most effective and were used most often. Twelve of the 14 subjects showed improved visual acuity for distant objects. The waking-suggestion group improved as easily and as quickly as the hypnotic group. The overall average improvement was equivalent to the difference between 20/50 and 20/20 acuity.

In an additional series of studies with three to five myopic subjects (Kelley, 1958), the same suggestive techniques were used to improve visual acuity while various optical procedures (haploscopy, retinoscopy, cycloplegia) were employed to delineate the mechanisms underlying the changes induced. These studies appeared to exclude the possibilities that the improvement in visual acuity induced by suggestions was cerebral (improved interpretation), pupillary (increased depth of field), or due to lens changes, and indicated that the improvement was due to changes in eyeball shape (refractive changes) produced by the action of the extrinsic eye muscles. Further studies are needed to confirm these interesting results.

VESTIBULAR NYSTAGMUS

Aschan, Finer, and Hagbarth (1962) studied the effects of hypnotic suggestions on the rapid eye movements produced by vestibular stimulation (vestibular nystagmus). Seventeen persons who were known to be good hypnotic subjects were selected for the experiment. Rapid eye movements produced by two types of vestibular stimulation (rotary and caloric stimulation) were measured with subjects' eyes closed under four experimental treatments: 1) a control treatment, 2) a hypnotic treatment, 3) a hypnotic treatment which included suggestions of decreased rotary sensation, and 4) a hypnotic treatment which included suggestions of increased rotary sensation. In most subjects the intensity of the induced nystagmus was lowest under Treatment 3 and highest under Treatment 4. No attempt was made to ascertain whether the intensity of the induced nystagmus could be altered in the desired direction by simply suggesting to unselected awake subjects that they would experience reduced and enhanced rotary sensations.

VISUAL HALLUCINATION

Barber and Calverley (1964e) and Spanos and Barber (1968) confirmed previous studies indicating that direct suggestions to see objects (that are not actually present) are effective when given under a hypnotic treatment in eliciting testimony that the objects are perceived. However, these investigators also found that ostensible visual hallucinations could be elicited almost as readily under a waking treatment which included suggestions that it was easy to see objects that are not present and instructions to try to perform maximally on assigned experimental tasks.

Prior to the above studies, Erickson (1958) and other investigators had contended that hypnotic visual hallucinations are similar if not identical with visual perceptions. This contentions received indirect support from the experiments of Erickson and Erickson (1938), Rosenthal and Mele (1952), and Barber (1959), which indicated that hypnotic color hallucinations resemble actual color preceptions in that they give rise to negative afterimages. In interpreting this finding the authors stated or implied that the complementary color afterimages were due to involuntary neurophysiological processes that were associated with or that were brought about by the hypnotic hallucination. However, the possibility was not excluded that the subjects, who were college students, may have had prior knowledge of complementary colored afterimages even though, in most instances, they denied such knowledge. To begin to demonstrate that negative afterimages associated with hypnotic color hallucinations are due to involuntary neurophysiological processes it is first necessary to exclude the possibility that subjects have prior knowledge of the phenomenon. Elsea (1961) presented a rigorous study along these lines conducted with adolescents attending an industrial training school. In the first part of the experiment, Elsea carefully excluded the possibility that subjects from this population possessed knowledge of complementary color phenomena. In the second part of the experiment, 32 volunteers who met criteria for deep trance, were assigned to the experimental group, and 32 volunteers who were not seen for hypnotic testing were assigned to the control group. The effects of several variables were investigated, including the following: the duration of the hypnotic-induction procedure (the control group was not exposed to a hypnotic-induction, half of the experimental group was exposed to a brief 5-minute hypnotic-induction, and the other half to a 30-minute induction); subject's knowledge of negative afterimages. Half of the subjects in each group were given information concerning complementary colored afterimages and the others were not given such information. Results were: Subjects exposed to the extended hypnotic-induction procedure reported no more correct afterimages to the hallucinated colors than those exposed to the brief induction; hypnotized subjects did not report a greater number of correct afterimages than expected by chance; subjects given information concerning the negative afterimage phenomenon did not report a greater number of correct afterimages to the hallucinated colors than those not given such information.

Elsea's negative results do not obviate the possibility that hypnotic color hallucinations may resemble actual color perceptions in giving rise to complementary colored afterimages. However, Elsea's null findings, taken together with the negative findings of Bernheim (1888), Dorcus (1937), Hibler (1935), Naruse (1962), Sidis (1906), and others, reviewed in detail elsewhere (Barber, 1964b, 1964d), clearly place the burden of proof upon those who wish to make this claim.

DEAFNESS

Black and Wigan (1961) reported that an autonomic response, which had been conditioned to an auditory stimulus, could not be elicited when deafness for the stimulus was suggested under a hypnotic experimental treatment. The procedure was as follows. Two selected subjects were presented with a tone paired with an electric shock until they showed cardiac acceleration when presented with the tone alone without shock. A hypnotic-induction procedure was then administered and, when the subjects appeared to be in a trance state, deafness for the tone was suggested and the tone was presented four times without shock. The subjects now did not show the conditioned cardiac acceleration response. Black and Wigan concluded that although the case is still in some respects unproven it seems that deafness to tones of specific frequency can be produced by suggestions of deafness given under hypnotic trance. However, since the experiment did not include a waking comparison group, it appears inappropriate to draw conclusions with respect to the effects of hypnotic trance.

Barber and Hahn (1968) recently presented an experiment carried out along similar lines. A cardiac response was conditioned to a tone by presenting the tone 30 times together with an electric shock. Next, half of the subjects were and half were not exposed to a hypnotic-induction procedure. Subjects who had and also those who had not received the hypnotic-induction procedure were then divided into four subgroups and each group received one of the following four sets of instructions or suggestions: "Try not to hear and to be deaf for the tone"; "You will not receive any more shocks when the tone is presented"; "Try to remain calm and relaxed when you expect the tone"; and no instructions.

When all subjects next received eight presentations of the tone alone without shock, the following results were obtained both with subjects who had and also with those who had not received the hypnotic-induction: The cardiac response that had been conditioned to an auditory stimulus was markedly reduced (71 per cent mean drop) by suggestions to try not to hear the tone, was practically extinguished (92 per cent mean reduction) by informing subjects that henceforth they would not be shocked when they heard the tone, was reduced to a small degree (26 per cent) by instructions to remain calm and relaxed when presented with the tone, and remained stable (was reduced only by 2 per cent) in the control subjects who were not given any instructions. In brief, one of the important findings in this experiment was that a conditioned cardiac response to an auditory stimulus can be markedly reduced by suggestions to try not to hear the auditory stimulus given either to a hypnotic group or a waking control group. Further studies are needed to determine to what extent the effects of suggestions on a conditioned cardiac response are mediated by changes in the subjects' respiratory pattern (Huttenlocher & Westcott, 1957; Shearn, 1961; Westcott & Huttenlocher, 1961; Wood & Obrist, 1964; Zeaman & Wegner, 1957).

Fisher (1932) and Erickson (1938b) had also studied the effect of hypnotically-induced deafness on conditioned responses to acoustic stimuli. Fisher found that during posthypnotic deafness one subject did not show a patellar response which had been conditioned to the sound of a bell. Erickson similarly demonstrated that after hypnotic suggestions of deafness two subjects failed to show a hand-withdrawal response conditioned to the sound of a buzzer. Although both investigators interpreted the failure to show conditioned responses to auditory stimuli as a sign of deafness, earlier experiments, reviewed by Hilgard and Marquis (1940, p. 35, pp. 269-270), which indicated that such conditioned responses can be voluntarily inhibited, suggest an alternative interpretation, namely, that the hypnotic deaf subjects perceived the sound stimulus but purposely inhibited the response. Some support for this interpretation was offered by the kymographic tracings reproduced in Fisher's paper which showed an aborted patellar response to some of the sound stimuli. Additional evidence was presented by Lundholm (1928) who, like Erickson, conditioned a hand-withdrawal response to an auditory stimulus; although the subject in this case did not show the conditioned response after hypnotic suggestions of deafness, he later admitted having heard the click, having felt an impulse to withdraw on click without shock, and having resisted and inhibited that impulse (p. 340).

As an additional index of deafness, Erickson (1938a) noted that his subjects did not show startle responses to sudden loud sounds. Other investigations, however, again suggest the possibility that the subjects may have perceived the sound and purposely inhibited the startle response. For instance, Dynes (1932) reported that three hypnotic deaf subjects, who did not show overt startle responses when a pistol was unexpectedly fired, admitted after the experiment that they heard the sound, and Kline, Guze, and Haggerty (1954) demonstrated that a hypnotic deaf subject who failed to show both conditioned responses to auditory stimuli and startle reflexes to sudden loud sounds showed clear-cut responses to auditory stimuli when tested by a method employing delayed auditory feedback.

The later experiment merits further comment. In the normal person, feeding back his speech through tape recording amplification and earphones with a delay of one-quarter second has been reported to produce an impairment in subsequent speech. Most commonly this speech disturbance involves stammering, stuttering, perseveration, and marked loss in speed and tempo (Yates, 1963). Kline et al. (1954) found that such delayed auditory feedback produced distinct impairment in speech performance in an excellent hypnotic subject who had been given suggestions of deafness. However, as compared with his waking performance, the subject showed less slurring, stuttering, and stammering, appeared more calm, and did not show discomfort. The investigators concluded that the hypnotic suggestions of deafness were effective in inducing a set, or in gearing the subject to give minimal response to the excruciating intensity and the constant interference of the feedback of his own voice without in any way inducing deafness in the usual sense. However, no attempt was made to determine if the subject would have shown a similar ability to tolerate the speech-disturbing delayed auditory stimulation during the waking experiment if he had been instructed and motivated to remain inattentive to or to concentrate away from the stimulation.

Barber & Calverley (1964d) presented an experiment that was designed to ascertain whether suggestions to try not to hear or to be deaf are effective in producing subjective deafness when given under both hypnotic and waking experimental treatments and whether suggested deafness produces similar objective consequences as actual deafness.

The experiment was conducted as follows:

Forty-two female students were pretested on an oral reading test with delayed auditory feedback, that is, while their utterances were delayed for a fraction of a second, amplified, and returned to their ears through a headphone. In harmony with previous studies, the delayed auditory feedback produced stuttering and other speech disturbances in these individuals who possessed normal hearing. Retests on an equivalent form of the oral reading test were then given, again with delayed auditory feedback, under three experimental treatments with 14 subjects randomly assigned to each treatment. Subjects assigned to Treatment 1 first received a 15-minute hypnotic-induction procedure, patterned after the procedures of Friedlander and Sarbin (1938), Marcuse (1959 pp. 52-53), and Weitzenhoffer and Hilgard (1959), and then received suggestions of deafness. Subjects assigned to Treatment 2 were simply told to try to the best of their ability not to hear and to be deaf. Subjects allocated to Treatment 3 (control) were retested without receiving either a hypnotic-induction or deafness suggestions. Significantly more subjects reported partial deafness (sounds were perceived as reduced in intensity) or total deafness (sounds were not heard at all) under Treatment 2 (93 per cent) than under Treatment 1 (64 per cent). Subjects under both Treatments 1 and 2 who claimed partial or total deafness responded to the delayed auditory feedback of their speech in the same way as subjects under Treatment 3 (control) who heard normally, that is, with stuttering, mispronunciations, increased vocal intensity, and slowed rate of speaking. In brief, this experiment indicated that: subjective reports of partial or total deafness can be elicited more effectively by simply instructing subjects under a waking experimental treatment to try to the best of their ability not to hear rather than by administering suggestions of deafness under a hypnotic experimental treatment; and the objective effects of partial or total suggested deafness, as evaluated by the method of delayed auditory feedback, closely resemble the objective effects of normal hearing and appear to be markedly dissimilar to the effects of actual deafness.

Sutcliffe (1961) also used delayed auditory feedback to assess hypnotic deafness objectively. The test performance consisted of adding aloud a series of 2-digit numbers under delayed auditory feedback distraction. The pertinent comparison in this complex experiment was the one made between eight subjects who were exposed to a hypnotic-induction procedure and then given suggestions of deafness for the auditory feedback and eight subjects who were tested under a waking treatment that did not include special suggestions or instructions. Hypnotic deafness did not prevent the impairment in performance which normally results from delayed auditory feedback; subjects who appeared to be in deep trance and who stated that they could not hear the feedback of their speech performed on the oral arithmetic test as poorly as the waking subjects who heard normally. Subsequent experiments (Kramer & Tucker, 1967; Scheibe, Gray & Keim, 1968), which also utilized the technique of delayed auditory feedback, similarly showed that the hypnotic deaf subject is affected by auditory stimuli in essentially the same way as the person with normal hearing. Although the hypnotic deaf subject may be trying not to hear, it appears that he simply does not succeed in blocking out sounds. The fact that the subject can hear is often obvious. For instance, although deaf individuals do not respond to spoken suggestions, hypnotic deafness usually ceases when the subject is given the suggestion, "Now you can hear again."

Malmo, Boag, and Raginsky (1954) reported comparable findings. After appropriate suggestions to induce deafness, two excellent hypnotic subjects denied auditory sensations and showed significantly reduced motor reactions to sudden auditory stimulation; however, myographic recordings from eye muscles showed a strong blink reaction in both subjects at each presentation of the auditory stimulus. Sternomastoid tracings indicated that one subject showed slight startle responses to all stimuli and the other subject showed a strong startle reaction to the first presentation of the stimulus and slight startle reactions to subsequent stimuli. Other data presented in the report (e.g., introspective reports and myographic tracings indicating a higher level of tension in the chin muscles under hypnosis as compared to the control condition) permit the following interpretation of the findings: the subjects were unable to inhibit blink responses to the auditory stimuli; since the first presentation of the auditory stimulus was more or less unexpected, one subject failed to inhibit the startle response; since the second and subsequent stimuli were expected, both subjects were able, to a great extent, to inhibit startle responses. In an earlier study, Malmo, Davis, and Barza (1952) found that, when unexpectedly presented with an intense auditory stimulus, a hysterical deaf patient also showed a gross startle response on the myograph; a control case of middle-ear deafness, studied by the same techniques, showed no blink reaction and no startle response to any presentation of the auditory stimulus.

In an earlier study, Pattie (1950) gave 12 excellent hypnotic subjects suggestions of unilateral deafness. Four subjects appeared to accept the suggestions, insisting that they could not hear in one ear. However, when auditory stimuli were presented in such a manner that they could not determine which ear was being stimulated, they showed normal hearing in both ears.

The above findings—that hypnotic deaf subjects purposely inhibit conditioned responses to auditory stimuli (Lundholm, 1928), appear to inhibit startle responses to sudden acoustic stimuli (Malmo et al., 1952), may show a calmer attitude and less tension during speech-disturbing delayed auditory stimulation but no sign of actual deafness (Barber & Calverley, 1964; Kline et al., 1954; Kramer & Tucker, 1967; Scheibe et al., 1968; Sutcliffe, 1961), and do not show deafness in one ear when unable to determine which ear is being stimulated (Pattie, 1950)—appear to indicate that the hypnotic deaf subject is very difficult if not impossible to distinguish from the non-hypnotic subject who is trying not to hear or is trying to ignore auditory stimuli but does not fully succeed in doing so.

HALLUCINATED (IMAGINED) PAIN

Barber and Hahn (1964) conducted an experiment to determine whether suggested painful stimulation evokes physiological and subjective responses which resemble those produced by actual painful stimulation. In the preliminary noncritical phase of the experiment, four groups of 12 subjects were exposed to a noxious stimulus (immersion of a hand in water at 2 degrees centigrade for one minute). Both Group 1, which had received a hypnotic-induction prior to stimulation, and Groups 2, 3, and 4 which had not received an induction, showed increased heart rate, elevated forehead muscle tension, and heightened levels of skin conductance during the stimulus period and subsequently stated that the stimulus had been experienced as painful. In the critical phase of the experiment the hypnotic group (Group 1) and a waking group (Group 2) were exposed to nonpainful stimulation (immersion of the hand in water at room temperature) after receiving suggestions to imagine vividly that the nonpainful stimulus was the same painful stimulus that was received in the first phase of the experiment. Groups 3 and 4 were exposed to the painful stimulus (water at 2 degrees centigrade) and the nonpainful stimulus (water at room temperature), respectively, without special instruction. Suggestions to imagine painful stimulation were more effective in eliciting verbal reports of discomfort and pain in the group that had received the hypnotic-induction (Group 1) rather than in the group that had not (Group 2). However, Groups 1 and 2 did not differ in physiological reactions to imagined pain; both groups manifested physiological responses (significantly increased heart rate and forehead muscle tension and a tendency toward increased skin conductance) which differed from the responses of the group exposed to the non-painful stimulus (Group 4) and were similar to the responses of the group exposed to the painful stimulus (Group 3).

Induction and Inhibition of Labor Contractions

Kelly (1962) used an intrauterine transducer to record the motility of the womb in five postpartum patients when they were given suggestions under a hypnotic treatment to recall vividly the pains that they had recently experienced during labor and delivery. Each patient showed a rise in intrauterine pressure which subsided and recurred in harmony with the remembered pains. No attempt was made to ascertain whether suggestions to recall previous labor were alone sufficient to produce these uterine effects or whether other variables incorporated into the hypnotic treatment also played a role.

Rice (1961) presented data indication that suggestions to reexperience previous labor pains, given under a hypnotic treatment, are effective with selected multiparous patients in inducing labor contractions, provided that the patient is at or near term and the cervix is 'ripe'. Carter (1963) similarly presented several case studies indicating that suggestions to recall previous labor given under a hypnotic experimental treatment are sufficient to induce labor in some pregnant women who are at term. The earlier report (Rice, 1961) included evidence indicating that, in some of the patients, voluntary contraction of the abdominal muscles may have indirectly brought about the uterine contractions. Further studies are needed to ascertain whether this is the mechanism involved.

Logan (1963) hypnotized two patients who were apparently in premature labor and suggested to them that the labor contractions would cease. (The fetal membranes had not as yet ruptured when the patients received the suggestions.) The contractions stopped and did not recur until the expected term date. Schwartz (1963) presented data indicating that some good hypnotic subjects in premature or full-term labor are able to stop uterine contractions voluntarily. One patient apparently deliberately stopped her contractions and another stopped her contractions on command. It is not clear from this report if the administration of a hypnotic trance induction procedure was relevant to producing these effects. Schwartz (1963) stated that: "Depth of trance apparently plays little part in the patient's ability to stop contractions purposefully. Some patients in deep trance are unable to stop labor; others in light trance are able to do so" (p. 213). It could also be, of course, that some patients who are not in hypnotic trance are able to stop labor contractions. Further studies are needed to delineate the necessary and sufficient conditions for producing this effect.

Circulatory Functions

VASOMOTOR FUNCTIONS

The evidence at present indicates that localized vasoconstriction and vasodilation (and a concomitant localized skin temperature alteration) can be induced in some hypnotized persons by appropriate suggestions. McDowell (1959) found that a good hypnotic subject showed erythema with vasodilation and increase in skin temperature of the right leg following suggestions that the leg was immersed in warm water. In another experiment, Chapman, Goodell, and Wolff (1959) suggested to 13 subjects as soon as a state of moderate to deep hypnosis had been established, that one arm was either normal or that it was numb, wooden, and devoid of sensation (anesthetic). The arm was then exposed on three spots, blackened with India ink, to a standard thermal stimulus (500 millicalories/second/centimeter^2 for 3 seconds). After an interval of 15 to 30 minutes during which time hypnosis was continued, it was suggested that the other arm was tender, painful, burning, damaged, and exceedingly sensitive (vulnerable) and the same standard noxious stimulation was applied. The results of 40 trials with the 13 subjects were as follows: In 30 trials the inflammatory reaction and tissue damage following the noxious stimulation was greater in the vulnerable arm, in two trials the reaction was greater in the anesthetic arm, and in eight trials no difference was noted. Plethysmographic and skin temperature recordings indicated that following the noxious stimulation local vasodilation and elevation in skin temperature was larger in magnitude and persisted longer in the vulnerable arm. This experiment should be repeated with unhypnotized subjects who are instructed to *imagine* one arm as devoid of sensation and the other arm as exceedingly sensitive. The data summarized below suggest that at least some of the effects reported in this study—localized vasodilation and elevation in skin temperature—can be induced by symbolic stimulation or suggestions in some individuals who do not appear to be in a state of hypnosis.

When attempting to condition local vasoconstriction and vasodilation to verbal stimuli, Menzies (1941) found that the conditioning procedure could be dispensed with in some cases; some persons, who had *not* participated in the experimental conditioning, showed vasodilation in a limb when recalling previous experiences involving warmth of the limb and local vasoconstriction when recalling experiences involving cold. In an earlier study, Hadfield (1920) found that localized changes in skin temperature could be induced by suggestions given to a person in the waking state. In this case, the subject had exercised vigorously before the experiment and the temperature of both hands, as measured with the bulb of the thermometer held firmly in the palm, had reached 95°F. Without a preliminary hypnotic procedure, it was suggested that the right arm was becoming cold. Within half an hour the temperature of the right palm fell to 68° while the temperature of the left palm remained at 94°. When subsequently given the suggestion that the right hand was becoming warm, the temperature of the hand rose within 20 minutes to 94°. Although this subject had previously participated in hypnotic experiments, Hadfield insisted that he did not hypnotize him during this experiment and that the temperature alterations occurred when the subject was entirely in the waking condition.

CARDIAC ACCELERATION AND DECELERATION

A number of experiments, reviewed by Gorton (1949) and Weitzenhoffer (1953), demonstrated that cardiac acceleration can be produced by hypnotic suggestions which activate the subject and that cardiac deceleration can be produced by hypnotic suggestions of relaxation, drowsiness, sleep. However, these results indicate no more and no less than that an alteration in the level of arousal or level of activation (Duffy, 1957, 1962; Woodworth & Schlosberg, 1954) — whether induced by stimuli present during various ongoing life situations or induced by suggestions during a hypnotic experiment — is correlated with an alteration in the heart rate. A more significant question is: Can the heart rate be accelerated or depressed by direct suggestions of such an effect without simultaneously inducing anxiety, emotion, or arousal?

Klemme (1963) conducted an experiment which attempted to answer the above question. The subjects were ten unselected volunteers, and ten selected individuals who had previously demonstrated that they were capable of deep trance. All subjects were first asked to accelerate their heart by simply thinking to themselves, "My heart is beating faster and faster." Next, all subjects were asked to accelerate and then to decelerate the heart by any means at their disposal. Finally, all subjects were exposed to a hypnotic-induction procedure and then received suggestions to accelerate and decelerate the heart in the same way as in the waking sessions. Suggestions to accelerate and decelerate the heart produced noticeable effects in the majority of subjects under both the waking and the hypnotic experimental treatments. There was a trend, which did not reach significance, for greater response to suggestions under the waking treatment. (This trend might have been due to failure to counterbalance the experimental treatments.) Klemme (1963) reported that: "In this experiment hypnosis did not enhance the ability of subjects to alter the heart rate as suggested despite rather deep trance states. This came as a surprise, for in the initial phase of the pilot experiment the author was convinced that contrary results would be obtained. Many of the good trance subjects . . . also expected the heart rate to be more effectively altered in the state of hypnosis." Klemme also noted that the observed alterations in heart rate may have been indirectly produced by variations in respiration. Under both the waking and the hypnotic treatments, respiratory rate was elevated when subjects were trying to accelerate the heart and was slowed by nearly 50 per cent when they were trying to produce cardiac deceleration.

To demonstrate a *direct* effect of suggestions or symbolic stimulation on heart rate it is necessary to control at least two factors, level of arousal and respiratory rate. One hypnotic experiment has been published which ostensibly satisfies these criteria: Van Pelt (1954) reported that an excellent hypnotic subject showed an accelerated cardiac rate following direct suggestions of such an effect without at the same time showing an altered respiratory rate or emotional arousal. After an hypnotic-induction procedure, this investigator spoke to the subject in a quiet tone as follows: "Your heart is beginning to beat faster. It is getting faster and faster. You are perfectly calm, but your heart is beating faster and faster." The electrocardiogram (EKG) showed that the heart rate increased immediately from 78 to 135 beats per minute. Van Pelt stated that he did not observe a change in the depth and rate of respiration during the tachycardia. Also, during the acceleration the subject appeared calm and the EKG tracing did not show somatic tremors which are typical of nervousness and fear. In a second experiment, in which the same subject showed cardiac acceleration following suggestions intended to arouse fear—"You are driving a car at a tremendous speed and are heading toward a second car and are going to crash"—the EKG recording showed clear evidence of somatic tremors.

The above study lacked an important control; no attempt was made to determine if the subject could voluntarily accelerate the heart without hypnosis. Since other workers employing similar procedures with equally good hypnotic subjects have failed to demonstrate cardiac acceleration (e.g., Jenness & Wible, 1937, failed in 30 attempts with eight excellent hypnotic subjects), it appears possible that the hypnotic procedure was not a necessary factor in producing this effect. Supporting evidence for this supposition is presented in a large number of studies which demonstrated that some apparently normal persons are able to accelerate the heart voluntarily (King, 1920). In most of the reported cases the voluntary tachycardia was on the order of 15 to 40 beats per minute; however, in some cases (Favell & White, 1917; Tarchanoff, 1885) the acceleration was as high as 63 or 75 beats per minute. In all cases the subjects denied that they induced the tachycardia by visualizing emotion-inducing situations and insisted that they produced the effect by voluntary effort. Some subjects showed changes in respiratory pattern during the voluntary tachycardia but in these cases the respiratory alterations varied and could not be correlated with the change in heart rate (Koehler, 1914; Pease, 1889; Tarchanoff, 1885; Van de Velde, 1897); other subjects could as readily induce the voluntary acceleration when breathing more or less normally as when showing changes in respiratory pattern (King, 1920; Taylor & Cameron, 1922); and some subjects showed no significant change in respiratory pattern on the pneumograph when inducing cardiac acceleration on the order of 40 beats per minute (Favill & White, 1917).

Voluntary acceleration of the heart may not be as uncommon as is generally assumed. Van de Velde found four cases and Tarchanoff five cases when confining their search to relatively small groups of individuals. Furthermore, a number of medical students discovered that they possessed this ability in physiology classes when they attempted to determine the validity of the lecturer's assertion that voluntary cardiac acceleration is possible (Ogden & Shock, 1939; West & Savage, 1918).

CARDIAC STANDSTILL

Raginsky (1959) demonstrated that hypnotic suggestions are effective in producing cardiac block for a brief period in an appropriately predisposed person. The subject in this case was a hospitalized patient whose carotid sinuses had been surgically removed because of periodic fainting episodes with cardiac arrest (Adams-Stokes disease). After the patient went into a medium to deep hypnotic state, he was instructed in a tone of considerable urgency to visualize with all clarity possible his worst attack of faintness. The patient turned pale, limp, and a cold perspiration appeared on his forehead. His pulse was unobtainable. The EKG tracing showed complete auricular and ventricular standstill for a time interval of four beats, followed by a normal sinu-auricular beat. After a rest period of ten minutes, the experiment was repeated with comparable results. However, no attempt was made to determine if cardiac arrest could be induced in this patient by asking him to visualize his worst attack of faintness *without* a preceding hypnotic-induction procedure. The case summarized below suggests that the hypnotic-induction and the medium to deep hypnotic state may have been unnecessary in producing this effect.

McClure (1959) found that an appropriately predisposed person could voluntarily produce cardiac standstill. The subject in this case, a 44-year-old airplane mechanic, had discovered that he could induce a progressive slowing of the pulse by relaxing completely. When asked to induce a diminution of the heart rate in the laboratory, the subject lay very quietly and allowed respiration to become extremely shallow. The EKG showed sinus arrest for a period of five seconds. An EKG tracing taken one hour after the experiment was within normal limits. Since the subject had rheumatic fever at age seven, McClure suggested the following tentative explanation of this performance:

> The underlying cardiac change is believed to be well compensated rheumatic heart disease with aortic valvulitis. The bradycardia and cardiac arrest are probably manifestations of exaggerated vagotonia, induced through some mechanism which, although under voluntary control, is not known to the patient himself. Careful observation did not reveal any breathholding or Valsalva maneuver in connection with the cessation of heartbeat. Apparently the patient simply abolished all sympathetic tone by complete mental and physical relaxation (pp. 440-441).

ELECTROCARDIOGRAM ALTERATIONS

Yanovski (1962a, 1962b) presented data indicating that various types of suggestions given under a hypnotic experimental condition were effective in producing alterations on the electrocardiogram (EKG). For instance, suggestions of relaxation at times produced cardiac deceleration, and suggestions intended to evoke anxiety at times produced tachycardia, ventricular extrasystoles, and flattening of the T wave. No attempt was made to ascertain whether the same suggestions would produce the same EKG effects in a waking comparison group.

    Bennett and Scott (1949) found that one of five excellent hypnotic subjects showed tachycardia and T wave abnormalities on the EKG — lowering or disappearance of T in Leads I, II, and III — within two minutes following suggestions intended to induce anxiety and anger. The subject in this case was an emotionally stable and well-adjusted young male with no history of cardiac disorders and with an otherwise normal EKG. Since such EKG abnormalities are not normally associated with tachycardia, two electrocardiographers, who were not informed of the experimental conditions under which the tracings were made, interpreted the records as indicating coronary artery disease or acute rheumatic fever. In a subsequent study with the same subject, subcutaneous administration of epinephrine elicited lower T waves in Leads I and II than those found during the control experiment. The authors concluded that the EKG alterations induced during the hypnotic experiment may have been an indirect result of sympathetic stimulation and release of epinephrine from the adrenal medulla. Berman, Simonson, and Heron (1954) confirmed this study; employing 14 susceptible hypnotic subjects with otherwise normal EKG, they found that during hypnotically-induced fear and anxiety, two showed elevation and five showed depression or inversion of T waves. In a second experiment these workers found that although deep hypnosis could not be induced in 11 patients with coronary sclerosis and angina pectoris, four showed T wave changes when given emotion-inducing suggestions.

The above experiments demonstrate that EKG alterations resembling those found in grave cardiac disorders can be induced in some hypnotized subjects by suggestions which evoke fear, anger, or anxiety; however, similar EKG abnormalities have been demonstrated in some normal persons during emotional arousal. Mainzer and Krause (1940) compared the EKG tracings of 53 unselected surgical patients recorded the day before surgery, and on the operating table immediately before the induction of general anesthesia. As compared with the earlier tracings, 40 per cent of the tracings recorded immediately before surgery showed various abnormalities such as S-T depression with T low, inverted, or absent. Along similar lines, Landis and Slight (1929) and Loftus, Gold, and Diethelm (1945) demonstrated that some persons with otherwise normal EKG show abnormalities of the ST segment and the T wave during startle or anxiety; Crede, Chivers, and Shapiro (1951) found that, in rare cases, mere anticipation of the EKG test is sufficient to produce inverted T waves in normal individuals; and Ljung (1949) published a study of 14 subjects with no evidence of cardiac disease who showed abnormal T waves during apparently slight emotional stimulation. After summarizing these and related investigations, Weiss (1956) suggested that such EKG effects are found during emotional stimulation in persons who are prone to show an elevation of sympathetic tone and an increase in cardiac metabolism without a corresponding increase in the coronary circulation.

In brief, the above studies on cardiac functions indicate the following:

Cardiac acceleration or deceleration can be produced in some subjects by various types of suggestions or instructions given under either hypnotic or waking conditions.

In extremely rare cases, i.e., in individuals who have a very unique predisposition, it appears possible to produce a complete stoppage of the heart for a very brief period by suggestions or instructions given under either hypnotic or waking conditions.

Although some hypnotic subjects show EKG alterations resembling those found in organic heart disease following suggestions designed to induce fear, anxiety, or anger, some persons who have not been exposed to a hypnotic-induction procedure and who do not appear to be in trance show similar EKG alterations during emotional stimulation.

Metabolic and Gastrointestinal Functions

BLOOD GLUCOSE LEVELS

A number of experiments appear to indicate that hypnotized persons show an elevation of blood glucose levels when given the direct suggestion that blood sugar will increase. Before discussing these studies, it is appropriate to note the following:

1. The level of blood glucose appears to be closely related to the level of arousal; blood sugar tends to increase during anxiety, emotion, or maintained activity and to decrease during relaxation, depression, or sleep (Dunbar, 1954, Ch. 8).

2. The blood glucose level is excessively labile in diabetics, i.e., as compared with normal persons, diabetics tend to show more extreme alterations in blood sugar content during periods of high or low arousal (Hinkle & Wolf, 1953; Mirsky, 1948).

The above postulates suggest that in diabetic patients any procedure (hypnotic or nonhypnotic) which induces relaxation or minimizes excitability will tend to depress the blood sugar level and minimize glycosuria and any procedure which induces arousal or excitability will tend to elevate the blood glucose level and increase glycosuria. Data supporting this hypothesis were presented by Bauch (1935) in a study of the effects of training in relaxation (Schultz's "autogene training") on seven diabetic patients. Each patient showed a significant decrease in blood sugar levels after becoming proficient in inducing relaxation—insulin dosage was reduced in each case by ten to 20 units. Apparently, healthy persons do *not* show the same degree of reduction in blood glucose content after achieving the same success in producing relaxation (Schultz & Luthe, 1959). Along similar lines, Mohr (1925) relieved a full-pledged diabetic of glycosuria by hypnotic suggestions which were effective in mitigating his affective excitability toward certain significant persons in his surroundings and was able to reinstate the glycosuria by suggesting that he would again be upset by these people. This experiment was repeated four times with the same results.

With the above findings in mind, the results reported in two hypnotic experiments become less mysterious. Gigon, Aigner, and Brauch (1926) found that blood sugar tended to be reduced in four hypnotized diabetic patients following suggestions of relaxation and suggestions that the pancreas would secrete insulin and that blood and urine sugar would markedly decrease. Although the reduction in blood glucose in these cases may have been due to the suggestion that the pancreas would secrete insulin, it appears equally possible that it was a secondary effect of the suggestions of relaxation. Along similar lines, Stein (quoted by Dunbar, 1954, p. 291) reported that direct suggestions that blood sugar would decrease given to six hypnotized diabetic patients resulted in reduced blood sugar in 47 out of 56 attempts. Again, it appears possible that the reduced blood glucose in these cases was an indirect result of the suggestions of relaxation given during the hypnotic-induction procedure. Supporting evidence for this supposition was presented in a second experiment by the same investigator; although Stein used only one diabetic patient in this study, he found that an hypnotic-induction (apparently consisting of suggestions of quietude, relaxation, and drowsiness) resulted in a significant fall in blood glucose content *without* suggesting that the blood sugar would fall.

Is it possible to elevate the blood sugar level by suggesting to a non-diabetic hypnotic subject that he is ingesting sugar? Marcus and Sahlgren (1925) found no rise in blood glucose content when four deeply hypnotized nondiabetics were given a saccharin solution which they were told was a sugar solution. Similarly, Nielsen and Geert-Jorgensen (1928) found no elevation in the fasting blood sugar level when six excellent hypnotic subjects (non-diabetics) were given the suggestion that a glass of water contained large amounts of sugar. In contradistinction to the above, Povorinskij and Finne (1930) found an elevated blood sugar content in two excellent hypnotic subjects after inducing an hallucination of ingesting sugar and honey; however, an elevation in blood glucose could be demonstrated in one of these subjects following similar suggestions given during the waking state. The data presented in the report did not exclude the possibility that the hypnotic suggestions which induced an hallucination of ingesting sugar and honey served to arouse the subjects or to induce emotional excitement.

GASTRIC FUNCTIONS

The evidence indicates that stomach secretions, hunger contractions, and various other gastrointestinal functions can be influenced by appropriate suggestions given to hypnotic subjects. Ikemi (1959) demonstrated that suggestions given under a hypnotic treatment of eating a delicious meal resulted in an increase in free acid, total acidity, and quantity of gastric secretion in 34 out of 36 healthy young persons. In an earlier experiment, Heyer (1925) introduced a tube into the stomach of a deeply hypnotized subject and removed the contents. If no secretion occurred within ten minutes, the subject was given the suggestion that he was ingesting either meat broth, bread, or milk and the gastric secretions were collected at 5-minute intervals and examined for quantity, acidity, and proteolytic activity. Each of the suggested meals evoked a secretion of approximately six to ten cubic centimeters of gastric juice within ten to 15 minutes and the acidity and proteolytic activity appeared to vary with each food suggested. Delhougne and Hansen (1927) reported a similar study with one excellent hypnotic subject. After the subject was placed in deep hypnosis, the stomach and duodenal secretions were aspirated by means of a Rehfuss tube. Following this, the subject was given the suggestion that he was ingesting a meal which was rich in protein (Schnitzel), rich in fat (a biscuit thickly covered with butter), or rich in carbohydrate (chocolate and marchpane). Each of the suggested meals evoked secretions of acid, pepsin, and lipase from the stomach and of trypsin, lipase, and diastase from the pancreas. Although the authors did not analyze the data statistically, they conclude that the hallucinated meals were as effective as actual meals in eliciting *specific* secretions from the stomach and pancreas, e.g., the hallucinated protein meal supposedly induced a specific increase in the secretion of pepsin and trypsin, and the hallucinated fatty meal supposedly induced a specific increase in the secretion of lipase. This startling conclusion, however, appears to be erroneous; a statistical analysis indicates that the quantity of each of the enzymes found after the three hallucinated meals was not significantly different.

The above studies did not answer a crucial question: Was the hypnotic-induction procedure and the appearance of deep trance on the part of the subjects necessary to produce these effects? If the subjects had been asked to vividly imagine or to think about eating certain foods (without an hypnotic-induction) would they have shown similar pancreatic and gastric secretory activity? That such may have been the case is suggested by an earlier experiment reported by Luckhardt and Johnston (1924). These investigators also found that when a hypnotized subject was given suggestions of eating a fictitious meal, he showed an increase in the volume and acidity of the digestive secretions comparable to that found when actually eating a meal; however, in the control experiment, when the investigators merely talked to the subject about an appetizing meal, he showed similar gastric secretory activity. This finding is not unusual. Miller, Bergeim, Rehfuss, and Hawk (1920) reported that in some normal subjects the sound and thought alone of a frying steak gave rise to gastric secretory activity. Employing a subject with a gastric fistula, Wolf and Wolff (1947) demonstrated that during the mere discussion of eating a certain food the output of hydrochloric acid from the parietal cells was essentially the same as when actually ingesting this food. Similar effects have been demonstrated in other parts of the gastrointestinal tract. Bykov (1957) found that in patients with a gall bladder fistula (but otherwise physiologically normal) "the sight of and even the mere mention of food evoked contraction of the gall bladder" (p. 119). Bykov also studied a patient with a fistula of the pancreatic duct but otherwise healthy and with a normal digestive tract; one or two minutes after being drawn into conversation about savory foods, this patient (who was kept on a special diet which served to inhibit secretions) "showed against this inhibitory background abundant pancreatic secretions." (The above patients had *not* participated in experimental conditioning procedures.)

Scantlebury and Patterson (1940) demonstrated that suggestions of eating a fictitious meal were effective in inducing a temporary and at times a complete cessation of gastric hunger contractions in a hypnotic subject. Lewis and Sarbin (1943) repeated this experiment, employing the Carlson balloon-manometer method with eight subjects who had fasted prior to the experiment. The subjects were first given the Friedlander-Sarbin hypnotic-induction procedure and rated on depth of hypnosis. Whenever the subjects showed gastric hunger contractions, they were given the suggestion of eating a meal. The kymographic tracings showed that the suggestions were effective in inhibiting the hunger contractions in the majority of trials with the deeply hypnotized subjects, in some of the trials, with the moderately hypnotized subjects, and in none of the trials with subjects who were slightly hypnotized or not hypnotized. However, a comparable inhibition of hunger contractions could be demonstrated in the deeply hypnotized subjects by asking them to solve an arithmetic problem silently. No attempt was made to determine if hunger contractions could be inhibited in unhypnotized persons by asking them to vividly imagine eating a delicious meal.

Earlier studies which did not employ hypnotic procedures found comparable effects. For example, Carlson (1916, p. 152) found that, after four days of fasting, the sight and smell of food inhibited his hunger contractions. Since acid in contact with the gastric mucosa apparently acts reflexly to produce inhibition of gastric contractions (Carlson, 1916, pp. 175-176) and since the mere thought of appetizing food gives rise to a significant amount of hydrochloric acid secretion in some normal persons (Miller et al., 1920), it can be hypothesized that suggestions of eating a meal are effective in some hypnotized subjects and some unhypnotized subjects in inducing gastric acid secretions which act reflexly to inhibit the hunger movements.

In summary, the above studies on metabolic and gastrointestinal functions appear to indicate that blood sugar levels can be altered in diabetic patients by hypnotic or nonhypnotic procedures which alter the level of arousal, and gastric and pancreatic secretions can be influenced by suggestions or symbolic stimulation in both hypnotized and unhypnotized persons.

Cutaneous Functions

HERPETIC BLISTERS (COLD SORES)

Ullman (1947) reported that a patient (who had been previously cured of hysterical blindness) showed multiple herpetic blisters on the lower lip 25 hours after it was suggested to him while in hypnotic trance that he appeared rundown and debilitated, he felt as if he were catching cold, and fever blisters were forming on his lower lip. Heilig and Hoff (1928) had previously demonstrated a similar effect in an experiment with three neurotic women. Their procedure was as follows: After an hypnotic-induction procedure, an intense emotional reaction was elicited from each subject by suggesting an extremely unpleasant experience related to her previous life history. During the excitement, the experimenter stroked the subject's lower lip and suggested a feeling of itch such as she had experienced previously when a cold sore was forming. Within 48 hours after the termination of the experiment small blisters had appeared on the lower lip of each subject. This report also included the following data: at least two of the subjects had a history of recurrent herpes labialis following emotional arousal; determination of the opsonic index before and after the hypnotic experiment indicated that the subjects' physiological resistance was reduced after the experiment; herpetic blisters could not be induced when the hypnotic subjects were given direct suggestions that such blisters were forming without at the same time eliciting an emotional reaction.

The above studies can be placed in broader context by noting the following: (a) The herpes simplex virus appears to be ubiquitous and ready to produce illness whenever the normal balance between it and the host is disturbed not only by fever, allergic reactions, sunburn, and so forth, but also by emotional stress and by symbolic stimulation which has significance for the person (Sulzberger & Zardens, 1948). (b) Some persons show recurrent attacks of herpes simplex in the same localized area (Veress, 1936); in some cases the attacks appear to be closely related to emotional conflicts or to stimulation which tends to elevate the level of arousal (Blank & Brody, 1950; Schneck, 1947). These findings suggest that an hypnotic-induction procedure and specific suggestions of blister formation may not be necessary to induce herpetic blisters in appropriately predisposed persons. An experiment along the following lines is indicated: An experimental group consisting of persons with a history of herpes labialis should be given appropriate stimulation to induce emotional arousal *without* an hypnotic-procedure. A second experimental group consisting of persons who do not have a history of herpes should be placed in deep hypnosis and given specific suggestions of cold sore formation. It can be hypothesized that some of the un-'hypnotized subjects in the first group will show herpetic blisters within a day or so after the experiment. It would be of interest to determine if any of the deeply hypnotized subjects in the second group will show cold sores after the experiment.

LOCALIZED (NONHERPETIC) BLISTERS

Pattie (1941) reviewed 11 experiments which ostensibly demonstrated that localized blisters (excluding cold sores) can be evoked by direct suggestions given to good hypnotic subjects. A relatively well controlled experiment reported by Hadfield (1917) can be taken as the prototype of these investigations: After the subject was hypnotized, an assistant touched his arm while Hadfield gave continuous suggestions that a red-hot iron was being applied and that a blister would form in the burned area. The arm was then bound in a sealed bandage and the subject was watched continuously during the following 24 hours. At the end of this period the bandage was opened in the presence of three physicians and, on the designated area, the beginning of a blister was noted which gradually developed during the day to form a large bleb surrounded by an area of inflammation. Although the other experiments followed this general pattern, there are numerous variations: in some instances, the experimenter stated that a blister would form after a definite time interval and in other instances no time was specified; some subjects were instructed to awaken immediately after the suggestion of bulla formation and others were not given such instructions until it was determined if the blister had formed; although in most instances the blister formed in the area specified, in at least two instances (Jendrassik, 1888; Smirnoff, 1912) the bleb formed in another body area. Also, in at least two experiments (Rybalkin, 1890; von Krafft-Ebing, 1889; pp. 26-27, 58-59) the controls were not satisfactory; the subjects were not observed during the intervening period and it is possible that they may have deliberately injured the area.

Two additional documented cases have been reported since the publication of Pattie's (1941) review. Ullman's (1947) subject, mentioned in the preceding section of the present chapter, had previously been cured of hysterical blindness and had previously shown herpetic blisters after hypnotic stimulation. In an additional hypnotic session, the subject was induced to recall the battle in which he had recently participated and was given the suggestion that a small particle of molten shell fragment had glanced off the dorsum of his hand. At this point in the procedure, the experimenter brushed the hand with a small flat file to add emphasis to the suggestion. Pallor followed immediately in the circumscribed area approximately one centimeter in diameter; after 20 minutes a narrow red margin was evident about the area of pallor and after one hour the beginning of a blister was noticable. The subject was then dismissed and returned approximately four hours later; at this time a bleb about one centimeter in diameter was evident. (The subject was not observed during the intervening period.)

Borelli and Geertz (Borelli, 1953) also succeeded in inducing dermatological alterations which superficially resembled blister formation in a 27-year-old patient with neurodermatitis. During deep hypnosis a coin was placed on the normal skin of the hand and it was suggested that a blister would form within a day at the spot where the fictitious burn was occurring. The next day the patient showed a sharply circumscribed and elevated area at the designated spot which superficially resembled a blister but could be more appropriately described as dermographism.

With few if any exceptions, investigators reporting positive results emphasized that they selected excellent hypnotic subjects for their experiments. However, a number of workers using similar procedures with excellent hypnotic subjects reported negative results in all cases (Sarbin, 1956; Wells, 1944) or reported negative results with the majority of such subjects and positive results only in rare cases (Hadfield, 1920). The negative findings appear to indicate that appropriate suggestions given to deeply hypnotized persons may be necessary but by no means sufficient conditions for this phenomenon.

An additional factor which appears necessary is indicated by the following. The 13 persons who gave ostensibly positive results were not a cross-section of the normal population; prior to the experiment, one had been cured of hysterical blindness and one had been cured of hysterical aphonia; during the time of experiment, six were diagnosed as hysterical and one was being treated for shell-shock. At least five of these subjects had histories of localized skin reactions: one had a delicate skin and showed labile vasomotor reactions (Doswald & Kreibich, 1906, Case 1), a second had suffered from neurotic skin gangrene and had a history of wheals following emotional arousal (Doswald & Kreibich, 1906, Case 2), a third had a delicate skin plus dermographia of medium grade (Heller & Schultz, 1909), a fourth had suffered from hysterical ecchymoses (Schindler, 1927), and a fifth was afflicted with atopic dermatitis (Borelli, 1953). This suggests that the induction of localized blisters by suggestions may be possible only in a small group of persons with a unique physiological predisposition. What is the nature of this predisposition? The data summarized below suggest a tentative answer.

Blister formation and wheal formation apparently involve similar physiological and biochemical processes: the circular wheal of urticaria, the linear wheals of dermographism, and the blister resulting from a burn can be viewed as variations of the triple response of the skin to injury, consisting of the release of histamine or a histamine-like substance such as 5-hydroxytryptamine (serotonin) from the Mast cells, a local dilation of the minute vessels, an increase in permeability of the vessels, and a widespread arteriolar dilation (Lewis, 1927; Nilzén, 1947). Nearly every type of stimulus that produces whealing when applied to the skin will lead to blistering if rendered more intense, and blister formation appears to differ from wheal formation primarily in that the increase permeability of the vessel walls is of greater degree, the transuded fluid typically forms a pool in the superficial layers of the skin, and the epidermal layers are gradually forced asunder (Lewis, 1927). This close relationship between wheals and blisters appears to be significant because of the following:

In at least two of the successful hypnotic experiments (Borelli, 1953; Doswald & Kreibich, 1906, Case 2) the dermatological changes induced were much more similar to wheals than to blisters.

A critical reading of the other reports suggests that the histological findings were rarely so clear-cut as to definitely conclude that blisters and not wheals were produced.

Some unhypnotized persons show localized wheals when recalling former experiences in which such dermatological effects occurred.

Some unhypnotized persons show localized wheals after mild mechanical stimulation.

Moody (1946, 1948) presented two case studies of patients who developed localized wheals when recalling former experiences in which wheals occurred. The first patient had been previously hospitalized for sleepwalking with agressive behavior. On one occasion, during this earlier hospitalization, the patient's hands had been tied behind his back during sleep and wheals had formed in the traumatized area. At a later time, when recalling this experience after hexobarbital administration, wheals appeared on both forearms in the area which had previously been tied. On at least 30 occasions when recalling earlier experience of physical injury, the second patient (who was being treated for nervous breakdown) showed swelling, bruising, and bleeding in the body parts where the original injury presumably occurred; for instance, when re-

membering a former occasion when she had been struck across the
dorsum of both hands with a cutting whip, the patient showed wheals on
both hands in the respective areas. Along similar lines, Graff and Wallerstein (1954) reported that during a therapeutic interview a 27-year-old
sailor, who had a tattoo of a dagger on his arm, suddenly showed a
wheal reaction sharply limited to the outline of the dagger. The wheal
subsided after this session but reappeared again in the same way during
a subsequent interview. The authors interpreted the patient's free associations as indicating that the wheal had symbolic significance for the
patient. Brandt (1950) reported similar cases of patients showing sharply
localized wheal reactions which appeared to be closely related to symbolic stimulation.

Dermographism (that is, wheal formation in response to a single
moderately strong stroking of the skin) is not as uncommon as is generally assumed. Testing 84 apparently normal young men, Lewis (1927)
found a detectable swelling of the skin as a reaction to a single firm
stroke in 25 per cent and in 5 per cent a full wheal developed. Some
persons also show wheal formation at sites of mild pressure stimulation
such as around a wristwatch strap, a belt, or a collar. Graham and Wolf
(1950) reported an experimental study of 30 such persons who had a
history of urticaria and showed spontaneous wheals in areas of mild
pressure. All of these subjects also showed dermographism although in
some this was not apparent until stressful interviews had altered the
condition of the skin vessels. Skin temperature measurements and indirect measurements of the state of the minute vessels (reactive hyperemia threshold) indicated that the subjects were prone to respond with
vasodilation of both arterioles and minute vessels to numerous stimuli.
Since in all but one of the successful hypnotic experiments tactual
stimulation was employed to localize the pseudotrauma and since in
many of the experiments the stimulus object was a small piece of metal
and was either allowed to remain in contact with the skin or was
replaced by a bandage, it appears possible, as Weitzenhoffer (1953, p.
144) suggested, that similar physiological mechanisms may be responsible for the above types of urticaria factitia and for at least some cases
of the hypnotic production of localized blisters.

Kaneko and Takaishi (1963) presented data that appear relevant to
the above considerations. These investigators worked with four selected
patients suffering from chronic urticaria (hives) and who were good
hypnotic subjects. Two patients were of the opinion that heat was a
causative factor in producing their urticarial wheals, and the other two
believed that their wheals were produced by emotional conflicts. The
former two patients were exposed to a hypnotic-induction procedure and

then given suggestions that wheals would be produced by heat, and the latter two were exposed to an induction and then given suggestions intended to produce emotional conflict. Kaneko and Takaishi reported that wheal formations were apparently produced in all cases during or right after trance. It should be noted that Kaneko and Takaishi did not give suggestions intended to produce emotional conflict to a waking comparison group. As stated above, previous investigations (Brandt, 1950; Graff & Wallerstein, 1954; Graham & Wolf, 1950; Moody, 1946, 1948) showed that, irrespective of hypnosis, some patients suffering from urticaria manifest new urticarial wheals while discussing their emotional problems.

The above data suggest an experiment as follows: Persons with urticaria, or persons who show gross vasomotor alterations during seemingly slight changes in the stimulating situation or who show dermographism under normal conditions or during stress, should be given the following instructions *without* a preliminary hypnotic-induction procedure: "Try to visualize a blister (in a specified area) and tell yourself repeatedly that such a blister is forming." If the subjects are adequately motivated to comply with these odd instructions, it can be hypothesized that some will show dermatological changes related to vesiculation. A second experimental group consisting of persons who do *not* show signs of vasomotor lability should be given suggestions of blister formation after an hypnotic-induction procedure and when they appear to be in the trance state. It would be of interest to determine if these hypnotized subjects will show any cutaneous reactions which are involved in the formation of a blister.

WARTS

Since the genesis of warts appears to be causally related to virus activity and since present day methods of treating warts are "roundabout and nonspecific" (Pillsbury, Shelley, & Kligman, 1956, p. 690), reports indicating that appropriate suggestions given to a hypnotized person are singularly effective in curing these benign epitheliomas are of unique interest. Asher (1956) found that suggestions of wart disappearance given to 25 hypnotizable patients resulted, after four to 20 treatments, in a complete cure in 15, a marked decrease in the number of warts in four and no apparent change in six patients. In these cases the warts before treatment varied from two to 53 and were present from three months to six years. Eight unhypnotizable patients given similar suggestions showed no diminution in the number of warts; however, in these cases the treatment was discontinued after ten sessions. In a more extensive investigation, Ullman and Dudek (1960) attempted to relieve warts by hypnotic suggestions in 62 adults attending an outpatient clinic. At weekly intervals each patient was given suggestions of sleep and drowsiness followed by suggestions to determine the depth of hypnosis; when the patient was judged to be at the period of maximum hypnotic effect, he was told that the warts would begin to disappear. Of the 47 patients rated as poor hypnotic subjects, only two showed wart regression within a 4-week period. However, six of the 15 patients rated as good hypnotic subjects has been cured of multiple common warts (or, in one case, of a single common wart) within two weeks following the initiation of treatment; within a 4-week period, eight of the 15 showed wart involution. In these successful cases the mean duration of the warts prior to treatment was 19 months with a range of three weeks to six years.

The foregoing investigations are open to the criticism that the warts may have shown spontaneous involution within the same period of time if no hypnotic treatment had been given. One study, however, appears to have satisfactorily controlled this factor. After an hypnotic-induction procedure consisting of eye fixation and suggestions of relaxation, Sinclair-Gieben and Chalmers (1959) suggested to 14 patients (with common warts present bilaterally for at least six months) that the warts on *one* side of the body would disappear. Ten of the 14 patients showed adequate depth of hypnosis as indicated by compliance with a simple posthypnotic suggestion and by partial or complete amnesia. Within five weeks to three months, nine of these ten hypnotizable patients showed wart involution on the treated side while the warts on the control side remained unchanged. (In one patient the untreated side showed wart regression six weeks after the treated side had been cured.) No benefit was observed from this treatment in the four patients who were not able to attain adequate hypnotic depth.

Although the above studies indicate that suggestions or symbolic stimulation are effective in inducing wart involution in some subjects who are able to attain a deep hypnotic state, equally successful results have been reported for a variety of suggestive procedures which do not involve an hypnotic-induction or the trance state (Dudek, 1967). Grumach (1927) found that 16 of 18 patients with longstanding warts showed complete regression of these structures within one to four months after being given, at intervals of eight to 14 days, an intramuscular placebo injection (normal saline) in the upper arm while, at the same time, being told that they were receiving a new and powerful wart remedy. Allington (1934) followed-up 84 patients with longstanding warts treated with an intragluteal placebo injection (distilled water); 35 (or 42 per cent) were relieved of common warts after only one injection, four were cured after two injections, and one after three injections. Bloch (1927) reported comparable results with a somewhat different procedure. The patient was blindfolded and his hand was placed on a table containing an electric apparatus; although the electricity was started no current reached the patient. The warts were then painted with an innocuous dye, the blindfold was removed, and the patient, now confronted with the luridly colored warts, was told that the warts were dead and must not be washed until they had disappeared. Of 179 patients thus treated and adequately followed-up, 55 (or 31 per cent) showed wart involution after the first session and an additional 43 patients (or 24 per cent) showed wart involution after additional sessions extending over a period varying from one week to three months. Using similar procedures, Bonjour (1929), Sulzberger and Wolf (1934), and Vollmer (1946) reported success in a comparable percentage of cases with warts of from two to six years duration. In general, these suggestive procedures were more effective when the patient showed multiple warts rather than a single wart and when the warts were of the juvenile type rather than the common type; this type of treatment also tended to be more successful with recent lesions and with younger patients.

Would a similar percentage of patients have shown spontaneous remission of warts if they had not been treated in the specified period of time involved in the above experiments? Memmescheimer and Eisenlohr (1931) matched 70 patients treated by a suggestive procedure—painting the warts with methylene blue and suggesting their disappearance—with 70 patients with similar warts of similar duration not given any treatment. The results were as follows: at the end of one month, 11 of the treated patients showed wart resolution as compared to only two of the patients in the control group; at the end of three months, 14 of the treated patients were cured as compared to only five of the untreated; however, at the end of six months, 20 patients in the control group showed wart involution as compared to only 17 patients in the treated group. The conclusion suggested by this study, namely, that suggestive treatment may accelerate a spontaneous physiological process leading to wart involution, is supported by additional investigations summarized below.

Similar physiological processes have been demonstrated when warts heal spontaneously and when they are cured in apparent response to suggestions. Unna (quoted by Samek, 1931) observed histologically that during spontaneous remission the normal cutis surrounding the wart showed a distinctive reaction consisting of hyperemia and cell proliferation. Other workers (Allington, 1952; Biberstein, 1944; Sulzberger & Wolf, 1934; Vollmer, 1946) have also noted a distinct inflammatory reaction immediately before spontaneous healing or before wart disappearance in apparent response to suggestion or to chemical treatment. In histological studies of warts undergoing involution in a patient treated by a suggestive procedure, Samek (1931) demonstrated a specific inflammatory reaction in the dermis consisting of dilation of blood vessels, hyperemia, edema, and perivascular infiltration of leucocytes (especially lymphocytes). Concomitant with this infiammatory reaction, mitoses became less frequent in the germinative epidermis (stratum mucosum); with mitoses almost at a standstill, the prickle-cell layer became thin, a normal stratum granulosum reformed, and the degenerated cells flaked off.

After a careful review of the above and related studies, Allington (1952) concluded that "at times the balance between susceptibility and immunity in warts must be a delicate one [and] only a slight shift may be needed to cause their disappearance." Volmer (1946) had similarly concluded from an earlier review that a labile equilibrium must exist between the physiological processes which maintain the wart and those which cause wart involution and that appropriate suggestions or verbal stimulation may alter the equilibrium in the direction of wart resolution by causing hyperemia in the surrounding tissue. A number of earlier workers (Sulzberger & Wolf, 1934; Zwick, 1932) had also pointed to vasomotor changes as crucial factors in wart remission and Ullman (1959) presented data indicating that, when warts are treated by suggestion, an affective response is induced in the patient and the mechanism of healing may be dependent on local vascular alterations which accompany the emotional reaction. Since a number of investigations reviewed in an earlier section of this chapter suggest that localized vasodilation and localized vasoconstriction can be induced in *some* individuals by suggestions or symbolic stimulation—e.g., by asking the individual to recall former experiences in which such vasomotor alterations occurred (Menzies, 1941)—further investigations are required to determine the following: Are local vasomotor changes consistently present when wart resolution is occurring after suggestive treatment? If so, do such vasomotor effects accelerate a natural physiological process of wart remission? If treatment of warts by suggestive procedures relatively more successful in persons who show vasomotor lability, that is, in persons who respond with a greater than average degree of vasodilation or vasoconstriction to suggestions, or to symbolic stimulation, or to emotion-inducing stimulation?

ICHTHYOSIS

Mason (1952) reported that a 16-year-old patient with fishskin disease (congenital ichthyosiform erythrodermia of Brocq) showed marked improvement in his condition during an extended series of hypnotic treatment sessions in which direct suggestions were administered that his skin would improve first in one limb and then in another. (The limb-by-limb improvement apparently ruled out the possibility of spontaneous resolution.) In a follow-up period extending over four years, it was noted that the patient continued to manifest improvement in his condition without further treatment of any sort (Mason, 1955). At the termination of the four-year period, the patient was hypnotized again and given suggestions that his legs would show further improvement. This time the suggestions were not efficacious.

Wink (1961) presented comparable findings. Two sisters with congenital fishskin disease were exposed to a hypnotic-induction procedure at weekly intervals for eight weeks and given suggestions that specific affected skin areas would soon start to grow soft and smooth and the thick skin would flake off. The skin condition of both patients improved in some designated areas but not in others. At the same time, improvement was noted in some undesignated areas. In the next phase of the experiment the patients were exposed to a hypnotic induction at fortnightly intervals for two months, and given suggestions that all affected areas of the skin would improve. Wink stated that: "Attempts at the assessment of skin changes can never be accurate and may be misleading. . . . With these reservations, the improvement in these two cases in tabulated as follows": both patients manifested a general reduction in skin thickness ranging from 20 per cent to 75 per cent in various areas (with an average reduction of 48 per cent), and a reduction in the circumference of specific affected areas ranging from 0 per cent to 90 per cent (with an average reduction of 24 per cent).

Unfortunately, neither Mason nor Wink attempted to ascertain whether the suggestions of improvement were effective alone (i.e., with or without hypnosis) or whether variables included in the hypnotic-induction procedure also played a role. Further studies are needed to determine which of the many variables incorporated into hypnotic experimental treatments are instrumental and which irrelevant in alleviating fishskin disease. Further studies that attempt to delineate the intervening hormonal, vascular, or neuronal mechanisms involved would also be of great interest to both psychologists and physicians.

ALLERGIC SKIN RESPONSES

Fry, Mason, and Bruce-Pearson (1964) presented two studies concerning the effects of hypnosis on allergic cutaneous responses. In the first study, 18 hypnotizable subjects, selected as manifesting asthma and/or hay fever and as showing positive skin reactions to extracts of either pollen or house dust, were randomly divided into a control and an experimental group. Both groups were skin tested with four strengths of pollen or house dust on two occasions separated by a two-week interval. The experimental subjects, but not the controls, were exposed to a hypnotic-induction procedure three times during the intervening two weeks and given suggestions that they would not manifest skin reactions when tested again. Both groups showed a reduction in the size of the wheals on second testing. At the two lower strengths of allergen, but not at the two higher strengths, the hypnotic group manifested significantly smaller wheal responses than the controls. Although this study indicated that a hypnotic treatment is effective with selected patients in reducing allergic responses to low strengths of allergens, it does not help in understanding which of the many variables subsumed under the term *hypnosis* are instrumental in producing this effect. Were the suggestions not to react to the allergen effective alone (with or without hypnotic-induction) or did other factors, such as the following, also play a rule: selection of subjects as hypnotizable, suggestions intended to produce relaxation, suggestions that the subject was entering a hypnotic state or trance, etc.?

In the second study, Fry *et al.,* assigned 29 patients randomly to three groups. All groups were exposed to a hypnotic-induction on three occasions at weekly intervals and given suggestions as follows: to one group it was suggested that the right arm would not react to skin tests, to another group it was suggested that neither arm would react, and to the third group no suggestions were given. Bilateral tests for response to allergens were made immediately before the first and immediately after the final hypnotic session. In general, all three groups showed a reduction in the size of the wheals on both arms during the second skin test. Since a waking control group was not employed, it cannot be stated with certainty whether a reduction in response to the specific allergens used in this experiment would have occurred on second testing if the hypnotic-induction procedure was not used.

Black (1963a) also evaluated the effects of hypnosis on an allergic response. Twelve subjects, comprising the experimental group, were selected as meeting three criteria: they gave histories of psychosomatic disorders, some of which were allergic; they were trained hypnotic subjects; and it was thought likely that they would show inhibition of an allergic response when given appropriate suggestions. The subjects were first tested on one arm for response to the selected allergen. They were subsequently exposed to a hypnotic-induction, given suggestions for five minutes that they would not react to the allergen, and then skin tested on the alternate arm. Eight of the 12 subjects manifested reduced response to the allergen on second testing, as indicated by temperature measurements at the site of the injection and by an observable reduction in edema. A control group excluded the possibility that subjects show reduced response on second testing to the selected allergens used in this experiment. However, Black did not attempt to ascertain whether suggestions not to react to the selected allergens, given with or without hypnotic-induction, were sufficient to reduce the allergic response.

In a second experiment, Black (1963b) set out to determine whether hypnotic suggestions can inhibit the Prausnitz-Küstner reaction, that is, the production of local hypersensitiveness in a nonallergic person by the intradermal injection of serum from an allergic person. Fourteen subjects were selected as meeting two criteria: they were not allergic to horse serum, and they were capable of hypnotic trance. There were two experimental phases. In the first phase the subject was inoculated on the arm with serial dilutions of a human serum containing skin-sensitizing antibodies against a component of horse serum. Horse serum was then pricked into each injection site and the size of the resultant wheal was measured. The second phase was carried out after an intervening period of two weeks to several months. The procedure was the same as in the first phase with the exception that before assessing the subject's reaction to the horse serum, he was placed in a supine position, exposed to a hypnotic-induction, and given suggestions for five minutes that he would not react. In general, the subjects showed smaller wheals in response to the horse serum in the second part of the experiment. No attempt was made to ascertain whether waking control subjects would have manifested a similar reduction in the Prausnitz-Küstner reaction if they were placed in a supine position during the second session, whether suggestions not to react were necessary and sufficient to produce the observed effects, or whether other variables included in or confounded with the hypnotic experimental treatment also played a role. These criticisms were also applicable to a further study carried out along similar lines by the same investigators (Black, Humphrey, & Niven, 1963).

West, Kierland, and Litin (1961) studied the effects of hypnosis on the following abnormal vascular responses that are typically present in patients with allergic eczema (atopic dermatitis): the delayed blanch, the absent histamine flare, and white dermographism. The subjects were 14 patients hospitalized with severe allergic eczema and capable of deep hypnosis. The vascular responses were assayed first under a waking treatment, then under a hypnotic treatment, and then again under a waking treatment. The hypnotic experimental treatment included the following confounded variables: the patients were deeply hypnotized, made comfortable and relaxed by suggestions, given suggestions that their skin was well and would react normally, and given a description of the expected normal reactions. Vascular responses were essentially the same in the two waking sessions. Results obtained during the hypnotic session were: three of the 14 patients did not show a delayed blanch reaction, a flare in response to histamine was present in three of the four patients who did not previously show a flare, and white dermographism was unaltered. Most subjects reported subjective improvement during and immediately after the hypnotic session, stating that tenseness and itching were relieved. However, there was no correlation between subjective improvement and alteration in the objective vascular responses. No attempt was made in the study to ascertain whether the objective effects on the abnormal vascular responses were produced by the suggestion that the skin would react normally, by the suggestions of comfort and relaxation, or by these suggestions in interaction with other suggestions included in the hypnotic experimental treatment.

Ikemi and Nakagawa (1962) included a necessary comparison group that was lacking in the above studies, namely, a waking group given suggestions not to react. These investigators selected 13 subjects who manifested high allergic sensitivity to the leaves of two common poisonous trees found in Japan (the lacquer tree and the wax tree). The leaves of the chestnut tree were used as a control. One group of five subjects were exposed to a hypnotic-induction procedure and then given suggestions that they were being touched by the leaves of the chestnut tree while they were actually touched with the leaves of one of the allerygy-producing trees. Chesnut leaves were applied to the alternate arm while the subjects received the suggestion that they were being touched by the leaves from one of the allergy-producing trees. Eight subjects assigned to the waking treatment were blindfolded and given the same suggestions. All hypnotic subjects and all waking subjects showed slight to marked degree of dermatitis—for example, flushing, erythema, papules—when exposed to the control leaves and given the suggestion that they were being exposed to the allergy-producing leaves. Four of the five subjects under the hypnotic treatment and seven of the eight under the waking treatment did not manifest noticable allergic responses to the leaves of the allergy-producing trees when given the suggestion that they were being exposed to the leaves of the chestnut tree. In brief, the data presented by Ikemi and Nakagawa strongly indicated that the effective variables in eliciting an allergic response to an innocuous substance were direct suggestions that the innocuous substance was an allergic substance, the effective variables in inhibiting an allergic response to an allergen were direct suggestions that the allergic substance was an innocuous substance, and the many other variables incorporated into the hypnotic experimental treatment appeared to be irrelevant to producing these effects. Further studies are clearly needed to confirm these striking experimental results.

Asthma

Several investigators used tests of respiratory function to measure the effects of hypnosis on asthma objectively. Smith and Burns (1960) worked with 25 selected hypnotizable asthmatic children. Suggestions that immediate and progressive relief from asthma would occur were given in four hypnotic treatment sessions conducted at weekly intervals. No evidence of improvement was obtained on objective tests of respiratory function (tests of vital capacity and of forced expiratory volume). In a similar study, Edwards (1960) administered suggestions that asthma would gradually disappear in several hypnotic treatment sessions conducted with six severe asthmatics. A one-year follow-up showed that two patients were not affected by the hypnotic sessions, two failed to show objective improvements on tests of respiratory function although they reported subjective improvement, and two showed both objective and subjective improvement. Edwards appropriately pointed out that, since a waking control group was not used, no clear-cut conclusions can be deduced from these results.

White (1961) conducted an extended study with ten patients suffering from moderate to severe asthma. Each patient participated in from seven to ten hypnotic treatment sessions extending over a four to six month period, and was subsequently hypnotized at irregular intervals for a further period of six to eleven months. During the hypnotic sessions, easier breathing, lessening of tension and bronchospasm, and increase in self-confidence were repeatedly suggested to the patient. Vital capacity along with mean and peak expiratory flow rates were measured before and after each hypnotic session. The subjects also made their own subjective evaluation of whether their breathing was easier, unaltered, or worse. The most striking finding was the disparity between the objective effects of the hypnotic treatment and the subjective improvement reported by the subjects. Subjective improvement was reported in 58 per cent of the hypnotic sessions, whereas respiratory functioning was objectively improved in only 19 per cent of the sessions. The subjects stated that their condition was worse in only 6 per cent of the sessions, whereas the objective tests showed deterioration in 29 per cent. (In the remaining sessions there was no change subjectively or objectively.) White speculated that the frequent objective deterioration in respiratory function, if not due to chance, may have been due to the fact that the patients were in a semirecumbent position during the hypnotic sessions. (It appears likely that the semirecumbent position is accompanied by a fall in vital capacity due to redisposition of abdominal viscera.) However, this explanation is not entirely convincing since the patients were tested in the sitting position, two minutes after completion of the hypnotic session, when it appears possible that the effects of recumbency on vital capacity would have ceased.

Maher-Loughnan, MacDonald, Mason, and Fry (1962) assigned 55 asthmatic patients at random to a hypnotic and a control treatment. The 27 patients assigned to the hypnotic treatment were exposed to a hypnotic-induction procedure in ten sessions extending over a 6-month interval. During each hypnotic session, symptom-removal suggestions were administered and, whenever possible, the patients were taught autohypnotic methods of relaxation. The 28 patients assigned to the waking control group were given symptomatic bronchodilators and were seen at the same intervals and for the same length of time as the hypnotic group. The hypnotic treatment was associated with improvement in the asthmatic condition according to subjects' entries in diaries, but not according to objective measurements. After two months of treatment and extending up to the six months duration of the study, the hypnotic group reported a greater reduction in wheezing and in use of bronchodilators that the control group. With respect to objective measurements, both the hypnotic and the control group failed to show clear-cut changes in sputum or blood eosinophil counts, and in vital capacity, forced expiratory volume, and peak flow. Further investigations are needed along similar lines to ascertain whether the subjective improvement attributed to the hypnotic treatment is accompanied by any objectively measured physiological criteria of improvement. Further studies should also use an additional waking comparison group given suggestions of symptom removal, but not given the many other suggestions commonly subsumed under the term *hypnosis*.

Secretory Functions

SALIVATION

Bowles and Pronko (1949) and Hill (1949) presented data indicating that, under a hypnotic experimental treatment, suggested taste stimuli tended to affect salivary secretions in a similar manner as actual gustatory stimuli. For instance, as compared to the base-level salivary secretory response to drops of water placed on the tongue, subjects showed enhanced salivation when it was suggested that the water was sour or acid. Barber, Chauncey, and Winer (1964) set out to confirm and extend these findings, asking: Are suggestions to imagine vividly that water is sour or that an acidic solution is tasteless effective in elevating and depressing salivary secretions, respectively? Are such suggestions more effective when given under a hypnotic or a waking experimental treatment? Under counterbalanced hypnotic and waking treatments, 16 subjects were given suggestions to imagine vividly specified taste stimuli ("Disregard the actual taste of the solution we are using today, and vividly imagine that [water is sour or that a sour solution is tasteless]"). The parotid gland salivary response to water was enhanced by the suggestion that the water was sour whereas the response to an acidic solution was depressed by the suggestion that the solution was tasteless, and the effects of suggestions on salivation did not differ significantly when given with and without a preceding hypnotic-induction procedure.

URINE SECRETION

To assess the effects of "hypnotically hallucinated water ingestion" on urine flow, Hulet, Shapiro, Schwarcz, and Smith (1963) selected nine hypnotizable subjects (five females from a psychiatric ward and four males from a surgical ward). After 12-15 hours of fluid restriction the subjects were put to bed for one hour and then the bladder was catheterized and the catheter was left in place. After an additional 1½-hour rest period in bed, the bladder was emptied and two or more 20-minute urine samples were collected (base-level measurements). The subject was next placed in a deep hypnotic trance for 20 minutes, an empty glass was then placed in his hand, and satiation of thirst was suggested repeatedly while the subejct "drank" for a period of 10 minutes. Following this, the bladder was emptied and urine samples were collected every 15 minutes during an experimental period extending over 45-75 minutes. Four of the five females, but none of the males, manifested an increase in urine osmotic concentration during the experimental period as compared to the base-level period. No significant increase in sodium excretion, sodium excretion fraction, or inulin clearance (a measure of filtration rate) was observed in any instance. No attempt was made to ascertain which of the many variables incorporated into the hypnotic experimental treatment were effective in producing water diuresis in the female subjects. When urine samples were collected during the experimental period the subjects had been lying down for at least 3.5 hours. It may be that lying quietly for an extended period of time may itself produce water diuresis. Best and Taylor (1950) point out that: "the urine volume is less in the standing position than in recumbency; this is due chiefly to the concentration of plasma protein which occurs in the former position" (p. 440). Further studies are needed to ascertain whether the water diuresis was due to: the long-maintained recumbent position, the suggestions of water ingestion, or one or more of the many other variables incorporated into the hypnotic experimental treatment.

Corson, Corson, Rosen, Reese, and Dykman (1960) had previously conducted an experiment similar to that of Hulet et al. However, the findings obtained by Corson and co-workers were presented only in abstract form and are thus difficult to evaluate. Corson et al. stated simply that "hypnotic suggestions of drinking water was made to hydropenic subjects. This often led to diuresis. In most cases, the response did not have the characteristics of a water diuresis. The urine osmolarity did not decrease: $^{U}N_a$, and $^{U}C_l$, and ^{u}K often increased."

Cold-Stress

Reifler (1964) used five trained hypnotic subjects in an experiment designed to evaluate the effects of hypnosis on response to a cold-stress situation. The subjects were placed in a thermal chamber at 40 degrees Fahrenheit for one hour under counterbalanced hypnotic and waking experimental treatments. Under the hypnotic treatment, but not under the waking treatment, suggestions were administered "related to techniques which the subject might utilize to increase his feelings of comfort." Under both treatments the subjects showed falling skin and rectal temperatures during the hour in the cold chamber. However, the subjects showed markedly reduced shivering, lower levels of skin conductance, and slower heart rate under the hypnotic treatment than under the waking treatment. It was not determined whether suggestions "related to techniques which the subject might utilize to increase his feelings of comfort" were alone sufficient (with or without hypnotic-induction) to reduce shivering, etc., or whether other variables incorporated into the hypnotic treatment also played a role.

Inhibition and Elicitation of
Narcotic Drug Effects

Ludwig and Lyle (1964) attempted to counteract the physiological effects or morphine by hypnotic suggestions. Five hospitalized patients, who were being treated for narcotic addiction, were first exposed to a hypnotic-induction procedure and then given 15 milligrams of morphine. Next, it was suggested to the subject that he had received only sugar water and that, after awakening, all of the effects of the shot would leave and he would feel perfectly normal. Although three of the five subjects stated after awakening that they felt normal, the attempt to reverse the physiological effects of morphine was unsuccessful; systolic blood pressure, pulse rate, and pupillary constriction were not significantly different prior to and after the suggestions to feel normal.

In another phase of the same investigation Ludwig and Lyle set out to ascertain whether suggestions given with and without a preceding hypnotic-induction procedure are effective in reproducing the behavioral and physiological effects produced by a narcotic drug and by abrupt narcotic withdrawal. The experimental subjects, 11 hospitalized postaddicts, were exposed to a hypnotic-induction and then given the suggestion that they had received a shot of their addicting drug. In a later session the same subjects were again exposed to a hypnotic-induction procedure and given the suggestion that they were going back to a previous time when they were experiencing sudden withdrawal from the drug and that they would again experience all of the withdrawal symptoms. In a subsequent session the same subjects were asked under a "waking-acting" treatment to act as if they had just received the narcotic drug and, later, to act as if they were experiencing withdrawal symptoms. Another group of 5 postaddicts ("faking" group) were first instructed to simulate hypnosis and were then given suggestions that they had received the addicting drug and, subsequently, were given suggestions of experiencing withdrawal symptoms. The experimental subjects behaved as if they had received a narcotic and also as if they were experiencing abstinence symptoms more convincingly under the hypnotic treatment that under the waking-acting treatment. Furthermore, the faking group did not perform as realistically as the experimental group had performed under the hypnotic treatment. When given the suggestion that they had received a narcotic, some subjects under the hypnotic treatment but no subjects under the waking-acting or faking treatments showed flushing, gagging, vomiting, mouth dryness, or slurred speech. When reexperiencing of the narcotic withdrawal syndrome was suggested, some subjects under the hypnotic treatment, but no subjects under the waking-acting or faking treatments, cried, hiccuped, yawned, and vomited. However, certain aspects of the narcotic abstinence syndrome, for example, gooseflesh, piloerection, diarrhea, and bowel incontinence, were not observed in any instance.

Ludwig and Lyle pointed out that they were aware during the experiment as to which subjects were actually hypnotized and which were faking or acting and that it would have been preferable if a blind condition had been used. They also noted that they may have conveyed "a bias to perform in an inferior manner" to the faking group and to the experimental group under the waking-acting treatment. Further studies are needed to exclude the possibility that it was these variables which produced the differences in performance.

Emotional Responses

A relatively large number of investigators have recently attempted to delineate the physiological concomitants of hypnotically-induced emotions.

Persky and collaborators reported that suggestions intended to produce anxiety, given under a hypnotic experimental treatment, were effective in one study (Persky, Grosz, Norton, & McMurtry, 1959) but not in another (Levitt, den Breeijen, & Persky, 1960) in producing a physiological effect commonly observed during anxiety or stress, namely, increased concentration of plasma hydrocortisone. These discrepant results were explained as due to differences in the preanxiety levels of hydrocortisone. The degree of increase in the plasma hydrocortisone level with stress appears to be negatively related to the pre-stress levels. In the first experiment the pre-anxiety level of hydrocortisone was low whereas in the second experiment it was relatively high.

Weller, Linder, Nuland, and Kline (1961) reported that hypnotic suggestions intended to produce anxiety, anger, and excitement failed to affect blood glucose levels in diabetic patients and in normal subjects. Dudley, Holmes, Martin, and Ripley (1964) found that hypnotic suggestions of deep relaxation and depression were associated with decreased respiratory ventilation and oxygen consumption whereas hypnotic suggestions of exercise, anger, and anxiety or pain were associated with elevated ventilation and oxygen consumption. Martin and Grosz (1964) measured muscle action potentials, heart rate, and palmar resistance when it was suggested to three subjects, who had received a hypnotic-induction, that they were becoming relaxed, anxious, and depressed. In general, physiological reactivity was highest during suggested anxiety and lowest during suggested relaxation. Hirose, Hirayama, and Ikemi (1961) presented data indicating that suggestions of anxiety and fear given under a hypnotic treatment produced a significant reduction in liver blood flow (as measured indirectly by the disappearance rate of colloidal radiogold). Graham and co-workers (Graham, Kabler, & Graham, 1962; Graham, Stern, & Winokur, 1958; Stern, Winokur, Graham, & Graham, 1961) demonstrated that specific attitudes, suggested under a hypnotic treatment, produced specific physiological effects. For instance, suggestions that the subject felt that he was being treated unjustly but could do nothing about it produced a rise in skin temperature but very little rise in blood pressure; whereas suggestions that he felt as if he had to be on guard against bodily assault produced a rise in blood pressure, but not in skin temperature.

It cannot be determined from the above investigations whether the suggestions intended to induce emotions were the only instrumental variables in producing the observed physiological effects or whether other variables incorporated into the hypnotic treatment also played a role. Several experiments that provide a tentative answer to this question are summarized next.

Vanderhoof and Clancy (1962) asked five selected hypnotizable subjects to specify an experience that they found stressful and emotional. The subjects were then asked to recall the emotional experiences under noncounterbalanced hypnotic and waking treatments, while blood flow through a limb was measured continuously by a venous occlusion plethysmograph. In general, blood flow was elevated during recall of the emotional experiences under both hypnotic and waking treatments, with a greater increase occurring under the first (hypnotic) treatment in three of the five subjects.

Kehoe and Ironside (1963) measured the secretory rate of gastric acid in seven subjects under noncounterbalanced hypnotic and waking treatments. Under both treatments, the subjects were first asked to report their ongoing thoughts and imagery and their dominant emotional states and, subsequently, were given suggestions to experience a specified emotion. After the experiment was completed, eight judges studied the subject's tape-recorded verbalizations and, using the method of paired comparisons, succeeded in rating reliably several emotional states. Significant correlations were obtained between the secretory rate of total gastric acid and the dominant emotional states, the secretory rate being highest with anger and lowest with helplessness-hopelessness. Comparable correlations were obtained between gastric secretory rate and emotional states under both the hypnotic and the waking treatments.

Damaser, Shor, and Orne (1963) suggested fear, calmness, happiness, and depression to eight trained hypnotic subjects under counterbalanced hypnotic and waking treatments. A second group, comprised of nine poor hypnotic subjects, was given the same emotion-inducing suggestions under a faking-hypnosis treatment. Consistent alterations in heart rate, forehead muscle activity, and palmar skin potential were observed in response to the suggested emotions under the hypnotic treatment, with fear tending to produce the highest and calmness the lowest activity on the physiological measures. However, very similar physiological responses were observed when the good hypnotic subjects were asked to produce the emotion under the waking treatment and also when the faking subjects were asked to simulate the emotion.

In summary, the experiments reviewed in this section indicate that suggestions designed to evoke emotional responses are at times effective in producing alterations in heart rate, skin conductance, respiration, gastric secretions and other physiological variables. Although suggestions to manifest the emotions are clearly instrumental variables in producing these effects, it remains to be demonstrated that other variables incorporated into hypnotic experimental treatments also play an important role.

Physiological Correlates of The Hypnotic State Per Se

The studies reviewed above indicate the general conclusion that many if not all of the *suggested* physiological effects that can be produced in some subjects during hypnosis can also be produced in some subjects without hypnosis. The experiments reviewed below indicate that, when suggestions that might produce physiological changes are *not* administered, it is very difficult if not impossible to find a physiological index that can clearly distinguish the subject who is in a hypnotic state from the subject who is in a waking state.

An extensive number of experiments have been designed to determine if hypnosis *per se* (without suggestions for physiological changes) is characterized by an elevated or depressed metabolic rate, heart rate, blood pressure, skin conductance, respiratory rate, digital blood volume, etc. All of these investigations lead to a similar conclusion: Physiological functions vary in the same way during hypnosis as they do during waking behavior. Taking energy expenditure as the example, the evidence indicates that metabolic rate may be elevated, may be depressed, or may not be significantly altered during the hypnotic state: Grafe and Mayer (1923) found that hypnotized subjects tended to show an elevated metabolic rate: von Eiff (1950) found that 16 subjects showed an average depression of 7 per cent in basal metabolic rate during hypnosis; and Whitehorn, Lundhold, Fox, and Benedict (1932) reported that oxygen consumption was not significantly affected by hypnosis. Since the metabolic rate is elevated during emotional arousal and is depressed during relaxation and sleep (Best & Taylor, 1950, p. 622), these results are only superficially contradictory: Experimenters finding that hypnosis depresses metabolism (von Eiff, 1950) had instructed their subjects to become relaxed, drowsy, and sleepy and had not given additional suggestions that could lead to arousal; investigators reported that the hypnotic states does not affect metabolism (Whitehorn et al., 1932) had trained their subjects over a period of days to insure maximal relaxation when the metabolic rate was determined during the control experiment; experimenters finding that heat production was elevated during hypnosis (Grafe & Mayer, 1923) had activated the subjects by suggesting various emotional experiences.

Investigations designed to determine if hypnosis is characterized by an elevated or depressed level of skin conductance have produced comparable results; during the hypnotic trance subjects may show an elevation, a slight decrease, or no significant change in palmar conductance (Barber & Coules, 1959; Davis & Kantor, 1935; Estabrooks, 1930; Levine, 1930). Since an elevated conductance level generally indicates an elevated activation level and a low level of conductance generally indicates a low level of arousal (Duffy, 1957, 1962; Woodworth & Schlosberg, 1954), these results are in agreement as follows: Hypnotic subjects show an elevated level of palmar conductance when they *carry out* suggestions which involve effort or activity (Barber & Coules, 1959; Davis & Kantor, 1935). When given suggestions of relaxation and drowsiness, subjects participating in hypnotic experiments may show a decrease or no significant change in palmar conductance; if the subject accepts the suggestion literally and relaxes, he shows a fall in conductance (David & Kantor, 1935; Estabrooks, 1930; Levine, 1930); if the subject is aware that suggestions of drowsiness and relaxation are not meant to be taken literally, i.e., if he has learned from previous participation in hypnotic experiments that to carry out subsequent suggestions properly he must remain alert, he generally shows no significant change in conductance (Barber & Coules, 1959). Investigations along similar lines which support the general conclusion that the hypnotized person cannot be clearly differentiated from the normal person by changes in heart rate, respiratory rate, blood pressure, digital blood volume, oral temperature, etc. have been reviewed by Gorton (1949) Weitzenhoffer (1953), Sarbin (1956), Crasilneck and Hall (1959), Levitt and Brady (1963), Barber (1965c), Jana (1965a, 1965b, 1967), and Timney and Barber (1969).

Some years ago it seemed that the electroencephalograph would prove to be a valuable tool for determining when a person was or was not hypnotized. This hope has not been realized. Extensive work in this area, reviewed by Weitzenhoffer (1953) and Chertok and Kramarz (1959), has demonstrated that in the great majority of instances the hypnotized person continues to show his characteristic waking pattern on the EEG. However, if the experimenter makes it clear to the subject that he should actually sleep—for example, by not disturbing the subject after instructing him to sleep – some subjects participating in hypnotic experiments show delta activity on the EEG, indicating that they have literally gone to sleep (Barker & Burgwin, 1948; Schwarz et al., 1955), and others show "periods of brief flattening out of the record . . . sometimes accompanied by infrequent isolated theta rhythms," indicating that they have gone into a light sleep (Chertok & Kramarz, 1959, p. 233). However, when the subject is once more stimulated verbally by the hypnotist, he again shows his characteristic waking pattern on the EEG. In brief, studies employing the EEG indicate that the hypnotized person remains normally awake until it is made clear that he should literally go to sleep and is then permitted to sleep.

Lovett Doust (1953) and Ravitz (1951, 1959) proposed two additional physiological indices of the hypnotic state. Employing three hysterics and one psychopath as subjects, Lovett Doust found that the induction of hypnosis was consistently accompanied by a significant fall in arterial oxygen saturation levels as measured by discontinuous spectroscopic oximetry at the fingernail fold. However, the term induction of hypnosis, as used in this report, does *not* imply that the subjects carried out one or more of the classical hypnotic behaviors, e.g., limb rigidities, negative or positive hallucinations. On the contrary, by this term the author refers to no more than the following: After being given suggestions of drowsiness, lethargy, and sleep, the subjects appeared passive and lethargic. Since a person who appears passive and lethargic is not necessarily hypnotized (that is, does not necessarily carry out any of the classical hypnotic behaviors) and since a person who carries out all of the classical hypnotic behaviors does not necessarily appear drowsy or passive (Barber, 1960a; Barber & Coules, 1959; Wells, 1924), Lovett Doust's findings are open to the following interpretation: A relative anoxemia is found during drowsiness or passivity and is not necessarily found when a person is in the hypnotic state, i.e., when he carries out the classical hypnotic behaviors. Supporting evidence for this interpretation is presented in a previous study by the same investigator (Lovett Doust & Schneider, 1952) which demonstrated a similar fall in oximetric values during sleep.

Measuring standing potentials between the forehead and the palm of the hand, Ravitz (1951, 1959) found that a hypnotic-induction procedure was accompanied by either a gradual increase or decrease in mean potential and "the trance state itself, following induction" was typically characterized by a voltage decrease and by an increased regularity of the direct current (DC) tracings. However, additional data presented in the reports suggest that a decrease in voltage and an increased regularity of the DC tracings may be present whenever a person is relaxed and shows a low arousal level. For example, Ravitz noted that a decrease in voltage and an increase in regularity of the tracings are found during sleep and that increased voltage and decreased regularity are found during changes in energy level, excitability, loquaciousness, grief, anxiety, and so forth.

The above investigations and other speculations concerning the neurophysiological correlates of hypnosis (Arnold, 1959; Robert, 1960; West, 1960) appear to be based on the following implicit assumptions: When a person carries out the type of behavior which has been historically associated with the term *hypnosis* he is in an altered state from his normal self, specifically, in a trance state or an hypnotic state. This altered state is such as to include a distinct and consistent type of physiological functioning which is rarely is ever present when a person is not carrying out hypnotic behavior. Although these assumptions are by no means limited to recent investigations (they are present in many if not all theories of hypnotism since the days of Mesmer), the evidence summarized below suggests that they are open to question.

Hypnotic Behavior Without an Hypnotic-Induction Procedure

Since subjects participating in hypnotic experiments are almost always given an hypnotic-induction consisting of suggestions of relaxation, drowsiness, and sleep, and since such a procedure is generally effective in inducing an appearance of lethargy or trance, it often seems as if hypnotic behavior is a function of, or closely related to, the trance state. However, in a pioneering study, Wells (1924) demonstrated that direct commands (e.g., "Your arm is insensitive to pain," "You cannot speak your name"), repeated emphatically for a few seconds, were sufficient to elicit anesthesia, amnesia for name, limb rigidity, hallucinatory pain, total amnesia, automatic writing, and posthypnotic behavior in a large proportion of male college students. Wells insisted that his subjects did not appear relaxed, drowsy, or lethargic and that he obtained results more quickly and with a larger proportion of subjects by such a direct procedure than by an hypnotic induction procedure designed to induce trance.

Wells' results were confirmed in a series of subsequent studies (reviewed in Chapter VII). For instance, in one study (Barber, 1960a) a female student research assistant (untrained as a hypnotist) gave 236 students at a girl's college direct suggestions (each suggestion requiring either 30 or 45 seconds) of body immobility—"Your body is heavy, rigid, solid; it's impossible for you to stand up; try, you can't,"—arm heaviness, arm levitation, hand rigidity, inability to say name, hallucination of thirst, selective amnesia, and post-hypnotic behavior. Although an hypnotic-induction procedure was not employed, 49 subjects (21 per cent) immediately carried out at least six of the eight suggestions and a total of 109 subjects (46 per cent) carried out at least half of the suggestions. The postexperimental reports of these subjects were indistinguishable from the reports of persons who are said to be hypnotized, e.g., "I just couldn't get up from the chair," "I was amazed when I couldn't speak my name," "I felt I was dying from thirst." In another study (Barber, 1960a, 1960b) the results of such a direct procedure were compared with the results of a formal hypnotic-induction procedure. In the first part of this experiment 70 attendants, nurses, and clerical workers at a state hospital (who agreed to participate in an experiment on imagination) were given a series of suggestions (each suggestion requiring 30 seconds) appropriate to induce arm rigidity, arm levitation, limb heaviness, limb anesthesia, hallucinations of thirst, heat, and cold, eye catalepsy, and hypnotic dream. Similar results were obtained as in the above study; 20 subjects (29 per cent) immediatedly carried out at least seven of the nine suggestions and a total of 34 subjects (49 per cent) carried out at least five of the suggestions. In the second part of this experiment the same subjects were given an hypnotic-induction procedure (consisting of suggestions of relaxation, drowsiness and sleep) and then given the suggestions of arm rigidity, arm levitation, limb anesthesia, etc., as in the preceding experiment. Although the subjects now appeared to be in trance (and stated, after the experiment, that they had "felt hypnotized") a high correlation (r=.84) was obtained between scores in the two session; in general, subjects who carried out one or two suggestions in the first part of the experiment carried out the same one or two suggestions after the hypnotic-induction procedure and subjects who responded positively to all of the suggestions in the second part of the experiment had also carried out all of the suggestions without the hypnotic-induction procedure.

Related to the above are the results of other investigations (Barber 1958a; Fisher, 1954) which indicate the following:

If subjects participating in hypnosis experiments show lethargy, drowsiness, or other signs of trance, these characteristics can be readily removed and the good subject will continue to carry out the hypnotic performances if instructed: "Be perfectly awake. Come out of 'trance' but continue to obey my commands."

Many if not all good hypnotic subjects carry out all suggestions given during the posthypnotic period, i.e., after they are told to wake up, as long as they believe that their relationship with the operator remains that of subject and hypnotist.

In brief: Investigations which propose to find the physiological correlates of hypnosis uncritically assume that hypnotic behavior is a function of the trance state; this assumption is open to question. Appropriately predisposed persons do not need an hypnotic-induction procedure and need not appear to be in trance to carry out many if not all of the behaviors which have been historically associated with the term *hypnosis*.

Summary and Conclusions

The investigations cited indicate that a wide variety of physiological effects can be elicited by suggestions administered under a hypnotic experimental treatment. Allergic responses can be inhibited, physiological reactions to cold-stress can be minimized, labor contractions can apparently be induced and inhibited in some women at term, some features of the narcotic withdrawal syndrome and some narcoticlike drug effects can be produced in postaddicts, water diuresis can be elicited in some hydropenic female subjects, ichthyosis can be mitigated, and wheals can be produced in patients suffering from urticaria.

However, in most instances, the experimental treatment whose consequences were under investigation (hypnosis) incorporated many variables whose separate contributions were not assessed. In the majority of investigations no attempt was made to evaluate the relative contributions of suggestions that certain physiological effects were forthcoming, instructions intended to produce positive motivation to respond to suggestions, suggestions of relaxation, and suggestions that the subject was entering a deep trance or a state of hypnosis. Further, no attempt was made to ascertain the role of such variables as the practice received by the subject in the preceding training sessions, the eyes-closed recumbent position adopted by the subject during the hypnotic session, and the bias introduced into the experiment by variations in the tone of voice in which the suggestions were administered to the subjects (Barber, 1961, 1962, 1967; Barber & Calverley, 1963a, 1964a, 1964b; Barber & Hahn, 1962).

In a few investigations an attempt was made to isolate the effects of some of the many variables confounded with the hypnotic experimental treatment, namely, the variable comprised of direct or indirect suggestions intended to elicit behaviors which would give rise to the desired physiological effects. In most instances it was found that the direct or indirect suggestions, given under either hypnotic or waking treatments, were sufficient to produce the physiological manifestations. Heart acceleration and heart deceleration were observed when both hypnotic and control subjects received direct suggestions to increase and then to decrease their heart rate. Direct suggestions to try not to see red or green or to try to respond as if color-blind, given to awake subjects, were sufficient to produce some responses to the Ishihara test which resemble those given by congenitally color-blind individuals. Direct suggestions to try not to hear were sufficient to produce partial or total subjective deafness in the majority of hypnotic and awake subjects. Suggestions to experience specified emotions, given to either hypnotic or awake subjects, were sufficient to produce various autonomic changes generally associated with emotions. Irrespective of the presence or absence of hypnotic-induction, suggestions to imagine pleasant scenes and then to open the eyes and keep the frame of mind developed during imagining were sufficient to improve visual acuity in myopic subjects. Suggestions to imagine that a sour solution was tasteless or that water was sour were sufficient to depress and enhance salivary secretion rate, respectively, in both hypnotic and awake subjects. Suggestions to try to imagine painful stimulation, given to hypnotic subjects and to awake subjects, were sufficient to elicit some autonomic effects which are commonly observed during painful stimulation. Suggestions to try to see objects not present, given to hypnotic and awake subjects, were sufficient to elicit apparent visual hallucinations. Suggestions given to hypnotic and awake subjects that they were being exposed to an allergy-producing substance (when they were actually exposed to an innocuous substance) were sufficient to produce allergic dermatitis. Suggestions given to hypnotic and awake subjects that they were being stimulated by an innocuous substance (when they were actually stimulated by an allergen) were sufficient to inhibit an allergic response.

In brief, a wide variety of physiological functions can be influenced by directly or indirectly suggesting to either hypnotic or awake subjects that certain physiological effects are forthcoming. Whether other variables commonly incorporated into hypnotic experimental treatments also play a role in producing these functional alterations remains to be determined. Also to be determined are the hormonal, vascular, and neuronal mechanisms which intervene in the production of these physiological manifestations.

The data reviewed in this chapter also indicate the following five supplementary conclusions:

A number of physiological effects which have been considered as peculiar to the hypnotic state appear to be *relatively commonplace performances;* e.g., although suggestions of eating a delicious meal are at times effective in evoking gastric and pancreatic secretions and in inhibiting gastric hunger contractions in some deeply hypnotized subjects, it is not uncommon for normal persons to show similar gastrointestinal effects when they visualize the ingestion of savory food.

A group of so-called hypnotic phenomena — production of localized blisters, cure of warts, alteration of blood glucose levels, production of cardiac block — can apparently be elicited with or without an hypnotic-induction *in only a small number of individuals who possess a specific lability of the physiological systems involved.*

An extensive series of experiments has failed to find a physiological index which differentiates the hypnotic state *per se* from the waking state.

A series of experiments comparing the results of an hypnotic induction procedure with the results of a direct suggestive procedure indicate that appropriately predisposed persons do not need an hypnotic-induction and need not appear to be in the trance state to carry out the typical behaviors which have been historically associated with the word *hypnosis*.

Further investigations into the nature of hypnosis might well bypass the concepts of hypnotic-induction and trance state and focus on biographical, biological or psychosomatic, and situational factors which may account for certain individuals responding to suggestions or symbolic stimulation from another person with so-called hypnotic behavior, whether primarily motor responses (e.g., limb rigidity, eye catalepsy) or primarily physiological responses (e.g., tachycardia, wart involution).

References

Allington, H. V. Sulpharsphenamine in the treatment of warts. *Arch Dermatol. Syphilol.*, 1934, *29*, 687-690.

Allington, H. V. Review of psychotherapy of warts. *Arch. Dermatol. Syphilol.*, 1952, *66*, 316-326.

Arnold, M. B. Brain function in hypnosis. *Int. J. Clin. Exp. Hypn.*, 1959, *7*, 109-119.

Aschan, G., Finer, B. L., and Hagbarth, K. E. The influence of hypnotic suggestion on vestibular nystagmus. *Acta Oto-Laryng.*, 1962, *55*, 97-110.

Asher, R. Respectable hypnosis. *Brit. Med. J.*, 1956, *1*, 309-313.

Barber, T. X. Hypnosis as perceptual-cognitive restructuring: II. "Post"-hypnotic behavior. *J. Clin. Exp. Hypn.*, 1958, *6*, 10-20 (a)

Barber, T. X. Hypnosis as perceptual-cognitive restructuring: IV. "Negative hallucinations". *J. Psychol.*, 1958, *46*, 187-201. (b)

Barber, T. X. The afterimages of "hallucinated" and "imagined" colors. *J. Abnorm. Soc. Psychol.*, 1959, *59*, 136-139.

Barber, T. X. The necessary and sufficient conditions for hypnotic behavior. *Amer. J. Clin. Hypn.*, 1960, *3*, 31-42. (a)

Barber, T. X. The reality of hynotic behavior and the fiction of "hypnosis". Paper presented at American Psychological Association, Annual Meeting, Chicago, September 1960. (b)

Barber, T. X. Antisocial and criminal acts induced by "hypnosis": A review of experimental and clinical findings. *Arch. Gen. Psychiat.*, 1961, *5*, 301-312.

Barber, T. X. Experimental controls and the phenomena of "hypnosis": A critique of hypnotic research methodology. *J. Nerv. Ment. Dis.*, 1962, *134*, 493-505.

Barber, T. X. "Hypnosis" as a causal variable in present-day psychology: A critical analysis. *Psychol. Rep.*, 1964, *14*, 839-842. (a)

Barber, T. X. Hypnotically hallucinated colors and their negative afterimages. *Amer. J. Psychol.*, 1964, *77*, 313-318. (b)

Barber, T. X. Hypnotizability, suggestibility, and personality: V. A critical review of research findings. *Psychol. Rep.*, 1964, *14*, (Monogr. Suppl. 3-V14), 299-320. (c)

Barber, T. X. Toward a theory of "hypnotic" behavior: Positive visual and auditory hallucinations. *Psychol. Rec.*, 1964, *14*, 197-210. (d)

Barber, T. X. Experimental analysis of "hypnotic" behavior: A review of recent empirical findings. *J. Abnorm. Psychol.*, 1965, *70*, 132-154. (a)

Barber, T. X. Effects of "hypnosis" on learning and recall: A methodological critique. *J. Clin. Psychol.*, 1965, *21*, 19-25. (b)

Barber, T. X. Physiological indices of "neutral hypnosis": A critical evaluation. Harding, Mass.: Medfield Foundation, 1965. (Mimeo) (c)

Barber, T. X. Effects of "hypnosis" and suggestions on strength and endurance: A critical review of research studies. *Brit. J. Soc. Clin. Psychol.*, 1966, *5*, 42-50.

Barber, T. X. "Hypnotic" phenomena: A critique of experimental methods. In J. E. Gordon (Ed.), *Handbook of clinical and experimental hypnosis*, New York: Macmillan, 1967. Pp. 444-480.

Barber, T. X., and Calverley, D. S. "Hypnotic behavior" as a function of task motivation. *J. Psychol.*, 1962, *54*, 363-389.

Barber, T. X., and Calverley, D. S. "Hypnotic-like" suggestibility in children and adults. *J. Abnorm. Soc. Psychol.*, 1963, *66*, 589–597. (a)

Barber, T. X., and Calverley, D. S. The relative effectiveness of task motivating instructions and trance induction procedure in the production of "hypnotic-like" behaviors. *J. Nerv. Ment. Dis.*, 1963, *137*, 107-116. (b)

Barber, T. X., and Calverley, D. S. Toward a theory of hypnotic behavior: Effects on suggestibility of task motivating instructions and attitudes toward hypnosis. *J. Abnorm. Soc. Psychol.*, 1963, *67*, 557-565. (c)

Barber, T. X., and Calverley, D. S. Comparative effects on "hypnotic-like" suggestibility of recorded and spoken suggestions. *J. Consult. Psychol.*, 1964, *28*, 384. (a)

Barber, T. X., and Calverley, D. S. Effect of E's tone of voice on "hypnotic-like" suggestibility. *Psychol. Rep.*, 1964, *15*, 139–144. (b)

Barber, T. X., and Calverley, D. S. Empirical evidence for a theory of "hypnotic" behavior: Effects of pretest instructions on response to primary suggestions. *Psychol. Rec.,* 1964, *14,* 457-467. (c)

Barber, T. X, and Calverley, D. S. Experimental studies in "hypnotic" behaviour: Suggested deafness evaluated by delayed auditory feedback. *Brit. J. Psychol.,* 1964, *55,* 439-446. (d)

Barber, T. X., and Calverley, D. S. An experimental study of "hypnotic" (auditory and visual) hallucinations. *J. Abnorm. Soc. Psychol.,* 1964, *68,* 13-20. (e)

Barber, T. X., and Calverley, D. S. Toward a theory of hypnotic behavior: Effects on suggestibility of defining the situation as hypnosis and defining response to suggestions as easy. *J. Abnorm. Soc. Psychol.,* 1964, *68,* 585-592. (f)

Barber, T. X., and Calverley, D. S. Toward a theory of "hypnotic" behaviour: Enhancement of strength and endurance. *Canad. J. Psychol.,* 1964, *18,* 156-167. (g)

Barber, T. X., and Calverley, D. S. Empirical evidence for a theory of "hypnotic" behavior: Effects on suggestibility of five variables typically included in hypnotic induction procedures. *J. Consult. Psychol.,* 1965, *29,* 98-107. (a)

Barber, T. X., and Calverley, D. S. Empirical evidence for a theory of "hypnotic" behavior: The suggestibility-enhancing effects of motivational suggestions, relaxation-sleep suggestions, and suggestions that the subject will be effectively "hypnotized". *J. Pers.,* 1965, *33,* 256-270. (b)

Barber, T. X., Chauncey, H. H., and Winer, R. A. Effect of hypnotic and nonhypnotic suggestions on parotid gland response to gustatory stimuli. *Psychosom. Med.,* 1964, *26,* 374-380.

Barber, T. X., and Coules, J. Electrical skin conductance and galvanic skin reponse during "hypnosis". *Int. J. Clin. Exp. Hypn.,* 1959, *7,* 79-92.

Barber, T. X., and Deeley, D. S. Experimental evidence for a theory of hypnotic behavior: I. "Hypnotic color-blindness" without "hypnosis". *Int. J. Clin. Exp. Hypn.,* 1961, *8,* 79-86.

Barber, T. X., and Hahn, K. W., Jr. Physiological and subjective responses to pain producing stimulation under hypnotically-suggested and waking- imagined "analgesia." *J. Abnorm. Soc. Psychol.,* 1962, *65,* 411-418.

Barber, T. X., and Hahn, K. W., Jr. Experimental studies in "hypnotic" behavior: Physiological and subjective effects of imagined pain. *J. Nerv. Ment. Dis.,* 1964, *139,* 416-425.

Barber, T. X., and Hahn, K. W., Jr. Effects of hypnotic procedures and suggestions of deafness on a cardiac response that has been conditioned to an auditory stimulus. Paper presented at the American Psychosomatic Society, Annual Meeting, Boston, March 29, 1968.

Barber, T. X., Karacan, I., and Calverley, D. S. "Hypnotizability" and suggestibility in chronic schizophrenics. *Arch. Gen Psychiat.,* 1964, *11,* 439-451.

Barker, W., and Burgwin, S. Brain wave patterns accompanying changes in sleep and wakefulness during hypnosis. *Psychosom. Med.,* 1948, *10,* 317–326.

Bauch, M. Beeinflussung des Diabetes mellitus durch psychophysche Entspannungsübungen. *Dtsch. Arch. Klin. Med.,* 1935, *2,* 149-166.

Beck, E. G. The variability of potentials evoked by light in man; the effect of hypnotic suggestion. *Utah Acad. Sci. Arts Let.,* 1963, *40,* 202–204.

Beck, E. C. Dustman, R. E., and Beier, E. G. The effects of hypnotic suggestion

194 *Yoga and a Theory of Hypnotism*

on the variability of visually evoked potentials. Salt Lake City, Utah: Veterans Administration Hospital, 1964. (Mimeo)

Bennett, L. L., and Scott, N. E. The production of electrocardiographic abnormalities by suggestion under hypnosis: A case report. *Amer. Practit.*, 1949, *4*, 189-190.

Berman, R., Simonson, E., and Heron, W. Electrocardiographic effects associated with hypnotic suggestion in normal and coronary sclerotic individuals. *J. Appl. Physiol.*, 1954, *7*, 89-92.

Berheim, H. *Suggestive therapeutics.* (Orig. Publ. 1888) Westport, Conn.: Associated Booksellers, 1957.

Best, C. H., and Taylor, N. B. *The physiological basis of medical practice.* (5th ed.) Baltimore, Md.: Williams & Wilkins, 1950.

Biberstein, H. Immunization therapy of warts. *Arch. Dermatol., Syphilol.*, 1944, *50*, 12-22.

Black, S. Inhibition of immediate-type hypersensitivity response by direct suggestion under hypnosis. *Brit. Med. J.*, 1963, *1* 925-929. (a)

Black, S. Shift in dose-response curve of Prausnitz-Küstner reaction by direct suggestion under hypnosis. *Brit. Med. J.*, 1963, *1*, 990-992. (b)

Black, S., Humphrey, J. H., and Niven, J. S. F. Inhibition of Mantoux reaction by direct suggestion under hypnosis. *Brit. Med. J.*, 1963, *1*, 1649-1652.

Black, S., and Wigan, E. R. An investigation of selective deafness produced by direct suggestion under hypnosis. *Brit. Med. J.*, 1961, *2*, 736-741.

Blank, H., and Brody, M. Recurrent herpes simplex: A psychiatric and laboratory study. *Psychosom. Med.*, 1950, *12*, 254-260.

Bloch, B. Ueber die Heilung der Warzen durch Suggestion. *Klin. Wschr.*, 1927, *6*, 2271-2275, 2320-2325.

Bonjour, J. Influence of the mind on the skin. *Brit. J. Dermatol.*, 1929, *41*, 324-326.

Borelli, S. Psychische Einflüsse and reactive Hauterscheinungen. *Münch. Med. Wschr.*, 1953, *95*, 1078-1082.

Bowles, J. W., Jr., and Pronko, N. H. Reversibility of stimulus function under hypnosis. *J. Psychol.*, 1949, *27*, 41-48.

Brandt, R. A tentative classification of psychological factors in the etiology of skin diseases. *J. Invest. Derm.*, 1950, *14*, 81-90.

Bravin, M. Role-play and direct suggestion in hypnotically induced color blindness. Unpublished doctoral dissertation, University of Denver, 1959.

Bykov, K. M. *The cerebral cortex and the internal organs.* New York: Chemical Publishing, 1957.

Callahan, A., and Redlich, F. C. Electroencephalography and ophthalmology. *Amer. J. Ophthal.*, 1946, *29*, 1522-1533.

Carlson, A. J. *The control of hunger in health and disease.* Chicago: Univer. Chicago Press, 1916.

Carter, J. E. Hypnotic induction of labor: A review and report of cases. *Amer. J. Clin. Hypn.*, 1963, *5*, 322-325.

Chapman, L. F., Goodell, H., and Wolff, H. G. Increased inflammatory reaction induced by central nervous system activity. *Trans. Ass. Amer. Physicians*, 1959, *72*, 84-109.

Chertok, L., and Kramarz, P. Hypnosis, sleep and electro-encephalography. *J. Nerv. Ment. Dis.*, 1959, *128*, 227-238.

Corson, S. A., Corson, E. O., Rosen, H., Reese, W. G., and Dykman, R. A. The effects of hypnotic suggestion on renal function in human subjects. *Physiologist*, 1960, *3* (3), 40.

Crasilneck, H. B., and Hall, J. A. Physiological changes associated with hypnosis: A review of the literature since 1948. *Int. J. Clin. Exp. Hypn.*, 1959, *7*, 9-50.

Crede, R. H., Chivers, N. C., and Shapiro, A. P. Electrocardiographic abnormalities associated with emotional disturbances. *Psychosom. Med.*, 1951, *13*, 227-288.

Damaser, E. C., Shor, R. E., and Orne, M. T. Physiological effects during hypnotically requested emotions. *Psychosom. Med.*, 1963, *25*, 334-343.

Davis, L. W., and Husband, R. W. A study of hypnotic susceptibility in relation to personality traits. *J. Abnorm. Soc. Psychol.*, 1931, *26*, 175-182.

Davis, R. C., and Kantor, J. R. Skin resistance during hypnotic states. *J. Gen. Psychol.*, 1935, *13*, 62-81.

Delhougne, R., and Hansen, K. Die suggestive Beeinflussbarkeit der Magen-und Pankreassekretion in der Hypnose. *Dtsch. Archiv. Klin. Med.*, 1927, *157*, 20-35.

Dorcus, R. M. Modification by suggestion of some vestibular and visual responses. *Amer. J. Psychol.*, 1937, *49*, 82-87.

Doswald, D. C., and Kreibich, K. Zur Frage der posthypnotischen Hautphänomene. *Mh. Prakt. Dermatol.*, 1906, *43*, 634-640.

Dudek, S. Z. Suggestion and play therapy in the cure of warts in children: A pilot study. *J. Nerv. Ment. Dis.*, 1967, *145*, 37-42.

Dudley, D. L., Holmes, T. H., Martin, C. J., and Ripley, H. S. Changes in respiration associated with hypnotically induced emotion, pain, and excercise. *Psychosom. Med.*, 1964, *24*, 46-57.

Duffy, E. The psychological significance of the concept of "arousal" or "activation". *Psychol. Rev.*, 1957, *64*, 265-275.

Duffy, E. *Activation and behavior*. New York: Wiley, 1962.

Dunbar, F. *Emotions and bodily changes*. (4th ed.) New York: Columbia Univer. Press. 1954.

Dynes, J. B. An experimental study in hypnotic anesthesia. *J. Abnorm. Soc. Psychol.*, 1932, *27*, 79-88.

Edwards, G. Hypnotic treatment of asthma: Real and illusory results. *Brit. Med. J.*, 1960, *2*, 492-497.

Elsea, O. C., Jr. A study of the effect of hypnotic suggestion on color perception. Unpublished doctoral dissertation, University of Oklahoma, 1961.

Erickson, M. H. A study of clinical and experimental findings on hypnotic deafness: I. Clinical experimentation and findings. *J. Gen. Psychol.*, 1938, *19*, 127-150. (a)

Erickson, M. H. A study of clinical and experimental findings on hypnotic deafness: II. Experimental findings with a conditioned response technique. *J. Gen. Psychol.*, 1938, *19*, 151-167. (b)

Erickson, M. H. The induction of color blindness by a technique of hypnotic suggestion. *J. Gen. Psychol.*, 1939, *20*, 61-89.

Erickson, M. H. Deep hypnosis and its induction. In L. M. LeCron (Ed.), *Experimental hypnosis*. New York: Macmillan, 1958. Pp. 70-112.

Erickson, M. H. Basic psychological problems in hypnotic research (and panel discussion). In G. H. Estabrooks (Ed.), *Hypnosis: Current problems*. New York: Harper & Row, 1962. Pp. 207-223, 238-272.

Erickson, M. H. and Erickson, E. M. The hypnotic induction of hallucinatory color vision followed by pseudo negative after-images. *J. Exp. Psychol.*, 1938, *22*, 581-588.

Erickson, M. H., Hershman, S., and Secter, I. I. *The practical application of medical and dental hypnosis*. New York: Julian Press, 1961.

Estabrooks, G. H. The psychogalvanic reflex in hypnosis. *J. Gen. Psychol.*, 1930, *3*, 150-157.

Favill, J., and White, P. D. Voluntary accerlation of the rate of the heart beat. *Heart*, 1917, *6*, 175-188.

Fisher, S. The role of expectancy in the performance of post-hypnotic behavior. *J. Abnorm. Soc. Psychol.*, 1954, *49*, 503-507.

Fisher, V. E. Hypnotic suggestion and the conditioned reflex. *J. Exp. Psychol.*, 1932, *15*, 212-217.

Ford, W. L., and Yeager, C. L. Changes in electroencephalogram in subjects under hypnosis. *Dis. Nerv. Syst.*, 1948, *9*, 190-192.

Friedlander, J. W., and Sarbin, T. R. The depth of hypnosis. *J. Abnorm. Soc. Psychol.*, 1938, *33*, 453-475.

Fry, L., Mason, A. A., and Bruce-Pearson, R. S. Effect of hypnosis on allergic skin responses in asthma and hay fever. *Brit. Med. J.*, 1964, *1*, 1145-1148.

Gerard, R. W. General discussion of symposium. In L. A. Jeffress (Ed.) *Cerebral mechanisms in behavior: The Hixon symposium*. New York: Wiley, 1951, P. 94.

Gigon, A., Aigner, E., and Brauch, W. Ueber den Einfluss der Psyche auf körperliche Vorgänge: Hypnose and Blutzucker. *Schwiez. Med. Wschr.*, 1926, *56*, 749-750.

Gill, M. M. and Brenman, M. *Hypnosis and related states*. New York: International Universities Press, 1959.

Gorton, B. E. The physiology of hypnosis. *Psychiat. Quart.*, 1949, *23*, 317-343, 457-485.

Grafe, E., and Mayer, L. Ueber den Einfluss der Affekte auf den Gesamtstoffwechsel. *Z. Ges. Neurol. Psychiat.*, 1923, *86*, 247-253.

Graff, N. I., and Wallerstein, R. S. Unusual wheal reaction in a tattoo. *Psychosom. Med.*, 1954, *16*, 505-515.

Graham; D. T., Kabler, J. D., and Graham, F. K. Physiological response to the suggestion of attitudes specific for hives and hypertension. *Psychosom. Med.*, 1962, *24*, 159-169.

Graham, D. T., Stern, J. A., and Winokur, G. Experimental investigation of the specificity of attitude hypothesis in psychosomatic disease. *Psychosom. Med.*, 1958, *20*, 446-457.

Graham, D. T., and Wolf, S. Pathogenesis of urticaria: Experimental study of life situations, emotions, and cutaneous vascular reactions. *J. Amer. Med. Assoc.*, 1950, *143*, 1396-1402.

Grether, W. F. A comment on "The induction of color blindness by a technique of hypnotic suggestion." *J. Gen. Psychol.*, 1940, *23*, 207-210.

Grumach, L. Ueber Suggestivbehandlung von Warzen. *Münch. Med. Wschr.*, 1927, *74*, 1093-1094.

Hadfield, J. A. The influence of hypnotic suggestion on inflammatory conditions. *Lancet*, 1917, *2*, 678-679.

Hadfield, J. A. The influence of suggestion on body temperature. *Lancet,* 1920, *2,* 68-69.

Harriman, P. L. Hypnotic induction of color vision anomalies; I. The use of the Ishihara and the Jensen tests to verify the acceptance of suggested color blindness. *J. Gen. Psychol.,* 1942, *26,* 289-298.

Heilig, R., and Hoff, H. Ueber Psychogene Entstehung des Herpes labialis. *Med. Klin.,* 1928, *24,* 1472.

Heller, F., and Schultz, J. H. Ueber einen Fall hypnotisch erzeugter Blasenbildung. *Münch. Med. Wschr.,* 1909, *56,* 2112.

Hernandez-Peon, R., and Donoso, M. Influence of attention and suggestion upon subcortical evoked electrical activity in the human brain. In L. van Bogaert and J. Radermecker (Eds.), *First International Congress of Neurological Sciences.*Vol. III. London: Pergamon, 1959. Pp. 385-396.

Heyer, G. R. Psychogene Functionsstörungen des Verdauungstraktes. In O. Schwarz (Ed.), *Psychogenese and Psychotherapie körperlicher Symptome.* Wien: Springer, 1925, Pp. 229-257.

Hibler, F. W. An experimental study of positive visual hallucinations in hypnosis. Unpublished doctoral dissertation. Ohio State University, 1935.

Hilgard, E. R. and Marquis, D. G. *Conditioning and learning.* New York: Appleton-Century, 1940.

Hinkle, L. E., Jr., and Wolf, S. A summary of experimental evidence relating life stress to diabetes mellitus. *J. Mt. Sinai Hosp.,* 1953, *19,* 537–570.

Hirose, S., Hirayama, C., and Ikemi, Y. The influence of emotional stress on the liver blood flow. *Kyushu J. Med. Sci.* 1961, *12,* 319–323.

Hulet, W. H., Shapiro, T., Schwarcz, B. E., and Smith, H. W. Water diuresis after hypnotic suggestion in hydropenic subjects. *J. Appl. Physiol.,* 1963, *18,* 186-188.

Huttenlocher, J., and Westcott, M. R. Some empirical relationships between respiratory activity and heart rate. *Amer. Psychologist,* 1957, *12,* 414. (Abstract)

Ikemi, Y., Akagi, M., Maeda, J., Fukumoto, K., Kawate, K., Hirakawa, K., Gondo, S., Nakagawa, T., Honda, T., Sakamoto, A., and Kumagai, M. Hypnotic experiments on the psychosomatic aspects of gastrointestinal disorders. *Int. J. Clin. Exp. Hypn.,* 1959, *7,* 139–150.

Ikemi, Y., and Nakagawa, S. A psychosomatic study of contagious dermatitis. *Kyushu J. Med. Sci.,* 1962, *13,* 335-350.

Jana, H. Biochemical changes in blood during hypnotic trance. *Ind. J. Med. Res.,* 1965, *53,* 1000-1002. (a)

Jana, H. Energy metabolism in hypnotic trance and sleep. *J. Appl. Physiol.,* 1965, *20,* 308-310.

Jana, H. Effect of hypnosis on circulation and respiration. *Ind. J. Med. Res.,* 1967, *55,* 591-598.

Jasper, H. H., and Carmichael, L. Electrical potentials from the intact human brain. *Science,* 1935, *81,* 51-53,

Jasper, H. H., and Cruikshank, R. M. Electro-encephalography:
II. Visual stimulation and the after-image as affecting the occipital alpha rhythm. *J. Gen. Psychol.,* 1937, *17,* 29-48.

Jendrassik, E. Einiges über suggestion. *Neurol. Zbl.,* 1888, *7,* 281-283, 321-330.

Jenness, A., and Wible, C. L. Respiration and heart action in sleep and hypnosis. *J. Gen. Psychol.,* 1937, *16,* 197-222.

Kaneko, Z., and Takaishi, N. Psychosomatic studies on chronic urticaria. *Folia Psychiat. Neurol. Japonica,* 1963, *17,* 16-24.

Kehoe, M., and Ironside, W. Studies on the experimental evocation of depressive response using hypnosis: II. The influence of depressive responses upon the secretion of gastric acid. *Psychosom. Med.,* 1963, *25,* 403-419.

Kelley, C. R. Psychological factors in myopia. Unpublished doctoral dissertation, New School for Social Research, New York, 1958.

Kelley, C. R. Psychological factors in myopia. Paper presented at American Psychological Association, Annual Meeting, New York, August 31, 1961.

Kelly, J. V. Effect of hypnotically induced anxiety on uterine muscle. *Amer. J. Obst. Gynec.,*1962, *83,* 582-587.

King, J. T., Jr. An instance of voluntary acceleration of the pulse. *Bull. Johns Hopkins Hosp.,* 1920, *31,* 303-304.

Klemme, H. L. Heart rate response to suggestion in hypnosis. Topeka, Kans.: Verterans Administration Hospital, 1963. (Mimeo)

Kliman, G., and Goldberg, E. L. Improved visual recognition during hypnosis. *Arch. Gen. Psychiat.,* 1962, *7,* 155-162.

Kline, M. V., Guze, H., and Haggerty, A. D. An experimental study of the nature of hypnotic deafness: Effects of delayed speech feedback. *J. Clin. Exp. Hypn.,* 1954, *2,* 145-156.

Koehler, M. Ueber die willkürliche Beschleunigung des Herzschlages beim Menschen. *Arch. Ges. Physiol.,* 1914, *158,* 579-622.

Kramer, E., and Tucker, G. R. Hypnotically suggested deafness and delayed auditory feedback. *Int. J. Clin. Exp. Hypn.,* 1967, *15,* 37-43.

Landis, C., and Slight, D. Studies of emotional reactions: VI. Cardiac responses. *J. Gen. Psychol.,* 1929, *2,* 413-420.

Levine, M. Electrical skin resistance during hypnosis. *Arch. Neurol. Psychiat.,* 1930, *24,* 937-942.

Levitt, E. E., and Brady, J. P. Psychophysiology of hypnosis. In J. M. Schneck (Ed.) *Hypnosis in modern medicine* (3d ed.) Springfield, Ill.: C. C. Thomas, 1963, Chap. 10.

Levitt, E. E., Den Breeijen, A., and Persky, H. The induction of clinical anxiety by means of a standardized hypnotic technique. *Amer. J. Clin. Hypn.,* 1960, *2,* 206-214.

Lewis, J. H., and Sarbin, T. R. Studies in psychosomatics: I. The influence of hypnotic stimulation on gastric hunger contractions. *Psychosomatic Med.,* 1943, *5,* 125-131.

Lewis, T. *The blood vessels of the human skin and their responses.* London: Shaw, 1927.

Ljung, O. Ekg-Koronarinsuffiizienz bei vegetativer Labilität. *Cardiologia,* 1949, *14,* 191-218.

Loftus, T. A., Gold, H., and Diethelm, O. Cardiac changes in the presence of intense emotion. *Amer. J. Psychiat.,* 1945, *101,* 697-698.

Logan, W. G. Delay of premature labor by the use of hypnosis. *Amer. J. Clin. Hypn.,* 1963, *5,* 209-211.

Loomis, A. L., Harvey, E. N., and Hobart, G. Electrical potentials of the human brain. *J. Exp. Psychol.,* 1936, *19,* 249-279.

Lovett Doust, J. W. Studies on the physiology of awareness: Oximetric analysis of emotion and the differential planes of consciousness seen in hypnosis. *J. Clin. Exp. Psychopathol.,* 1953, *14,* 113-126.

Lovett Doust, J. W., and Schneider, R. A. Studies on the physiology of awareness: Anoxia and the levels of sleep. *Brit. Med. J.,* 1952, *1,* 449-453.

Luckhardt, A. B., and Johnston, R. L. Studies in gastric secretions: I. The
psychic secretion of gastric guice under hypnosis. *Amer. J. Physiol.,* 1924, *70,*
174-182.

Ludwig, A. M., and Lyle, W. H., Jr. The experimental production of narcotic
drug effects and withdrawal symptoms through hypnosis. *Int. J. Clin. Exp.
Hypn.,* 1964, *12,* 1-17.

Lundholm, H. An experimental study of functional anesthesias as induced by
suggestions in hypnosis. *J. Abnorm. Soc. Psychol.,* 1928, *23,* 337-355.

Lundholm, H., and Lowenbach, H. Hypnosis and the alpha activity of the
electroencephalogram. *Charact. Pers.,* 1942, *11,* 144-149.

McClure, C. M. Cardiac arrest through volition. *Calif. Med.,* 1959, *90,* 440-441.

McDowell, M. Hypnosis in dermatology. In J. M. Schneck (Ed.), *Hypnosis in
modern medicine.* (2nd ed.) Springfield Ill.: Charles C. Thomas, 1959. Pp.
101-115.

Madow, L. Cortical blindness. *J. Neuropathol.,* 1958, *17,* 324-332.

Maher-Loughnan, G. P., MacDonald, N., Mason, A. A., and Fry, L. Controlled
trial of hypnosis in the symptomatic treatment of asthma. *Brit. Med. J.,* 1962,
2, 371-376.

Mainzer, F., and Krause, M. The influence of fear on the electrocardiogram.
Brit. Heart J., 1940, *2,* 221-230.

Malmo, R. B., Boag, T. J., and Raginsky, B. B. Electromyographic study of
hypnotic deafness. *J. Clin. Exp. Hypn.,* 1954, *2,* 305-317.

Malmo, R. B., Davis, J. F., and Barza, S. Total hysterical deafness: An
experimental case study. *J. Pers.,* 1952, *21,* 188-204.

Marcus, H., and Sahlgren, E. Untersuchungen über die Einwirkung der Hypnotischen Suggestion auf die Funktion des vegetativen Systemes. *Münch. Med.
Wschr.,* 1925, *72,* 381-382.

Marcuse, F. L. *Hypnosis: Fact and fiction.* Baltimore, Md.: Penguin Books,
1959.

Martin, I., and Grosz, H. J. Hypnotically induced emotions: Autonomic and
skeletal muscle activity in patients with affective illnesses. *Arch. Gen. Psychiat.,* 1964, *11,* 203-213.

Mason, A. A. A case of congenital ichthyosiform erythrodermia of Brocq
treated by hypnosis. *Brit. Med. J.,* 1952, *2,* 422-423.

Mason, A. A. Ichthyosis and hypnosis. *Brit. Med. J.,* 1955, *2,* 57.

Memmesheimer, A. M., and Eisenlohr, E. Untersuchungen über die Sugges-
tivebehandlung der Warzen. *Dermatol. Z.,* 1931, *62,* 63-68.

Menzies, R. Further studies of conditioned vasomotor responses in human
subjects. *J. Exp. Psychol.,* 1941, *29,* 457-482.

Miller, R. J., Bergeim, O., Rehfuss, M. E., and Hawk, P. B. Gastric response to
food: X. The psychic secretion of gastric juice in normal men. *Amer. J.
Physiol.,* 1920, *52,* 1-27.

Mirsky, I. A. Emotional factors in the patient with diabetes mellitus. *Bull.
Menninger Clin.,* 1948, *12,* 187-194.

Mohr, F. *Psychophysische Behandlungs-methoden.* Leipzig: Hirzel, 1925.

Moody, R. L. Bodily changes during abreaction. *Lancet,* 1946, *2,* 934-935.

Moody, R. L. Bodily changes during abreaction. *Lancet,* 1948, *1,* 964.

Naruse, G. Hypnosis as a state of meditative concentration and its relationship to the perceptual process. In M. V. Kline (Ed.), *The nature of hypnosis*. New York: Institute for Research in Hypnosis, 1962. Pp. 37-55.

Nielsen, O. J., and Geert-Jorgensen, E. Untersuchungen über die Einwirkung der hypnotischen Suggestion auf den Blutzucker bei Nichtdiabetikern. *Klin. Wschr.*, 1928, *7*, 1467-1468.

Nilzen, A. Studies in histamine. *Acta Dermat. Venereol. Stockh.*, 1947, *27*, Suppl. 17, 1-67.

Ogden, E., and Shock, N. W. Voluntary hyper-circulation. *Amer. J. Med. Sci.*, 1939, *198*, 329-342.

Parker, P. D., and Barber, T. X. "Hypnosis", task motivating instructions, and learning performance. *J. Abnorm. Soc. Psychol.*, 1964, *69*, 499-504.

Pattie, F. A. A report of attempts to produce uniocular blindness by hypnotic suggestion. *Brit. J. Med. Psychol.*, 1935, 15, 230-241.

Pattie, F. A. The production of blisters by hypnotic suggestions: A review. *J. Abnorm. Soc. Psychol.*, 1941, *36*, 62-72.

Pattie, F. A. The genuineness of unilateral deafness produced by hypnosis. *Amer. J. Psychol.*, 1950, *63*, 84-86.

Pattie, F. A. Methods of induction, susceptibility of subjects, and criteria of hypnosis. In R. M. Dorcus (Ed.), *Hypnosis and its therapeutic applications*. New York: McGraw-Hill, 1956, Ch 2.

Pease, E. A. Voluntary control of the heart. *Boston Med. Surg. J.*, 1889, *120*, 525-529.

Persky, H., Grosz, H. J., Norton, J. A., and McMurtry, M. effect of hypnotically-induced anxiety on the plasma hydrocortisone level of normal subjects. *J. Clin. Endocr. Metab.*, 1959, *19*, 700-710.

Pillsbury, D. M., Shelley, W. B., and Kligman, A. M. *Dermatology*. Philadelphia: Saunders. 1956.

Povorinskij, J. A., and Finne, W. N. Der Wechsel des Zuckergehalts des Blutes unter dem Einfluss einer hypnotisch suggerierten Vorstellung. *Z. Ges. Neurol. Psychiat.*, 1930, *129*, 135-146.

Pronko, N. H., and Hill, H. A study of differential stimulus function in hypnosis. *J. Psychol.*, 1949, *27*, 49-53.

Raginsky, B. B. Temporary cardiac arrest induced under hypnosis. *Int. J. Clin. Exp. Hypn.*, 1959, *7*, 53-68.

Ravitz, L. J. Standing potential correlates of hypnosis and narcosis. *Arch. Neurol. Psychiat.*, 1951, *65*, 413-436.

Ravitz, L. J. Application of the electro-dynamic field theory in biology, psychiatry, medicine, and hypnosis. *Amer. J. Clin. Hypn.*, 1959, *1*, 135-150.

Reifler, C. B. Hypnotic alteration of thermoregulatory response to cold. Paper presented at American Psychosomatic Society, Annual Meeting, San Francisco, April 4, 1964.

Rice, F. G. The hypnotic induction of labor: Six cases. *Amer. J. Clin. Hypn.*, 1961, *4*, 119-122.

Roberts, D. R. An electrophysiological theory of hypnosis. *Int. J. Clin. Exp. Hypn.*, 1960, *8*, 43-55.

Rock, N. L., and Shipley, T. Ability to "fake" color blindness under hypnosis. Philadelphia: Temple University Medical Center, Department of Psychiatry, 1961. (Mimeo)

Rosenthal, B. G., and Mele, H. The validity of hypnotically induced color hallucinations. *J. Abnorm. Soc. Psychol.*, 1952, *47*, 700-704.

Rybalkin, J. Brûlure du second degré provoquée par suggestion. *Rev. Hypn.,* 1890, *4,* 361-362.

Samek, J. Zum wesen der Suggestiven Warzenheilung. *Dermatol. Wschr.,* 1931, *93,* 1853-1857.

Sarbin, T. R. Physiological effects of hypnotic stimulation. In R. M. Dorcus (ed.), *Hypnosis and its therapeutic applications.* New York: McGraw-Hill, 1956. Ch. 4.

Scantlebury, R. E., and Patterson, T. L. Hunger motility in a hypnotized subject. *Quart. J. Exp. Physiol.,* 1940, *30,* 347-358.

Scharf, B., and Zamansky, H. S. Reduction of word-recognition threshold under hypnosis. *Percept. Motor Skills,* 1963, *17,* 499–510.

Scheibe, K. E., Gray, A. L., and Keim, C. S. Hypnotically induced deafness and delayed auditory feedback: A comparison of real and simulating sujects. *Int. J. Clin. Exp. Hypn.,* 1968, *16,* 158-164.

Schindler, R. *Nervensystem und spontane Blutunge.* Berlin: Karger, 1927.

Schneck, J. M. Psychogenic component in a case of herpes simplex. *Psychosom. Med.,* 1947, *9,*62-64.

Schultz, J. H., and Luthe, W. *Autogenic training.* New York: Grune and Stratton, 1959.

Schwartz, M. M. The cessation of labor using hypnotic techniques. *Amer. J. Clin. Hypn.,* 1963, *5,* 211-213.

Schwarz, B. E., Bickford, R. G., and Rasmussen, W. C. Hypnotic phenomena, including hypnotically activated seizures, studied with the elec-troencephalogram. *J. Nerv. Ment. Dis.,* 1955, *122,* 564-574.

Shearn, D. Does the heart learn? *Psychol. Bull.,* 1961, *58,* 452–458.

Sidis, B. Are there hypnotic hallucinations? *Psychol. Rev.,* 1906, *13,* 239-257.

Sinclair-Gieben, A. H. C., and Chalmers, D. Evaluation of treatment of warts by hypnosis. *Lancet,* 1959, *2,* 480-482.

Smirnoff, D. Zur Frage der durch hypnotische Suggestion hervorgerufenen vasomotorischen Störungen. *Z. Psychother. Med. Psychol.,* 1912, *4,* 171-175.

Smith, J. M., and Burns, C. L. C. The treatment of asthmatic children by hypnotic suggestions. *Brit. J. Dis. Chest,* 1960, *54,* 78-81.

Spanos, N. P., and Barber, T. X. "Hypnotic" experiences as inferred from subjective reports: Auditory and visual hallucinations. *J. Exp. Res. Pers.,* 1968, *3,* 136-150.

Stern, J. A., Winokur, G., Graham, D. T., and Graham, F. K. Alterations in physiological measures during experimentally induced attitudes. *J. Psychosom. Res.,* 1961, *5,* 73-82.

Sulzberger, M. B., and Wolf, J. The treatment of warts by suggestion. *Med. Rec.,* 1934, *140,* 552-557.

Sulzberger, M. B., and Zardens, S. H. Psychogenic factors in dermatologic disorders. *Med. Clin. N. Amer.,* 1948 (May), 669-685.

Sutcliffe, J. P. "Credulous" and "skeptical" views of hypnotic phenomena: Experiments in esthesia, hallucination, and delusion. *J. Abnorm. Soc. Psychol.,* 1961, *62,* 189-200.

Tarchanoff, J. R. Ueber die willkürliche Acceleration der Herzschläge beim Menschen. *Arch. Ges. Physiol.,* 1885, *35,* 109-137.

Taylor, N. B., and Cameron, H. G. Voluntary acceleration of the heart. *Amer. J. Physiol.,* 1922, *61,* 385-398.

Timney, B. N., and Barber, T. X. Hypnotic induction and oral temperature. *Int.*

J. Clin. Exp. Hypn., 1969, *17*, 121-132.

Ullman, M. Herpes simplex and second degree burn induced under hypnosis. *Amer. J. Psychiat.*, 1947, *103*, 828–830.

Ullman, M. On the psyche and warts: I. Suggestions and warts: A review and comment. *Psychosom. Med.*, 1959, *21*, 473-488.

Ullman, M., and Dudek, S. On the psyche and warts: II. Hypnotic suggestion and warts. *Psychosom. Med.*, 1960, *22*, 68-76.

Underwood, H. W. The validity of hypnotically induced visual hallucinations. *J. Abnorm. Soc. Psychol.*, 1960, *61*, 39-46.

Vanderhof, E., and Clancy, J. Peripheral blood flow as an indicator of emotional reaction., *J. Appl. Physiol.*, 1962, *17*, 67-70.

Van De Velde, T. H. Ueber willkürliche Vermehrung der Pulsrequenz beim Menschen. *Arch. Ges. Physiol.*, 1897, *66*, 232-240.

Van Pelt, S. J. The control of heart rate by hypnotic suggestion. In L. M. LeCron (Ed.) *Experimental hypnosis*. New York: Macmillan, 1954. pp. 268-275.

Veress, F. V. Beiträge zur Pathogenese des Herpes simplex. *9th Int. Conv. Dermatologists*, 1936, *2*, 242.

Vollmer, H. Treatment of warts by suggestion. *Psychosom. Med.*, 1946, *8*, 138-142.

Von Eiff, A. W. Ueber die Moglichkeit einer Grundumsatzenkung durch Psychische Beeinflussung. *Artzl. Forsch.*, 1950, *4*, 611.

Von Krafft-Ebing, R. *Eine experimentelle Studie auf dem Gebiete des Hypnotismus*. (2nd ed.) Stuttgart: 1889.

Weiss, B. Electrocardiographic indices of emotional stress. *Amer. J. Psychiat.*, 1956, *113*, 348-351.

Weitzenhoffer, A. M. *Hypnotism: An objective study in suggestibility*. New York: Wiley, 1953.

Weitzenhoffer, A. M. *General techniques of hypnotism*. New York: Grune & Stratton, 1957.

Wietzenhoffer, A. M., and Hilgard, E. R. *Stanford hypnotic susceptibility scale*. Palo Alto, Calif.: Consulting Psychologists Press, 1959.

Weller, C., Linder, M., Nuland, W., and Kline, M. V. The effects of hypnotically-induced emotions on continuous uninterrupted blood glucose measurements. *Psychosomatics*, 1961, *2*, 375-378.

Wells, W. R. Experiments in waking hypnosis for instructional purposes. *J. Abnorm. Soc. Psychol.*, 1924, *18*, 389-404.

Wells, W. R. The hypnotic treatment of the major symptoms of hysteria: A case study. *J. Psychol.*, 1944, *77*, 269-297.

West, H. F., and Savage, W. E. Voluntary acceleration of the heart beat. *Arch. Intern. Med.*, 1918, *22*, 290-295.

West, J. R., Kierland, R. R., and Litin, E. M. Atopic dermatitis and hypnosis: Physiologic stigmata before, during, and after hypnosis. *Arch. Derm.*, 1961, *84*, 579-588.

West, L. J. Psychophysiology of hypnosis. *J. Amer. Med. Ass.*, 1960, *172*, 672-675.

Westcott, M. R., and Huttenlocher, J. Cardiac conditioning: The effects and implications of controlled and uncontrolled respiration. *J. Exp. Psychol.*, 1961, *61*, 353-359.

White, H. C. Hypnosis in bronchial asthma. *J. Psychosom. Res.,* 1961, *5,* 272-279.

Whitehorn, J. C., Lundholm, H., Fox, E. L., and Benedict, F. G. Metabolic rate in "hynotic sleep". *New England J. Med,* 1932, *206,* 777-781.

Wink, C. A. S. Congenital ichthyosiform erythrodermia treated by hypnosis: Report of two cases. *British Med. J.,* 1961, *2,* 741-743.

Wolf, S., and Wolff, H. G. *Human gastric function: An experimental study of a man and his stomach.* (2nd ed.) New York: Oxford University Press, 1947.

Wood, D. M. and Obrist, P. A. Effects of controlled and uncontrolled respiration on the conditioned heart rate response in humans. *J. Exp. Psychol.,* 1964, *68,* 221-229.

Woodworth, R. S., and Schlosberg, H. *Experimental psychology.* (Rev. ed.) New York: Holt, 1954.

Yanovski, A. G. Feasibility of alteration of cardiovascular manifestations in hypnosis. *Amer. J. Clin. Hypn.,* 1962, *5,* 8-16. (a)

Yanovski, A. G. Hypnosis as a research tool in cardiology. In G. H. Estabrooks (Ed.), *Hypnosis: Current problems.* New York: Haper & Row, 1962. Pp. 76-108. (b)

Yates, A. J. Delayed auditory feedback. *Psychol. Bull.,* 1963, *60,* 213-232.

Yeager, C. L., and Larson, A. L. A study of alpha desynchronization in the elctroencephalogram utilizing hypnosis. Paper presented at American Electroencephalographic Society, Santa Fe, October, 1957.

Zamansky, H. S., and Brightbill, R. Modification of the word-recognition threshold by hypnotic suggestion and monetary reward. *Percept. Motor Skills,* 1964, *18,* 805-812.

Zamansky, H. S., Scharf, B., and Brightbill, R. The effect of expectancy for hypnosis on pre-hypnotic performance. *J. Pers.,* 1964, *32,* 236–248.

Zeaman, D., and Wegner, N. A further test of the role of drive reduction in human cardiac conditioning. *J. Psychol.,* 1957, *43,* 125-133.

Zwick, C. G. Hygiogenesis of warts disappearing without topical medication. *Arch. Dermatol. Syphilol.,* 1932, *25,* 508-521.

"Hypnosis" and Pain

CONTENTS

"Hypnosis" and Pain

Some investigators contend that hypnotically-suggested analgesia reduces or obliterates pain and others are of the opinion that hypnotic suggestions produce verbal denial of pain experience without affecting pain and suffering. This chapter critically evaluates the effects of hypnosis on pain. Relevant clinical and experimental studies are reviewed to answer two questions: Does hypnotically-suggested analgesia refer to reduction of pain, to verbal denial of pain experienced, or to a combination of both of these effects? Of the many independent and intervening variables subsumed under the term *hypnotically-suggested analgesia* — e.g., the suggestions of analgesia, the hypnotic trance state, the close relationship between patient and physician — which are effective and which are superfluous to producing pain relief?

Denotations of Critical Terms

THE TERM 'HYPNOSIS'

When investigators report that analgesia was produced under hypnosis or in a hypnotized subject, they appear to be saying in an abbreviated way that pain and suffering were ameliorated in a subject who was selected as meeting criteria of hypnotizability; who was placed in a state of trance; and who was given suggestions of pain relief by a prestigeful person with whom he had a close interpersonal relationship (Barber, 1962a). This confounding of a number of independent and intervening variables under the single term hypnosis leads to serious problems. It may be that one or two of these variables (e.g., suggestions of pain relief given in a close interpersonal setting) are sufficient to reduce pain and that the other variables — the hypnotic trance state, the selection of

207

subjects as hypnotizable — are extraneous. The following discussion first uses the word hypnosis as it is commonly used, to refer to all of these variables in combination. After reviewing clinical and experimental investigations concerned with hypnotically-suggested analgesia, I shall turn again to the term hypnosis and will place this concept under critical analysis.

THE TERM "PAIN"

Pain is a multidimensional concept. First, pain refers to a unpleasant sensation which varies not only in intensity (from mild to excruciating) but also in quality (from the lancinating sensation associated with trigeminal neuralgia, to the burning sensation found in causalgia, to the deep, aching sensation of abdominal cramps). Secondly, the term pain subsumes not only these various sensations of pain but also a reaction pattern which is generally categorized by such terms as anxiety or concern over pain. Although these two components of the pain experience — sensation of pain, and anxiety or reaction to pain — are normally intimately interrelated, a series of studies, summarized below, suggests that they can be partly dissociated under certain conditions.

Beecher (1946, 1956) presented cogent evidence that similar wounds which presumably produce similar pain sensations may give rise to strikingly different reaction patterns. He studied 215 seriously wounded soldiers in a combat zone hospital. Two-thirds of the men did not show signs of suffering, were in an "optimistic, even cheerful, state of mind," and refused pain-relieving drugs. This apparent lack of anxiety and suffering was not due to shock, and it was not due to a total pain block; the men were clear mentally and complained in a normal manner to rough handling of their wounds or to inept venipunctures. Beecher compared the reaction pattern of the wounded soldiers with the reactions shown by 150 male civilians who had undergone major surgery. Although the postoperative patients were suffering from less tissue trauma, only one-fifth of these patients (as compared to two-thirds of the soldiers) refused medication for relief of pain. The striking difference in reaction to injury in the two groups was apparently due to differences in significance of the wound. The soldier viewed his wound as a good thing; it enabled him to leave the battlefield with honor. The civilian viewed his surgery as a calamitous event. Beecher (1959) noted that "one cannot know whether in the above instances [of the wounded soldiers] the pain sensation or the reaction to pain is blocked; however, since the conscious man badly wounded in warfare often does not suffer at all from his great wound, yet is annoyed by, and suffers apparently normally from, a venipuncture, one can conclude that the nervous system can transmit pain sensations but that somehow the reaction to them is the altered element."

Hill, Kornetsky, Flanary, and Wikler (1952a, 1952b) and Kornetsky (1954) presented evidence to support the hypothesis that pain relief following morphine administration is closely related to relief of anxiety or reduction in fear of pain. Cattel (1943), Beecher (1959), and Barber (1959, 1960) reviewed other studies which suggest that morphine and other opiates at times alleviate suffering by minimizing anxiety and concern over pain without necessarily elevating the pain threshold or altering awareness of pain. Data indicating that placebos also at times ameliorate pain experience by alleviating anxiety or reaction to pain have been reviewed by Beecher (1955) and by Barber (1959).

Additional evidence that the reaction component of the pain experience can be at least partly dissociated from pain sensation is found in the effects of such surgical procedures as prefrontal leukotomy and topectomy of Brodmann's areas 9 and 10. These and other operations on the frontal areas at times appear to ameliorate intractable pain by alleviating anxiety, worry, and concern over pain (Barber, 1959; Dynes, 1949; LeBeau, 1950). Leukotomized patients characteristically state that their pain is the same, but it does not bother them anymore. Investigators who have studied the effects of frontal operations appear to agree with Ostenasek's (1948) conclusion that "when the fear of pain is abolished, the perception of pain is not intolerable."

The above and other data (Barber, 1959; Shor, 1959) suggest that, in attempting to delineate the effects of hypnotically-suggested anesthesia or analgesia, it may be more relevant to focus on the reaction component of the pain experience rather than on pain sensation per se. If hypnotically-suggested analgesia relieves anxiety or concern over pain but does not affect pain as a sensation or exerts only an indirect effect or a minor effect on pain sensation, it can be said that it affects a major component of the "pain experience", and it may be exerting as much effect on pain experience as powerful analgesics such as morphine (Shor, 1959).

Hypnotic Analgesia, Posthypnotic Amnesia, and Denial of Pain

A series of clinical reports indicates that suggestions of analgesia given under hypnotic trance at times result not in a reduction in pain and suffering but in an apparent amnesia for the pain and suffering experienced. In a number of investigations (Hull, 1933, p. 252; LaFontaine, 1860) the hypnotized patients cried, moaned, or showed signs of shock during surgery or parturition but maintained afterwards that they had forgotten the experience. For instance, Schultze-Rhonhof (1922) reported that obstetric patients who had received extensive antenatal training in entering deep trance showed overt behavioral signs of pain during labor—some groaned, others cried, others showed marked agitation—but the patients maintained on awakening that they were not aware of having suffered. This investigator interpreted his findings as indicating that hypnotic suggestions of pain relief rarely if ever produce a complete suppression of pain: "In the majority of cases, the complete analgesia which is claimed on awakening is the result of the amnesia."

Raginsky (1951) referred to cases of minor surgery performed under hypnosis in which the patients appeared amnesic immediately after surgery; however, when hypnotized at a later date, the patients could ". . . usually recall the site of pain and describe accurately the pain experienced at the time of the operation." Myers (1903), Perchard (1960), and Dorcus and Shaffer (1945) also presented data indicating that posthypnotic amnesia for pain experienced during surgery or during parturition is temporary and easily reversible.

Many other studies (Banister & Zangwill, 1941; Bitterman & Marcuse, 1945; Bramwell, 1903; Life, 1929; Mitchell, 1932; Moll, 1889; Patten, 1932) indicate that posthypnotic amnesia is labile and superficial. These additional studies, reviewed in detail elsewhere (Barber, 1962b), can be summarized as follows:

With few if any exceptions, investigators report that amnesic hypnotic subjects recall the forgotten events if the hypnotist states, "Now you remember" (Bramwell, 1903, p. 106). Subjects who have been deeply hypnotized also recall the forgotten events when given *implicit* permission to remember. Such tacit permission may be given by asking, "Do you remember?," with the intonation that the subject is permitted to remember; by giving a hint; by instructing the subject to allow his hand to write automatically; and so forth (Moll, 1889; Weitzenhoffer, 1957, p. 347; Wells, 1940).

Experimental evidence indicates that amnesic hypnotic subjects *recognize* the material which they claim not to remember; this recognition is indicated by overt behaviors—e.g., avoidance of amnesic material but not of similar control material—and by alterations in pulse and respiration when presented with the forgotten material but not when presented with comparable control material (Banister & Zangwill, 1941; Bitterman & Marcuse, 1945; Wells, 1940).

Experimental evidence indicates that excellent hypnotic subjects who show complete amnesia when interviewed by the hypnotist show very little if any effects of the amnesia when tested by indirect methods which do not depend on verbal reports, such as assessment of practice effects or of retroactive inhibition effects (Life, 1929; Mitchell, 1931; Patten, 1932).

Amnesic hypnotic subjects characteristically make such statements as: "I haven't any inclination to go back over it;" "I do remember but I can't say;" "I know it but I can't think about it—I know what it is but I just kind of stop myself before I think of it" (Blum, 1961, p. 162; White, 1941). These and other remarks made by amnesic hypnotic subjects can be interpreted as supporting " . . . not a dissociation theory, but rather a motivational theory, a theory that such amnesia is due to an unwillingness to remember, an attempt to occupy oneself with other things than an effort to recall" (Pattie, 1956b, p.8).

The above and other data (Barber, 1962b) suggest that posthypnotic amnesia for pain may be more labile and temporary than is at times supposed and may be difficult to differentiate from purposive denial of the pain experienced or from unwillingness to admit to the hypnotist that pain was experienced. It should be noted here that the verbal reports of good hypnotic subjects often appear to be closely correlated with what the hypnotist leads the subject to believe he is expected to report (Barber, 1962a). If the hypnotist implies when interviewing the subject that he should state that no pain was experienced, the good hypnotic subject may comply on a verbal level even though pain was experienced. On the other hand, if the hypnotic subject is given a means of stating what occurred without at the same time directly contradicting the hypnotist's explicit suggestions and the hypnotist's apparent desires and expectations, he may give a different report. Kaplan (1960) presented an interesting case study which can be interpreted along these lines. A highly trained hypnotic subject was placed in a very deep trance and given two suggestions: that his left arm was analgesic and insensitive and that his right hand would continously perform automatic writing. The analgesic left arm was pricked four times with a hypodermic needle; when receiving this stimulation, the subject's right hand wrote, "Ouch, damn it, you're hurting me." After a minute or two, the subject asked the experimenter, "When are you going to begin?", apparently having forgotten that he had received the painful stimuli. Kaplan interpreted these findings as indicating that hypnotic suggestions of analgesia produce " . . . an artificial repression and/or denial of pain, but that at *some level* pain *is* experienced—moreover, experienced as discomfort at that level."

The motivation for denial of pain is present in the clinical hypnotic situation. The physician who has invested time and energy hypnotizing the patient and suggesting that pain will be relieved, expects and desires that his efforts will be successful, and by his words and manner commu-

nicates his desires and expectations to the patient. The patient in turn
has often formed a close relationship with the physician-hypnotist and
would like to please him or at least not to disappoint him. Furthermore,
the patient is aware that if he states that he suffered, he is implying that
the physician's time and enery were wasted and his efforts futile. The
situation is such that even though the patient may have suffered, it may
be difficult or disturbing for him to state directly to the physician-hypnotist that he experienced pain and it may be less anx-
iety-provoking to say that he did not suffer.

It should be noted that the motivation to deny pain is not necessarily
a function of the patient's having been hypnotized. Similar findings may
be obtained in any situation, hypnotic or nonhypnotic, in which the
physician invests time and effort attempting to support the patient and to
ameliorate the patient's suffering. These conditions making for denial of
pain appear to be present, for instance, in situations described as natural
childbirth. Mandy, Mandy, Farkas, and Scher (1952) presented data
indicating that the natural childbirth patient who reports to the physician
and to the physician's associates that she was "delighted with natural
childbirth" may state, when interviewed by an independent observer,
that her delivery was more painful than she had anticipated or believed
was necessary "but she couldn't admit it to the house staff for fear of
disappointing them."

Carefully controlled studies are needed in which patients who have
ostensibly experienced hypnotic analgesia are interviewed not only by
the hypnotist but also by a person who is not associated with hypnosis
and to whom the patient is willing to confide. It can be hypothesized
from the data presented above that *some* hypnotic subjects who deny
pain or who appear to have amnesia for pain when questioned by the
hypnotist will state that they experience pain and that they suffered
when interviewed by a person whom they trust and who is not associated with the hypnosis.

Overt Behavioral Reactions as Criteria
of Analgesia or Pain Relief

The data cited above suggest caution in using the hypnotic patient's
verbal report as given to the hypnotist as an index of pain relief. Caution
is also necessary in using the hypnotic patient's lack of overt behavioral
reactions to noxious stimulation as indicating that pain and suffering
have been abolished; as noted above the hypnotic subject is often
motivated to please the hypnotist and this may at times be sufficient for

him to try to inhibit overt signs of pain such as moaning, wincing, or restlessness.

The findings presented by Javert and Hardy (1951) with respect to natural childbirth may also apply to the patient undergoing labor under hypnosis. The subjects consisted of 26 untrained labor patients and five patients who had been trained in natural childbirth by others (not by Javert or Hardy). During labor the untrained patients showed evidence of anxiety and pain, while the natural childbirth patients appeared relatively serene. Between uterine contractions both groups were asked to compare the pain of labor with the pain produced by application of radiant heat to the forelimb. (These measurements were made in both groups prior to the administration of analgesic or anesthetic drugs). The natural childbirth patients did not differ from the untrained patients in estimates of pain intensity; both groups rated the pain of labor as relatively severe and equal in maximal intensity to blister-producing thermal stimulation. Javert and Hardy interpreted these findings as indicating that natural childbirth produces a satisfactory reaction pattern but has little if any effect on the intensity of the pain experienced during labor.

An additional consideration whould be noted here: Velvovski, Platonov, Plotitcher and Chougom (1954) claim that from 7 to 14 percent of *unselected* patients in the Soviet Union give birth without medications, without showing signs of pain, anxiety, or suffering, and without receiving any training or preparation. Are more than 14 percent of *unselected* hypnotized patients able to perform as well? No data are available to answer this question; reports concerned with the effects of hypnosis in parturition are in all cases based on volunteer or *selected* patients.

The proportion of *selected* hypnotic patients able to deliver without medications and without exhibiting signs of suffering may not greatly exceed the 7 to 14 percent of *unselected* patients, which Velvovski et al. claim can deliver in this way without any training at all. Although some investigators (Clark, 1956; Michael, 1952; Mody, 1960) report that more than one-third of selected hypnotic patients are able to deliver without anodynes, others (Asin, 1961; Callan, 1961; Winkelstein, 1948) find that no more than 14 percent of patients who volunteer for hypnotic training are able to deliver without medicaments and without showing gross signs of pain.

Similar considerations may apply in surgery: The proportion of *selected* patients who are able to undergo surgery with hypnoanesthesia alone may not greatly exceed the proportion of *unselected* patients who were able to undergo surgery in the preanesthetic period without manifesting signs of pain. Data presented by Trent, (1946), Leriche (1939, pp. 55-56) Elliotson (1843, pp. 15-17), and Chertok (1959, pp. 3-4) indicate that although many surgical patients, prior to the advent of anesthetics, struggled and screamed, a small proportion of patients "... bravely made no signs of suffering at all." Although it is often stated that at the present time approximately 10 per cent of the population is able to undergo surgery under hypnotic trance, Wallace and Coppolino (1960) note the following:

"Our percentage of success in the complete substitution of hypno-anesthesia for chemoanesthesia has been less than the previously quoted 10 per cent. There have not been any published series of cases in which a statistical analysis would indicate that approximately 10 per cent of the patients are able to withstand a surgical intervention with hypnoanesthesia as a sole modality. Therefore, it is our conclusion that the 10 per cent estimate is an often-repeated but unsubstantiated quantity and that the true percentage of successful cases is much below that figure."

The above data suggest two conclusions:

Caution is necessary in accepting the hypnotic patient's verbal report of his lack of behavioral reactions as valid indices that the patient did not suffer. The hypnotic situation is often structured in such a manner that the patient is motivated to inhibit overt signs of pain and to deny pain experience.

The proportion of *selected* hypnotized patients who are able to undergo labor or surgery without manifesting signs of pain and without receiving drugs may not greatly exceed the proportion of *unselected* patients who are able to do the same thing without any preparation at all. Careful controls are needed to determine if the effects attributed to hypnosis are due to the selection of patients.

Physiological Indices of Anxiety and Pain

The data presented above suggest that an objective index of pain which is difficult or impossible to affect voluntarily is needed in studies concerned with hypnotically-suggested analgesia. Unfortunately, there appears to be no single index and no combination of indices which unequivocally indicate the presence of absence of pain and suffering. However, a series of studies demonstrate that a useful objective index of anxiety and pain consists of an alteration in one or more systemic physiological functions which are difficult to alter by voluntary effort.

In normal subjects painful stimulation almost always produces alterations in one or more of the following: blood pressure, heart rate, respiration, digital vasomotor tone, skin resistance, and degree of tension in localized muscles (Barber & Hahn, 1962, 1964; Beecher, 1959; Cannon, 1951; Cohen & Patterson, 1937; Goetzl, Bien, & Lu, 1951; Gold, 1943; Hilgard, 1969; Schwartz, Sata, & Laszlo, 1950). Although nonpainful stimuli at times also produce alterations in these physiological indices, they rarely produce the same degree or the same pattern of alteration as painful stimuli (Barber & Hahn, 1962; Engel, 1956; Lacey, 1959). There is also evidence to indicate that morphine, meperidine, nitrous oxide, and other analgesics and anesthetics drastically reduce these normally expected responses to noxious stimulation. The galvanic skin response to painful stumulation is apparently markedly reduced by morphine at low dose levels (8 mg.) and is apparently abolished by nitrous oxide anesthesia, by merperidine (100 mg.), and by morphine at higher dose levels (20-100 mg.) (Andrews, 1943; Brown & Vogel, 1938). It also appears that morphine (8-16 mg.) and codeine (32-64 mg.) reduce the vasoconstriction response to noxious stimulation to near the vanishing point and that the elevation in blood pressure which normally follows painful stimulation is eliminated by anesthetic doses of barbiturates (Goetzl et. al, 1951; Schwartz et. al, 1950).

Before turning to experimental studies which used physiological variables to assess the effects of hypnotically-suggested analgesia, two considerations should be emphasized. Subjects differ in their physiological patterns of response to the same noxious stimulus, and the same subject may show different patterns of physiological response to different types of noxious stimuli (Lacey, 1959). When physiological variables are used to assess hypnotic analgesia, it is necessary to take inter- and intra-subject variability into account. Alterations in physiological variables during painful stimulation appear to be more closely correlated with the anxiety or reaction component of the pain experience than with pain sensation per se (Barber & Coules, 1959; Doupe, Miller, & Keller, 1939; Hardy, Wolff, & Goodell, 1952; Levine, 1930; Sattler, 1943). The latter consideration, however, is not a major objection to the use of autonomic indices to assess the effects of hypnotically-suggested analgesia. Anxiety or concern over pain appears to be a major component of the total pain experience, and if hypnotic analgesia reduces anxiety and concern over pain, it can be said to exert an important effect on pain experience even if it does not significantly affect pain as a sensation (Barber, 1959, 1960; Beecher, 1959; Hall & Stride, 1954; Hill et al, 1952a, 1952b; Kornetsky, 1954; Shor, 1959).

Experimental Studies of Hypnotic Analgesia

Experimental studies pertaining to hypnotic analgesia can be subdivided

into two sets: studies that employed short-lasting pain stimuli that endured for only one to three seconds; and studies that employed longer
lasting pain stimuli. Since the results obtained with pain stimuli of brief
duration differ in some respects from those obtained with pain stimuli of
longer duration, I will review the two sets of studies separately.

STUDIES EMPLOYING SHORT-LASTING PAIN STIMULI

Dynes (1932) monitored heart rate, respiratory rate, and change in skin
resistance in response to pinch and pinprick in seven excellent hypnotic
subjects (trained somnambules) under control conditions and after suggestions of analgesia were given under hypnotic trance. The noxious
stimulation produced an average increase in respiratory rate of three
cycles per minute under the control condition and of one cycle per
minute under the trance condition. Heart rate showed a mean increase
of 2.5 beats per minute under the control condition and failed to show an
increase under the trance condition. All subjects showed galvanic skin
responses (GSR) of the same order of magnitude under the control and
trance conditions. This study is open to at least one major criticism: The
stimuli were always administered first under the control condition and
then under trance. As Shor (1959) pointed out, since physiological
reactions to painful stimulation generally show a habituation or adaptation effect, tending to decrease during a second and subsequent stimulations, the possibility was not excluded that a similar reduction in heart
rate and respiratory rate might have been observed during the second
stimulation if the subjects had not been placed in hypnotic trance and
had not been given suggestions of analgesia.

Sears (1932) employed facial flinch, respiratory depth, respiratory
variability, pulse amplitude, pulse variability, and GSR as indices of
pain. Seven carefully selected deep trance subjects participated. The
pain stimulus consisted of a sharp steel point pressed against the calf of
the leg for one second with a pressure of 20 ounces without breaking the
skin. This stimulus was first applied in a waking control series to determine which of the physiological variables were reliable indices of pain.
In a subsequent hypnotic series the subjects were placed in deep trance,
suggestions of anesthesia were given for the left leg, the right leg was
employed as a control, and the stimulus was applied alternately to the
two legs. In a third series of experiments (voluntary inhibition), the
subjects were instructed to try to inhibit reactions to the painful stimulus.

Sears presented the following findings with respect to the critical
hypnotic series: When the painful stimulus was applied to the 'anesthet-

ic' leg, the hypnotized subjects showed significantly less facial flinch, respiratory depth, respiratory variability, pulse variability, and GSR than when the stimulus was applied to the control leg. The amplitude of the pulse did not differ significantly when the 'anesthetic' and control limbs were stimulated.

Sear's findings have been generally interpreted as a convincing demonstration of the effect of hypnotic analgesia on physiological reactions to pain stimuli (Gorton, 1949; Heron, 1954; Kirkner, 1956; Weitzenhoffer, 1953). However, Shor (1959) reanalyzed Sears' data and found that some of the computations were incorrect. Shor's analysis showed that respiratory depth, pulse variability, and pulse amplitude were not significantly different when the stimulus was applied under trance to the 'anesthetic' and control limbs. Facial flinch, respiratory variability and GSR differed significantly under the 'anesthetic' and control conditions. A further problem arose when the probabilities for the waking control series were recomputed: Shor found that in this series respiratory variability was not significantly different before and after painful stimulation and was thus of questionable adequacy as a criterion of physiological response to painful stimulation. In brief, Shor's careful reanalysis of Sears' original data indicated that only three measures, instead of six as reported originally, were significantly affected by hypnotically-suggested analgesia. However, of these three measures, one (respiratory variability) was of questionable adequacy under the conditions of the experiment as an index of response to painful stimulation and other (facial flinch) is not a physiological variable and is amenable to voluntary control. Sear's major finding, then, was that the GSR to painful stimulation was reduced by 22 per cent under hypnotically-suggested analgesia. This mean reduction in GSR was due to 4 of the 7 subjects; the other 3 subjects showed a GSR of the same order of magnitude when the stimulus was applied to the 'anesthetic' and control limbs.

As mentioned above, Sears performed an additional series of experiments in which the same subjects were instructed to try to inhibit all responses to the painful stimulus. In this voluntary inhibition series significant physiological reactions were found and the subjects showed facial flinch. Sears interpreted these findings as indicating that "Voluntary inhibition of reaction to pain does not present a picture even remotely resembling the reaction under true hypnotic anesthesia." However, the subjects' failure to inhibit flinching renders this conclusion questionable. In pilot studies Sears had found that the flinch response to the stimulus could be inhibited "by most people with little difficulty." As Hull (1933) pointed out, since the flinching response is normally under voluntary control, it appears possible that the trained hypnotic subjects participating in Sears' experiment did not actually try to suppress reactions to pain when instructed to do so. Sears' study thus appears to be open to the same criticism that applies to other studies in hypnosis which employed trained hypnotic subjects "as their own controls," namely, when a single group of trained hypnotic subjects is tested under both the experimental and the control conditions, it is difficult to exclude the possibility that the subjects may purposively give an inferior performance under the control condition in order to comply with what they correctly or incorrectly surmise are the wishes or the expectations of the experimenter (Barber, 1962a; Sutcliffe, 1960).

Doupe et al. (1939) studied the effect of hypnotically-suggested analgesia on the vasoconstriction response to painful stimulation. Eight subjects were used, but data are presented only on five subjects. These five subjects participated in 11 experiments. After the subject was deeply hypnotized, digital vasodilation was produced by placing his legs in warm water. Suggestions were then given that one arm was insensitive and analgesic with the understanding that the alternate arm would remain normally sensitive. Pin-prick stimulation (and, at times, ice stimulation) was then applied alternately to the 'anesthetic' and normal limbs. From six to 40 stimulations were applied to each limb in each experiment. Eight of the 11 experiments failed to show a significant difference between the 'anesthetic' and normal limbs in vasoconstriction response to the noxious stimuli. In the remaining three experiments, stimulation of the 'anesthetic' limb produced less vasoconstriction than stimulation of the control limb, the reductions ranging from 36 per cent to 40 per cent. Doupe et al. also recorded respiration and pulse in these experiments but did not present the data obtained on these measures. They state only that "No significant changes in pulse rate were recorded" and "A slight alteration in respiratory rhythm was caused by stimuli applied to either [the "anesthetic" or normal] side, but this tended to be greater when then normal side was stimulated."

In addition to performing reanalyses of the data of previous experiments, Shor (1959) also carried out an experimental study of his own. The experimental group consisted of eight very good hypnotic subjects (somnambulists); the control group consisted of eight subjects who had demonstrated in a series of preliminary sessions that they were not susceptible to hypnosis. Prior to the experiment proper all subjects chose a level of electric shock which they found painful but which they were willing to tolerate with equanimity for an extended series of experiments. Each subject was then presented with his chosen level of electric shock under five experimental conditions while skin resistance, respiration, and heart rate were recorded continuously on a polygraph. The experimental conditions (counterbalanced to control for order effects) were as follows: wake control (the effect of the wake state alone); hypnotic control (the effect of hypnosis alone); wake inhibition (voluntary suppression of reactions to pain in the waking state); hypnotic inhibition (voluntary suppression of reactions to pain in the hypnotic state); and hypnotically-suggested analgesia. The experimental group (somnambulistic hypnotic subjects) was hypnotized under conditions of hypnotic control, hypnotic inhibition, and hypnotically-suggested analgesia; the controls (subjects insusceptible to hypnosis) were instructed to pretend they were hypnotized under these three experimental conditions. Shor presented the following findings: The experimental group did not show significantly different physiological responses to the noxious stimuli under any of the five experimental conditions. The control group also failed to show significant differences in physiological responses under any of the experimental conditions. There appeared to be a trend (not significant) for overall reactivity to be less under the waking inhibition condition. Shor concluded that his data offered no support to the hypothesis that hypnotically-suggested analgesia has special effects on physiological responses to painful stimuli which are beyond the bounds of waking volitional control.

Since skin-resistance change (GSR) is easily monitored and is markedly responsive to painful and to anxiety-arousing stimulation, it has been employed in an extensive series of studies concerned with the effects of hypnotic analgesia. Five early studies which used the GSR as the sole criterion of physiological response to pain reported contradictory findings. Peiper (1924), working with four subjects, Prideaux (1920), with four subjects, and Levine (1930), with one subject, reported that noxious stimulation applied to a skin area for which analgesia had been suggested under trance produced a normal GSR. Georgi (1921), working with three subjects, and Moravesik (1912), with one subject, reported that hypnotic suggestions of analgesia reduced the GSR to painful stimuli. In these early studies the experimental procedures were not presented in detail, and the data were not analyzed statistically. Two more recent sudies, summarized below, were carried out more rigorously; here again, contradictory results were obtained.

West et al. (1952) monitored skin resistance in an extensive series of repeated sessions with seven subjects. (A total of 45 experimental sessions was held, an average of more than six session per subject). Each experimental session included a waking control condition followed by a hypnotic condition. Under the control condition each subject received a series of painful stimuli of increasing intensity produced by radiant heat applied to a forelimb for no more than three seconds; following these control trials, hypnosis was induced, suggestions were given that the limb was anesthetic, and the painful stimuli were again presented in the same order. The mean GSR to the painful stimuli was significantly reduced under the hypnotic analgesia condition for all subjects, the reductions ranging from 26 to 67 per cent. West et al. note that the GSR was at times reduced, even when "... there was no alteration in pain perception, according to subjective reports," and during control periods a stimulus evoking reports of relatively severe pain at times failed to produce a GSR. The findings thus appear to be consistent with earlier reports that the galvanic skin response to noxious stimulation may be more closely related to the threat-content or anxiety aroused by a noxious stimulus rather than to "pain perception per se" (Furer & Hardy, 1950). The study by West et al. appears to be open to one major criticism: The control trials always preceded the hypnotic trials with three subjects and were only occasionally reversed with the other four subjects; since the GSR to noxious stimulation tends to decrease over a series of trials (Furer & Hardy, 1950; Seward & Seward, 1934), the effects of hypnotically-suggested analgesia may have been confounded with possible adaptation effects (Shor, 1959). In a more recent experiment which controlled adaptation effects, Sutcliffe (1961) presented contradictory findings.

Sutcliffe (1961) recorded the galvanic-skin response to noxious stimulation under waking conditions, hypnotically-suggested analgesia, and waking simulation of analgesia. Adaptation of the GSR to the noxious stimuli was controlled by employing different subjects under each experimental condition. In pre-experimental sessions, 24 subjects were given a series of electric shocks, and a level of shock was established which invariably produced pain. The subjects were then randomly assigned to three experimental groups with eight subjects (four somnambulists and four nonsomnambulists) in each group. Group 1 received four electric shocks at intervals of one minute under normal waking conditions. Group 2 received the four electric shocks after suggestions of analgesia were given under hypnosis. Group 3 received the four shocks after receiving instructions under waking conditions to act as if the shocks were nonpainful. The GSR to the shocks was the same under the waking control condition, the hypnotic analgesia condition, and the waking action condition. The somnambulists did not differ from the nonsomnambulists under any of the experimental conditions.

The findings reviewed above appear to indicate that hypnotically-suggested analgesia at times has some effect on physiological reactions to noxious stimuli, but this effect is by no means as drastic as was implied in earlier reviews (Gorton, 1949; Kirkner, 1956; Weitzenhoffen, 1953). Sutcliffe (1961) and Shor (1959) failed to reject the null hypothesis of no difference in autonomic responses to painful stimuli under hypnotically suggested analgesia and a waking control condition. Doupe et al. (1939) found that hypnotically-suggested analgesia reduced the vasoconstriction response to pin-prick in three experiments but failed to do so in eight experiments. Sears (1932) observed a 22 per cent reduction in mean GSR to noxious stimuli under hypnotic analgesia. In Dynes' (1932) experiment, hypnotically-suggested analgesia reduced the expected increase in heart rate, and in respiratory rate, by 2.5 beats per minute, and by 2 cycles per minute, respectively. West et al. (1952) observed a 26-67 per cent reduction in galvanic-skin response to painful heat under hypnotically-suggested analgesia. However, in the Dynes experiment and in the West et al. experiment, the hypnotic trials almost always followed the control trials, and it appears possible that some of the observed reduction in autonomic reactivity associated with hypnotic analgesia was produced by adaptation to the stimuli.

In each of the experiments described above, the subjects were exposed to pain-producing stimuli for a very brief period at any one time; the noxious stimuli—pinch, pinprick, application of a sharp point, electric shock or radiant heat—were applied to the body surface for only one to three seconds. The results obtained with these momentary or very short-lasting pain stimuli, may be difficult to generalize to situations in which the pain is of longer duration. To estimate the effectiveness of hypnotically-suggested analgesia in reducing longer-lasting pain, I will next review experiments in which pain stimuli were applied for a period of minutes instead of seconds.

STUDIES EMPLOYING
LONGER-LASTING PAIN STIMULI

To produce an aching type of pain which continues for one or more minutes, the subjects participating in the experiments described below were exposed to one or more of the following: immersion of a limb in ice water or in very hot water (Barber & Hahn, 1962; Brown & Vogel, 1938; Hilgard, 1969); occlusion of the blood supply in a limb while the subject exercised the limb (Hilgard, 1969; McGlashan, Evans, & Orne, 1969); and application of a heavy weight or a weighted thumbtack on a limb or a digit (Barber & Calverley, 1969; Brown & Vogel, 1938; Spanos, Barber, & Lang, 1969).

In a series of studies carried out by Hilgard and associates (Hilgard, 1967; Hilgard, 1969; Hilgard, Cooper, Lenox, Morgan, & Voevodsky,

1967), pain was produced either by immersing a limb in ice water, or by exercising a limb in which the blood supply had been occluded by means of a tourniquet (ischemic pain). The results included the following: Hypnotic-induction alone (without suggestions of analgesia) at times produced a small reduction in reported pain. Suggestions of analgesia given after a hypnotic-induction procedure generally produced a further reduction in verbally reported pain; the pain reduction was slight for the low hypnotizable subjects and greater for the high hypnotizable subjects. Under hypnotically-suggested analgesia, the great majority of the highly hypnotizable subjects reported that pain was reduced but still present and a few reported that pain was gone. With some highly hypnotizable subjects, hypnotically-suggested analgesia was apparently effective in reducing the anxiety associated with pain; with other highly hypnotizable subjects, hypnotically-suggested analgesia was apparently effective in reducing the experience of pain per se. A few nonhypnotizable subjects were apparently able to divert their attention from the painful stimulus and thus reported little pain in the waking state.

McGlashan, Evans, and Orne (1969) worked with two groups of selected subjects; a group of good hypnotic subjects who had scored in the upper 5 per cent on hypnotic susceptibility scales and had met criteria for hypnotic analgesia (as measured by response to moderate electric shock); and a group of poor hypnotic subjects who had scored in the lowest 5 per cent on hypnotic susceptibility scales. In the formal experiment, each subject was tested three times on responses to ischemic pain: first under a control condition, then under hypnotically-suggested analgesia and, finally, under a condition in which a placebo was administered that was described to the subjects as a powerful analgesic drug. Half of the good hypnotic subjects and also half of the poor hypnotic subjects rated the pain as the same, or even greater, during hypnotically-suggested analgesia as compared to the control condition. However, half of the good hypnotic subjects and also half of the poor hypnotic subjects rated the pain as less intense during hypnotically-suggested analgesia than during the control condition. Although the same proportion (50 per cent) of the good and poor hypnotic subjects stated that pain was reduced during hypnotically-suggested analgesia, the good subjects stated that it was significantly more reduced than the poor subjects. The good hypnotic subjects who reported that pain was reduced under hypnotically-suggested analgesia apparently experienced less pain under this condition than under the placebo condition. However, the other good and poor hypnotic subjects apparently experienced no greater reduction in pain under hypnotically-suggested analgesia than under the placebo condition. In brief, this study appeared to indicate that hypnotically-suggested analgesia may reduce pain to a certain degree in some good hypnotic subjects and also in a few poor hypnotic subjects, reduces reported pain more in good hypnotic subjects than in poor hypnotic subjects, and reduces reported pain more than a placebo only in a very small proportion of hypnotic subjects (about half of the subjects from the upper 5 per cent of susceptibility or in the upper 2-3 per cent of the subjects).

Although the experiments by Hilgard and associates and by McGlashan et at., which were summarized above, indicated that hypnotically-suggested analgesia at times reduces pain, they did not demonstrate that hypnotic-induction procedures or hypnosis was necessary to produce the effect. In these experiments, the direct suggestions of analgesia were always confounded with a hypnotic-induction procedure. Although, in the McGlashan et al. experiment, placebo instructions were given under a waking condition, in both the McGlashan et al. experiment and in the experiments by Hilgard and associates, the direct suggestions of analgesia were always given to subjects after they had been exposed to a hypnotic-induction procedure. Consequently, it cannot be determined whether the reduction in reported pain was due to hypnosis, to suggestions of analgesia, or to a combination of hypnosis with suggestions of analgesia. Attempts to separate these variables were made in the experiments described next.

Brown and Vogel (1938) compared physiological responses to noxious stimulation under local analgesia produced by Novocain, general anesthesia produced by nitrous oxide, suggestions of analgesia given after a hypnotic-induction procedure, and suggestions to try to imagine or to think of a limb as analgesic given under waking conditions. Three pain stimuli were used (immersion of a limb in water at 49° C., weighted thumbtack applied to a limb for a period of time, and application of a lancet point to the skin); three physiological measures were monitored (GSR, pulse, and blood pressure); and three carefully selected good hypnotic subjects participated. Brown and Vogel presented their results in the form of raw data without statistical analysis. From the raw data they deduced the following conclusions: Suggestions to imagine analgesia given under waking conditions may be as effective as suggestions of analgesia given under hypnosis in reducing physiological responses to noxious stimulation. Nitrous oxide anesthesia is totally dissimilar to hypnotically-suggested analgesia; nitrous oxide anesthesia but not hypnotically-suggested analgesia abolishes physiological reactions to noxious stimulation. It is difficult to determine from the raw data presented in the report if these conclusions are justified. However, a careful analysis of Brown and Vogel's data was performed by Shor

(1959) who reported the following: Physiological responses to the noxious stimuli did not differ significantly under hypnotically-suggested, waking-imagined, and Novocain analgesia. Given the small number of subjects and the variability of the data, it was not possible for statistically significant effects to emerge. With respect to the conclusion that nitrous oxide anesthesia is totally dissimilar to hypnotic analgesia, it appears that this is valid for the galvanic skin response, but it is not clear if it also applies to the pulse and blood-pressure responses. The GSR to noxious stimulation dropped out under nitrous oxide but not under hypnotic analgesia. With respect to the conclusion that waking-imagined analgesia may be as effective as hypnotically-suggested analgesia in attenuating physiological reactions to noxious stimulation, it appears that what is being said is that since neither waking-imagined nor hypnotically-suggested analgesia had any measurable effect, they both by default had about equal effectiveness.

Although the Brown and Vogel (1938) experiment yielded inconclusive results, it suggested an interesting hypothesis for further research, namely, that pain can be reduced to a comparable degree either by suggestions of analgesia given under hypnotic conditions or by suggestions to try to imagine or to think of a noxious stimulus as non-painful given under waking conditions. The hypothesis was tested in an experiment by Barber and Hahn (1962) which was conducted as follows:

Prior to the experiment proper, the Barber Suggestibility Scale was administered under nonhypnotic conditions to 192 female students. The 48 most suggestible subjects (ranking in the upper quartile with respect to scores on the suggestibility scale) were selected to participate in the formal experiment. These selected subjects, who were homogeneous with respect to sex, age, social background, and level of pre-existing suggestibility, were allocated at random to one of four experimental conditions (hynotic analgesia, uninstructed condition, control condition, and waking analgesia) with 12 subjects to each condition. Subjects assigned to the hypnotic condition were given a standardized 20-minute hypnotic induction procedure followed by a series of tests to assess suggestibility. All subjects in this group appeared to enter hypnosis (i.e., appeared drowsy, showed psychomoter retardation and lack of spontaneity, and responded positively to the test-suggestions). Suggestions were then given for a period of one minute to induce anesthesia and analgesia of the left hand; following these suggestions the hypnotized subject immersed the anesthetic hand in water near the freezing point (2° C.) for three minutes. Subjects assigned to the uninstructed, control, and waking analgesia conditons were not hypnotized. Under the uninstructed and control conditions the subjects were simply asked to immerse the left hand in water: The uninstructed group immersed the hand in water near the freezing point (2° C.) for three minutes, and the control group immersed the hand in water at room temperature for the same period of time. Subjects allocated to the waking analgesia condition were instructed and motivated for a one-minute period to imagine and to think of a pleasant situation when the noxious stimulus (water at 2 ° C.) was applied (" . . . try to imagine that the water is pleasant and try to think of it as *not* uncomfortable . . . ").

Soon after stimulation all subjects completed a questionnaire designed to assess subjective experiences. This questionaire yielded the following findings: the hypnotic and waking analgesia groups did not differ in subjective reports, stating that, on the average, the stimulus was experienced as uncomfortable but not painful. The hypnotic and waking analgesia groups differed significantly from the uninstructed group which rated the stimulus as painful, and from the control group, which rated the stimulus as not uncomfortable. Physiological variables (heart rate, skin resistance, forehead-muscle tension, and respiration) monitored prior to and during stimulation were analyzed in terms of Lacey's autonomic lability scores (1956) to control for differences in base (prestimulus) levels of physiological functioning. This analysis showed the following: The hypnotic and waking analgesia groups did not differ on any physiological response to the noxious stimulus. As compared to the uninstructed condition, both hypnotic analgesia and waking analgesia were effective in reducing muscle tension and respiratory irregularities during the noxious stimulation. Under hypnotic and waking analgesia, muscle tension but not respiratory irregularity was reduced to the low level found under the control condition. Heart rate and skin-resistance level during the period of noxious stimulation did not differ under the hypnotic analgesia, waking analgesia, and uninstructed conditions; under these conditions the subjects showed significantly faster heart rate and significantly lower skin resistance than under the control condition. In brief, the Barber and Hahn experiment indicated that hypnotically-suggested analgesia is effective in attenuating pain experience as indicated by subjective reports and by reduction in forehead muscle tension and respiratory irregularities; although pain experience is reduced under hypnotically-suggested analgesia, it is rarely abolished; and the experience of pain can be reduced to about the same degree either by suggesting anesthesia under a hypnotic condition or by suggesting to subjects under a waking condition that they try to imagine and to think of the noxious stimulus as non-painful.

In the above experiment (Barber & Hahn, 1962) the suggestions of analgesia were worded differently for the hypnotic group and the waking group. To ascertain if *identically-worded suggestions of analgesia* are as effective in reducing pain in waking subjects as in hypnotic subjects, Barber and Calverley (1969) and Spanos, Barber, and Lang (1969) carried out experiments as follows:

Barber and Calverley (1969) compared subjective reports of pain (produced by a heavy weight applied to a finger for a period of one minute) in subjects who were given suggestions of anesthesia after they had received a hypnotic-induction procedure and in a comparable group of subjects who received the identical suggestions of anesthesia without a preceding hypnotic-induction. The suggestions of anesthesia were equally effective when given with or without the hypnotic-induction procedure in reducing reports of pain below the level obtained under an uninstructed control condition. The Barber and Calverley (1969) experiment also included addtional groups of subjects who were distracted during the pain stimulation by having them listen to and try to remember an interesting story presented on a tape-recording. Pain was reduced to a comparable degree by distraction under waking conditions, distraction under hypnosis, suggestions of anesthesia given under waking conditions, and suggestions of anesthesia given under hypnosis. In addition, this experiment showed that a hypnotic-induction procedure alone (without suggestions of anesthesia or distraction) is also effective in reducing reported pain.

Spanos, Barber, and Lang (1969) carried out an experiment which also used a heavy weight, applied to a finger for one minute, as the pain stimulus. They found that suggestions of anesthesia given without a hypnotic-induction and suggestions of anesthesia given after a hypnotic induction were equally effective in reducing subjective reports of pain below the level obtained under a control condition. Another variable assessed in this study was the effects of demands for honesty. Half of the subjects under both the hypnotic and non-hypnotic conditions gave their pain reports after a person other than the experimenter had told them that it was very important to give completely honest reports. In both hypnotic and non-hypnotic subjects, the degree of pain reduction reported under suggested anesthesia was not affected by the demands for honesty; that is, the subjects rated the pain as reduced to the same degree under suggested anesthesia regardless of whether or not honest ratings were demanded and regardless of whether or not they had been exposed to a hypnotic-induction procedure.

A substantial number of hypnotic-analgesic and waking analgesic subjects participating in the above experiments manifested physiological responses to pain stimuli which are indicative of anxiety or pain. This raises a crucial question: Does the hypnotic analgesic subject under-going surgery show autonomic responses indicative of anxiety or pain? In searching the literature, no studies were found which presented data on a series of physiological variables recorded continuously during sur-gery performed under trance. A small number of surgical studies were found which presented a few discontinuous pulse or blood-pressure measurements; these studies are reviewed next.

Surgery Under Hypnotically-Suggested Analgesia

Discussions concerned with the effectiveness of hypnot-ically — suggested analgesia in surgery (Anderson, 1957; Butler, 1954; Heron, 1955; Raginsky, 1951; Tinterow, 1960) generally follow an outline as follows: It is first stated that the effectiveness of hypnosis is beyond dispute since Esdaile performed amputations and many other operations "painlessly" under "mesmeric trance" in India during the years 1845 to 1851; the authors then present a few subsequent cases of surgery performed under trance and then conclude that hypnotic anal-gesia produces a drastic reduction in pain experience. The argument to support this contention almost always relies heavily on Esdaile's series.

Although Esdaile's cases are generally referred to as painless surgery performed under trance, a close look at Esdaile's (1850) original report suggests that his operations may not have been free of anxiety and pain. Esdaile did not claim that all or even a majority of his patients remained quiet during surgery (Marcuse, 1947). Some patients showed "disturbed trances" and others awakened from trance: "She moved and moaned" (Esdaile, 1850, p. 200); "He moved, as in an uneasy dream" (p. 204); "About the middle of the operation he gave a cry" (p. 222); "He awoke, and cried out before the operation was finished" (p. 232); "The man moved, and cried out before I had finished . . . on being questioned he said that he had felt no pain" (pp. 145-146). Esdaile claimed that many of his operations were successful even though pain may have been experienced because the patients forgot the pain: " . . . the trance is sometimes completely broken by the knife, but it can occasionally be reproduced by continuing the process, and then the sleeper remembers nothing; he has only been disturbed by a night-mare, of which on waking he retains no recollection" (pp. 145-146).

In 1846, the governor of Bengal appointed a committee consisting of the inspector-general of hospitals, three physicians, and three judges to investigate Esdaile's claims (Braid, 1847). Esdaile removed scrotal tu-mors from six carefully selected patients who had been placed in "mes-meric trance" by "passes" made over the body for a period of about 6-8 hr. (Three additional patients who were to undergo surgery before the committee were dismissed when it was found that they could not be mesmerized after repeated attempts extending up to 11 days.) The committee reported (Braid, 1847) that during surgery three of the six patients showed "convulsive movements of the upper limbs, writhing of the body, distortions of the features, giving the face a hideous expression of suppressed agony; the respiration became heaving, with deep sighs." The other three patients did not show gross signs of pain; however, two of these three showed marked elevations in pulse rate during the surgery on the order of 40 beats per in minute.

In brief, it appears that some of Esdaile's surgical cases awakened from trance and suffered and some remained in trance but showed either "a hideous expression of suppressed agony" or marked tachycardia. However, a certain number of Esdaile's surgical patients did *not* show overt signs of pain and stated on awakening that they had *not* suffered. Although this is indeed remarkable, caution should be exercised in generalizing from these cases. In the first place, the proportion of Esdaile's patients who fell into this category cannot be determined from the data presented in his report. Secondly, if facilities had been available for recording blood pressure, pulse, skin resistance, and other autonomic variables continuously, it appears possible that these patients may also have shown physiological reactions indicative of anxiety and pain. Thirdly, it cannot be assumed that these patients would have moaned or cried during the surgery if they had *not* been in mesmeric trance; although many of Esdaile's nonmesmerized surgical patients cried and struggled, his report suggests that a few of his surgical patients who could *not* be placed in mesmeric trance did *not* show gross signs of pain (Esdaile, 1850, pp. 214-215.)

Following Esdaile's report, scattered cases have been published of surgery performed under hypnosis (Bramwell, 1903; Cochran, 1955; Cooper & Powles, 1945; Crasilneck, McCranie, & Jenkins, 1956). Typically these reports state that an operation was performed under hypnotically suggested analgesia, e.g., dental extraction, avulsion of fingernail, incision of infected digit, removal of cervicouterine tumors and the " . . . cooperation of the patient was perfect, the operation was painless and there was no post-operative pain" or the patient " . . . woke up without pain or any physiological disturbance" (Rose, 1953; Sampimon & Woodfuff, 1946). The procedures employed and the patient's overt behavior and subjective reports are not presented in detail, and physiological measures monitored during the surgery are not reported.

The few reports that present some physiological data suggest the possibility that the hypnotic-analgesic surgical patient may experience some degree of anxiety and pain. Finer and Nylen (1961) presented a successful case of excisions and skin grafts performed upon a severely burned patient under hypnoanesthesia; although the patient did not show overt motoric signs of pain, blood pressure and pulse showed significant elevations. Kroger (1957) and Kroger and DeLee (1957) employed hypnotic analgesia in the removal of breast tumor, in subtotal thyroidectomy, in excision biopsy for breast tumor, and in cesarean section and hysterectomy; no physiological data are presented with the exception of the cesarean section and hysterectomy; in this case, Kroger and Delee (1957) write that during the surgery the blood pressure varied from 125/85 to 80/60 and pulse varied from 76 to 100. Taugher (1958) presented three cases of surgery (tonsillectomy, curettage, and cesarean section) performed under trance. Although the patients did not complain of pain, blood pressure and pulse showed marked variability; in the cesarean section, for instance, blood pressure varied from 140/90 to 80/20, and pulse rate varied from 86 to 120.

Mason (1955) presented a case of mastoplasty performed under hypnotically-suggested analgesia. With the exception of sodium amytal, administered the night before surgery, no other medications were given. During the operation the entranced patient did not show noticeable signs of pain; on awakening, she appeared to be amnesic for any pain that may have been experienced. Mason writes that at some point during the operation — the precise time is unspecified — the patient's " . . . pulse rate stabilized at 96 and respiratory rate at 24 per minute" with the implication that these measures may have been unstable prior to this period.

In other recent surgical cases the effects of hypnotically — suggested analgesia were confounded with the effects of sedative and analgesic drugs: For instance, Marmer (1959) employed hypnosis in an extensive series of surgical cases (bunionectomy, laminectomy, thyroidectomy, hemorrhoidectomy), but substantial quantities of analgesic agents (nitrous oxide, meperidine, caudal block with lidocaine) were always used, no control cases are reported, and it is difficult to separate the effects of hypnosis from the effects of the drugs. Tinterow (1960) presented seven cases of hypnotic surgery (cesarean section, bilateral vein ligation, vaginal hysterectomy, debridements and skin grafts, hemorroidectomy, appendectomy, and open-heart surgery); in most of these cases, secobarbital, atropine sulfate, chlorpromazine, and promethazine were administered singly or in combination. Similary, Owen-Flood (1959) presented a case of appendectomy performed under hypnoanesthesia in which the effects of hypnosis were confounded with the effects of a regular dose of scopolamine and one-half the routine dose of morphine.

In other surgical cases, hypnotic suggestions of analgesia were sufficient to produce a satisfactory reaction pattern during part of the operation, but chemical agents were required before surgery was completed. Anderson (1957) reported that an entranced subject showed little if any overt signs of pain at the commencement of an abdominal exploration; however, before the operation was completed, the patient " . . . practically broke his hypnotic trance," and thiopental was administered. Butler (1954) presented similar findings concerning an abdominal exploration: As the fascia was being incised, the hypnotized patient showed signs of pain and was given cyclopropane.

The above data suggest the possibility that surgery performed under hypnotic trance may not be as painless and as free from anxiety as has at times been supposed. Although highly selected subjects were used in all of these studies, some subjects showed physiological reactions which appear to be indicative of anxiety and pain, others broke the trance, and others required the assistance of chemical agents. These findings appear not to contradict Bernheim's (1887, p. 116) contention that "hypnotism only rarely succeeded as an anesthetic, that absolute insensibility is the exception among hypnotizable subjects, and that the hypnotizing itself generally fails in persons disturbed by the expectations of an operation." The findings also do not contradict Moll's (1889, p. 105) contention that "a complete analgesia is extremely rare in hypnosis, although authors, copying from one another, assert that it is common."

An additional experimental invesigation is needed to delineate more precisely the effects of hypnotic and waking suggestions of analgesia on surgical pain. Although it appears practically impossible to carry out such an investigation during major surgery it may be possible to carry it out when certain types of minor surgery are preformed. A study along these lines would be extremely useful if it were conducted as follows: A series of physiological variables that vary with pain and anxiety, e.g., blood pressure, pulse, skin resistance, and respiration, should be recorded on a polygraph during minor surgery performed on four randomized groups of subjects: a group given suggestions of analgesia after a hypnotic-induction procedure; a group given suggestions of analgesia *without* a hypnotic-induction; a group under chemical analgesia or anesthesia; and a control group which is carefully treated in such a way so as to minimize anxiety but is not exposed either to hypnosis, to suggestions of analgesia, or to analgesic or anesthetic drugs. If subjects in the control group or in the groups given suggestions of analgesia report severe pain at some point during the surgical procedure, they could be given the analgesic or anesthetic drugs. However, the amount of time the subjects are able to undergo the surgical procedure before reporting severe pain will be treated as a dependent variable. The polygraph data should be analyzed by appropriate statistical techniques to take into account differences in physiological base levels under the four conditions (Benjamin, 1967; Dykman, Reese, Galbrecht & Thomasson, 1959; Lacey, 1956). The studies reviewed in this chapter suggest the following hypotheses:

Suggestions of analgesia given either with or without a hypnotic-induction procedure will reduce both reported pain and the physiological measures that vary with pain below the level obtained in the control group.

Verbal reports of pain and the polygraph indices will be more drastically reduced under chemical analgesia or anesthesia than under suggested analgesia.

Suggestions of analgesia given under waking conditions will reduce verbal reports of pain and physiological correlates of pain to about the same degree as suggestions of analgesia given under hypnotic conditions.

Judging from personal experience in this area, I would also venture to predict that investigators may be surprised at the results they obtain with the control subjects; the control subjects may report much less pain than investigators now expect. Stated otherwise, I believe that the degree of pain per se that is actually experienced during minor surgery (and also during major surgery) is usually overestimated by present-day investigators and is often confused with anxiety. Although pain is certainly produced when the skin is cut, this pain is more limited than is commonly believed and the underlying muscles and internal organs are relatively insensitive to pain. If the experimental-surgical situation is structured in such a way that anxiety is minimized in the control subjects, I believe they will report only a limited amount of pain.

Reduction in Drug Requirements as an Index of Pain Relief

Some patients in labor, some postoperative patients, and some terminal cancer patients, who are given suggestions of pain relief under hypnotic trance, state to the hypnotist that their pain has been reduced or abolished. Since the statements of the hypnotic subject, as given to the hypnotist, do not always correspond to the true state of affairs (Barber, 1962a, 1969) a number of investigators have focused on a reduction in the hypnotic patient's need for drugs as a somewhat more objective and somewhat more reliable index of pain relief.

August (1961) compared drug requirements during labor in two groups of patients: 850 trained hypnotic patients who had chosen hyp-

nosis as the preferred form of anesthesia, and 150 control patients who
had refused hypnosis. The control group received an average of 53.7 mg.
of meperidine (Demerol) and 22.7 mg. of barbiturates (Seconal or Nem-
butal); the hypnotic group received on the average 30.3 mg. of meperidine and 2.2 mg. of barbiturate. Abramson and Heron (1950) compared
narcotics requirements during labor of 100 hypnotic patients and of 88
controls picked at random from the hospital files. The hypnotic group
had participated on the average in four prelabor hypnotic training sessions, each session requiring a period of 30 minutes; the controls had
been delivered previously by other obstetricians and had not received
antenatal training. The control group on the average received 123.6 mg.
of meperidine; the hypnotic group received an average of 103.5 mg. of
merperidine, a reduction of 16 per cent.

The studies of August (1961) and of Abramson and Heron (1950) are
open to a number of criticisms: The hypnotic group consisted of vol-
utneers who may have represented a selected group of patients who
were likely to be more cooperative during labor. The obstetricians gave
more time and attention to the hypnotic patients than to the control
patients. The hypnotic group was apparently given medication only on
demand, while the control group received medicaments more or less
routinely. Perchard (1960) carried out a large-scale study which attempted to control some of these variables. A total of 3083 primigra-
vidas were observed, of whom 1703 did not volunteer for antenatal
classes. The other 1380 primiparas, who volunteered for classes, were
assigned to three experimental treatments as follows. Group 1 (268
patients) received three instructional talks concerning parturition plus
a visit to the labor wards. Group 2 (126 patients) was given the three
instructional talks, plus a visit to the labor wards, plus three physical
relaxation classes conducted by a physio-therapist. Group 3 (986
patients) received the three instructional talks, the visit to the labor
wards, plus three training sessions in hypnosis. In the hypnotic training
sessions this group was given practice in hypnosis; practice in responding to suggestions of anesthesia; suggestions that labor would be painless; and suggestions that amnesia would follow the labor. (Fifty-six per
cent, 26 per cent and 18 per cent of the subjects in Group 3 were rated
as "good," "moderately good," and "poor" hypnotic subjects, respectively.) There were no significant differences among the four groups
(nonvolunteers, Group 1, Group 2, and Group 3) in: duration of labor;
calmness, relaxation, and cooperation during labor; number of patients
judged to have had severe pain; incidence of amnesia for labor; and
proportion of patients eager to have more children. There was a small
difference in the amount of sedation requested during labor: 40 per cent

of the hypnotic group and 32, 34, and 35 per cent of Groups 1, 2, and nonvolunteers, respectively, requested less than 100 mg. of meperidine. (The 40 per cent figure for the hypnotic group was increased to 44 per cent in the subgroup rated as "good" hypnotic subjects.) Perchard concluded that "It would appear that no detectable benefits were derived from the simple relaxation exercises and that not more than a limited subjective benefit with slightly reduced need for sedation resulted from the hypnosis."

Papermaster, Doberneck, Bonello, Griffen, and Wangensteen (1960), Bonilla, Quigley, and Bowers (1961) and Laux (1953) assessed the effects of hypnotically suggested pain relief on narcotics requirements in postoperative cases. Papermaster et al. (1960) worked with 33 unselected patients undergoing major surgery. An attempt was made to hypnotize each patient three times, twice prior to and once after surgery; during the hypnotic sessions it was suggested that the area of incision would produce no post operative discomfort. A matched control group, consisting of 33 patients undergoing surgery but not receiving hypnotic training, was selected from the hospital files. The hypnotic group requested and received an average of 4.21 doses of meperidine (50 mg. per dose) postoperatively as compared to 7.57 doses for the control group, a reduction in narcotics requirements of 45 per cent. The authors did not present data for the individual subjects, stating only that the range in doses of meperidine received varied from 0 to 44 and from 0 to 29 in the control and hypnosis groups, respectively.

Bonilla et al., (1961) worked with ten male patients undergoing uncomplicated arthrotomy of the knee. Each patient participated in from one to four 30-minute hypnotic sessions prior to surgery and received suggestions that he would experience no post-operative discomfort; in some, hypnotic sessions were also conducted in the post-operative period. This group was compared on postoperative narcotics requirements with 40 preceding male patients undergoing uncomplicated arthrotomy for similar knee afflictions. The control group received an average of 360 mg. of peperdine postoperatively as compared to 275 mg. for the hypnotic group, a reduction of 24 per cent.

It appears that in the Papermaster et al. (1960) and Bonilla et al. (1961) studies the hypnotic group received medicaments only on demand while the control group was given medication routinely. Laux (1953) presented an experimental study which controlled this factor. Forty veterans undergoing urological surgery were assigned either to an experimental hypnotic group (20 subjects) or to a non-treated control group (20 subjects). The two groups were matched with respect to type of surgery, age, sex, and socio-economic status. The emperimental subjects received suggestions intended to relieve postoperative pain in three presurgery and one postsurgery hypnotic sessions. Criteria for postoperative pain relief included: number of requests for pain-relieving drugs; amount of drugs given; and the charge nurse's evaluation of the amount of pain suffered. The assessment period extended over five days. During the first postoperative day the number of requests for pain-relieving drugs by the hypnotic group was 34 per cent less than for the control group. There were no significant differences between the two groups on any of the criteria during the remaining four days of the assessment period.

Butler (1954), Cangello (1962) and Perese (1962) assessed the effect of suggestions given under trance on pain associated with terminal cancer. Butler found that after a series of intensive hypnotic sessions with 12 selected hypnotizable cancer patients, one patient showed a 50 per cent reduction in narcotics requirements for a few days and another showed a 100 per cent reduction for 3 weeks. (Of the remaining 10 patients, eight manifested subjective relief of pain during and, at times, for a brief period following the trance sessions.) Cangello (1962) reported that after a series of intensive hypnotic sessions 18 of 31 selected cancer patients manifested from 25 to 100 per cent reduction in narcotics for a period extending from two days to twelve weeks. Perese (1961) reported that hypnosis was useful in relieving pain in two of 16 cancer patients and that with another four patients it diminished narcotic requirements slightly. In these sudies the physicians worked intensively with their hypnotic patients, and a control group receiving a similar amount of attention was not used for comparison. It is thus difficult to determine to what extent the reported pain relief was due to the support the patients received from the physician and to what extent it was due to other factors subsumed under the term hypnosis. This factor—the support and attention received by the patient from the physician—will be discussed again below.

In summary, the studies reviewed above appear to indicate that hypnotically-suggested pain relief produces some degree of reduction in anxiety and pain in some patients undergoing surgery or parturition and in some patients suffering from postoperative pain or cancer pain. However, these studies also suggest that although pain experience is at times ameliorated, it is only in very rare cases abolished. A more precise statement of the effects of hypnotically-suggested analgesia in surgery, in labor, and in chronic pain appears to be that when given suggestions of pain relief under hypnotic trance, some patients are able to endure whatever degree of pain is present, are not overly anxious, and do not seem to suffer to the degree expected when anxiety is present.

The Effects of Hypnotic
Suggestions on Functional or Conditioned Pain

Although it appears that hypnotic suggestions rarely if ever abolish pain experience in conditions in which noxious stimulation is continually present—e.g. in surgery or in chronic pain—this does not exclude the possibility that hypnotic suggestions may at times eliminate some types of pain, specifically, those types of pain which appear to be produced by a "conditioning or learning process." Dorcus and Kirkner (1948) presented experimental findings which support this contention. These investigators worked with two groups of selected patients: a group of five males suffering from pain associated with spinal-cord injuries and a group of five females suffering from chronic dysmenorrhea. (No pathology could be found in the latter group that could account for the chronic painful menstrual condition.) Each of the spinal-cord cases participated in approximately 16 hypnotic sessions; the dysmennorheics participated in from one to five hypnotic sessions. The method of treatment included: induction of hypnosis; suggestions of anesthesia to needle pricks and burns; suggestions to induce hallucinatory pain; and posthynotic suggestions that whenever pain arose in the waking state, it would disappear immediately. The spinal-cord cases showed a reduction in requests for pain-relieving drugs and reported less pain, but none were free from pain. The dysmenorrheics, on the other hand, " . . . were relatively free from pain upon discontinuance of therapy and have remained relatively free from pain for at least two years." The authors presented the following interpretation of these findings:

> We believe that dysmenorrhea is a conditioned process brought about in the following manner. Pain above threshold levels has been present at some time during menstruation. When the experience has once occured, such changes as extra-cellular edema, basal temperature change, muscle tonicity, vascular changes, and breast change which were originally associated with the painful experience reinstate the pain even in the absence of the organic factors that originally brought it about . . . In the dysmenorrheic, when we break the chain of expectancy and tension, we break down the conditioned process, whereas in the spinal nerve injury cases we are not destroying a conditioned process, but suppressing the primary pain-arousing mechanism. This is held in abeyance only insofar as the factors that tend to focus the individual's attention on the pain is concerned and in that respect the pain may appear abated. It does not remain inhibited because the source is continually present.

Dorcus and Kirkner's findings with respect to dysmenorrhea may be relevant to other functional painful conditions such as certain types of headaches or backaches. There is evidence to indicate that some headaches are associated with "emotional tension, anxiety, and conflict" and with prolonged contraction of the muscles of the head and neck, and that alleviation of the conflicts and anxieties and/or relief of the muscle hyper-function at times relieves the headache (Wolff, 1948). There is also evidence to indicate that some backaches are associated with sustained contraction in the muscles of the back; the sustained skeletal-muscle hyper-function is one component of a more generalized pattern of response to "anxiety, hostility, and conflict;" and the backache may be ameliorated by relieving either the anxiety or the muscular contractions (Holmes & Wolff, 1950). The findings presented by Dorcus and Kirkner (1948), Wolff (1948) and Holmes and Wolff (1950) suggest the hypothesis that some types of headaches and backaches can be effectively relieved with or without hypnotic trance, by suggestions designed to eliminate the tension-anxiety-conflict pattern and the sustained muscle contractions in the neck or back. Experiments are needed to test this hypothesis.

Significant Variables in Hypnotic Analgesia

One conclusion indicated by this review is that some degree of reduction in pain experience can at times be produced by suggestions given under hypnosis. The question may now be raised: Which of the many variables subsumed under the term hypnosis are effective and which are irrelevant in producing this effect? To answer this question, it is necessary first to specify the referents of the term hypnosis.

Although formal definitions of hypnosis, hypnotized, and hypnotic trance differ widely, in practice the terms are used more or less interchangeably and appear to derive meaning from a consensual frame of reference; that is, when it is stated that subjects were hypnotized or placed in hypnotic trance, it is implied that: one of various types of procedures that have been historically categorized as trance inductions was administered, and that the subjects manifested a number of characteristics which by consensus are presumed to signify the presence of the hypnotic trance. These two interrelated referents of the term hypnosis can be further specified as follows:

Investigators agree that a wide variety of procedures can be classified as trance-inductions. At the present time such induction procedures generally include verbal suggestions of relaxation, drowsiness, and sleep, and often also include some type of physical stimulation such as the sound of a metronome or eye-fixation on a 'hypnodisk.' However, other types of induction procedures, comprehensively described by Weitzenhoffer (1957) and Teitelbaum (1965), have been used in the past and are at times used now, including hyperventilation, compression of the carotid sinus, stimulation of hypnogenic zones, and use of 'passes' or hand gestures. Although one of these induction procedures is employed to induce an inexperienced subject to enter the hypnotic trance, a consensus exists that after a subject has had experience with or training in hypnosis, he may be induced to enter trance by a drastically abbreviated induction procedure consisting of a prearranged signal or cue word.

Numerous attempts have been made to find physiological indices of the state of trance which is said to be produced when the induction procedure is successful. These attempts have failed to yield an acceptable criterion and the presence of the trance state is inferred from the subject's observable characteristics and behaviors (chapter IV). These trance characteristics according to Erickson, Hershman, and Secter (1961, pp. 55-58) include a loss in mobility, tonicity throughout the body, rigid facial expression, and literalness in response. Other investigators list similar indices (Barber, 1969). Pattie (1956a) refers to "... passivity, a disinclination to talk ... a great degree of literal-mindedness, and a lack of spontaneity and initiative." Weitzenhoffer (1957) notes that "There seems to be some agreement that hypnotized individuals, even when behaving in a most natural manner, still show a constriction of awareness, a characteristic literal-mindedness, some psychomotor retardation, and possibly a degree of automatism."

It has often been assumed that hypnotic trance, as inferred from the characteristics and behaviors described above, is a crucial factor in producing pain relief by suggestions. A series of recent investigations, summarized below, suggest that this assumption is open to question.

THE HYPNOTIC TRANCE AS A
FACTOR IN HYPNOTIC ANALGESIA

The presence of hypnotic trance is not sufficient to produce analgesia by suggestions. Esdaile (1850) presented cases of patients manifesting many if not all of the characteristics of deep trance who "shrunk on the first incision" and showed normal responses to painful stimulation. Winkelstein and Levinson (1959), Anderson (1957) Butler (1954), Liebeault (1885), and others also found that some deeply entranced patients did not respond positively to suggestions intended to produce pain relief. The crucial question, however, is not, Is hypnotic trance sufficient to produce analgesia by suggestions?, but, Is hypnotic trance a necessary or an extraneous factor in producing this effect? Contrary to what the early literature on hypnosis might lead one to expect, recent studies indicate that subjects who are in a very light trance and subjects who are not in trance are often as responsive and at times more responsive to suggestions of pain relief than deep-trance subjects.

Barber and Hahn (1962) found that waking control subjects instructed to imagine a pleasant situation during painful stimulation showed as much reduction in pain experience, as indicated by subjective reports and by reduction in muscle tension and respiratory irregularities, as entranced subjects given suggestions of anesthesia. Two recent studies (Barber & Calverley, 1969; Sponos, Barber, & Lang, 1969) demonstrated that a waking group reports as much reduction in pain as a hypnotic group when the two groups are given *identical* suggestions of anesthesia. Von Dedenroth (1962) presented a series of cases in which patients who manifested the characteristics of deep trance did not respond to suggestions of pain relief, and patients who appeared at best to be in a light hypnoidal state and patients who insisted that they were not hypnotized at all, showed dramatic relief of stubborn headache or underwent dentistry without analgesics even though these agents had been demanded consistently for prior dental work. Von Dedenroth interpreted his data as indicating that "each instance of hypnotherapy is dependent upon the patient's inner responsiveness and the character and nature of his motivation rather than upon trance level or depth." Lea, Ware, and Monroe (1960) arrived at a similar conclusion in an investigation concerned with the effects of hypnosis on chronic pain: "We assumed that our success would depend upon the depth of hypnosis, but, to our surprise, we found that this was not necessarily the case. As a matter of fact, two of our best patients obtained only light to medium trances, and significant responses were noted in even the very lightest hypnoidal states." Along similar lines, Cangello (1962) found in a study of the effects of hypnosis on pain associated with cancer that "an individual who entered a deep trance might be unable to obtain relief of pain while another who was at best in a hypnoidal or light state experienced complete pain relief." Laux (1953) presented comparable results in an experimental investigation on postoperative pain: "Some of those who appeared to be the most deeply hypnotized had marked pain, and some who showed little response to the hypnosis had little pain and attributed their comfort to the effect of hypnosis."

Comparable findings have been presented in a series of recent studies employing hypnosis in obstetrics. Michael (1952) found that some patients who at best attained only a very light hypnotic trance underwent labor without medications and without manifesting overt signs of pain while others who attained a deep trance experienced severe pain and required standard doses of narcotics. Winkelstein (1958) observed that "Some women, hypnotized only to the lightest degree managed their delivery successfully, while others, deep in the somnambulistic state were unable to cope with the discomfort of labor." Similarly, Mody (1960) noted no relationship in his sample of 20 selected patients between the depth of hypnosis and the degree of pain experienced during parturition.

The data cited above suggest that the hypnotic trance state may not be a critical factor in producing pain relief by suggestions. The data reviewed below suggest that the critical factors in so-called hypnotic analgesia may include: suggestions of pain relief; which are given in a close interpersonal setting.

THE INTERPERSONAL RELATIONSHIP

Butler (1954) attempted to relieve pain associated with carcinoma in 12 selected patients who were able to attain a medium or deep trance. Each patient received suggestions of pain relief in a series of trance sessions held daily and at times two to four times per day. Ten of the 12 patients stated that their pain was reduced during and, at times, for a brief period following the hypnotic sessions; however, when hypnosis and the relationship between patient and physician were terminated, the patients showed a return of the original pain syndrome. The significant finding in these cases was that when hypnosis was discontinued, but the physician continued to give the same amount of personal attention to the patient, the patient continued to show pain relief. Marmer (1957) has also pointed to the attention and support given to the patient as a significant variable, writing that "The realization that the anesthesiologist is willing to invest time, effort, warmth and understanding in an attempt of hypnosis, will give most patients added security and trust in the physician and will result in decreased tension and anxiety." Lea et al. (1960) reported similar observations in a study on chronic pain: "At times it was hard to decide whether benefit was actually being derived from hypnosis itself or such extraneous factors as the secondary gain a patient would derive from an unusual amount of personal attention from the hypnotherapist."

Recent reports concerned with the effects of hypnosis on the pain of parturition also emphasize the significance of interpersonal factors. In a study with 200 obstetrical patients, Winkelstein (1958) found that to produce some measure of pain relief by suggestions, it was necessary for the physician to devote a great amount of time and attention to each patient. This investigator de-emphasized the importance of the trance state in producing pain relief by suggestions, pointing to the following variables as crucial: the suggestions themselves; the mental attitude of the patient toward pregnancy and delivery; the will to succeed; the confidence of the patient in the procedure as well as in the obstetrician; and the patient-obstetrician rapport. Chlifer (1930) had similarly observed that the effectiveness of pain relief in labor is not correlated with the depth of trance; pain may be ameliorated by suggestions given to nontrance subjects and "the success of verbally induced analgesia is closely related to the personality of the subject and the relationship established between the doctor and the parturient woman." After wide experience in the use of hypnosis for relief of labor pain, Kroger and Freed (1956) proffered the hypothesis that if a close relationship exists between patient and obstetrician, about 10 to 15 per cent of nonmedicated patients will be free of discomfort during labor even though the hypnotic trance is not induced.

The above studies suggest that the critical factors in so-called hypnotic analgesia may include suggestions of pain relief given in a close interpersonal setting. The interpersonal variable has been emphasized above; the "suggestions of pain relief" require further comment.

SUGGESTIONS OF PAIN RELIEF AS A
CRITICAL FACTOR IN HYPNOTIC ANALGESIA

The effects of suggestions of pain relief per se have at times been confounded with the effects of hypnotic trance. In a number of studies (Abramson & Heron, 1950; August, 1951; Bonilla et al., 1961) the experimental group was placed in hypnotic trance and then given suggestions to relieve pain; the control group was not placed in trance and was not given pain-relieving suggestions. These studies failed to exclude the possibility that the effective factor in ameliorating pain in the experimental group was not the hypnotic trance but the suggestions of pain relief per se; if the control group had been given suggestions of pain relief without trance, it might also have shown a reduction in pain experience. Supporting evidence for this supposition is found in the recent experiments by Barber and Calverley (1969) and by Spanos *et. al* (1969) in which nontrance control groups given instructions or suggestions intended to ameliorate pain showed a similar reduction in pain experience as entranced subjects given the same suggestions for pain amelioration.

Sampimon and Woodruff (1946) presented data indicating that direct suggestions given without hypnotic trance are at times sufficient to alleviate pain. In 1945 these investigators were working under primitive conditions in a prisoner of war hospital near Singapore. Anesthetic agents were not available, and hypnosis was employed for surgery. Two patients could not be hypnotized; since the surgical procedures (incision for exploration of the abscess cavity and extraction of incisor) had to be performed without drugs, Sampimon and Woodruff proceeded to operate after giving "the mere suggestion of anesthesia." To their surprise they found that both patients were able to undergo the normally painful procedures without complaints and without noticeable signs of pain. These investigators write that "As a result of these cases two other patients were anesthetized by suggestions only, without any attempt to induce true hypnosis, and both had teeth removed painlessly." Klopp (1961), Wolfe (1961), and Barber (1969) have presented comparable findings with respect to the effectiveness of direct suggestions given without the induction of hypnotic trance.

Similar findings have been presented in studies concerned with the effects of placebos. Hardy et al. (1952) found that two subjects given an inactive drug with the suggestion that it was a strong analgesic showed elevations in pain threshold over 90 per cent above the control levels; blisters were produced in these subjects without reports of pain. Beecher (1955), Dodson and Bennett (1954), Houde and Wallenstein (1953), and Keats (1956) presented evidence indicating that about one-third of post-operative patients receive satisfactory relief of pain when inert agents are adminstered as pain-relieving drugs. Laszlo and Spencer (1953) found in a study with 300 cancer patients that "over 50 per cent of patients who had received analgesics for long periods of time could be adequately controlled by placebo medication." Although few if any studies on the placebo effect report detailed data concerning the relationship between patient and physician and the suggestions given to the patient, it appears likely that in some if not many of these studies the patients were given suggestions of pain relief in a close interpersonal setting.

Indications for Further Research

To determine the significance of hypnotic trance as a factor in relieving pain by suggestions, additional experiments are needed which control three critical variables noted above: the selection of subjects; the inter-personal relationship between subject and experimenter; and the suggestions of pain relief per se. These experiments should be conducted as follows:

The effects of hypnotic trance should not be confounded with differences between subjects. In a number of studies cited above (Abramson & Heron, 1950; August, 1961; Bonilla et al, 1961; Shor, 1959) subjects meeting criteria of hypnotizability were assigned to the trance treatment, and unselected subjects or nonhypnotizable subjects were assigned to the control treatment. The criterion used for selecting the experimental group, that the subjects were hypnotizable, is difficult if not impossible to differentiate from an interrelated implicit criterion, namely, that the subjects were highly responsive to suggestions with or without hypnotic trance. If suggestible subjects are allocated to the trance treatment and less suggestible subjects to the control treatment, it is impossible to determine if greater response to suggestions of pain relief in entranced subjects, as compared to control subjects, is due to their being in trance or to their being more suggestible to begin with. To control this factor, it is necessary that subjects be randomly assigned to the trance and non-trance treatments from an original group of subjects who show a similar level of suggestibility (Barber, 1962a; Sutcliffe, 1960).

Subjects allocated to the trance and nontrance treatments should be given comparable time and attention by the experimenter and should have a comparable opportunity to form a close relationship with him.

Both groups should be given similar suggestions of pain relief, one group to be given the suggestions under trance and the other under non-trance conditions.

The data presented in this chapter suggest that if these criticial variables are controlled, it will be difficult to reject the null hypothesis of no difference in response to suggestions of analgesia in nonentranced and deeply entranced subjects.

Variables Intervening Between Suggestions of Pain Relief and Reduction in Pain Response

Halliday and Mason (1964) showed that cortical evoked potentials produced by stimulation of a limb were the same when the stimulation was applied either under normal conditions or under 'hypnotic anesthesia.' They concluded that "no part of the [subjectively reported] loss of sensation in hypnotic anesthesia can be attributed to attenuation of the sensory messages in the afferent pathways on their way to the cortex." In other words, the reduction in reported pain experience which is associated with 'hypnotic anesthesia' is apparently due to processes going on at the highest or cortical levels of the central nervous system. These higher processes have been conceptualized in terms of attention, attitude, anxiety, distraction, and similar concepts. Let us now turn to these intervening or mediating variables.

A number of investigators have postulated that suggestions of analgesia are effective in diminishing subjective and physiological responses to pain if and when they lead the subject to stop thinking about or to stop attending to the pain. Liebeault (1885) hypothesized that the process of suggested analgesia can be described simply as the focusing of attention on ideas other than those concerning pain. Young (1926) presented a similar hypothesis. Pain relief produced by hypnosis or by suggestive procedures is due to a "taking of an attitude and consequently *refusing* to feel the pain or even to take cognizance of it." August (1961) postulated that "Hypnoanesthesia results from directing attention away from pain response towards pleasant ideas." These hypotheses receive support from recent experimental studies which found that the subjective and physiological responses to painful stimuli which characterize hypnotic analgesic subjects can be elicited from control subjects either by asking them to think about and to imagine a pleasant situation when noxious stimulation is applied (Barber & Hahn, 1962) or by distracting them during the noxious stimulation (Barber & Calverley, 1969).

The intervening variables in so-called hypnotic analgesia may be similar to those which presumably operate in the placebo situation and in other nontrance situations in which pain experience is abated without medications. These intervening variables have been summarized succinctly by Cattell (1943):

> The intensity of the sensation produced by a painful stimulus is determined to a large extent by circumstances which determine the attitude towards its cause. If there is no worry or other distressing implications regarding its source, pain is comparatively well tolerated and during important occasions injuries ordinarily painful may escape notice. On the other hand, in the absence of distraction, particularly if there is anxiety, the patient becomes preoccupied with his condition, and pain is badly tolerated.

It appears unnecessary to hypothesize additional intervening or mediating variables in so-called hypnotic analgesia. In any situation (hypnotic or nonhypnotic) in which anticipation or fear of pain is dispelled, and anxiety is reduced, and the subject does not attend to or think about the painful stimulus, noxious stimulation is apparently experienced as less painful and less distressing than in situations in which anxiety and concern over pain are present (Barber, 1959; Beecher, 1959; Hall, 1953, 1957; Hall & Stride, 1954; Hill et al., 1952a, 1952b; Shor, 1959).

Summary

This chapter has documented six major points: In some instances, suggestions of pain relief given under hypnotic trance appear to produce some degree of diminution in pain experience as indicated by reduction in physiological responses to noxious stimuli and by reduction in requests for pain-relieving drugs. In other instances, however, hypnotically-suggested analgesia produces, not a reduction in pain experience, but an unwillingness to state directly to the hypnotist that pain was experienced and/or an apparent amnesia for the pain that was experienced.

The motivation for denial of pain is present in the hypnotic situation. The physician has invested time and energy hypnotizing the patient and suggesting that pain will be relieved; expects and desires that his efforts will be successful and communicates his desires to the patient. The patient in turn has often formed a close relationship with the physician-hypnotist and does not want to disappoint him. The situation is such that even though the patient may have suffered, it is at times difficult or distrubing for him to state directly to the physician that pain was experienced and it is less anxiety provoking to state that he did not suffer.

A series of experiments that monitored heart rate, skin resistance, respiration, blood pressure, and other physiological responses which are normally associated with painful stimulation found that in some instances hypnotically-suggested analgesia reduced some physiological responses to noxious stimuli and in other instances physiological responses were not affected. However, experiments which found reduced autonomic responses to noxious stimuli under hypnotic analgesia compared reactivity under the hypnotic condition with reactivity under an *uninstructed* waking condition. In an experiment in which physiological reactions to painful stimulation were compared under hypnotically-suggested analgesia and a waking condition in which subjects were instructed to imagine a pleasant situation when noxious stimulation was applied, it was found that both conditions were equally effective in reducing subjective and physiological responses to painful stimulation.

Studies concerned with surgery performed under hypnoanesthesia alone rarely present any physiological data; the small number of studies that presented a few pulse or blood pressure measurements suggest the possibility that hypnotic-analgesic subjects undergoing surgery may show autonomic responses indicative of anxiety and pain. In other studies concerned with surgery performed under hypnosis the effect of hypnotically-suggested analgesia was confounded with the effects of sedative and analgesic drugs.

The data appear to indicate that in surgery, in chronic pain, and in other conditions in which noxious stimulation is continually present pain experience is at times reduced but is rarely if ever abolished by hypnotically-suggested analgesia. However, the data also indicate that suggestions given under hypnotic trance (and also without hypnotic trance) may at times drastically reduce or eliminate some painful conditions, such as dysmenorrhea and certain types of headaches and backaches, which appear to be produced by a conditioning or learning process.

This review suggests that the critical variables in so-called hypnotic analgesia include: suggestions of pain relief, which are given in a close interpersonal setting. Additional research is needed to determine if the hypnotic trance state is also a relevant variable. Further experiments should control: the preexisting level of suggestibility among subjects assigned to the trance and control treatments; the interpersonal relationship between subject and experimenter; and the suggestions of pain relief per se. Recent studies indicate that, when these variables are controlled, suggestions of pain relief given either to waking control subjects or to hypnotized subjects produce a comparable reduction in pain experience.

References

Abramson, M., and Heron, W. T. An objective evaluation of hypnosis in obstetrics. *Amer. J. Obstet. Gynec.*, 1950, *59*, 1069-1074.

Anderson, M. N. Hypnosis in anesthesia. *J. Med. Ass. Alabama*, 1957, *27*, 121-125.

Andrews, H. L. Skin resistance change and measurements of pain threshold. *J. Clin. Invest.*, 1943, *22*, 517-520.

Asin, J. The utilization of hypnosis in obstetrics, *J. Amer. Soc. Psychosom. Dent. Med.*, 1961, *8*, 63-68.

August, R. V. *Hypnosis in obstetrics.* New York: McGraw-Hill, 1966.

Banister, H., and Zangwill, O. L. Experimentally induced visual paramnesias. *Brit. J. Psychol.*, 1941, *32*, 30-51.

Barber, T. X. Toward a theory of pain: Relief of chronic pain by prefrontal leucotomy, opiates, placebos, and hypnosis. *Psychol. Bull.*, 1959, *56*, 430-460.

Barber, T. X. "Hypnosis," analgesia, and the placebo effect. *J. Amer. Med. Ass.*, 1960, *172*, 680-683.

Barber, T. X. Experimental controls and the phenomena of "hypnosis": A critique of hypnotic research methodology. *J. Nerv. Ment. Dis.*, 1962, *134*, 493-505 (a).

Barber, T. X. Toward a theory of hypnosis: Posthypnotic behavior. *Arch. Gen. Psychiat.*, 1962, *7*, 321-342. (b)

Barber, T. X. *Hypnosis: A scientific approach.* New York: Van Nostrand Reinhold, 1969.

Barber, T. X., and Calverley, D. S. Effects of hypnotic induction, suggestions of anesthesia, and distraction on subjective and physiological responses to pain. Paper presented at Eastern Psychological Association, Annual Meeting, Philadelphia, April 10, 1969.

Barber, T. X., and Coules, J. Electrical skin conductance and galvanic skin response during "hypnosis." *Int. J. Clin. Exp. Hypn.*, 1959, *7*, 79-82.

Barber, T. X., and Hahn, K. W., Jr. Physiological and subjective responses to

pain-producing stimulation under hypnotically-suggested and waking-imagined "analgesia." *J. Abnorm. Soc. Psychol.,* 1962, *65,* 411-418.

Barber, T.X., and Hahn, K. W., Jr. Experimental studies in "hypnotic" behavior: Physiological and subjective effects of imagined pain. *J. Nerv. Ment.
Dis.,* 1964, *139,* 416-425.

Beecher, H. K. Pain in men wounded in battle. *Ann. Surg.,* 1946, *123,* 96-105.

Beecher, H. K. The powerful placebo. *J. Amer. Med. Ass.,* 1955, *159,*
1602-1606.

Beecher, H. K. Relationship of significance of wound to pain experienced. *J.
Amer. Med. Ass.,* 1956, *161,* 1609-1613.

Beecher, H. K., *Measurement of subjective responses.* New York: Oxford
Univ. Press, 1959.

Benjamin, L. S. Facts and artifacts in using analysis of covariance to "undo" the
law of initial values. *Psychophysiology,* 1967, *4,* 187-206.

Bernheim, H. *Suggestive therapeutics.* Westport, Conn.: Associated Booksellers, 1957. (Original date of publication: 1887.)

Bitterman, M. E., and Marcuse, F. L. Autonomic responses in posthypnotic
amnesia. *J. Exp. Psychol.,* 1945, *35,* 248-252.

Blum, G. S. *A model of the mind.* New York: Wiley, 1961.

Bonilla, K. B., Quigley, W. F., and Bowers, W. F. Experience with hypnosis on
a surgical service. *Milit. Med.,* 1961, *126,* 364-366.

Braid, J. Facts and observations as to the relative value of mesmeric and
hypnotic coma, and ethereal narcotism, for the mitigation or entire prevention
of pain during surgical operations. *Med. Times,* 1847, *15,* 381-382.

Bramwell, J. M. *Hypnotism.* New York: Julian Press, 1956, (Original date of
publication: 1903.)

Brown, R. R., and Vogel, V. H. Psychophysiological reactions following painful
stimuli under hypnotic analgesia, contrasted with gas anesthesia and Novocain block. *J. Appl. Psychol.,* 1938, *22,* 408-420.

Butler, B. The use of hypnosis in the care of the cancer patient. *Cancer,* 1954, *7,*
1-14.

Callan, T. D. Can hypnosis be used routinely in obstetrics? *Rocky Mountain
Med. J.,* 1961, *58,* 28-32.

Cangello, V. W. Hypnosis for the patient with cancer. *Amer. J. Clin. Hypn.,*
1962, *4,* 215-226.

Cannon, W. B. *Bodily changes in pain, hunger, fear, and rage.* New York:
Appleton, 1915.

Cattell, M. The action and use of analgesics. *Res. Publ. Ass. Nerv. Ment. Dis.,*
1943, *23,* 365-372.

Chertok, L. *Psychosomatic methods in painless childbirth.* New York: Pergamon, 1959.

Chlifer, R. I. Verbal analgesia in childbirth. *Psychotherapia* (Kharkov) 1930,
307-318.

Clark, R. N. Training method for childbirth utilizing hypnosis. *Amer. J. Obstet.
Gynec.,* 1956, *72,* 1302-1304.

Cochran, J. L. The adaptability of psychosomatic anesthesia for the performance
of intermediate surgery on certain types of patients. *Brit. J. Med. Hypn.,*
1955, *7,* (1), 26-34.

Cohen, L. H., and Patterson, M. Effects of pain on heart rate of normal and
schizophrenic individuals. *J. Gen. Psychol.,* 1937, *16,* 273-289.

Cooper, S. R., and Powles, W. E. The psychosomatic approach in practice. *McGill Med. J.,* 1945, *14,* 415-438.

Crasilneck, H. B., McCranie, E. J., and Jenkins, M. T. Special indications for hypnosis as a method of anesthesia. *J. Amer. Med. Ass.,* 1956, *162,* 1606-1608.

Dodson, H. C., Jr., and Bennett, H. A. Relief of postoperative pain. *Amer. Surg.,* 1954, *20,* 405-409.

Dorcus, R. M., and Kirkner, F. J. The use of hypnosis in the suppression of intractable pain. *J. Abnorm. Soc. Psychol.,* 1948, *43,* 237-239.

Dorcus, R. M., and Shaffer, G. W. *Textbook of abnormal psychology,* (3rd Ed.) Baltimore: Williams & Wilkins, 1945.

Doupe, J., Miller, W. R., and Keller, W. K. Vasomotor reactions in the hypnotic state. *J. Neurol. Psychiat.,* 1939, *2,* 97-106.

Dykman, R. A., Reese, W. G., Galbrecht, C. R., and Thomasson, P. J. Psychophysiological reactions to novel stimuli: Measurement, adaptation, and relationship of psychological and physiological variables in the normal human. *Ann. N. Y. Acad. Sci.,* 1959, *79,* 43-61.

Dynes, J. B. An experimental study of hypnotic anesthesia. *J. Abnorm. Soc. Psychol.,* 1932, *27,* 79-88.

Dynes, J. B., and Poppen, J. L. Lobotomy for intractable pain. *J. Amer. Med. Ass.,* 1949, *140,* 15-18.

Elliotson, J. *Numerous cases of surgical operations without pain in the mesmeric state.* London: H. Bailliere, 1843.

Engel, B. T. Physiological correlates of pain and hunger. Unpublished doctoral dissertation. Univ. of California at Los Angeles, 1956.

Erickson, M. H., Hershman, S., and Secter, I. I. *The practical application of medical and dental hypnosis.* New York: Julian Press, 1961.

Esdaile, J. *Hypnosis in medicine and surgery.* New York: Julian Press, 1957. (Originally entitled *Mesmerism in India* and published in 1850.)

Finer, B. L., and Nylen, B. O. Cardiac arrest in the treatment of burns, and report on hypnosis as a substitute for anesthesia. *Plast. Reconstr. Surg.,* 1961, *27,* 49-55.

Furer, M., and Hardy, J. D. The reaction to pain as determined by the galvanic skin response. *Res. Publ. Ass. Nerv. Ment. Dis.,* 1950, *29,* 72-89.

Georgi, F. Beiträge zur Kenntnis des psycho-galvanischen Phänomens. *Arch. Psychiat.,* 1921, *62,* 571-597.

Goetzl, F. R., Bien, C. W., and Lu, G. Changes in blood pressure in response to presumably painful stimuli. *J. Appl. Physiol.,* 1951, *4,* 161-170.

Gold, H., The effect of extracardiac pain on the heart. *Res. Publ. Ass. Nerv. Ment. Dis.,* 1943, *23,* 345-357.

Gorton, B. E. The physiology of hypnosis. *Psychiat. Quart.,* 1949, *23,* 317-343 and 457-485.

Hall, K. R. L. Studies of cutaneous pain: A survey of research since 1940. *Brit. J. Psychol.,* 1953, *44,* 279-294.

Hall, K. R. L. Pain and suffering. *South Afr. Med. J.,* 1957, *31,* 1227-1231.

Hall, K. R. L., and Stride, E. The varying response to pain in psychiatric disorders: A study in abnormal psychology. *Brit. J. Med. Psychol.,* 1954, *27,* 48-60.

Halliday, A. M., and Mason, A. A. The effect of hypnotic anesthesia on cortical responses. *J. Neurol. Neurosurg. Psychiat.,* 1964, *27,* 300-312.

Hardy, J. D., Wolff, H. G., and Goodell, H. *Pain sensations and reactions.* Baltimore: Williams & Wilkins, 1952.

Heron, W. T. Hypnosis as an anesthetic. *Brit. J. Med. Hypn.,* 1954, *6,* 20-26.

Hilgard, E. R. A quantitative study of pain and its reduction through hypnotic suggestion. *Proc. Nat. Acad. Sci.,* 1967, *57,* 1581-1586.

Hilgard, E. R. Pain as a puzzle for psychology and physiology. *Amer. Psychol.,* 1969, *24,* 103-113.

Hilgard, E. R., Cooper, L. M., Lenox, J., Morgan, A. H., and Voevodsky, J. The use of pain-state reports in the study of hypnotic analgesia to the pain of ice water. *J. Nerv. Ment. Dis.,* 1967, *144,* 506-513.

Hill, H. E., Kornetsky, C. H., Flanary, H. G. and Wikler, A. Effects of anxiety and morphine on discrimination of intensities of painful stimuli. *J. Clin. Invest.,* 1952, *31,* 473-480. (a)

Hill, H. E., Kornetsky, C. H. Flanary, H. G., and Wikler, A. Studies on anxiety associated with anticipation of pain. I. Effects of morphine. *Arch. Neurol. Psychiat.,* 1952, *67,* 612-619. (b)

Holmes, T. H., and Wolff, H. G. Life situations, emotions and backache. *Res. Publ. Ass. Nerv. Ment. Dis.,* 1950, *29,* 750-772.

Houde, R. W., and Wallenstein, S. L. A method for evaluating analgesics in patients with chronic pain. *Drug. Addict. Narcot. Bull.,* 1953, Appendix F., 660-682.

Hull, C. L. *Hypnosis and suggestibility: An experimental approach.* New York: Appleton-Century-Crofts, 1933.

Javert, C. T., and Hardy, J. D. Influence of analgesics on pain intensity during labor (with a note on "natural childbirth"). *Anesthesiology,* 1951, *12,* 189-215.

Kaplan, E. A. Hypnosis and pain. *Arch. Gen. Psychiat.,* 1960, *2,* 567-568.

Keats, A. S. Postoperative pain: Research and treatment. *J. Chron. Dis.,* 1956, *4,* 72-80.

Kirkner, F. J. Control of sensory and perceptive functions by hypnosis. In R. M. Dorcus (Ed.) *Hypnosis and its therapeutic applications.* New York: McGraw-Hill, 1956. Chap. 3.

Klopp, K. K. Production of local anesthesia using waking suggestion with the child patient. *Int. J. Clin. Exp. Hypn.,* 1961, *9,* 59-62.

Kornetsky, C. Effects of anxiety and morphine in the anticipation and perception of painful radiant heat stimuli. *J. Comp. Physiol. Psychol.,* 1954, *47,* 130-132.

Kroger, W. S. Introduction and supplemental reports: In J. Esdaile *Hypnosis in medicine and surgery.* New York: Julian Press, 1957.

Kroger, W. S., and DeLee, S. T. Use of hypnoanaesthesia for cesarean section and hysterectomy. *J. Amer. Med. Ass.,* 1957, *163,* 442-444.

Kroger, W. S., and Freed, S. C. *Psychosomatic gynecology.* Glencoe, Ill.: Free Press, 1956.

Lacey, J. I. The evaluation of autonomic responses: Toward a general solution. *Ann. N. Y. Acad. Sci.,* 1956, *67,* 123-164.

Lacey, J. I. Psychophysiological approaches to the evaluation of psychotherapeutic process and outcome. In E. A. Rubinstein and M. B. Parloff (Eds.) *Research in psychotherapy.* Washington, D. C.: American Psychol. Ass., 1959. Pp. 160-208.

LaFontaine, C. *L'art de magnetiser ou le magnetisme animal* (3rd Ed.). Paris: Bailiere, 1860.

Laszlo, D., and Spencer, H. Medical problems in the management of cancer. *Med. Clin. N. Amer.,* 1953, *37,* 869-880.

Laux, R. An investigation of the analgesic effects of hypnosis on postoperative pain resulting from urological surgery. Unpublished doctoral dissertation, Univ. of Southern Calif., 1953.

Lea, P. A., Ware, P. D., and Monroe, R. R. The hypnotic control of intractable pain. *Amer. J. Clin. Hypn.,* 1960, *3,* 3-8.

LeBeau, J. Experience with topectomy for the relief of intractable pain. *J. Neurosurg.,* 1950, *7,* 79-91.

Leriche, R. *The surgery of pain.* Baltimore: Williams & Wilkins, 1939.

Levine, M. Psychogalvanic reaction to painful stimuli in hypnotic and hysterical anesthesia. *Bull. Johns Hopkins Hosp.,* 1930, *46,* 331-339.

Liebeault, A. A. Anesthesia par suggestion. *J. Magnetisme* 1885, *64.* (Cited by Chertok, 1959.)

Life, C. The effects of practice in the trance upon learning in the normal waking state. Bachelor's thesis, Univ. of Wisconsin, 1929.

Mandy, A., J., Mandy, T. E., Farkas, R., and Scher, E. Is natural childbirth natural? *Psychosom. Med.,* 1952, *14,* 431-438.

Marcuse, F. L. Hypnosis in dentistry. *Amer. J. Orthodont. Oral. Surg.,* 1947, *33,* 796-809.

Marmer, M. J. Hypnoanalgesia: The use of hypnosis in conjunction with chemical anesthesia. *Anesth. Analg.,* 1957, *36,* 27-31.

Marmer, M. J. *Hypnosis in anesthesiology.* Springfield, Ill.: C. C. Thomas, 1959.

Mason, A. A. Surgery under hypnosis. *Anesthesia,* 1955, *10,* 295-299.

McGlashan, T. H., Evans, F. J., and Orne, M. T. The nature of hypnotic analgesia and placebo response to experimental pain. *Psychosom. Med.,* 1969, *31,* 227-246.

Michael, A. M. Hypnosis in childbirth. *Brit. Med. J.,* 1952, *1,* 734-737.

Mitchell, M. B. Retroactive inhibition and hypnosis. *J. Gen. Psychol.,* 1932, *7,* 343-358.

Mody, N. V. Report on twenty cases delivered under hypnotism. *J. Obstet. Gynec., India,* 1960, *10,* 348-353.

Moll, A. *The study of hypnosis.* New York: Julian Press, 1958. (Original date of publication: 1889.)

Moravcsik, E. E. Experiments über das psychogalvanische Reflexphänomen. *J. Psychol. Neurol.,* 1912, *18,* 186-199.

Myers, F. W. H. *Human personality and its survival of bodily death.* Vol. 1. New York: Longmans, Green, 1954. (Original date of publication: 1903.)

Ostenasek, F. J. Prefrontal lobotomy for the relief of intractable pain. *Johns Hopk. Hosp. Bull.,* 1948, *83,* 229-236.

Owen-Flood, A. Hypnosis in anaesthesiology. In J. M. Schneck (Ed.) *Hypnosis in modern medicine* (2nd Ed.). Springfield, Ill.. C. C. Thomas, 1959, Pp. 89-100.

Papermaster, A. A., Doberneck, R. C., Bonello, F. J., Griffen, W. O., Jr., and Wangensteen, O. H. Hypnosis in surgery: II. Pain. *Amer. J. Clin. Hypn.,* 1960, *2,* 220-224.

Patten, E. F. Does post-hypnotic amnesia apply to practice effects? *J. Gen. Psychol.,* 1932, *7,* 196-201.

Pattie, F. A. Methods of induction, susceptibility of subjects, and criteria of hypnosis. In R. M. Dorcus (Ed.) *Hypnosis and its therapeutic applications.* New York: McGraw-Hill, 1956, Chap. 2.(a).

Pattie, F. A. Theories of hypnosis. In R. M. Dorcus (Ed.) *Hypnosis and its therapeutic applications.* New York: McGraw-Hill, 1956, Chap. 1. (b)

Peiper, A. Untersuchungen über den galvanischen Hautreflex (psychogalvanischen Reflex) in Kindesalter, *Jahrb. Kinderheilkunde,* 1924, *107,* 139-150.

Perchard, S. D. Hypnosis in obstetrics. *Proc. Royal Soc. Med.,* 1960, *53,* 458-460.

Perese, D. M. How to manage pain in malignant disease. *J. Amer. Med. Ass.,* 1961, *175,* 75-81.

Prideaux, E. The psychogalvanic reflex. *Brain,* 1920, *43,* 50-73.

Raginsky, B. B. The use of hypnosis in anesthesiology. *J. Pers.,* 1951, *1,* 340-348.

Rose, A. G. The use of hypnosis as an anaesthetic, analgesic, and amnesic agent in gynaecology. *Brit. J. Med. Hypn.,* 1953, *5,* (1), 17-21.

Sampimon, R. L. H., and Woodruff, M. F. A. Some observations concerning the use of hypnosis as a substitute for anesthesia. *Med. J. Australia,* 1946, *1,* 393-395.

Sattler, D. G. Absence of local sign in visceral reactions to painful stimulation. *Res. Publ. Ass. Nerv. Ment. Dis.,* 1943, *23,* 143-153.

Schultze-Rhonhof, F. Der hypnotische Geburtsdämmerschlaf. *Zbl. Gynäk.* 1922, *247.* (Cited by Chertok, 1959.)

Schwartz, A. M., Sata, W. K., and Laszlo, D. Studies on pain. *Science.* 1950, *111,* 310-311.

Sears, R. R. Experimental study of hypnotic anesthesia. *J. Exp. Psychol.,* 1932, *15,* 1-22.

Seward, J. P., and Seward, G. H. The effect of repetition on reaction to electric shock. *Arch. Psychol.,* 1934, No. 168.

Shor, R. Explorations in hypnosis: A theoretical and experimental study. Unpublished doctoral dissertation, Brandeis Univ., 1959.

Spanos, N. P., Barber, T. X., and Lang, G. Effects of hypnotic induction, suggestions of analgesia, and demands for honesty on subjective reports of pain. Department of Sociology, Boston University, 1969. (Mimeo)

Sutcliffe, J. P. "Credulous" and "sceptical" views of hypnotic phenomena: A review of certain evidence and methodology. *Int. J. Clin. Exp. Hypn.,* 1960, *8,* 73-101.

Sutcliffe, J. P. "Credulous" and "skeptical" views of hypnotic phenomena: Experiments on esthesia, hallucination and delusion. *J. Abnorm. Soc. Psychol.,* 1961, *62,* 189-200.

Taugher, V. J. Hypno-anesthesia. *Wisc. Med. J.,* 1958, *57,* 95-96.

Teitelbaum, M. *Hypnosis induction technics.* Springfield, Ill.: C. C. Thomas, 1965.

Tinterow, M. M. The use of hypnoanalgesia in the relief of intractable pain. *Amer. Surg.,* 1960, *26,* 30-34.

Tinterow, M. M. The use of hypnotic anesthesia for major surgical procedures. *Amer. Surg.,* 1960, *26,* 732-737.

Trent, J. C. Surgical anesthesia, 1846-1946. *J. Hist. Med.,* 1946, *1,* 505-511.

Velvovski, I. Z., Platonov, K. I. Plotitcher, V. A., and Chougom, E. A. *Psychoprophylactic.* Leningrad: Medguiz, 1954.

Von Dedenroth, T. E. A. Trance depth: An independent variable in therapeutic results. *Amer. J. Clin. Hypn.,* 1962, *4,* 174-176.

Wallace, G., and Coppolino, C. A. Hypnosis in anesthesiology. *New York J. Med.,* 1960, *60,* 3258-3273.

Witzenhoffer, A. M. *Hypnotism: An objective study in suggestibility.* New York: Wiley, 1953.

Weitzenhoffer, A. M. *General techniques of hypnotism.* New York: Grunes & Stratton, 1957.

Wells, W. R. The extent and duration of post-hypnotic amnesia. *J. Psychol.,* 1940, *2,* 137-151.

West, L. J., Niell, K. C., and Hardy, J. D. Effects of hypnotic suggestion on pain perception and galvanic skin response. *Arch. Neurol. Psychiat.,* 1952, *68,* 549-560.

White, R. W. A preface to the theory of hypnotism. *J. Abnorm. Soc. Psychol.,* 1941, *36,* 477-505.

Winkelstein, L. B. Routine hypnosis for obstetrical delivery: An evaluation of hypnosuggestion in 200 consecutive cases. *Amer. J. Obstet. Gynec.,* 1958, *76,* 152-160.

Winkelstein, L. B., and Levinson, J. Fulminating pre-eclampsia with Cesarean section performed under hypnosis. *Amer. J. Obstet. Gynec.,* 1959, *78,* 420-423.

Wolfe, L. S. Hypnosis in anesthesiology. In L. M. LeCron (Ed.) *Techniques of hypnotherapy.* New York: Julian Press, 1961, Pp. 188-212.

Wolff, H. G. *Headache and other head pain.* New York: Oxford Univ. Press, 1948.

Young, P. C. An experimental study of mental and physical functions in the normal and hypnotic states. *Amer. J. Psychol.,* 1926, *37,* 345-356.

CHAPTER 6

Hypnotic Age-Regression

CONTENTS

Hypnotic Age-Regression

When given the suggestion that he is five months old, the hypnotized person at times indulges in infantile acts such as thumbsucking, babbling, and feeding from a bottle. Pertinent to on-going research in the behavioral and physiological sciences are reports indicating that during such hypnotic age-regression subjects manifest some infantile reflex responses and some overt behavioral responses that are not within the range of knowledge of infant or child behavior available, under normal conditions, to the adult. An example of the first is the apparent reinstatement of the infantile plantar reflex under hypnotic regression to an age of five months (Gidro-Frank & Bowersbuch, 1948); an example of the latter is the recall by subjects, under hypnotic regression to age four, of the exact day of the week on which their fourth birthday fell (True, 1949). To form an estimate as to the validity and possible significance of such reported effects of hypnotic age-regression, the present chapter will review relevant clinical and experimental studies.

Role-Playing

Previous surveys of the literature (Gebhard, 1961; Gorton, 1959; Kline, 1953; Pattie, 1956; Weitzenhoffer, 1953) asked: Is hypnotic age-regression real or is it role-playing? The question, as stated, is amenable to more than one answer, depending on how we conceive of the critical terms. For instance, hypnotic age-regression is not real if this word connotes a reinstatement of all behaviors typical of an earlier chronological age; under regression to infancy, the hypnotized person does not topple from his chair; he understands the spoken word, and he obeys instructions to return to the present time. But hypnotic age-regression is

255

also not necessarily role-playing if this term implies deception, pretense, or dissimulation; available evidence appears to indicate that when return to an earlier life-period is suggested, some good hypnotic subjects may remain, for a time, relatively unconcerned with the immediate experimental situation and may vividly imagine and think about an earlier time. Since words such as 'real' and 'role-playing' lead to semantic problems which are difficult to resolve empirically, I shall, in the following discussion, focus on a somewhat different question: When return to infancy or childhood is suggested, does the good hypnotic subject exhibit some behaviors that are characteristic of infancy or childhood and difficult or impossible for the normal adult to perform voluntarily?

Studies Using Physiological Criteria

A series of studies attempted to determine whether hypnotic age-regression reinstates physiological responses that are characteristic of the suggested age. These studies were concerned with one of four types of responses: an 'unconditioned infantile reflex'; an 'involuntary' conditioned response; an electroencephalographic response; and other types of physiological responses such as homonymous hemianopsia. Studies falling under each of these four headings will now be reviewed in turn.

ELICITATION OF AN 'UNCONDITIONED INFANTILE REFLEX'

Gidro-Frank and Bowersbuch (1948) carried out a study that was based on the following assumption: Up to about five months of age the infant responds to stimulation of the sole of the foot with upturning (dorsiflexion) of the large toe and fanning of the other toes (the Babinski toe response); and, from the age of seven months and above, flexion of the toes is the normal plantar response. Gidro-Frank and Bowersbuch asked: Is the Babinski toe response revived under hypnotic regression to early infancy? Working with three carefully selected subjects, they found that, under hypnotic regression to below five months of age, each subject showed the Babinski response; and, under hypnotic regression to an age of seven months and above, each subject showed normal plantar flexion. Although Mesel and Ledford (1959) were unable to confirm these results, True and Stephenson (1951) and McCranie, Crasilneck, and Teter (1955) reported that they obtained the Babinski response with some subjects who were hypnotically-regressed to early infancy.

Since in each of these experiments the Babinski response appeared spontaneously without being suggested, the experimenters concluded that hypnotic regression to early infancy is sufficient to revive an unconditioned infantile reflex. This interpretation is open to question. Dorsiflexion of the large toe (the Babinski sign) is *not* the characteristic response of the infant to plantar stimulation; the characteristic response from a few days after birth to about seven months of age consists of a sudden total withdrawal of the extremity. In a careful study with 75 infants, McGraw (1941) found that withdrawal of the limb followed plantar stimulation in all infants up to about three months of age and in 60 per cent of infants up to about seven months of age. In earlier studies, Wolff (1930) had observed a typical Babinski in only 13 of 389 observations made on infants below seven months of age, and Burr (1921) had noted such wide variation in the digital response of 69 infants as to conclude that no specific movements of the toes could be considered as characteristic of the infantile response to plantar stimulation.

Why was hypnotic regression to early infancy associated with the uncharacteristic Babinski toe response? There are at least two possibilities:

In the normal adult, it is possible to elicit a Babinski response under conditions which involve depressed muscle tone such as in sleep, drowsiness, fatigue, and narcosis (DeJong, 1958). Indirect evidence also suggests that the Babinski response (in non-neurological conditions) may be a function of depressed tonicity: e.g., small doses of scopolamine, which depress tonus, may give rise to a Babinski, while physiological doses of physostigmine (eserine), which apparently elevate tonus, may abolish a positive Babinski (Zador, 1927); deep hypnosis, which is associated at times with relaxation and depressed tonus (Ford & Yeager, 1948), is sufficient at times (without suggestions of age-regression) to produce a Babinski response (Jolowicz & Heyer, 1931; Kline, 1960; Sarbin, 1956). Since, during hypnotic regression to early infancy, the subjects assumed the relaxed "sleeping posture of an infant" (Gidro-Frank & Bowersbuch, 1948), it appears possible that, in these instances also, the Babinski response was due to a general depression of muscle tone. But how can one explain Gidro-Frank and Bowersbuch's observation that normal plantar flexion was present during hypnotic regression to all ages above seven months and that the Babinski response was present only during hypnotic regression to below five months of age? It is possible that suggestions of increased relaxation and deeper sleep were given concurrently with suggestions to regress to below five months of age. It is also possible that the hypnotized subjects interpreted the suggestion, "You are now five months old", as meaning, "You are now more relaxed and more deeply asleep than before" (Zeckel, 1950). In either case, the suggestions could have given rise to a sufficient fall in tonicity to attain the threshold for elicitation of the Babinski response.

Sarbin (1956) has pointed to an alternative possibility: the subjects may have become aware of the purpose of the experiment and may have voluntarily performed the Babinski response. Data presented in the original reports suggest that this possibility should not be summarily dismissed. For instance, Gidro-Frank and Bowersbuch write that their subjects, when not hypnotized, could not by voluntary effort produce dorsiflexion on plantar stimulation. Since the normal person is able to "turn his large toe up" any time he so desires, Gidro-Frank and Bowersbuch's subjects may have purposively responded in accordance with what they surmised was expected of them, namely, to show dorsiflexion under hypnotic regression to early infancy and to show normal flexion under all other conditions.

In brief, the elicitation of the Babinski response does not indicate (as has been assumed) that an unconditioned infantile reflex was reinstated during hypnotic regression to early infancy. The characteristic response of an infant to plantar stimulation is not the Babinski but withdrawal of the limb, with variability in the response of the toes. The elicitation of the Babinski sign in the regression experiments may have been due to diminution of tonicity associated with assumption of the infantile sleeping posture or to realization by the subject of what was wanted, followed by voluntary performance of the dorsiflexor toe response.

ABOLITION AND REVIVIFICATION OF 'INVOLUNTARY' CONDITIONED RESPONSES

A number of experimenters have asked: Can an involuntary conditioned response be abolished by returning the hypnotized subject to a time preceding its establishment? LeCron (1952) conditioned hand-withdrawal and eye-blink to the sound of a buzzer in four subjects; under hypnotic regression to a time preceding the conditioning, both conditioned responses were abolished. However, in a similar experiment with 12 subjects, McCranie and Crasilneck (1955) found that, although the conditioned hand-withdrawal was abolished under hypnotic regression, the conditioned eye-blink was not affected. Similarly, Krotkin and Suslova (1956) found, with three subjects, that a conditioned eye-blink response was not abolished under hypnotic regression to a time preceding the conditioning.

Edmonston (1960) reversed the question: Can an involuntary conditioned response which has been extinguished be revived by hypnotically-regressing the subject to the time when it was present? The eye-blink response produced by a puff of air on the eye was conditioned in six experimental subjects to a concurrent presentation of a click and an increase in brightness; some weeks later the conditioned response was abolished by sufficient extinction trials to meet a criterion. When regressed hypnotically to the time of the original conditioning, all subjects again manifested the eye-blink response but not "in exactly the same manner as it had been established".

The criterion measures (conditioned hand-withdrawal and conditioned eye-blink) were categorized by the experimenters as involuntary responses, and the findings were interpretated as indicating that involuntary responses can (or cannot) be abolished or re-established by hypnotic age-regression. In actuality, the experiments indicate little if anything concerning the fate of involuntary responses: a series of investigations, summarized by Hilgard and Marquis (1940), demonstrated that such responses as conditioned hand-withdrawal and conditioned eye-blink, can be voluntarily inhibited and voluntarily performed.

ELECTROENCEPHALOGRAPHIC ALTERATIONS

To determine if the slow and arrythmic brain waves found during the early months of life are revived under hypnotic regression to a neonatal period, True and Stephenson (1951) suggested an age of one month to six hypnotized adults; no change was observed on the electroencephalogram (EEG). Subsequently, Schwarz, Bickford, and Rasmussen (1955) regressed five hypnotized subjects to various infant age levels, and McCranie *et al.* (1955) regressed ten adults to one month of age; in all cases, the EEG continued to show normal adult patterns.

Under different circumstances, Kupper (1945) found EEG alterations associated with hypnotic age-regression. The 24-year-old subject in this case was hospitalized for convulsive seizures which had existed since age 18. On admission, the patient had an EEG that showed "diffuse abnormalities" consistent with a convulsive disorder. Psychiatric interviews indicated that the seizures were related to an emotional problem which involved hostility toward the father. The critical study was conducted as follows: Age 12 (antedating the seizures) was suggested; the EEG was within normal limits. Serial EEGs remained normal through succeeding suggested years until age 18 (following the first attack) was suggested; at this point "diffuse abnormalities" were observed. The EEG record was then brought to within normal limits by reassuring the patient. Subsequently, a convulsive seizure was produced under hypnosis by bringing forth material related to the patient's conflict with his father.

Hypnotic age-regression may have been helpful, but it was not necessary to produce the effects. Kupper writes: "In this man, the trigger to a convulsive seizure centered about a personal conflict whose resolution could lower the emotional danger point enough for clinical improvement. Under hypnosis *and in interviews,* only this emotional problem could produce an attack or a perceptible change in the electroencephalogram" (italics added). In subsequent studies, Barker and Barker (1950) and Stevens (1959) also produced convulsions in unhypnotized epileptic patients by inducing emotional conflict. In addition, Barker and Barker found that by inducing distressing thoughts and feelings it was possible to produce previously unobserved EEG abnormalities in some patients with epilepsy, and Stevens found that by provoking intense emotional response it was possible "to precipitate previously unobtained epileptiform abnormalities in the electroencephalogram of one-third of a group of [30] patients with convulsive disorders and to reduplicate or exaggerate previously demonstrated pathological electroencephalogram changes in another third".

USE OF OTHER PHYSIOLOGICAL CRITERIA

Ford and Yeager (1948) worked with a patient who had manifested a right homonymous hemianopsia prior to undergoing craniotomy for removal of a colloid cyst from the floor of the third ventricle; following the surgery, vision gradually returned to normal. In the critical experiment, the patient was hypnotically-regressed to a period shortly before the operation. The authors write that under this condition the patient "showed a right homonymous hemianopsia"; although this statement has been used in support of the contention that involuntary physiological functions are revived under hypnotic regression to a time when they were originally present (Gorton, 1949), the operations on which the statement is based are not specified. Apparently, the hypnotically-regressed subject stated that he could not see in certain parts of his visual field; however, objective tests appropriate to demonstrate the presence of hemianopsia were either not performed or, if performed, were not reported.

Erickson (1937) worked with a 19-year-old patient who, during his seventeenth year, was drugged and beaten into unconsciousness and did not regain full consciousness for approximately 48 hours. Under hypnotic regression to the traumatic day, the patient appeared to re-enact the forced drugging and beating. At one point during the re-enactment, he suddenly collapsed; patellar and pupillary reflexes seemed absent and muscle tonus, pulse, and respiration appeared markedly diminished. Before accurate counts of pulse, respiration, and blood pressure could be made, the patient recovered. After several minutes of confusion, he apparently collapsed again, and then again recovered. Erickson interpreted these data as indicating that by means of hypnotic age-regression, it is possible to relive a former experience "as if in the course of the actual original development." However, alternative interpretations exist; for example, the patient may have been simulating unconsciousness, or he may have fainted at the recall of former traumatic experiences; unhypnotized persons have also been known to faint during emotional arousal.

Studies Using Psychological Criteria

A rather large number of studies used psychological tests to determine whether hypnotic age-regression gives rise to behaviors which are appropriate for the suggested age. The psychological tests used in these studies included memory tests (recall of specific days), optical illusion tests, intelligence tests, and the Rorschach, drawings, and other tests. Studies which utilized each of these kinds of psychological tests will now be reviewed in turn and, at the conclusion of this section, studies will be reviewed that utilized a variety of psychological tests and reported positive findings.

RECALL OF SPECIFIC DAYS

True (1949) used 50 college students as subjects, each of whom was regressed hypnotically to Christmas day and his birthday at the ages of ten, seven, and four. On each suggested day, the subject was asked: "What day of the week is this?", and his reply was scored against a 200-year calendar. In 81 per cent of the cases, the replies were accurate. Of the total answers, 93 per cent were correct at the suggested age of ten, 82 per cent at the suggested age of seven, and 69 per cent at the suggested age of four.

Subsequent studies, which were designed to confirm True's findings, reported contrary results. Best and Michaels (1954) hypnotically regressed five subjects to two past birthdays that had fallen on either a Saturday or a Sunday. The regressed subjects were asked to describe the events of the selected day. Nine of the ten birthdays in question were misidentified, the subjects stating that they had attended school when a week-end was actually involved. The one birthday that was identified correctly under hypnotic age-regression was also identified correctly under normal conditions; in this case, the subject's grandfather had died on the specified day (her fourteenth birthday) and she was able to recall (with and without hypnosis) the exact day of the week and the associated events. Subsequently, Reiff and Scheerer (1959) asked five subjects, regressed to their tenth and seventh birthdays, to identify the day of the week. At the suggested age of ten, three subjects named the wrong day, one said "I don't know", and one was correct; at the suggested age of seven, three named the correct day, one was incorrect, and one answered "I don't know". Barber (1961) regressed nine excellent hypnotic subjects (selected from an original group of 70 hospital employees) to their tenth birthdays. After the subject gave a realistic and detailed description (in the present tense) of the events of the birthday, he was asked to name the day of the week. One subject said it was "a schoolday", one said "I don't know", and seven replied with a specific day; six of the seven answers were incorrect. Burke, as reported by Barber (1961), also regressed nine excellent hypnotic subjects (selected from an original group of 104 women college students) to their tenth birthday; when asked to name the day of the week, three answered "I don't know" and the others named a specific day; all answers were incorrect. Mesel and Ledford (1959), Fisher (1962), and Leonard (1963) also failed to confirm True's results.

The results of the above experiments suggest that True's findings may be difficult to confirm; this supposition is strengthened by the following four observations:

It is reported that of the 50 subjects participating in True's study, better than 60 per cent correctly identified the day of the week on which their fourth birthday fell, and better than 75 per cent correctly identified the day on which Christmas fell when they were four years old. What these data signify is an open question in light of a study with American nursery school children (Barber, 1961), which found that only about 25 per cent of 4-year-olds (or 5-year-olds) are able to give correct answers to such questions as, "What day of the week is today?" or, "What day of the week was yesterday?".

True has pointed out in a personal communication to the present writer that his 50 subjects were tested over a period of many months; they may have discussed the experiment with each other.

Sutcliffe (1960) noted that it is possible to compute mentally the day of the week on which any past birthday or Christmas day fell, as follows: A birthday or a Christmas which fell on a particular day (say, a Monday) on a certain year, fell one day earlier (that is, on Sunday) on the previous year, provided the previous year was not a leap year; if it was a leap year, it fell two days earlier (that is, on Saturday). (It should be emphasized that proper use of this relationship enables one to compute mentally a past Christmas or birthday within seconds.) To determine if subjects are aware of this relationship, Yates (1960) asked 49 college students (under normal conditions) on which day of the week their tenth, seventh, and fourth birthdays fell. Two minutes were permitted for each answer. After the subject replied, he was asked how he arrived at his answers. The percentage of correct replies (31 per cent for age ten, 29 per cent for age seven, and 20 per cent for age four) ran consistently above the 14 per cent of correct answers expected by chance. Forty-two subjects (86 per cent) stated that they had tried to use the above or a similar method to figure out the answers.

In my own attempts to validate True's results, I finally found one subject who named the exact day of the week at each regressed chronological birthdate. This subject stated, after the hypnotic session, that she was able to perform the feat simply because she knew that the days of the week go backward one day each year and two on leap years, and knowing the day of the week on which her birthdate fell in a recent year, she could easily and quickly figure out the day of the week it must have fallen in an earlier year.

Further studies which set out to confirm True's findings should control for foreknowledge of the purpose of the experiment on the part of the subject, and should use appropriate interview techniques to determine if accurate answers are due to mental computation performed as described above.

OPTICAL ILLUSION TESTS

Parrish, Lundy, and Leibowitz (1968) reported that good hypnotic subjects who were hypnotically-regressed to the ages of nine and five performed on two optical illusions (the Ponzo and Poggendorff illusions) in a manner which closely resembled the performances of children of ages nine and five. However, the results of this study could not be confirmed in two subsequent investigations carried out in my own laboratory. Ascher and Barber (1968) closely replicated the experimental procedures used by Parrish et al. When the good hypnotic subjects were regressed to ages nine and five, their performance on the Ponzo and Poggendorff illusions was virtually the same as their adult performance and did not at all resemble the performance of children. Spanos and Barber (1969) also replicated the experimental procedures of Parrish et al. with one change; only very exceptional hypnotic subjects were used who had previously passed a large number of test-suggestions. Again, under hypnotic regression to ages nine and five, these unusually good hypnotic subjects performed on the Ponzo and Poggendorff illusions in a manner which was practically the same as their adult performance and which did not remotely resemble the performance of children.

INTELLIGENCE TESTS

The Binet Tests, which are based on standard norms for children of various age levels, have been widely employed in studies of hypnotic age-regression. In an early experiment, Platonow (1933) administered the Binet-Simon to three hypnotic subjects under the assigned ages of 10, 6, and 4. In two cases, the mental ages under hypnotic age-regression were roughly parallel to (but somewhat higher than) the suggested chronological ages; however, the third subject did not approach the norms for the suggested ages (e.g., he passed all tests for an average 7-year-old when assigned an age of four).

Young (1940) carried out two related experiments. In the first, five subjects, hypnotically-regressed to age three, were given 25 items from the 1916 version of the Stanford-Binet. Under regression all subjects attained a mental age which was higher than the suggested age (average mental age, four years and eight months). Young criticized this study in that group hypnosis was employed and the 25 test items gave only a rough approximation of the mental age. A better-controlled experiment was subsequently performed; the standard procedure for administering the Stanford-Binet was used in individual sessions to test nine subjects hypnotically-regressed to age three, and seven "unhypnotizable" subjects instructed to simulate age three. Hypnotized subjects regressed to age three responded on the Binet as if they were six years old (average mental age, five years and eleven months). Unhypnotized subjects simulating age three performed as well as the hypnotically regressed subjects (average mental age, five years and five months). Correnti (1958) reported similar results.

Spiegel, Shor, and Fishman (1945) gave the Stanford-Binet to a 25-year-old patient under normal conditions and under hypnotic regression to 12 chronological levels ranging from 1.5 to 20 years of age. Under regression the IQ ranged from 95 to 134 (normally the IQ was 123). Marked discrepancies were noted at certain age levels; for example, the mental age attained under the suggested age of five years and nine months differed by 17 months from the mental age attained under the suggested age of six years; the authors note that in reality, such a 17-month leap in mental age hardly ever occurs in three months.

In these studies the score obtained by the hypnotized subject under regression to a specified chronological age was compared with standard norms for children of that age. This procedure is open to criticism since the subject as a child may have deviated markedly from the standard norms. A more appropriate procedure would involve comparing a subject's performance under hypnotic age-regression with the performance given by the same subject on the same test when he was actually a child of the stipulated age. This procedure has been followed in two experiments. In the study by Spiegel et al., mentioned above, the Stanford-Binet had been administered on one occasion under normal waking conditions. Eighteen months later, the subject was hypnotically-regressed back to the day of the original testing, and given a re-test. He did not repeat his earlier performance; the pattern of responses and the total score differed markedly on the two occasions. Subsequently, Sarbin (1950) succeeded in finding nine adults who had taken the Stanford-Binet at the age of eight or nine (the records of which were still available), were willing to be hypnotized, and were excellent hypnotic subjects. Each subject was hypnotically-regressed to the specific day during his eighth or ninth year when he had originally taken the Binet, and the test was readministered. In a control session, the same subjects were given the Binet under instructions to simulate the behavior of an eight- or nine-year-old child. All scores under hypnotic age-regression were higher than scores on the original testing. (Average overestimation of the mental age under hypnosis was 3.5 years.) Subjects approached more closely their earlier performances under regression than under simulation. (Average overestimation of the mental age under simulation was 5.25 years.)

Evidently, performance on the Binet under hypnotic age-regression tends to be superior to the norms for the assigned age, or to the subject's actual performance at an earlier age.

Contrary results have been reported with the Otis Self-Administering Test of Mental Ability. Kline (1950) administered equivalent forms of the Otis to 10 college students under normal conditions and under hypnotic regression to ages 15, 10, and eight. The scores under regression were appropriate to the norms for the suggested age. The IQ of all subjects remained practically constant, no variation exceeding four IQ points. The mean IQ was 117 under the normal condition and 118 at each of the suggested ages. The lack of variation in IQ, however, does not necessarily indicate that the regressed subjects duplicated their performance at earlier age-levels. As Kline himself pointed out, such constancy in IQ is not found on the Otis (or on any other standard test of intelligence) on retesting under normal conditions. Failure to include a control condition — e.g., administering the Otis under instructions to imitate the performance of children at the three age-levels — renders Kline's results equivocal. In a later study, Barber (1961) found that hypnotic age-regression was not only unnecessary but also not helpful in inducing a performance on the Otis which was in accord with the norms for the assigned age. In this experiment, nine excellent hypnotic subjects were given equivalent forms of the Otis under normal conditions and under hypnotic regression to age ten; as a control, nine normal subjects were given equivalent forms of the Otis under normal conditions and under instructions to perform as they would have at age ten. (To motivate the control group, a 10-dollar reward was offered for the best performance.)

The IQ of one hypnotically-regressed and of three simulating subjects remained "practically constant", i.e., did not vary more than four IQ points under the two conditions. The mean IQ of the experimental group was 118 under the normal condition and 136 under hypnotic regression to age ten; the mean IQ of the control group was 112 under the normal condition and 118 under simulation of age ten. Further replication of Kline's experiment with the addition of a motivated control group is indicated; the results of Barber's study suggest that, if appropriately motivated, simulating subjects will not differ from hypnotically-regressed subjects on the criterion measure.

RORSCHACH, DRAWINGS, AND OTHER TESTS

Taylor (1950) gave the Goodenough Draw-a-Man Test to 12 hypnotized adults under the assigned ages of ten, eight, and six. In a second session, the same subjects were instructed to draw a man in the manner of a 10-, 8-, and 6-year-old child. Goodenough's norms were used to score the drawings. All drawings showed both mature and immature features. Scores on the regressed drawings did not differ significantly from scores on the drawings made under simulation.

In addition to a drawing test, Orne (1951) administered the Rorschach to nine hypnotized college students under the suggested age of six. In a second session, both the Rorschach and the drawing test were administered under normal conditions and the drawings were repeated under instructions to simulate age six. Drawings actually made at age six by one subject and a Rorschach administered at the age to another subject were available for comparison; no similarity was noted between the original and the regressed protocols. All drawings and all Rorschachs made under hypnotic regression to age six showed some childlike features and some features which are never found in the record of a 6-year-old child. In a number of instances, the drawings made under regression were practically identical with those made under simulation.

Along similar lines, Sarbin and Farberow (1952) gave the Rorschach and a drawing test to six adults under hypnotic regression to ages 18, 13, six, and three. As in the previous studies, the Rorschach protocols showed both childlike and adultlike responses and the drawings tended to be superior to the norms for the suggested ages.

Crasilneck and Michael (1957) instructed ten student nurses to copy the Bender-Gestalt figures under normal conditions, under normal conditions with instructions to pretend to be four years old, hypnotized and instructed to pretend to be four, and hypnotically-regressed to four. Three clinical psychologists, unaware of the nature of the experiment, rated the maturational level of the Bender protocols. (Interjudge reliability was satisfactorily high, $r = .84-.90$.) The mean maturational levels were rated as follows: 11.2 years (normal condition); 9.9 years (pretending to be four); 7.8 years (pretending to be four under hypnosis); and 7.3 years (hypnotically-regressed to age four). (The ratings for the last two conditions did not differ significantly.) The authors concluded that although hypnotized subjects try to comply with suggestions that they are children of a certain age, they do not reach the actual age level suggested.

Staples and Wilensky (1968) administered the Rorschach test to good hypnotic subjects who were hypnotically-regressed to six years of age and to subjects who were instructed to respond as if they were 6-year-old children (simulators). Using a counterbalanced order, all subjects were also tested on the Rorschach under normal conditions (without hypnotic procedures or simulation instructions). As compared to their normal performance, all hypnotically-regressed subjects and also all of the simulators showed significantly more childlike responses on the Rorschach. The hypnotically-regressed subjects did not differ from the simulators in their Rorschach performance.

In brief, in experiments in which the Rorschach or drawings were used as the criterion measures, the performance of hypnotically-regressed subjects and the performance of subjects who were asked to imitate or to simulate a younger age level did not differ significantly, included a mixture of childlike and adultlike responses, and was generally at a level that was superior to the norms for the suggested age. Similar results were obtained in a series of five recent studies that used a wide variety of criterion measures:

Hoskovec and Horvai (1963) compared the speech of adults hypnotically-regressed to the age of 2 years, 1 year, and 6 months, adults asked to imitate the speech of children of 2 years, 1 year, and 6 months, and children of the same respective ages. In all cases of hypnotic regression and imitation, the subjects markedly overestimated the speech of children. Subjects hypnotically-regressed to early childhood did not differ in their speech from subjects who were asked, under nonhypnotic conditions, to imitate young children.

Gordon and Freston (1964) tested good hypnotic subjects on a word association task after the subjects had been deeply hypnotized and given suggestions to regress to seven years of age. The comparison groups were comprised of three types of subjects (good, poor, and inexperienced hypnotic subjects) who were told, under a nonhypnotic condition, to play the role of a seven-year-old child and were then tested on the word-associations. Instructions to play the role of a child given under a nonhypnotic or waking condition were as effective as hypnotic regression in eliciting childlike word-associations.

Greenleaf (1969) tested good hypnotic subjects twice on four developmental tasks. Under one condition, the subjects were placed in a deep state of hypnosis and regressed to age four (hypnotic regression). Under the other condition, the same subjects were again placed in deep hypnosis and instructed to "act the way you think a four-year-old child acts, while *always knowing* you are really [an adult]" (hypnotic simulation). In general, subjects under both hypnotic regression and hypnotic simulation did not successfully approximate the performance of children; under both hypnotic regression and hypnotic simulation the subjects gave a mixture of childlike and adult responses to the developmental tasks. However, under hypnotic regression the subjects gave somewhat more childlike responses than under hypnotic simulation.

Troffer (1966) assigned subjects who had obtained high scores on a suggestibility scale either to a hypnotic group or to a simulating group. When given suggestions to regress to the ages of seven and four, the hypnotic subjects did not differ from the simulators on a variety of tests (e.g., an arithmetic test, a word-association test, and a draw-a-man test). Under suggested regression, both the high-suggestible hypnotic subjects and the high-suggestible simulating subjects performed on the tests in a manner which is found, not in children of ages seven and four, but in older individuals. Also, after receiving the suggestions to regress, both the hypnotic subjects and the simulators tended to talk in a childlike way and to show childlike mannerisms when the experimenter spoke to them as if they were children and tended to talk in the manner of an adult when the experimenter did not speak to them as if they were children.

Barber and Calverley (1966) gave identical suggestions to regress to an earlier time to a group that had been exposed to a hypnotic-induction procedure (hypnotic-regression group) and to a group that had *not* been exposed to a hypnotic-induction (waking-regression group). All of the subjects who had received the hypnotic-induction and 70 per cent of those who had *not* received the hypnotic-induction, accepted the suggestions to regress, that is, they testified that it was the specified (earlier) time. However, when the subjects in both the hypnotic-regression and the waking-regression groups were asked to recall material that they had actually learned at the earlier time, they did not recall the material any better than a control group that was not exposed to a hypnotic-induction or to suggestions to regress. Along similar lines, Leonard (1965) demonstrated that good hypnotic subjects who are regressed to an earlier time do *not* perform on a learning-recall task in the way they had actually performed at the earlier time.

STUDIES REPORTING POSITIVE FINDINGS

A number of reports presented detailed findings obtained with one subject. In each case, the performance of the hypnotically-regressed subject—on the Rorschach (Bergmann, Graham, & Leavitt, 1947; Gakkebush, Polinkovsii, & Fundiller, 1930; Mercer & Gibson, 1950; Norgarb, 1952), on the Binet (Gakkebush *et al.*, 1930; Leeds, 1949), on the Wechsler-Bellevue (Kline, 1951), on handwriting (Dolin, 1934), or on drawings (Bergmann *et al.*, 1947; Leeds, 1949)—seemed to parallel the performance expected from a child of the suggested age. However, each study lacks a necessary control; the subject was not instructed under normal conditions to imitate the performance of a child.

Reiff and Scheerer (1959) and Kline and Guze (1951) have published experiments which are open to criticism on other grounds. The former investigators used eight perceptual-cognitive tests, two of which (The Hollow Tube Test and the Left and Right Test) were selected from Piaget's work with European children, and six of which (e.g., a word-association test, an arithmetic test, a time-clock test) were especially constructed for the experiment by the authors. The test battery was administered to five hypnotized subjects under the suggested ages of 10, 7, and 4. As a control, 15 subjects were divided into three groups of five subjects, and each group was given the battery under instructions to simulate one of the age levels. Performance under hypnotic age-regression and under simulation was rated as appropriate to the assigned age level in 86 and 43 per cent of the cases, respectively. However, the validity of the norms used in rating performance is open to question. McCarthy (1930), Deutsche (1937), and Isaacs (1930) have published data indicating that Piaget's norms may be inapplicable to American and British children, and the most that Reiff and Scheerer claim for the six tests they constructed is that they "presumably fit the cognitive structures" of children at various age levels. Until norms for American children are established, valid conclusions cannot be drawn from this study.

Kline and Guze (1951) administered Buck's House-Tree-Person drawing test to a 23-year-old subject under normal conditions; under normal conditions with instructions to simulate age six; hypnotized and instructed to simulate age six; and hypnotically-regressed to age six. Drawings made under normal conditions and under simulation (conditions one to three) were adultlike and difficult to differentiate from each other; drawings made under hypnotic age-regression (condition four) contained some childlike features. Although the authors concluded that striking alterations in "neuropsychological organization" were found under hypnotic age-regression, they did not attempt to explain why the drawings made under instructions to simulate were practically indistinguishable from drawings made under normal (nonsimulating) conditions. Did the subject actually try to perform like a child when asked to imitate the performance of a 6-year-old? This question is related to the problem of controls in regression experiments and is discussed more fully below.

Controls in Hypnotic Age-Regression Experiments

In a few of the experiments described above, subjects approximated more closely the norms for the assigned age under regression than under simulation. In these instances, the following three factors may have played a role in producing a 'better' performance under the hypnotically-regressed condition:

The control group (simulators) was selected haphazardly. In contradistinction, the experimental group was carefully selected from a large original group as the most hypnotizable; this explicit criterion for selection, however, is difficult if not impossible to differentiate from an interrelated implicit criterion, namely, that the subjects chosen for the experimental group were able or motivated to carry out the experimenter's suggestions regardless of whether or not they were in hypnosis or trance. The pre-existing differences between the subjects assigned to the experimental (hypnotic) and control (simulating) groups may thus account for the findings in some of the regression experiments, that is, the experimental subjects may have given a better performance than the control subjects, not because they were hypnotized, but because they were selected as being more willing or able to accept suggestions.

Since subjects assigned to the experimental group had participated in preliminary training sessions in which they had become familiar with the experimental situation, had formed an interpersonal relationship with the experimenter, and had received practice in performing activities involving imagination and fantasy in the presence of another person, it seems likely that they were comfortable in the critical experiment (hypnosis) and motivated to give a good performance. In contrast, subjects assigned to the control group had not participated in preliminary training sessions and had not had prior experience in carrying out imaginative behavior in an experimental setting. Since, in addition, subjects in the control group were instructed, without preliminaries, to imitate the behavior of a child, and *immediately afterward* given the criterion tests, it seems possible that they were not prepared to carry out instructions, were relatively ill at ease in the experimental situation, and were not motivated to give their best performance.

The above contentions apply to studies in which the performance of an experimental group was compared with the performance of an independent control group. Other factors may have played a role in experiments in which the subject's performance under hypnosis was compared with his own performance under simulation. In these instances, the better performance found (on some occasions) under hypnotic age-regression may have been due to an awareness by the subject that the experimenter not only expected but also desired better results under hypnosis. Experimental evidence suggests that good hypnotic subjects characteristically strive to fulfill the expectations and desires of the experimenter and, in some instances, purposively give their best possible performance under the hypnotic condition and purposively give an inferior performance under the control condition (Barber, 1967; Pattie, 1935). Indirect evidence suggests that this factor may have been responsible for the results obtained in some of the regression experiments; for example, since the normal adult is able to imitate a child's manner of drawing and to raise his large toe, this factor may have played a role in Kline and Guze's (1951) experiment, in which the subject was apparently unable to draw in a childlike manner when instructed to simulate the age of six, and in Gidro-Frank and Bowersbuch's (1948) experiment, in which subjects were apparently unable to imitate the Babinski response under normal conditions.

Experimental studies which explicitly recognize the significance of the above three factors are in order. Subjects serving as their own controls should be unequivocally informed that as good a performance is expected and desired under simulation as under hypnosis. If the experimental design calls for comparison of the performance of an experimental group with the performance of an independent control group, subjects should not, as in many previous investigations, be assigned to the control group haphazardly. On the contrary, the control group should be selected and treated in a manner similar to that used in the experimental group (with the exception that no attempt be made to induce hypnosis); e.g., the control group should be selected for proficiency in carrying out suggested tasks and should receive practice in carrying out suggestions in an experimental setting. The data surveyed suggest that, under carefully controlled conditions, simulating subjects will not differ from hypnotically age-regressed subjects on the criterion measures.

AGE-PROGRESSION AND REGRESSION TO PRENATAL LIFE
A discussion of the phenomenon of age-regression is not complete without mention of two complementary phenomena—age-progression to a future time and age-regression to a previous life.

Kline (1951) showed that hypnotic subjects who give a childlike performance when regressed to childhood also give a convincing portrayal of themselves as older individuals when hypnotically-progressed to a future time. Rubenstein and Newman (1954) obtained similar results with five excellent hypnotic subjects who were able to 'relive' past experiences when they were hypnotically-regressed to childhood. Each of the five subjects "consistently and without exceptions" was also able to live out 'future' experiences during hypnotic age-progression to the age of 70 or 80.

Furthermore, some subjects who give a childlike performance when hypnotically-regressed to childhood also give a convincing portrayal when hypnotically-regressed to prenatal life in the womb or to a time which preceded their present life (the Bridey Murphy phenomenon) (Bernstein, 1956; Kelsey, 1953).

Summary and Conclusions

The contents and conclusions of this chapter can be summarized as follows:

When told that he is a child of a certain chronological age, the good hypnotic subject typically tries to imagine vividly and to think that he is a child and typically tends to behave in a childlike manner. However, when assessed on standard physiological or psychological tests, the behavior of the hypnotically age-regressed subject either shows discrepancies from the norms for the suggested age, or, if in accord with the norms, is of such a kind as to be amenable to simulation by the normal adult.

Specifically, physiological studies do not indicate (as has been assumed) that involuntary functions characteristic of an earlier age level are revived under hypnotic age-regression: In no case has regression to infancy been associated with the revival of the infantile EEG pattern. (Although, in one experiment with an epileptic patient, abnormal patterns on the EEG were abolished and reinstated under hypnotic age-regression, similar EEG effects were produced in the same patient, and in other epileptic patients, without hypnosis.) The assertion that involuntary conditioned responses can be abolished under hypnotic age-regression is based on a questionable interpretation of experimental data. The so-called involuntary conditioned responses which were assessed in the regression experiments (conditioned hand withdrawal and conditioned eye-blink) are amenable to voluntary inhibition. Although a Babinski response to plantar stimulation has been demonstrated in some subjects under hypnotic regression to early infancy, this does not indicate (as has been assumed) that an unconditioned infantile reflex is recoverable under regression. The characteristic response of the infant to stimulation of the sole of the foot is not the Babinski, but withdrawal of the limb with variability in response of the toes.

On standard psychological tests such as the Binet, the Rorschach, and Goodenough drawings, hypnotically age-regressed subjects generally manifest some responses that are atypical of a child, and attain scores that are superior to the norms for the assigned age, or to the scores they had actually attained at the earlier age.

In one experiment, subjects under regression to ages ten, seven, and four were able, in 81 per cent of the cases, to state the exact day of the week on which Christmas and their birthday fell in the particular year involved. Indirect evidence suggests that failure to control crucial experimental variables may have been responsible for these results: e.g., the experiment was carried out over a period of many months and it is possible that the subjects discussed the experiment with each other; seven subsequent experimental studies failed to confirm the findings; the overwhelming majority of American 4-year-olds do not distinguish the days of the week: normal persons can deduce on which day of the week an earlier birthday (or Christmas) fell by counting back from a known birthday (or Christmas), one day of the week for each intervening year and an additional day for each intervening leap-year.

In a few experiments the regressed subjects approximated more closely the norms for the stipulated age than subjects instructed to simulate. In these instances, the better performance found under the hypnotic condition may have been due to such factors as the following: The experimental group was selected under the implicit criterion of proficiency in carrying out suggested tasks and had received practice, in preliminary training sessions, in carrying out suggestions in an experimental setting. In contradistinction, the control group was selected haphazardly and did not participate in prior experiments. The data reviewed suggest a need for further experiments in which control groups are selected and treated in a manner similar to that used for the hypnotic groups. It can be hypothesized that under such conditions, no difference will be found between hypnotically-regressed and control subjects on the criterion behaviors.

Most subjects who give a convincing performance when hypnotically-regressed to childhood also usually give a convincing performance when hypnotically-progressed to the age of 70 or 80 or when hypnotically-regressed to prenatal life in the womb or to a time which preceded their present life.

One possible theoretical formulation that can tie together the data presented in this chapter is as follows: When it is suggested to subjects in a hypnotic group, a simulating group, or a control group that they are in the past or in the future, some subjects in each group try to imagine or to think of themselves as in the past or in the future and, when imagining or trying to think of themselves as in an earlier or in a future time, some subjects in each of the three groups behave to a certain limited extent as if they are in the past or future.

References

Ascher, L. M., and Barber, T. X. An attempted replication of the Parrish-Lundy-Leibowitz study on hypnotic age-regression. Harding, Mass.: Medfield Foundation, 1968.

Barber, T. X. Experimental evidence for a theory of hypnotic behavior. II. Experimental controls in hypnotic age-regression. *Int. J. Clin. Exp. Hypn.*, 1961, *9*, 181-193.

Barber, T. X. "Hypnotic" phenomena: A critique of experimental methods. In J. E. Gordon (Ed.) *Handbook of clinical and experimental hypnosis*. New York: Macmillan, 1967. Pp. 444-480.

Barber, T. X., and Calverley, D. S. Effects on recall of hypnotic induction, motivational suggestions, and suggested regression: A methodological and experimental analysis. *J. Abnorm. Psychol.*, 1966, *71*, 169-180.

Barker, W., and Barker, S. Experimental production of human convulsive brain potentials by stress-induced effects upon neural integrative function: Dynamics of the convulsive reaction to stress. *Res. Publ. Ass. Nerv. Ment. Dis.*, 1950, *29*, 90-100.

Bergmann, M. S., Graham, H., and Leavitt, H. C. Rorschach exploration of consecutive hypnotic chronological age level regression. *Psychosom. Med.*, 1947, *9*, 20-28.

Bernstein, M. *The search for Bridey Murphy*. New York: Doubleday, 1956.

Best, H. L., and Michaels, R. M. Living out "future" experience under hypnosis. *Science*, 1954, *120*, 1077.

Burr, C. W. The reflexes of early infancy. *Brit. J. Child. Dis.*, 1921, *18*, 152-153.

Correnti, S. Concept formation and intelligence under hypnotic and simulated age regression. Unpublished Ph. D. dissertation, Univ. of Denver, 1958.

Crasilneck, H. B., and Michael, C. M. Performance on the Bender under hypnotic age regression. *J. Abnorm. Soc. Psychol.*, 1957, *54*, 319-322.

DeJong, R. N. *The neurologic examination.* New York: Hoeber, 1958. Pp. 591-593.

Deutsche, M. The development of children's concepts of causal relations. Monograph No. 13, Institute of Child Welfare, 1937.

Dolin, A. O. A physiological analysis of the elements of individual personality experience. The Johns Hopkins University Applied Physics Laboratory, Library Bulletin (Translation Series), Report No. TG-230-T-139, 1960. Translation from *Arkhiv. Biologich. Nauk.,* 1934, *36,* 25-52.

Edmonston, W. E. An experimental investigation of hypnotic age regression. *Amer. J. Clin. Hypn.,* 1960, *3,* 127-138.

Erickson, M. H. Development of apparent unconsciousness during hypnotic reliving of a traumatic experiment. *Arch. Neurol. Psychiat.,* 1937, *38,* 1282-1288.

Fisher, S. Problems of interpretation and controls in hypnotic research. In G. H. Estabrooks (Ed.) *Hypnosis: Current problems.* New York: Harper & Row, 1962. Pp. 109-126.

Ford, W. L., and Yeager, C. L. Changes in the electroencephalogram in subjects under hypnosis. *Dis. Nerv. Syst.,* 1948, *9,* 190-192.

Gakkebush, V. M., Polinkovskii, S. I., and Fundiller, R. I. Experimental study of personality development by hypnotic inhibition. The Johns Hopkins University Applied Physics Laboratory, Library Bulletin (Translation Series), Report No. TG-230-T-152, 1960. Translation from *Trudy Instit. Psikhonevrol.,* 1930. *2,* 236-272.

Gebhard, J. W. Hypnotic age-regression: A review. *Amer. J. Clin. Hypn.,* 1961, *3,* 139-168.

Gidro-Frank, L., and Bowersbuch, M. K. A study of the plantar response in hypnotic age regression. *J. Nerv. Ment. Dis.,* 1948, *107,* 443-458.

Gordon, J. E., and Freston, M. Role-playing and age regression in hypnotized and nonhypnotized subjects. *J. Pers.,* 1964, *32,* 411-419.

Gorton, B. E. The physiology of hypnosis. *Psychiat. Quart.,* 1949, *23,* 317-343 and 457-485.

Greenleaf, E. Developmental-stage regression through hypnosis. *Amer. J. Clin. Hypn.,* 1969, *12,* 20-36.

Hilgard, E. R., and Marquis, D. G. *Conditioning and learning.* New York: Appleton-Century, 1940, Pp. 35 and 269-270.

Hoskovec, J., and Horvai, I. Speech manifestations in hypnotic age regression. *Activ. Nerv. Super.,* 1963, *5,* 13-21.

Isaacs, S. *Intellectual growth in young children.* New York: Harcourt, Brace, 1930.

Jolowicz, E., and Heyer, G. *Suggestion therapy and hypnosis and hypnotherapy.* London: Daniel, 1931. P. 141.

Kelsey, D. E. R. Phantasies of birth and prenatal experiences recovered from patients undergoing hypnoanalysis. *J. Ment. Sci.,* 1953, *99,* 216-223.

Kline, M. V. Hypnotic age regression and intelligence. *J. Genet. Psychol.,* 1950, *77,* 129-132.

Kline, M. V. Hypnosis and age progression: A case report. *J. Genet. Psychol.,* 1951, *78,* 195-206.

Kline, M. V. Hypnotic retrogression: A neuropsychological theory of age regression and progression. *J. Clin. Exp. Hypn.,* 1953, *1,* 21-28.

Kline, M. V. Hypnotic age regression and psychotherapy: Clinical and theoretical observations. *Int. J. Clin. Exp. Hypn.,* 1960, *8,* 17-25.

Kline, M. V., and Guze, H. The use of a projective drawing technique in the investigation of hypnotic age regression and progression. *Brit. J. Med. Hypn.*, (Winter) 1951, *3*, 10-21.

Krotkin, I. I., and Suslova, M. M. Changes in conditioned and unconditioned reflexes during suggestion states in hypnosis. *Central nervous system and human behavior.* (Translations from the Russian Medical Literature). Washington, D. C.: U. S. Dept. of Health, Education, and Welfare, Public Health Service, 1959. Pp. 653-669. Translated from *Trudy Instit. Fiziol. Pavlov.* 1956, *5*, 267.

Kupper, H. I. Psychic concomitants in wartime injuries. *Psychosom. Med.*, 1945, *7*, 15-21.

LeCron, L. M. The loss during hypnotic age regression of an established conditioned reflex. *Psychiat. Quart.*, 1952, *26*, 657-662.

Leeds, M. An hypnotic regression series *Personality*, 1949, *1*, 13-16.

Leonard, J. R. An investigation of hypnotic age-regression. Unpublished Ph. D. dissertation, University of Kentucky, 1963.

Leonard, J. R. Hypnotic age regression: A test of the functional ablation hypothesis. *J. Abnorm. Psychol.*, 1965, *70*, 266-269.

McCarthy, D. Language development of the pre-school child. Monograph No. 4, Institute of Child Welfare, 1930.

McCranie, E. J., and Crasilneck, H. B. The conditioned reflex in hypnotic age regression. *J. Clin. Exp. Psychopath.*, 1955, *16*, 120-123.

McCranie, E. J., Crasilneck, H. B., and Teter, H. R. The electroenc phalogram in hypnotic age regression. *Psychiat. Quart.*, 1955, *29*, 85-88.

McGraw, M. B. Development of the plantar response in young infants. *Amer. J. Dis. Child.*, 1941, *61*, 1215-1221.

Mercer, M., and Gibson, R. W. Rorschach content in hypnosis: Chronological age level regression. *J. Clin. Psychol.*, 1950, *6*, 352-358.

Mesel, E., and Ledford, F. F., Jr. The electroencephalogram during hypnotic age regression (to infancy) in epileptic patients. *Arch. Neurol.*, 1969, *1*, 516-521.

Norgarb, B. A. Rorschach psychodiagnosis in hypnotic regression. In L. M. LeCron (Ed.) *Experimental hypnosis*, New York: Macmillan, 1952. Pp. 178-214.

Orne, M. T. The mechanism of hypnotic age regression: An experimental study. *J. Abnorm. Soc. Psychol.*, 1951, *46*, 213-225.

Parrish, M., Lundy, R. M., and Leibowitz, H. W. Hypnotic age-regression and magnitudes of the Ponzo and Poggendorff illusions. *Science*, 1968, *159*, 1375-1376.

Pattie, F. A. A report of attempts to produce uniocular blindness by hypnotic suggestion. *Brit. J. Med. Psychol.*, 1935, *15*, 230-241.

Pattie, F. A. The genuineness of some hypnotic phenomena. In R. M. Dorcus (Ed.) *Hypnosis and its therapeutic applications*, New York: McGraw-Hill, 1956. Chap. 6.

Platonov, K. I. On the objective proof of the experimental personality age regression. *J. Gen. Psychol.*, 1933, *9*, 190-209.

Reiff, R., and Scheerer, M. *Memory and hypnotic age regression.* New York: Internat. Univ. Press, 1959.

Rubenstein, R., and Newman, R. The living out of "future" experiences under hypnosis. *Science*, 1954, *119*, 472-473.

Sarbin, T. R. Mental changes in experimental regression. *J. Pers.*, 1950, *19*, 221-228.

Sarbin, T. R. Physiological effects of hypnotic stimulation. In R. M. Dorcus (Ed.) *Hypnosis and its therapeutic applications*. New York: McGraw-Hill, 1956. Chap. 4.

Sarbin, T. R., and Farberow, N. L. Contributions to role-taking theory: A clinical study of self and role. *J. Abnorm. Soc. Psychol.*, 1952, *47*, 117-125.

Schwarz, B. E., Bickford, R. G., and Rasmussen, W. C. Hypnotic phenomena, including hypnotically activated seizures, studied with the electroencephalogram. *J. Nerv. Ment. Dis.*, 1955, *122*, 564-574.

Spanos, N. P., and Barber, T. X. A second attempted replication of the Parrish-Lundy-Leibowitz study on hypnotic age-regression. Harding, Mass.: Medfield Foundation, 1969.

Spiegel, H., Shor, J., and Fishman, S. An hypnotic ablation technique for the study of personality development. *Psychosom. Med.*, 1945, *7*, 273-278.

Staples, E. A., and Wilensky, H. A controlled Rorschach investigation of hypnotic age regression. *J. Proj. Techn.*, 1968, *32*, 246-252.

Stevens, J. R. Emotional activation of the electroencephalogram in patients with convulsive disorders. *J. Nerv. Ment. Dis.*, 1959, *128*, 339-345.

Sutcliffe, J. P. "Credulous" and "skeptical" views of hypnotic phenomena: A review of certain evidence and methodology. *Int. J. Clin. Exp. Hypnos.*, 1960, *8*, 73-101.

Taylor, A. The differentiation between simulated and true hypnotic regression by figure drawings. Master's thesis, The College of the City of New York, 1950.

Troffer, S. A. H. Hypnotic age regression and cognitive functioning. Unpublished Ph. D. dissertation, Stanford University, 1966.

True, R. M. Experimental control in hypnotic age regression states. *Science*, 1949, *110*, 583-584.

True, R. M., and Stephenson, C. W. Controlled experiments correlating electroencephalogram, pulse, and plantar reflexes with hypnotic age regression and induced emotional states. *Personality*, 1951, *1*, 252-263.

Weitzenhoffer, A. M. *Hypnotism: An objective study in suggestibility*. New York: Wiley, 1953.

Wolff, L. V. The response to plantar stimulation in infancy. *Amer. J. Dis. Child.*, 1930, *39*, 1176-1185.

Yates, A. J. Simulation and hypnotic age regression. *Int. J. Clin. Exp. Hypn.*, 1960, *8*, 243-249.

Young, P. C. Hypnotic regression—fact or artifact? *J. Abnorm. Soc. Psychol.*, 1940, *35*, 273-278.

Zador, J. Ueber die Beeinflussbarkeit und Pathogenese des Babinskischen Reflexes. *Monatschr. Psychiat. Neurol.*, 1927, *64*, 336-342.

Zeckel, A. Authenticity and advantages of age regression in hypnotherapy. *Folia Psychiat.*, 1950, *53*, 906-915.

CHAPTER 7

An Empirically Based
Theory of Hypnotism

CONTENTS

SEVEN

An Empirically Based
Theory of Hypnotism

The term *hypnotism* is multidimensional. It refers to: a variety of antecedent variables including, for example, repeated suggestions of relaxation, drowsiness, and sleep; a hypothesized altered state of consiousness or hypnotic trance; and a series of consequent behaviors such as analgesia, age-regression, hallucination and amnesia. Since the time of Mesmer, theories in this area have typically focused on the hypothesized altered state (trance or hypnosis); they have been concerned with the essential properties of the hypnotic state, how this state differs from the waking state and the sleeping state, and whether the phenomena associated with the hypnotic trance state are genuine or artifactual. These traditional theoretical formulations, which pivot around the terms *hypnosis* (or *hypnotic state* or *trance*), have been subjected to criticism in recent years. Barber (1964a) noted that such formulations involve circular reasoning in that the factor (hypnosis) which is said to give rise to the behaviors is itself inferred from the same behaviors that it is supposed to explain. Along related lines, Sarbin and Andersen (1967) pointed out that the pivotal term *trance* is never clearly denoted but is treated as a primitive word that everyone presumably understands. However, theories are highly resistant to these kinds of criticisms; the history of science shows that theories succumb, not to criticisms, but to new theoretical approaches which prove to be more explanatory, more parsimonious, and more useful (Conant, 1951; Kuhn, 1962).

The purpose of this chapter is to present an alternative approach toward a theory of hypnotism. The alternative formulation differs from those that have historically dominated this area of inquiry in several important respects: It does not postulate a special state of consciousness to account for analgesia, age-regression, hallucination, and the other behaviors that have been traditionally associated with hypnotism. Such behaviors are viewed as due to denotable antecedent variables of the type found in a wide variety of interpersonal test-situations. Different questions are placed at the forefront of inquiry. Instead of asking questions such as, "What are the essential characteristics of the state of hypnosis?", the alternative approach asks "What denotable antecedent variables are effective in eliciting the behaviors that have been historically subsumed under the rubric *hypnotism*?"

Since the fundamental assumption underlying the present formulation is that the behaviors associated with the term *hypnotism* are functionally related to *denotable* antecedent variables, the important methodological features of the approach are as follows:

First, the behaviors that are to be explained (consequent variables) are specified and quantified.

Next, denotable antecedent variables are specified that might be functionally related to the consequent behaviors.

Functional relations holding between the antecedent and consequent variables are delineated by empirical investigations.

Attempts are made to subsume the empirically-determined antecedent-consequent relations under general principles.

The reader will note that the four methodological features of the present approach aim to give rise to an empirically-based theory of hypnotism. Glaser and Strauss (1967) have presented a rationale for such grounded approaches that derive general principles from ongoing empirical research which relates antecedents to consequents. Such empirically-grounded approaches to theory construction differ markedly from hypothetico-deductive methods (Koch, 1954). As Koch (1959), Marx (1963) and Glaser and Strauss (1967) have emphasized, it appears preferable at the present time to proceed toward general principles by a series of gradual steps which allow concepts to be closely tied to empirical data rather than by attempting in one stroke to formulate an all-encompassing theory. The issues involved here, which are far too many and too complex to discuss in the space available, have been succinctly stated by Marx (1951), as follows: "The most immediate need of psychology would rather plainly seem to be the careful development of a large number of low-level empirical laws and low-order theories based upon the use of intervening constructs of the more operational type. Higher-order theoretical generalizations may then be built upon a sound empirical framework . . .rather than developed from above, as too often been attempted in the past . . .".

Although the formulation to be presented here differs markedly from those that have historically dominated this area of inquiry, it has many features which parallel Sarbin's formulation (Andersen & Sarbin, 1964; Coe & Sarbin, 1966; Sarbin, 1964; Sarbin & Andersen, 1967) and a few features which parallel the recent formulation of Edmonston (1967), Hilgard (1965), London (1967), Orne (1959), Rosenhan (1967), Shor (1967), and Sutcliffe (1960). The similarities and differences between the present formulation and other representative recent approaches to hypnotism are analyzed in a recent paper (Spanos & Chaves, 1968).

I will now discuss in turn each of the four major features of my own approach. I will first specify the consequent variables and the antecedent variables. Next, functional relations between antecedent-consequent variables will be delineated. Finally, an attempt will be made to subsume the empirically-determined relations between antecedent and consequent variables under general principles and directions will be noted for further research.

Specification of Consequent Variables

The term *hypnotism* subsumes a series of behaviors that are elicited by suggestions (or by instructions, requests, or commands) given to the subject by the experimenter (or hypnotist). For instance, the experimenter may suggest to the subject that he is insensitive to pain; when the subject is then exposed to a normally painful stimulus, he may not wince or show other noticable overt reactions and may report that the stimulus was not painful (analgesia). Similarly, the experimenter may attempt to elicit behaviors that have been traditionally labeled as *limb rigidity, hallucination* and *amnesia* by suggesting to the subject that he cannot move his arm, that he perceives objects that are not present, and that he will forget the experimental events. These and other behaviors, which we view as consequent or dependent variables, are listed at the top of column 2 in Table 2. Since each of the behaviors is elicited by suggesting to the subject that certain events are occurring or will occur, they are labeled as *responses to test-suggestions.* It is clearly this class of behaviors that has made the topic *hypnotism* of marked interest not only to psychologist, physicians, and other professionals, but also to laymen. (Other classes of consequent variables subsumed under the term *hypnotism,* in addition to those labeled as *responses to test-suggestions,* are listed at the bottom of column 2 in Table 2 and discussed later in this chapter.)

*TABLE 2 Antecedent and Consequent Variables Subsumed
under the Term* Hypnotism

(1)	(2)
Antecedent Variables	Consequent Variables

A. *Instruction-suggestion variables*
  1. Wording and tone of direction sug-
    gestions
  2. Task-motivational instructions
  3. Definition of the situation
  4. Relaxation-sleep suggestions
  5. Wording and tone of inquiry

B. *Subject variables*
  6. Subjects' attitudes (toward hyp-
    notism or test-situation)
  7. Subjects' expectations (pertaining
    to their own hypnotic depth, wheth-
    er the tasks are easy to perform,
    and what behaviors are appropriate)
  8. Subject's personality character-
    istics

C. *Experimenter variables*
  9. Experimenter's role behavior
  10. Experimenter's personal charac-
    teristics

D. *Subject-experimenter variables*
  11. Interpersonal relationship between
    subject and experimenter

A. *Responses to test-suggestions* (for
limb or body rigidity, analgesia, hallucination, age-regression,
time-distortion, deafness, color-
blindness, blindness, amesia,
post-hypnotic behavior, etc.)

B. *Reports of having been hypnotized*

C. *Hypnotic appearance* (e.g., lack of
spontaneity, limpness-relaxation,
trance stare, and psychomotor retardation)

At first glance, the behaviors associated with hypnotism appear rather extraordinary — subjects seem to be analgesic, hallucinated, regressed to childhood, amnesic, deaf, colorblind, blind, and so on. Since the behaviors appeared to be extraordinary, a special factor — an altered state of consciousness labeled as *hypnotic state, hypnosis,* or *trance* — has been traditionally invoked to account for them. However, the data summarized in Chapters III-VI and also other data summarized elsewhere (Barber, 1969), indicate that the behaviors are not what they seem to be superficially and that it may be possible to explain them without positing a special state of consciousness. The remainder of this chapter will attempt to provide an explanation of the behaviors associated with the term *hypnotism* in terms of variables that are an integral part of present-day psychology.

QUANTIFICATION OF CONSEQUENT VARIABLES

To conduct a scientific program of research in this area, it is very useful to have a standardized scale for measuring the degree to which subjects respond to test-suggestions for body immobility, halluncination, amnesia, post-hypnotic behavior, and so on. An ideal scale would fulfill three requirements: It would be reliable. Since responses to test-suggestions include two aspects or dimensions (overt performances, and subjective reports that the suggested effects were actually experienced), it would quantify both dimensions. It would be constructed in such a way that it could be administered with equal facility to subjects who have and also those who have not received a hypnotic-induction procedure. To meet the need for an instrument that fulfilled each of these three requirements, a scale was constructed by the present author and his collaborators and was named the Barber Suggestibility Scale (BSS).[1]

Since the BSS was used to quantify responses to test-suggestions in a substantial number of the studies described below, it is appropriate at this point to summarize its major characteristics.

The BSS includes eight standardized test-suggestions of the type that have been commonly used in experiments subsumed under the term *hypnotism*. It includes a hallucination item, a post-experimental (post-hypnotic) item, an amnesia item, three challenge items (Body Immobility, Hand Clasp, and Verbal Inhibition), and two items which directly suggest that certain effects are occurring (Arm Heaviness and Arm Levitation). The scale includes criteria for scoring both the subject's overt performances (Objective scores) and also their subjective reports pertaining to the degree to which the suggested effects were experienced (Subjective scores). The scale is designed so that it can be administered either in the presence of or in the absence of any of the antecedent variables that are typically present in hypnotic situations, e.g., with or without suggestions of relaxation, drowsiness, and sleep. The BSS has been shown to have factorial validity, the test-retest and split-half reliabilities are satisfactory (*rs* ranging from .78 to .88), and norms are available for responses to the scale at various age-levels and under several experimental treatments (Barber, 1965b).

Methods have also been delineated for measuring the overt performances and the subjective reports elicited by other types of test-suggestions not included in the BSS, such as suggestions for analgesia, amnesia, age-regression, time-distortion, and deafness (Barber & Calverley, 1964e, 1964g, 1966a, 1966b, 1969a; Barber & Hahn, 1962; Hilgard, Cooper, Lenox, Morgan, & Voevodsky, 1967; Troffer, 1966; Williamsen, Johnson & Eriksen, 1965).

1. Weitzenhoffer and Hilgard (1959, 1962) had previously constructed a series of scales, the Stanford Hypnotic Susceptibility Scales, which met the first criterion mentioned above but failed to satisfy the latter two criteria (Barber, 1965b).

Specifications of Antecedent Variables

Having specified and proposed methods for quantifying the consequent behaviors that require explanation, we can now ask: Of the many denotable antecedent variables present in hypnotic situations, which are relevant and which extraneous in eliciting these behaviors? Let us first emphasize that, since the presence of an altered state of consciousness—trance, hypnosis, hypnotic state—is an *inference* made by observing the subject's behaviors (consequent variables) (Barber, 1964a; Chaves, 1968; Edmonston, 1968), the presumed altered state cannot be satisfactorily treated as an antecedent variable. However, at the beginning of inquiry we can point to four classes of *denotable* antecedent variables that are present in hypnotic situations and that might play a role in producing body immobility, hallucination, amnesia, analgesia, and the other behaviors that are to be explained. These four sets of antecedent variables, listed in summary form in Table 2, column 1, comprise the following:

Instruction-suggestion variables. Hypnotism differs from other experimental situations in that the experimenter *continually* proffers instructions and suggestions which are designed to influence the subject's ongoing behavior. These instruction-suggestion variables include: direct suggestions that certain behaviors and experiences are occurring or will occur (for instance, suggestions that the subject's arm is rigid and immovable); instructions intended to produce positive task-motivation (for example, "cooperate . . . concentrate on my words . . . try to follow my suggestions"); instructions which define the situation to the subject (as hypnotism, as a test of imagination, etc.); and repeated suggestions of eye-closure, relaxation, drowsiness, and sleep.

Subject variables.   The subjects' attitudes and expectations with respect to the test-situation and their personality traits may also play a role in determining their responses to test-suggestions. Several investigators (Andersen, 1963; Barber & Calverley, 1966c; Dermen & London, 1965; Melei & Hilgard, 1964) have constructed scales for measuring the subjects' attitudes and expectancies with respect to the test-situation. A wide variety of personality scales have been used in recent studies to measure subjects' long-enduring traits and characteristics (Barber, 1964c; Hilgard, 1965).

Experimenter variables. Another class of quantifiable antecedent variables that may influence the subject's performance includes the experimenter's prestige, his personality attributes, and his attitudes, expectancies, and biases with respect to the experimental situation.

Subject-experimenter variables. This class subsumes those variables which involve both the subject and the experimenter, such as the type of interpersonal relationship that is formed between the two individuals.

We will begin our inquiry by hypothesizing that each of the antecedent variables listed above plays a role in eliciting limb rigidity, analgesia, hallucination, amnesia, and the other consequent behaviors that have been historically associated with the word *hypnotism*. As we proceed we will differentiate other antecedent variables that may also be functionally related to the behaviors.

Functional Relations between Antecedent and Consequent Variables

Functional relations between the antecedent variables listed in Table 2, column 1, and the consequent variables listed in Table 2, column 2, have been delineated in several dozen experiments conducted during recent years. Since the present approach to theory construction proposes to derive its theoretical propositions from the empirically-determined functional relationships between antecedent and consequent variables, these relationships will now be specified in detail. I will first summarize the lawful relations that have been delineated experimentally between each of the antecedent variables listed in Table 2, column 1, and the first consequent variable listed in Table 2, column 2 (response to test-suggestions). Then I will summarize empirical data relating the antecedent variables to the remaining two consequent variables listed in Table 2, column 2 (reports of having been hypnotized and hypnotic appearance). It might be advisable for the reader to refer frequently to Table 2 as he reads this section of the chapter.

FUNCTIONAL RELATIONS BETWEEN ANTECEDENT VARIABLE I (WORDING AND TONE OF DIRECT SUGGESTIONS) AND RESPONSE TO TEST-SUGGESTIONS

It is very easy to overlook a factor that is of utmost importance in eliciting the behaviors associated with the word *hypnotism*. This powerful, and yet easily-neglected variable, consists of *directly suggesting* to the subject, in a firm or expectant tone of voice, that his arm is rigid and immovable, that he sees or hears objects (not present), that he is insensitive to pain, and so on. When given suggestions firmly and directly, without any special preliminaries, many subjects exhibit some of the behaviors traditionally associated with the word *hypnotism* and some subjects exhibit many of the behaviors. Let us look at a few examples.

Stage-hypnotists typically suggest to the entranced subject that his body is becoming stiff and rigid. When the subject appears rigid, he is suspended between two supports—one at the back of the head and the other at the ankles. Typically, the subject remains suspended for two or three minutes while the orchestra plays a crescendo. As pointed out in Chapter III, it has been commonly assumed that the subject is able to perform the human-plank feat because the hypnotist has placed him in a trance. This assumption is unnecessary. Barber (1969) found that the great majority (at least 80 per cent) of unselected male and female subjects are able to perform this feat when told firmly and directly to make their body rigid and not to bend under any circumstances. Similar results were obtained by Collins (1961); when given direct suggestions to become and to stay rigid, subjects in an experimental (hypnotic) group and those in a control group performed in the same way, remaining suspended for two to four minutes. In post-experimental interviews, most of the subjects in both the hypnotic and control groups reported that they were amazed at their own performance since they did not believe initially that they had the ability to perform the feat.

Similar results were obtained in a series of studies in which the eight standardized test-suggestions of the BSS were administered to unselected college undergraduates without special preliminaries—under a direct suggestion or control condition (Barber, 1965a, 1965b). Two items on the BSS, Thirst "Hallucination" and Hand Lock, were passed by about half of the subjects; for example, with respect to Hand Lock, about half of the subjects tested without special preliminaries failed to take their hands apart when they tried to do so (Objective score) and also reported that they did not compliantly keep their hands together but actually felt that they could not unclasp them (Subjective scores). Furthermore, at least 24 per cent of the subjects who were given the suggestions directly under a control condition passed the Arm Lowering, Arm Levitation, Body Immobility, and Verbal Inhibition items of the BSS and at least one in eight passed the "Post hypnotic-Like" Response and Selective Amnesia items.

A rather large number of recent studies have demonstrated that many other overt performances and subjective reports that have been historically subsumed under the rubric *hypnotism* can also be elicited in a substantial number of subjects by suggestions given firmly and directly in a control situation. For instance, the majority of unselected control subjects who received direct suggestions that time was slowing down (time-distortion) reported post-experimentally that a short period was experienced as a long period of time (Barber & Calverley, 1964g). Also, the majority of unselected control subjects who received direct suggestions to regress to a previous time testified post-experimentally that they felt they had gone back to the earlier time "to some extent" and 11 per cent testified that they "thoroughly felt" they were back at the earlier time (Barber & Calverley, 1966a). With respect to suggested hallucinations, approximately 50 per cent of unselected control subjects who received direct suggestions to hear a specified song reported that they clearly heard the (suggested) music and about 33 per cent of unselected controls who received direct suggestions to see an object reported that they clearly saw the (suggested) object (Barber & Calverley, 1964a; Bowers, 1967). In a subsequent experiment (Spanos & Barber, 1968), in which honest reports were demanded from the subjects by another person (not the experimenter), the same proportion of unselected control subjects, about 50 per cent and 33 per cent, respectively, reported that they clearly heard the (suggested) music and clearly saw the (suggested) object. Along similar lines, a series of investigations has demonstrated that most experimental subjects proceed to carry out ostensibly antisocial or harmful acts when given direct emphatic suggestions or instructions to do so (Calverley & Barber, 1965; Milgram, 1963; Orne & Evans, 1965). Also, at least as many subjects in a control group as in an experimental (hypnotic) group comply with direct suggestions to perform a post-experimental or post-hypnotic act (Damaser, 1964; Kellogg, 1929; Patten, 1930).

In brief, these findings, and related data presented elsewhere (Andersen & Sarbin, 1964; Barber, 1969; Barber & Calverley, 1963a), support two conclusions: When unselected subjects are exposed to direct suggestions of limb or body rigidity, hallucination, time-distortion, age-regression, selective amnesia, and so on, they typically manifest some of the behaviors that have been historically associated with the word *hypnotism*. To formulate a general theory of hypnotism, we must begin with the fact that subjects are more responsive to direct suggestions than has been commonly assumed and then we must go on to delineate the factors that are effective in raising this rather high base-level response.

It needs to be emphasized that direct suggestions can vary in wording and can be presented in several tones of voice. The *wording and tone of direct suggestions* play an important role in determining to what extent subjects will manifest the behaviors associated with the term *hypnotism*. A recent study (Barber & Calverley, 1966b) showed that subjects manifest more apparent forgetting on tests of recall and recognition when the suggestions for amnesia are worded permissively ("try to forget") rather than peremptorily ("you will forget"). Similarly, subjects report more nocturnal dreams on a specified topic when the suggestions to dream at night on the selected topic are permissive ("try to dream") rather than peremptory ("you will dream") (Barber & Hahn, 1966). Also, subjects are markedly more reponsive to the test-suggestions of the BSS when the suggestions are presented in a firm tone of voice rather than in a lackadaisical tone (Barber & Calverley, 1964c).

FUNCTIONAL RELATIONS BETWEEN ANTECEDENT VARIABLE 2
(TASK-MOTIVATIONAL INSTRUCTIONS) AND RESPONSE TO
TEST-SUGGESTIONS

As stated above, to formulate a theory of hypnotism, we must begin with the fact that base-level response to test-suggestions is higher than has been assumed, and then we must go on to specify the factors that are present in hypnotic experiments which produce further increments in the rather high base-level response. One factor, which is typically present in hypnotic experiments, that can raise response above the base-level, has been labeled *task-motivational instructions*. Let us first specify the referents for this term.

Present-day experimenters who take the role of hypnotists attempt to motivate their subjects to perform maximally. For example, they may use the Stanford Hypnotic Susceptibility Scale to instruct their subjects along the following lines: " . . . in participating here you are contributing to scientific knowledge . . . It will be useful if you can do everything I ask you to do . . . I assume that you are willing and that you are doing your best to cooperate . . . pay close attention to what I tell you, and think of the things I tell you to think about . . . Most people find this a very interesting experience. . . You are going to experience many things I will tell you to experience . . ." (Weitzenhoffer & Hilgard, 1959).

A series of experiments (Barber & Calverley, 1962, 1963b. 1963c, 1968) indicate that these kinds of instructions, which can be labeled as *task-motivational instructions,* make it easier for subjects to exhibit behaviors of the type traditionally associated with the word *hypnotism*. Each of these experiments included at least two randomly-selected groups. Subjects in one group were assessed individually on response to the eight test-suggestions of the BSS without special preliminaries (base-level condition). Subjects in another group were tested individually on the BSS after receiving task-motivational instructions patterned after those quoted above; that is, each subject was told that his performance would depend on his willingness to try to experience those things which would be described to him, that previous subjects were able to experience the effects, and that if he cooperated fully and tried to perform maximally he would experience interesting things and would be helping the experiment. The task-motivational instructions produced enhanced suggestibility (Barber, 1965b, Table 3). For instance, although nearly half the subjects passed the Hand Lock and Thirst "Hallucination" items under the base-level condition, more than 75 per cent of the subjects who received task-motivational instructions obtained passing Objective and Subjective scores on these items. Furthermore, about twice as many subjects under the task-motivational instructions condition, as compared to the base-level condition, passed the remaining six test-suggestions of the BSS (Arm Lowering, Arm Levitation, Verbal Inhibition, Body Immobility, "Posthypnotic-Like" Response, and Selective Amnesia).

In general, task-motivational instructions appear to be sufficient to elicit other types of hypnotic performances. For instance, in most, but not all, of the pertinent experiments, task-motivational instructions were sufficient to elicit the type of heightened physical endurance that has at times been associated with hypnotism (Barber, 1966; Barber & Calverley, 1964i; Levitt & Brady, 1964; London & Fuhrer, 1961; Orne, 1959; Slotnick & London, 1965).

Although task-motivational instructions generally augment response to test-suggestions, we might expect that this effect will not be obtained if subjects are highly motivated prior to their participation in the experiment. For instance, we might predict that if all subjects have volunteered for an experiment in hypnotism, that is, all subjects are presumably motivated to be hypnotized, it may not be especially important whether or not they receive task-motivational instructions. An experiment which supports this conjecture was recently presented by Hartman (1967).

FUNCTIONAL RELATIONS BETWEEN ANTECEDENT VARIABLE 3 (DEFINITION OF THE SITUATION) AND RESPONSE TO TEST-SUGGESTIONS

Three sets of experiments indicate that responsiveness to test- suggestions is also functionally related to another antecedent variable, namely, to how the situation is defined to the subjects:

An experiment by Barber and Calverley (1964f) demonstrated that subjects are markedly more responsive to the test-suggestions of the BSS when the situation is defined as a test of imagination rather than as a test of gullibility. Although hypnotists do not define the situation to their subjects as a test of gullibility, some subjects may define it in this way to themselves and it appears likely that these subjects will show a very low level of response to test-suggestions.

Secter (1960) showed that a higher level of response to suggestions for anesthesia, hyperaesthesia, and post-hypnotic behavior is obtained when the hypnotic situation is defined permissively ("Is there anyone who would object to learning how to enter hypnosis through his own efforts?") rather than authoritatively ("I propose that we hypnotize you").

In recent experiments (Barber & Calverley, 1964h, 1965a), subjects were randomly assigned to one of two groups. One group was told that it was participating in a hypnotic experiment and the other group was told that it was to be tested for ability to imagine. Subjects in both groups were then treated identically; they were tested individually on response to the BSS. Subjects told that they were participating in a hypnotic experiment were significantly more responsive on the BSS than those told they were being tested for imaginative ability.

The last-mentioned experiments raise an important question: Why are subjects more responsive to suggestions when the situation is defined to them as hypnotism? An answer to this question will be provided when I will attempt to integrate the empirical data.

FUNCTIONAL RELATIONS BETWEEN ANTECEDENT VARIABLE 4 (RELAXA-TION-SLEEP SUGGESTIONS) AND RESPONSE TO TEST-SUGGESTIONS

In a hypnotic situation the experimenter typically tells the subject repe-atedly that he is becoming "relaxed . . . more and more re-laxed . . . drowsy . . . drowsier and drowsier . . . sleepy . . . very, very sleepy." Do suggestions of this type which I shall label as *relaxa-tion-sleep suggestions,* raise response to other types of test-suggestions above the level found when the subject is simply told that he is partici-pating in a hypnotic experiment? In three studies (Barber & Calverley, 1965a, Exp. 3, 1965b, Exps. 1 and 2) subjects assigned at random to experimental groups were tested on response to the BSS after they were told only that they were participating in a hypnotic experiment or, in addition, were told repeatedly that they were becoming relaxed, drowsy, and sleepy. Each of the three experiments showed that, when other variables are held constant or are counterbalanced, repeated relaxa-tion-sleep suggestions significantly raise Objective and Subjective scores on the 8-point BSS by about one or two points. In addition, two ex-periments (Barber & Calverley, 1965a, Exp. 2; Klinger, 1968) showed that scores on the BSS are raised to about the same degree when the relaxation-sleep suggestions are administered either for a brief period (one minute) or for a longer period (five or ten minutes).

The effectiveness of relaxation-sleep suggestions in raising subject's responsiveness to other test-suggestions is open to several inter-pretations which will be discussed later in this chapter.

FUNCTIONAL RELATIONS BETWEEN ANTECEDENT VARIABLE 5
(WORDING AND TONE OF INQUIRY)
AND SUBJECTIVE RESPONSES TO TEST-SUGGESTIONS

A recent experiment by Barber, Dalal and Calverley (1968) showed that the subjects' subjective reports are also dependent, in part, on another antecedent variable, namely, on *the wording and tone of the inquiry*. The rationale and design of this experiment were as follows:

In an important paper Orne (1959) had concluded that the essence of hypnosis will be found in the subject's "report of alterations in his experiences" as indicated, for example, by his report of "an inability to resist a cue [a suggestion] given by the hypnotist" and of having experienced the "[hypnotic] state as basically different from the normal one." The experiment by Barber *et. al.* was designed to determine to what extent subjective reports of this type are influenced by the wording of the questions that are submitted to the subjects. Fifty-three nursing students were exposed individually to the Stanford Hypnotic Suscepti-bility Scale (Form A) which includes repeated relaxation-sleep sugges-tions and a series of standardized test-suggestions. After the subjects were told to awaken, they were randomly allocated to three ex-perimental groups and each group was asked questions that differed slightly in wording. Let us look closely at the results obtained with two of the random groups.

Subjects in Group A were asked individually, "Did you feel you could resist the suggestions?", whereas those in Group B were asked individually, "Did you feel you could not resist the suggestions?" The two questions elicited markedly different subjective reports: 22 per cent of the subjects in Group A and 83 per cent in Group B reported that they could not resist the suggestions. A separate analysis was performed for the very good subjects in each group (who had either or both judged themselves as deeply hypnotized and had passed all of the test-suggestions). Only *half* of the very good subjects in Group A and *all* of the very good subjects in Group B reported that they could not resist.

Next, subjects in Group A were asked, "Did you experience the hypnotic state as basically similar to the waking state?" and those in Group B were asked, "Did you experience the hypnotic state as bas-ically different from the waking state?" Only a minority of the subjects in Group A (17 per cent of all subjects in the group and 33 per cent of the very good subjects) reported that they experienced the two states as different whereas the great majority of subjects in Group B (72 per cent of all subjects and 75 per cent of the very good subjects) reported that they experienced the two states as different.

These results, and the results obtained with a third experimental group that was asked slightly different questions, strongly indicated that the subjective reports of hypnotic subjects are markedly affected by ostensibly small variations in the *wording* of the questions that are submitted to them. There is also evidence to indicate that the *tone* and *inflections* of the questions influence the subject's experimental reports. For instance, subjects can be asked "Do you remember what occurred?" with a tone of voice and with inflections implying that they can and should remember or with a tone of voice and with inflections implying that they cannot and should not. More subjects manifest amnesia (appear to be unable to verbalize the events) when the question is asked in the latter rather than in the former way (Barber, 1962).

The inconsistencies in subjective reports that are produced by seemingly slight changes in the wording and tone of the inquiry have important implications for formulating a theory of hypnotism. These implications will be discussed when I will attempt to integrate the data theoretically.

FUNCTIONAL RELATIONS BETWEEN ANTECEDENT VARIABLES 6 AND 7 (SUBJECTS' ATTITUDES AND EXPECTATIONS) AND RESPONSE TO TEST-SUGGESTIONS

The above discussion has been concerned with the effects of five instruction-suggestion variables (*wording and tone of direct suggestions, task motivational instructions, definition of the situation, relaxation-sleep suggestions,* and *wording and tone of inquiry*). Although these antecedent variables play an important role, they cannot, by themselves, account for the variability in performance among subjects. When exposed to the same instruction-suggestion variables, subjects will differ in the degree to which they exhibit behaviors of the type associated with the word *hypnotism*. To an important extent this variability appears to be due to variations among subjects in their attitudes and expectations.

Attitudes and expectations with respect to hypnotism. Andersen (1963) obtained a significant correlation of .47 between scores on a pre-experimental scale measuring attitudes and expectations (e.g., "I would feel uneasy or uncomfortable in the hypnosis situation") and scores on suggestibility tests administered in the hypnotic experiment. In another study (Barber and Calverley, 1966c), responses to test-suggestions in a hypnotic experiment were significantly correlated with subject's pre-experimental expectations (self-predictions) of their own hypnotic depth (average $r = .41$) and with a pre-experimental attitude to hypnosis measure (perceiving hypnotism as interesting) (average $r = .55$). Similarly, other studies (Barber & Calverley, 1969b; Dermen & London, 1965; London, Cooper & Johnson, 1962, Melei & Hilgard, 1964; Rosenhan & Tompkins, 1964; Shor, Orne & O'Connell, 1966) generally yielded small positive correlations (which were more often significant for females than for males) between subjects' scores on suggestibility tests given in a hypnotic situation and their pre-experimental attitudes toward hypnotism and their pre-experimental expectations (self-predictions) of their own hypnotic depth. A further study (Barber & Calverley, 1964d), in which attitudes toward the test-situation were manipulated experimentally, indicated that negative attitudes preclude responsiveness to test-suggestions of the type traditionally associated with the word *hypnotism;* or, stated in a different way, to manifest some degree of responsiveness to test-suggestions, it is necessary for the subject to hold at least neutral if not positive attitudes toward the test-situation.

Task-expectancy. Several experiments mentioned in the preceding paragraph evaluated the effects of one type of expectancy — subjects' expectancy pertaining to the depth of hypnosis they would attain. Hypnotists also typically attempt to induce another type of expectancy, namely, an expectancy that the tasks or things suggested will be rather easy to perform or to experience. Three recent experiments evaluated the effects of the latter type of expectancy, which can be labeled as *task-expectancy.*

The first experiment (Barber & Calverley, 1964h) showed that subjects are significantly more responsive to the test-suggestions of the BSS when they are told that the tests are easy rather than difficult to perform. In the second experiment (Klinger, 1968) each subject was assessed on response to the test-suggestions of the BSS after he had observed another person (a stooge) responding to the suggestions. Prior to the experiment, the stooge had been secretly instructed to role-play a very responsive person half of the time and a very unresponsive person the other half of the time. The subjects who had observed the highly responsive person obtained mean scores of 6.0 whereas those who had observed the unresponsive person obtained significantly lower mean scores of 2.6 on the 8-point BSS.

In the third study (Wilson, 1967) an experimental group was asked to imagine various suggested effects while ingenious methods were employed to help them experience the effects without their knowing that they were receiving such aid. For instance, the subject was asked to imagine that the room was red while a tiny bulb was lit secretly which provided a very faint red tinge to the room. Following these preliminaries, the subjects were assessed on the BSS. Another random group of subjects (controls) were tested on the BSS without receiving "external confirmation of the suggested effects". The experimental group obtained a mean score of 5 whereas the control group obtained a significantly lower mean score of 3 on the 8-point BSS.

In brief, three experiments, which employed different methods to induce an expectancy that the tasks are easy to perform, indicate that positive task-expectancy facilitates response to test-suggestions.

Expectancy of appropriate behavior. A study by Orne (1959) was concerned with another type of expectancy. An experimental group was told in a class lecture that hypnotic subjects typically manifest "catalepsy of the dominant hand" whereas a control group was not told anything about "*catalepsy*". Subsequently, subjects in both groups were tested individually on response to test-suggestions in a hypnotic experiment. Since 55 per cent of the subjects in the experimental group and none in the control group showed catalepsy of the dominant hand during the experiment, it appears that the subjects' expectations concerning what behaviors are appropriate in a hypnotic experiment play an important role in determining their performance.

In summary, the data indicate that response to test-suggestions of body immobility, hallucination, amnesia, etc., is functionally related to subjects' pre-experimental attitudes toward hypnotism, to their pre-experimental expectations (self-predictions) of their own hypnotic depth, and to their pre-experimental expectations of what behaviors are appropriate in a hypnotic situation. Furthermore, three studies indicate that responsiveness to test-suggestions is enhanced when an attempt is made to produce an expectancy that the tasks are easy to perform.

A FAILURE TO DEMONSTRATE FUNCTIONAL RELATIONS BETWEEN
ANTECEDENT VARIABLE 8 (SUBJECTS' PERSONALITY CHARACTERISTICS)
AND RESPONSE TO TEST-SUGGESTIONS

It has been commonly assumed that subjects' enduring traits of personality play an important role in determining their responsivity to test-suggestions in a hypnotic situation (hypnotizability) and also in a non-hypnotic situation (suggestibility). In fact, it has been hypothesized by one or more investigators that highly responsive subjects differ from those who are unresponsive in neuroticism, hysterical traits, extroversion, dominance, ego-strength, sociability, general cooperativeness, and other characteristics of personality. The numerous studies that have tested these hypotheses, reviewed in detail elsewhere (Barber, 1964b), yielded either negative or conflicting results. For instance, one study found a positive correlation between neuroticism and hypnotizability or suggestibility, another found a negative correlation, and at least five studies found no relationship between these variables (Cooper & Dana, 1964; Eysenck, 1947; Furneaux & Gibson, 1961; Heilizer, 1960; Hilgard & Bentler, 1963; Ingham, 1954, 1955; Lang & Lazovik, 1962; Thorn, 1961). Similarly, although some investigators (As, 1962; Shor, Orne & O'Connell, 1962) reported that response to test-suggestions was correlated with propensity to have natural hypnotic-like experiences such as vivid daydreams, other investigators (Barber & Calverley, 1965c; Dermen, 1964; London, Cooper & Johnson, 1962; Wilson, 1967) failed to confirm this relationship. In brief, the studies in this area either failed to demonstrate hypothesized relationships between personality traits and hypnotizability or suggestibility, or when a relationship was obtained and an attempt was made to cross-validate it, the confirmation failed to occur.

The failure to find consistent differences in personality between individuals who are and those who are not suggestible or hypnotizable has several important implications for formulating a theory of hypnotism which will be discussed later in this chapter.

FUNCTIONAL RELATIONS BETWEEN ANTECEDENT VARIABLES 9 AND 10 (EXPERIMENTER ROLE BEHAVIOR AND PERSONAL CHARACTERISTICS) AND RESPONSE TO TEST-SUGGESTIONS

Each of the instruction-suggestion variables that were discussed earlier are under the control of the experimenter. It is the experimenter who defines the situation and who administers the task-motivational instructions, the relaxation-sleep suggestions, the test-suggestions, and the inquiry questions. Speaking metaphorically, the experimenter can be viewed as a funnel through which many of the important antecedent variables must filter before they affect the subject's response.

When the experimenter's role in a hypnotic situation is permitted to vary, the subject's performance can be viewed from a *transactional* frame of reference, that is, the subject's performance is influenced by the experimenter's behavior and, conversely, the experimenter's behavior is influenced by the subject's performance (Barber, 1958). For example, when suggestions for regression to childhood have been administered and the experimenter's role is allowed to vary, subjects behave more or less in an age-regressed manner depending on whether the experimenter treats them as children or as adults (Troffer, 1966) and, presumably, the experimenter's behavior vis-à-vis the subject is in turn partly determined by the degree to which the subject performs appropriately to the suggested age.

It also appears possible that the subject's performance is affected by

the experimenter's attitudes, expectancies, and biases or, more generally, by the experimenter's investment in a given experimental outcome
(see Orne, 1959, 1962, for a discussion of "demand characteristics").
For instance, researchers in this area may have expected that behaviors
such as hallucination, age-regression, analgesia, and amnesia would be
elicited from a hypnotic group but not from a control group. In expecting
more dramatic results under the hypnotic treatment than under the
control treatment, investigators may have inadvertently given the
test-suggestions in a more forceful tone to the hypnotic group than to the
control group, worded the inquiry somewhat differently for the two
groups, and varied their procedures in other subtle ways (Troffer & Tart,
1964). Further studies are clearly needed to assess the effects of experimenters' expectancies or biases. For instance, experimenters could
be led to expect that some of their subjects will obtain high scores on a
standardized scale of test-suggestions and that others will obtain low
scores. The data available at present, which have been reviewed in detail
elsewhere (Barber & Silver, 1968a, 1968b; Rosenthal, 1968), suggest
two hypotheses that are open to empirical test: Experimenters tend to
obtain results in line with their expectancies when their procedures are
not rigorously standardized, for example, when they vary the wording,
tone, or inflections of the test-suggestions and of the inquiry questions.
And, experimenters' expectancies do not significantly affect the results
when the experimental procedures are rigorously standardized, for example, when the test-suggestions are administered to all subjects by a
tape-recording and the inquiry is conducted by written questionnaires.

It has also been hypothesized that the personal characteristics of the
experimenter—voice, prestige, age, sex, ethnic background, and personality characteristics—influence the subject's performance in a hypnotic
situation. Studies by Das (1960) and by Thorne & Beier (1968) indicated that either or both the experimenter's prestige or his accent may
affect the subject's response to test-suggestions. However, other studies
indicated that, in a standardized experimental situation, very similar
performances are elicited by different experimenters and that subjects do
not differ significantly in performance when the test-suggestions are
administered personally by an experimenter or impersonally by a
tape-recording (Barber & Calverley, 1964b, 1966b, Hoskovec, Svorad,
& Lanc, 1963; London & Fuhrer, 1961; Weitzenhoffer & Weitzenhoffer,
1958). Further investigations are needed to determine more conclusively
if experimenter's vocal characteristics, prestige, age, sex, ethnic background, and personality characteristics exert a main effect or interact
with other variables to affect subjects' performances.

SUGGESTED FUNCTIONAL RELATIONS BETWEEN ANTECEDENT VARIABLES
11 (INTERPERSONAL RELATIONSHIP BETWEEN SUBJECT AND EX-
PERIMENTER) AND RESPONSE TO TEST-SUGGESTIONS

The relationship between the subject and the hypnotist is listed in Table 2, column 1, as another antecedent variable that may affect the subject's performance. Since this variable appears to exert somewhat different effects in clinical and experimental settings, let us look at each setting in turn.

When hypnotic procedures are used in the clinic, the patient is typically seen many times by the clinician-hypnotist and strong interpersonal ties are often formed. In this context, the clinician administers repeated relaxation-sleep suggestions and, when the patient is judged to be in a trance, suggestions are administered which are intended to produce desired effects such as relief of pain. In some investigations in which the desired effects were elicited, it was concluded that the suggestions were effective because they were administered when the patient was in a trance (Fogelman & Crasilneck, 1956). However, the possibility was not excluded that the effective determinant was the close interpersonal relationship that had been formed between the patient and the clinician-hypnotist which included an "implicit demonstration by the hypnotist of his commitment to the patient and his desire to use all means and to enter into the most intimate contact with him to help him" (Gordon, 1967, p. 616).

The interpersonal relationship between subject and hypnotist may be less important in an experimental situation than in a clinical one (August, 1967). In experimental situations the subject and hypnotist typically meet only once or twice and they usually do not interact sufficiently to form strong ties. Further studies are needed to delineate reliable methods for rating both the nature and the intensity of the relationship between subject and hypnotist and to determine to what extent the relationship influences subjects' performance in both clinical and experimental situations.

FUNCTIONAL RELATIONS BETWEEN CONSEQUENT VARIABLE B (SUBJECTS'
REPORTS OF HAVING BEEN HYPNOTIZED) AND FIVE ANTECEDENT VARI-
ABLES

The preceding discussion related the 11 antecedent variables listed in Table 2, column 1, to the most important set of consequent variables that have been traditionally subsumed under the rubric *hypnotism,* namely, *responses to test-suggestions.* As Table 2, column 2, shows, another consequent variable is *the subject's report that he was hypno-*

tized to some degree. The evidence at present indicates that the antecedent variables which determine whether the subject will report that he was hypnotized to a deep, medium or light level or was not hypnotized at all include the wording and tone of the questions that are used to elicit the subject's report and whether the experimenter states or implies that he believes the subject was or was not hypnotized (Barber, Dalal, , & Calverley, 1968). Also, a substantial number of subjects judge to what degree they were hypnotized by observing to what degree they responded to relaxation-sleep suggestions or to suggestions of limb rigidity, hallucination, analgesia, amnesia, and so on (Barber & Calverley, 1969b). Subject's reports of having been hypnotized are also dependent, in part on their preconceptions of what hypnosis is supposed to involve. When other variables are held constant, subjects differing in preconceptions differ in their reports of having been hypnotized. For instance, one subject conceives hypnosis as a state of relaxation whereas another believes that a person is hypnotized when he does not remember the events that occurred. When both subjects become relaxed during the session and both remember the experimental events, the former will testify that he was hypnotized whereas the latter will testify that he was not hypotized (Barber, 1969). Finally, subject's reports of having been hypnotized are also functionally related to their pre-experimental expectations of their own performance. A recent study (Barber & Calverley, 1969b) showed that subject's pre-experimental expectations (self-predictions) pertaining to what degree they expected to be hypnotized were significantly correlated ($r = .45$ to $.49$) with their post-experimental self-ratings of the hypnotic depth they had attained.

In brief, a series of recent experiments indicate that subjects' reports pertaining to their being hypnotized are functionally related to at least five denotable antecedent variables. It now remains to be demonstrated, it cannot be assumed a priori without evidence, that subjects' reports pertaining to whether or not they were hypnotized are also functionally related to another factor—namely, the presence or absence of an "altered state of consciousness" (hypnosis or trance).

FUNCTIONAL RELATIONS BETWEEN CONSEQUENT VARIABLE C (HYPNOTIC APPEARANCE) AND FOUR ANTECEDENT VARIABLES

In addition to responding to test-suggestions and reporting that they were hypnotized, subjects in a hypnotic situation also typically appear to be in trance or in hypnosis. For instance, they characteristically manifest a lack of spontaneity, a type of limpness-relaxation, a trance stare (fixity of the eyes), and psychomotor retardation (slowed movements of the body or limbs) (Weitzenhoffer, 1957, p. 210, 1963, p. 42). Traditional theories of hypnotism typically assumed that the degree to which the subject manifests a hypnotic appearance is primarily determined by the degree to which he is in an altered state of hypnosis or trance. Two comments are relevant here. First of all, this traditional assumption has never been tested experimentally and, at the present time, it is not clear how it could be tested (Chaves, 1968). Secondly, when subjects in a hypnotic situation manifest loss of spontaneity, limpness-relaxation, trance stare, psychomotor retardation, and other characteristics of a hypnotic appearance, these characteristics can be removed by telling the subject to stop manifesting them and many subjects will continue to respond positively to test-suggestions.

The hypnotic appearance that is manifested by a substantial number of subjects in a hypnotic situation can be viewed as a third set of consequent variables (Table 2, column 2) that is related to denotable antecedent variables. A recent study (Barber & Calverley, 1969b) indicates that the degree to which subjects in a hypnotic situation appear to be in hypnosis or trance is functionally related to the subjects' preconceptions of what hypnosis is supposed to involve and to the suggestions that they have received (such as explicit or implicit suggestions to sit quietly for a period of time with eyes closed or repeated suggestions to become relaxed, drowsy, and sleepy). Furthermore, there is evidence to indicate that a hypnotic appearance is also related to subjects' pre-experimental attitudes toward hypnotism and their pre-experimental expectations of their own performance (Barber, 1969). Further studies are in order to isolate all of the important antecedent variables which determine whether or not and to what degree subjects will appear to be in hypnosis or trance.

CONVERGENCE AND INTERACTION OF ANTECEDENT VARIABLES

Each of the three sets of consequent behaviors subsumed under the term hypnotism is multidetermined; each set of behaviors—*responses to test-suggestions, reports of having been hypnotized, and hypnotic appearance*–is functionally related to more than one of the 11 antecedent variables listed in Table 2, column 1. For instance, data summarized above indicated that a least five classes of antecedent variables affect subjects' reports that they were hypnotized. Similarly, the degree to which subjects respond to test-suggestions and manifest a hypnotic appearance appears to be dependent upon many antecendent variables including the subjects' attitudes and expectancies toward the test-situation, the wording and tone of instructions and suggestions, and whether or not task-motivational instructions and relaxation-sleep suggestions are administered.

In a recent study (Barber & Calverley, 1965a), a triple interaction among the following three antecedent variables was shown to affect response to test-suggestions: the definition of the situation (as hypnotism or as a control experiment); task-motivational instructions; and instructions that it is easy to perform well on assigned tasks. It also appears likely that other antecedent variables also *interact* to affect the behaviors associated with the word *hypnotism*. For instance, although one antecedent variable—whether the subjects' eyes are open or closed—fails to exert a significant main effect on response to the test-suggestions of the BSS (Barber & Calverley, 1965a), it can be hypothesized that this variable *interacts* with the type of test-suggestions to affect response. That is, subjects may be more responsive to some types of test-suggestions (e.g., suggestions for heightened endurance) when their eyes are open and more responsive to other types of test-suggestions (e.g., suggestions to dream) when their eyes are closed. In brief, it appears that the effectiveness of a given antecedent variable depends upon the qualititative and quantitative properties of other antecedent variables that are simultaneously present and to attain a complete explanation of the behaviors of hypnotism it is necessary to delineate the many complex interactions that occur among all important antecedent variables.

Theoretical Integration

Having specified the functional relations between three sets of behaviors to be explained (consequent variables) and 11 antecedent variables typically present in hypnotic situations, the next step is to formulate general propositions that are based upon the empirically-determined antecedent-consequent relationships. Although much more work is needed to specify all important antecedent-consequent relations, a sufficient number have been delineated to justify preliminary attempts to provide a theoretical integration. We need to continue an active search for new variables and new relations among variables while simultaneously endeavoring to conceptualize the domain of empirical facts parsimoniously under a small number of general principals.

We can begin our endeavors toward formulating general theoretical principles by first interpreting the effects of the following four antecedent variables: *definition of the situation; relaxation-sleep suggestions; wording and tone of inquiry;* and *subjects' personality characteristics.* As pointed out in the preceding discussion, the effects exerted by each of these four antecedent variables on subjects' performance are open to several possible interpretations *and each interpretation has major repercussions for formulating a theory of hypnotism.*

INTERPRETATION OF EFFECTS OF FOUR ANTECEDENT VARIABLES

Definition of the situation. It was mentioned that most present-day subjects manifest a higher level of response to standardized test-suggestions when told that they are participating in a hypnotic experiment rather than in an experiment designed to test their imaginative ability. This experimental outcome can be interpreted in at least two ways:

One interpretation is that, when the situation is defined to subjects as hypnotism, they are more likely to enter an altered state of consciousness (a hypnotic state). Unfortunately, this interpretation cannot be unequivocally confirmed or disconfirmed at the present time because it is not clear how one could determine empirically whether the hypothesized alteration in consciousness is present or absent (Barber, 1964a; Chaves, 1968).

An alternative interpretation of the suggestibility-enhancing effect of defining the situation as hypnotism is as follows: When subjects are told that they are in a hypnotic experiment, they typically construe this to mean that they are in an unusual situation in which high response to test-suggestions and "unprecedented kinds of experiences" are to be expected (Gill & Brenman, 1959, p. 10). On the other hand, when subjects are told that they are to be tested for ability to imagine, they are being told by implication that they are not necessarily expected to show a high level of response to test-suggestions of the type associated with the word *hypnotism*. This interpretation can be tested experimentally by first ascertaining how subjects conceive a hypnotic situation and a test-of-imagination situation and then relating their pre-experimental conceptions to their responsiveness to test-suggestions when the experimental situation is defined to them in these two different ways.

Relaxation-sleep suggestions. I noted previously that subjects are more likely to respond positively to suggestions for analgesia, hallucination, amnesia, etc., if they are first exposed to repeated suggestions of relaxation, drowsiness, and sleep. The suggestibility-enhancing effect of relaxation-sleep suggestions is open to at least three possible interpretations:

One interpretation, not clearly testable, is that relaxation-sleep suggestions raise responsiveness to other suggestions because they produce an altered state of consciousness (a hypnotic state).

Another interpretation postulates that repeated suggestions of relaxation, drowsiness, and sleep tend to give rise to relaxation and that relaxation in turn facilitates responsiveness to suggestions. Empirical evaluation of this interpretation is possible by monitoring autonomic variables, such as skin resistance, respiration, and heart rate, which indirectly indicate whether the subject is relaxed or is aroused and activated (Duffy, 1962).

A third interpretation is that relaxation-sleep suggestions raise response to other test-suggestions because they effectively define the situation as hypnotism. There are three interrelated aspects to this interpretation: Present-day subjects (typically college students or nursing students) are aware that repeated relaxation-sleep suggestions are administered in a hypnotic situation. Although some subjects accept the situation as hypnotism when they are simply told that they have been assigned to the hypnotic group, practically all present-day subjects believe that they are truly participating in a hypnotic experiment if the experimenter goes on to suggest to them repeatedly that they are becoming more and more relaxed, drowsy, and sleepy. When the situation is effectively defined as hypnotism to present-day subjects, it is being implicitly defined as one in which a high level of response to test-suggestions of hallucination, amnesia, etc., is not only possible but is also desired and expected.

This definition of the situation interpretation can more readily account for two sets of empirical data that cannot be satisfactorily explained by the relaxation interpretation: Relaxation-sleep suggestions facilitate responsiveness even in those subjects who become alert and activated when they receive such suggestions (Barber & Coules, 1959).[2] Subjects who become relaxed when they receive relaxation-sleep suggestions do not remain relaxed when they are assessed on response to test-suggestions (Barber & Coules, 1959).

The relaxation and the definition of the situation interpretations give rise to different predictions concerning the outcome of an experiment with children, say around five or six years of age, of whom some are and some are not knowledgeable concerning the traditional implications of the word *hypnotism*. (By the term *knowledgeable* I refer to those chil-

---

2. This paradoxical reaction—alertness and activation produced by relaxation-sleep suggestion—is apparently found more often in inexperienced subjects (who are participating for the first time in a hypnotic experiment) rather than in experienced subjects (Barber & Coules, 1959; May & Edmonston, 1966). A possible explanation of this paradoxical reaction is that inexperienced subjects, told repeatedly that they are becoming relaxed, drowsy, sleepy, and are entering a hypnotic state, typically expect at any moment to experience a drastic alteration in their state of consciousness, and since this expected profound alteration is foreboding, they do not relax but instead become alert and activated while waiting for it to appear.

dren who have learned from television or from hearsay that relaxation-sleep suggestions are part of hypnotism and that hypnotic subjects are highly responsive to suggestions.) The relaxation interpretation would predict that repeated relaxation-sleep suggestions will be equally effective in producing relaxation in knowledgeable and non-knowledgeable children and, consequently, will be equally effective in raising response to test-suggestions above the base-level in both groups of children. Since the definition of the situation interpretation views the effectiveness of relaxation-sleep suggestions as due to their role in defining the situation as hypnotism, it would predict that relaxation-sleep suggestions will be significantly more effective in raising response above the base-level in knowledgeable rather than in non-knowledgeable children. Experiments are in order to test these contrasting predictions.

Wording and tone of inquiry. It was pointed out earlier that the subjective reports of hypnotic subjects vary with seemingly slight changes in the wording and tone of the questions that are submitted to them. These inconsistencies in experiential reports that are produced by minor variations in the inquiry may be due to one or both of the following:

The subjects may be misreporting their experiences in order to comply with the desires of the experimenter as indicated by the wording and tone of his questions.

The subjects may accept the categories for classifying their experiences (that are implicitly offered to them by the specific wording and tone of the experimenter's questions) because their experiences were ambiguous and they do not know how to categorize them. For instance, subjects may give inconsistent testimony when asked if they experienced the hypnotic state as similar to the waking state or as different from the waking state, because their experiences were multifaceted and difficult to classify. They may feel that their state during the hypnotic session was somewhat different from the waking state because they experienced various suggested effects that they had not previously experienced; however, they might also feel that their state was similar to the waking state because they were aware of what was going on and were continually thinking about their role in the situation.

Further studies are needed to determine to what extent the variability in subjects' verbal reports that is associated with changes in the wording and tone of the questions is due to each of the aforementioned possibilities or to other possibilities.

Subjects' personality characteristics. I noted previously that investigators have failed to demonstrate consistent differences in personality between individuals who are and those who are not suggestible or hypnotizable. These negative results require explanation.

It may be that subtle aspects of personality which are related to suggestibility or hypnotizability are not tapped by present-day methods of personality assessment. Another possibility is that the variability among individuals in suggestibility or hypnotizability is due primarily to differences in their attitudes, expectancies, and motivations with respect to the test-situation rather than to differences in their personality traits. Data which tend to support the latter possibility include the following:

Subjects show consistency in their hypnotizability when they are tested in the same way twice (test-retest correlations are around .72 to .82) (Barber, 1965b; Hilgard, 1965). However, subjects do not necessarily show a consistent level of hypnotizability when they are tested in the same way five or more times (correlations may drop to around .18 to .22) and there is evidence to indicate that the inter-individual variability in responsiveness with repeated testing is due to changes in subjects' attitudes toward the test-situation (Barber & Calverley, 1966c).

As noted earlier, small to moderate positive correlations have been found between subjects' pre-experimental attitudes or expectations with respect to the test-situation and their hypnotizability or suggestibility. Also, subjects' responsiveness to test-suggestions varies with ostensibly minor changes in the experimental situation, for example, with variations in the way the experimenter describes the purpose of the experiment and with changes in the experimenter's tone of voice when he is administering the test-suggestions (Barber & Calverley, 1964c, 1964f). These changes in response with ostensibly small changes in the situation cannot be attributed to changes in the subjects' personality traits (since such traits remain constant) but can be attributed to changes in subjects' attitudes, expectancies, or motivations with respect to the test-situation.

Although the data suggest that enduring personality traits may be less important than attitudes, expectancies, and motivations in determining response, this does not exclude the possibility that personality characteristics may exert a small effect on response. To ascertain how much of the variance is due to personality traits, new types of studies are needed which use covariance or statistical regression techniques to partial out or control for the effects of subjects' attitudes, expectancies, and motivations. If the latter three sets of variables were controlled or partialled out, we might be able to demonstrate more consistently than heretofore that some of the inter-individual variability in response to suggestibility tests is due to inter-individual differences in enduring personality charactersistics (Barber, 1964c).

FORMULATION OF THEORETICAL STATEMENTS WHICH ARE CLOSELY TIED
TO RESEARCH

The term *theory* is one of the most ambiguous terms in the behavioral sciences. As DiRenzo (1966) has aptly pointed out:

> Explanation is taken to be tentatively complete when it has become, or it has taken on the nature of, a theory. One is pressed to ask, however, what is theory? Various meanings have been given to "theory", and the term has been applied to a host of diversified, even though related, elements. It has been taken to imply a definition, a speculation, a postulate, a correlation, a deduction, an assumption, a general orientation, an ordered taxonomy, an empirical generalization, a conceptual scheme, a set of logically interrelated concepts, a set of propositions linked into a logical framework, a mathematical formula, an hypothesis, a model, a law, and so on (p. 246).

I cannot even begin to analyze the term *theory*. Leaving this task for another time, I will state baldly here that I see theory as a set of general statements which aim to unify the empirically-determined functional relations between antecedent and consequent variables in an area of inquiry. Having specified and clarified the functional relations between the antecedent and consequent variables listed in Table 2, we can now proceed to unify these relations under a set of general statements. There is a method available by which we could proceed toward unifying principles by gradual inductive-deductive steps. This method is based on the following considerations:

The data presented in this chapter indicate that the three sets of consequent behaviors (*responses to test-suggestions, reports of having been hypnotized,* and *hypnotic appearance*) are functionally related to at least eight sets of antecedent variables, namely, *wording and tone of direct suggestions, task-motivational instructions, definition of the situation, relaxation-sleep suggestions, wording and tone of inquiry, subjects' attitudes toward the test-situation, subjects' expectations pertaining to their own performance,* and *experimenter role behavior.* The empirically-established antecedent-consequent relations could be subsumed under a smaller number of broader principles if it could be demonstrated that the eight major antecedent variables can be subsumed under a smaller number of more broadly-defined variables. Three sets of empirical investigations that might be helpful are as follows:

As pointed out previously in this chapter, researchers may be able to demonstrate empirically that the variable labeled as *relaxation-sleep suggestions* can be subsumed under the variable labeled as *definition of the situation.* That is, it may be possible to show that repeated suggestions of relaxation, drowsiness, and sleep affect subjects' performance to

the extent that they effectively define the situation to the subjects as hypnotism.

Researchers may be able to demonstrate empirically that variations in the *definition of the situation* produce different attitudes, expectancies, and motivations toward the test-situation and toward the experimental tasks, and that differences on the latter three variables (different *task-attitudes, task-expectancies,* and *task-motivations*) give rise to different levels of response. More concretely, research utilizing the most proficient methods available at present for assessing how subjects construe the test-situation (Spielberger & DeNike, 1966) may be able to confirm empirically propositions such as the following: Subjects who are more responsive on the three sets of consequent variables when the situation is defined as hypnotism rather than as a test of imagination, view a hypnotic situation more so than a test-of-imagination situation as one in which it is appropriate for them to perform unusual behaviors and to experience unusual effects *(task-attitude),* in which they will find it rather easy to respond to suggestions and to experience unusual effects *(task-expectancy),* and in which they should not resist but instead should try to perform the suggested behaviors and try to experience the suggested effects *(task-motivation).* If propositions of this type are supported by empirical studies, the variable that was labeled in this chapter as *definition of the situation* could be subsumed under the more broadly-defined variables labeled as *task-attitude, task-expectancy,* and *task-motivation.*

Researchers may be able to show empirically that experimenters' attitudes, expectancies, and biases significantly affect subjects' behavior only when experimenters are free to vary the way they administer the suggestions and instructions and conduct the inquiry. If this can be demonstrated, the class of variables that has been labeled as *experimenter role behavior* might be subsumed under those labeled as *wording and tone of direct suggestions* and *wording and tone of inquiry.*

In brief, it appears that further investigations may be able to show that at least three of the eight important antecedent variables — *definition of the situation, relaxation-sleep suggestions,* and *experimenter role behavior* — can be subsumed under the remaining 5 variables, namely, under *task-attitude, task-expectancy, task-motivation, wording and tone of direct suggestions,* and *wording and tone of inquiry.* If this were to be accomplished, most of the functional relations between antecedent and consequent variables that were delineated in this chapter could be subsumed under a general principle worded as follows:

A substantial proportion of the variance in behaviors that have been traditionally associated with the word hypnotism *is due to a set of*

subject variables (subjects' attitudes, expectancies, and motivations toward the test-situation and toward the experimental tasks) and a set of instruction-suggestion variables (wording and tone of instructions, direct suggestions, and inquiry questions).

Two additional considerations are relevant here.

The broadly-defined variables specified above can be conceived as similar to those that operate in many types of interpersonal test-situations. For instance, when individuals are assessed on various types of tasks that do not involve special training—e.g., the Rorschach test, a draw-a-man test, a weight-holding endurance task, an unstructured spool-sorting task—it appears likely that performance is determined in part by *task-attitude, task-expectancy, task-motivation,* and *wording and tone of suggestions and instructions.* Also, subjects' reports pertaining to their experiences during the task-performance are partly determined by the *wording and tone of the inquiry.* The effective variables can also be viewed as overlapping with those which play a role in a variety of interpersonal situations in which a person in the more dominant role, such as a teacher or a psychotherapist, attempts to influence the behavior of a person in a less dominant role. For instance, the effective teacher presumably attempts to produce positive *task-attitude, task-expectancy,* and *task-motivation* in the pupil. Furthermore, the *wording and tone of suggestions, instructions,* and *inquiry questions* presumably influence the pupil's overt performance and subjective reports. There is also evidence to indicate that variables of this type play an important role in psychotherapy (Goldstein, Heller & Sechrest, 1966). In brief, the effective antecedent variables in hypnotism may be viewed as similar to those which affect performance in a wide variety of interpersonal test-situations. If this is valid, then it is just as unnecessary to posit an "altered state of consciousness" to explain the performances elicited in a hypnotic situation as it is to posit such a state to explain the performances elicited in a teacher-pupil situation, a psychotherapy situation, or in various other interpersonal test-situations.

If the experimental program outlined above succeeds in showing that the empirical antecedent variables can be reduced to a smaller number of more broadly-defined variables, further research will be required to determine how much of the behavior variance in a hypnotic situation can be accounted for by the reduced number of variables and to delineate additional variables that may account for the unexplained portion of the variance. Furthermore, if the experimental program demonstrates that the available empirical laws (functional relations between antecedents and consequents) can be subsumed under a smaller number of broader principles, empirical and theoretical endeavors will still be at an early stage. Further investigations will then be needed to test predictions that are deduced from the higher-order principles, to discard those principles that give rise to predictions which are not confirmed by empirical test, and to continue to formulate and test new principles until such time as the theoretical conceptualization closely covers the domain of empirical facts.

FUTURE PROSPECTS

The formulation presented in this chapter is simply one approach to an area of inquiry, not a closed theoretical system. It is hoped that it is a sufficiently systematic formulation to move researchers to undertake more focused investigations which ask continually more penetrating questions. Implementation of the approach is still at an early stage. Intensive investigations are now required which focus on the following.

Consequent variables. Methods are available at present for quantifying three sets of behaviors that have been historically subsumed under the rubric *hypnotism* (overt and subjective *responses to test-suggestions, reports of having been hypnotized,* and *hypnotic appearance*). There is reason to believe that further intensive work will yield more reliable and valid methods for measuring each of these sets of dependent variables. Also, further work is needed to delineate and to quantify additional consequent variables that may be associated with the topic *hypnotism.*

Antecedent variables. In some readers the formulation presented here may arouse a reaction along the following lines: Although the antecedent variables that have been considered may play a role in eliciting the behaviors, there still remains the possibility that there is something more, perhaps a "trance state", which is also instrumental in producing the behaviors.' Two considerations are relevant here:

A more complete explanation will be attained only after other variables that are hypothesized to play a role are quantified and related to the consequent behaviors. For instance, to demonstrate that a trance state plays a role in eliciting the behaviors traditionally associated with the word *hypnotism,* it is necessary first to denote the state and then to show that it is functionally related to and accounts for at least some of the variability in the behaviors. It should be clear to the reader that investigators who have attempted to explain the behaviors present in a hypnotic situation by positing an altered state of consciousness or hypnotic trance state have not as yet specified criteria for inferring the presence or absence of this state which are independent of the behaviors that are to be explained (Barber, 1964a; Chaves, 1968). Also, as pointed out in Chapter IV, although investigators have sought as unequivocal physiological index of the hypothesized hypnotic state for nearly 50 years, they have failed to find one.

Regardless of whether or not future investigators can successfully denote the hypnotic state without circularity and can show that it plays a role in eliciting the behaviors historically associated with the word *hypnotism,* there is little doubt that further research will discover other important variables that were not considered in the present chapter. For instance, other antecedent variables that may be important include: subjects' prior practice or training in hypnotic sessions (Barber & Calverley, 1966c); subjects' role-taking ability or dramatic ability (Coe & Sarbin, 1966; Sarbin & Lim, 1963); whether the subjects volunteered or were coerced to participate in the experiment (Boucher & Hilgard, 1962); whether the subjects were unselected or were selected as high or low in suggestibility, hypnotizability, or suceptibility (London, Conant & Davison, 1966; London & Fuhrer, 1961; Rosenhan & London, 1963); whether the subjects were tested individually or in a group (Sarbin, 1964, p. 201); whether or not the subject's performance was observed by an audience (Coe, 1966); whether or not the subjects were provided with a clear conception of the experiences desired and were given verbal reinforcement for each appropriate response (Giles, 1962; Sachs & Anderson, 1967); whether or not honest subjective reports were demanded during the post-experimental inquiry, and whether the post-experimental inquiry was conducted by the hypnotist or by another person (Bowers, 1967; Spanos & Barber, 1968).

Relations between antecedent-consequent variables. Research is needed to cross-validate each of the antecedent-consequent relations that has been presented in this chapter, to specify the complex interactions that occur among the antecedent variables, and to relate other antecedent factors to the overt performances and reports of subjective experiences that are associated with the term *hypnotism.*

Parsimonious conceptualization. Further endeavors are needed which aim toward a parsimonious codification of research findings. These endeavors will be successful to the degree that the empirically-established relations between antecedent and consequent variables are unified under a small number of broad principles and deductions are made from the general principles that are confirmed by empirical test.

When the present approach has been implemented—when a parsimonious conceptualization of all important antecedent-consequent relations has been attained—, we may expect the following to occur:

A series of useful effects that has been associated with the topic *hypnotism*—e.g., reduction of pain, heightened learning proficiency, enhanced physical endurance, heightened recall of earlier events—will be produced more simply and directly than at present, utilizing only those antecedent variables (that have been traditionally included in hypnotic situations) which are found to be actually effective and excluding those that are extraneous.

Principles developed in the sudy of hypnotism may be relevant to a deeper understanding of other topics in psychology. Research in hypnotism is more than the study of one isolated set of human behaviors. This area offers rewarding possibilities for the study of the effects of verbal stimulation on overt behavior and on physiological processes. It could also provide a deeper understanding of such broad psychological topics as *cognition, perception, emotion,* and *interpersonal relations.* Furthermore, the methodology developed in clarifying the topic hypnotism may also prove useful in clarifying other areas in psychology. For instance, in approaching various areas in abnormal psychology, subsumed under such headings as *schizophrenia, multiple personality,* and *hysteria,* researchers may find it profitable to hold in abeyance extant constructs and theories and to proceed along the following lines: first, they will specify and quantify the consequent variables (the overt performances and verbal reports that are to be explained); next, series of studies will be conducted to delineate denotable antecedent variables that are functionally related to the consequent behaviors; finally, proceeding gradually and always adhering closely to empirical data, attempts will be made to subsume the empirically-determined antecedent-consequent relations under a small number of general principles and deductions will be made from the network of general principles which, in turn, will be tested empirically.

Although research in hypnotism promises to provide a broader understanding of human behavior, the reverse is also true—as psychologists working on other problems develop general principles, their principles should help in attaining a deeper understanding of hypnotism. Finally, the topic *hypnotism* may lose its aura and separate status and may become an integral part of a future social-psychology in the same way as such topics as *attitude change, conformity,* and *persuasibility* are integrated into present-day social-psychology.

References

Andersen, M. L. Correlates of hypnotic performance: An historical and role-theoretical analysis. Unpublished doctoral dissertation, University of California, Berkeley, 1963.

Andersen, M. L., and Sarbin, T. R. Base rate expectancies and motoric alterations in hypnosis. *Int. J. Clin. Exp. Hypn.,* 1964, *12,* 147-158.

As, A. Non-hypnotic experiences related to hypnotizatility in male and female college student. *Scand. J. Psychol.,* 1962, *3,* 112-121.

August, R. V. Hypnosis: Viewed academically and therapeutically. *Amer. J. Clin. Hypn.,* 1967, *9,* 171-180.

Barber, T. X. The concept of "hypnosis". *J. Psychol.,* 1958, *45,* 115-131.

Barber, T. X. Toward a theory of hypnosis: Posthypnotic behavior. *Arch. Gen. Psychiat.,* 1962, *7,* 321-342.

Barber, T. X. "Hypnosis" as a causal variable in present-day psychology: A critical analysis. *Psychol. Rep.,* 1964, *14,* 839-842. (a)

Barber, T. X. Hypnotizability, suggestibility, and personality: V. A critical review of research findings. *Psychol. Rep.,* 1964, *14,* 299-320. (b)

Barber, T. X. Experimental analyses of "hypnotic" behavior: A review of recent empirical findings. *J. Abnorm. Psychol.,* 1965, *70,* 132-154. (a)

Barber, T. X. Measuring "hypnotic-like" suggestibility with and without "hypnotic induction"; psychometric properties, norms, and variables influencing response to the Barber Suggestibility Scale (BSS). *Psychol. Rep.,* 1965, *16,* 809-844. (b)

Barber, T. X. The effects of hypnosis and suggestions on strength and endurance: A critical review of research studies. *Brit. J. Soc. Clin. Psychol.,* 1966, *5,* 42-50.

Barber, T. X. *Hypnosis: A scientific approach.* New York: Van Nostrand Reinhold. 1969.

Barber, T. X. and Calverley, D. S. "Hypnotic" behavior as a function of task motivation. *J. Psychol.,* 1962, *54,* 363-389.

Barber, T. X. and Calverley, D. S. "Hypnotic-like" suggestibility in children and adults. *J. Abnorm. Soc. Psychol.,* 1963, *66,* 589-597. (a)

Barber T. X., and Calverley, D. S. The relative effectiveness of task motivating instructions and trance induction procedure in the production of "hypnotic-like" behaviors. *J. Nerv. Ment. Dis.,* 1963, *137,* 107-116. (b)

Barber, T. X., and Calverley, D. S. Toward a theory of hypnotic behavior: Effects on suggestibility of task motivating instructions and attitudes toward hypnosis. *J. Abnorm. Soc. Psychol.,* 1963, *67,* 557-565. (c)

Barber, T. X., and Calverley, D. S. An experimental study of "hypnotic" (auditory and visual) hallucinations. *J. Abnorm. Soc. Psychol.,* 1964, *63,* 13-20. (a)

Barber, T. X., and Calverley, D. S. Comparative effects on "hypnotic-like" suggestibility of recorded and spoken suggestions. *J. Cons. Psychol.,* 1964, *28,* 384. (b)

Barber, T. X. and Calverley, D. C. Effect of E's tone of voice on "hypnotic-like" suggestibility. *Psychol. Rep.,* 1964, *15,* 139-144. (c)

Barber, T. X., and Calverley, D. S. Empirical evidence for a theory of "hypnotic" behavior: Effects of pretest instructions on response to primary suggestions. *Psychol. Rec.,* 1964, *14,* 457-467. (d)

Barber, T. X., and Calverley, D. S. Experimental studies in "hypnotic" behavior: Suggested deafness evaluated by delayed auditory feedback. *Brit. J. Psychol.,* 1964, *55,* 439-446. (e)

Barber, T. X. and Calverley, D. S. The definition of the situation as a variable affecting "hypnotic-like" suggestibility. *J. Clin. Psychol.,* 1964, *20,* 438-440. (f)

Barber, T. X. and Calverley, D. S. Toward a theory of "hypnotic" behavior: An experimental study of "hypnotic time distortion". *Arch. Gen. Psychiat.*, 1964, *10*, 209-216. (g)

Barber, T. X., and Calverley, D. S. Toward a theory of hypnotic behavior: Effects on suggestibility of defining the situation as hypnosis and defining response to suggestions as easy. *J. Abnorm. Soc. Psychol.*, 1964, *68*, 585-592. (h)

Barber, T. X., and Calverley, D. S. Toward a theory of "hypnotic" behavior: Enhancement of strength and endurance. *Canad. J. Psychol.*, 1964, *18*, 156-167. (i)

Barber, T. X. and Calverley, D. S. Empirical evidence for a theory of "hypnotic" behavior; Effects on suggestibility of five variables typically included in hypnotic induction procedures. *J. Cons. Psychol.*, 1965, *29*, 98-107. (a)

Barber, T. X., and Calverley, D. S. Empirical evidence for a theory of "hypnotic" behavior: The suggestibility-enhancing effects of motivational suggestions, relaxation-sleep suggestions, and suggestions that the subject will be effectively "hypnotized". *J. Pers.*, 1965, *33*, 256-270. (b)

Barber, T. X. and Calverley, D. S. Hypnotizability, suggestibility, and personality: II. Assessment of previous imaginative-fantasy experiences by the As, Barber-Glass, and Shor questionnaires. *J. Clin. Psychol.*, 1965, *21*, 57-58. (c)

Barber, T. X., and Calverley, D. S. Effects on recall of hypnotic induction, motivational suggestions, and suggested regression: A methodological and experimental analysis. *J. Abnorm. Psychol.*, 1966, *71*, 169-180. (a)

Barber, T. X., and Calverley, D. S. Toward a theory of "hypnotic" behavior: Experimental analyses of suggested amnesia. *J. Abnorm. Psychol.*, 1966, *71*, 95-107. (b)

Barber, T. X., and Calverley, D. S. Toward a theory of hypnotic behavior: Experimental evaluation of Hull's postulate that hypnotic susceptibility is a habit phenomenon. *J. Pers.*, 1966, *34*, 416-433. (c)

Barber, T. X., and Calverley, D. S. Toward a theory of "hypnotic" behavior: Replication and extension of experiments by Barber and co-workers (1962-65) and Hilgard and Tart (1966) *Int. J. Clin. Exp. Hypn.*, 1968, *16*, 179-195.

Barber, T. X. and Calverley, D. S. Effects of hypnotic induction, suggestions of anesthesia, and distraction on subjective and physiological responses to pain. Paper presented at Eastern Psychol. Assoc., Annual Meeting, Philadelphia, April 10, 1969. (a)

Barber, T. X., and Calverley, D. S. Multidimensional analysis of "hypnotic" behavior. *J. Abnorm. Psychol.*, 1969, *74*, 209-220. (b)

Barber, T. X., and Coules, J. Electrical skin conductance and galvanic skin response during "hypnosis". *Int. J. Clin. Exp. Hypn.*, 1959, *7*, 79-92.

Barber, T. X., Dalal, A. S., and Calverley, D. S. The subjective reports of hypnotic subjects. *Amer. J. Clin. Hypn.*, 1968, *11*, 74-88.

Barber, T. X., and Hahn, K. W., Jr. Physiological and subjective responses to pain producing stimulation under hypnotically-suggested and waking-imagined "analgesia". *J. Abnorm. Soc. Psychol.*, 1962, *65*, 411-418.

Barber, T. X., and Hahn, K. W., Jr. Suggested dreaming with and without hypnotic induction. Harding, Mass.: Medfield Foundation, 1966. (Mimeo)

Barber, T. X., and Silver, M. J. Fact, fiction, and experimenter bias effect. *Psychol. Bull.*, 1968, *70*, (6, Pt. 2), 1-29. (a)

Barber, T. X., and Silver, M. J. Pitfalls in data analysis and interpretation: A reply to Rosenthal. *Psychol. Bull.,* 1968, *70,* (6, Pt. 2), 48-62. (b)

Boucher, R. G., and Hilgard, E. R. Volunteer bias in hypnotic experimentation. *Amer. J. Clin. Hypn.,* 1962, *5,* 49-51.

Bowers, K. S. The effect of demands for honesty on reports of visual and auditory hallucinations. *Int. J. Clin. Exp. Hypn.,* 1967, *15,* 31-36.

Calverley, D. S., and Barber, T. X. "Hypnosis" and antisocial behavior: An experimental evaluation. Harding, Mass.: Medfield Foundation, 1965. (Mimeo)

Chaves, J. F. Hypnosis reconceptualized: An overview of Barber's theoretical and empirical work. *Psychol. Rep.,* 1968, *22,* 587-608.

Coe, W. C. Hypnosis as role enactment: The role demand variable. *Amer. J. Clin. Hypn.,* 1966, *8,* 189-191.

Coe, W. C., and Sarbin, T. R. An experimental demonstration of hypnosis as role enactment. *J. Abnorm. Psychol.,* 1966, *71,* 400-406.

Collins, J. K. Muscular endurance in normal and hypnotic states: A study of suggested catalepsy. Honors thesis, Dept. of Psychology, University of Sydney, 1961.

Conant, J. B. *On understanding science.* New York: Mentor Books, 1951.

Cooper, G. W., Jr., and Dana, R. H. Hypnotizability and the Maudsley Personality Inventory. *Int. J. Clin. Exp. Hyn.,* 1964, *12,* 28-33.

Damaser, E. An experimental study of long-term post-hypnotic suggestion. Unpublished doctoral dissertation, Harvard University, 1964.

Das, J. P. Prestige effects in body-sway suggestibility. *J. Abnorm. Soc. Psychol.,* 1960, *61,* 487-488.

Dermen, D. Correlates of hypnotic susceptibility. Masters thesis, University of Illinois, 1964.

Dermen, D., and London, P. Correlates of hypnotic susceptibility. *J. Cons. Psychol.,* 1965, *29,* 537-545.

DiRenzo, G. J. Toward explanation in the behavioral sciences. In G. J. DiRenzo (Ed.) *Concept, theory, and explanation in the behavioral sciences.* New York: Random House, 1966, Pp. 239-291.

Duffy, Elizabeth, *Activation and behavior.* New York: John Wiley, 1962.

Edmonston, W. E., Jr. Stimulus-response theory of hypnosis. In J. E. Gordon (Ed.) *Handbook of clinical and experimental hypnosis.* New York: Macmillan, 1967, Pp. 345-387.

Edmonston, W. E., Jr. Hypnosis and electrodermal responses. *Amer. J. Clin. Hypn.,* 1968, *11,* 16-25.

Eysenck, H. J. *Dimensions of personality.* London: Routledge & Kegan Paul, 1947.

Fogelman, M. J., and Crasilneck, H. B. Food intake and hypnosis. *J. Amer. Diet. Assoc.,* 1956, *32,* 519-522.

Furneaux, W. D., and Gibson, H. G. The Maudsley Personality Inventory as a predictor of susceptibility to hypnosis. *Int. J. Clin. Exp. Hypn.,* 1961, *9,* 167-176.

Giles, E. A cross-validation study of the Pascal technique of hypnotic induction. *Int. J. Clin. Exp. Hyp.,* 1962, *10,* 101-108.

Gill, M. M., and Brenman, Margaret. *Hypnosis and related states.* New York: International Universities Press, 1959.

Glaser, B. G., and Strauss, A. L. *The discovery of grounded theory.* Chicago: Aldine, 1967.

Goldstein, A. P., Heller, K., and Sechrest, L. B. *Psychotherapy and the psychology of behavior change.* New York: John Wiley, 1966.

Gordon, J. E. Conclusions. In J. E. Gordon (Ed.) *Handbook of clinical and experimental hypnosis.* New York: Macmillan, 1967. Pp. 613-641.

Hartman, B. J. Hypnotizability as affected by attitudinal and motivational variables. *Int. J. Clin. Exp. Hypn.,* 1967, *15,* 89-91.

Heilizer, R. An exploration of the relationship between hypnotizability and anxiety and/or neuroticism. *J. Cons. Psychol.,* 1960, *24,* 432-436.

Hilgard, E. R. *Hypnotic susceptibility.* New York: Harcourt, Brace, & World, 1965.

Hilgard, E. R., and Bentler, P. M. Predicting hypnotizability from the Maudsley Personality Inventory. *Brit. J. Psychol.,* 1963, *54,* 63-69.

Hilgard, E. R., Cooper, L. M., Lenox, J., Morgan, A. H., and Voevodsky, J. The use of pain-state reports in the study of hypnotic analgesia to the pain of ice water. *J. Nerv. Ment. Dis.,* 1967, *144,* 506-513.

Hoskovec, J., Svorad, D., and Lanc, O. The comparative effectiveness of spoken and tape-recorded suggestions of body sway. *Int. J. Clin. Exp. Hyp.,* 1963, *11,* 163-166.

Ingham, J. G. Body-sway suggestibility and neurosis. *J. Ment. Sci.,* 1954, *100,* 432-441.

Ingham, J. G. Psychoneurosis and suggestibility. *J. Abnorm. Soc. Psychol.,* 1955, *51,* 600-603.

Kellogg, E. R. Duration of the effects of post-hypnotic suggestion. *J. Exp. Psychol.,* 1929, *12,* 502-514.

Klinger, B. I. The effects of peer model responsiveness and length of induction procedure on hypnotic responsiveness. Paper presented at the meeting of the Eastern Psychological Association, Washington, D.C., April 18, 1968.

Koch, S. Clark, L. Hull. *In Modern learning theory.* New York: Appleton-Century-Crofts, 1954. Chap. 1.

Koch, S. Epilogue. In S. Koch (Ed.) *Psychology: A study of a science.* (Vol. 3) New York: McGraw-Hill, 1959, Pp. 729-738.

Kuhn, T. S. *The structure of scientific revolutions.* Chicago: University of Chicago Press, 1962.

Lang, P. J., and Lazovik, A. D. Personality and hypnotic susceptibility. *J. Cons. Psychol.,* 1962, *26,* 317-322.

Levitt, E. E., and Brady, J. P. Muscular endurance under hypnosis and in the motivated waking state. *Int. J. Clin. Exp. Hypn.,* 1964, *12,* 21-27.

London, P. The induction of hypnosis. In J. E. Gordon (Ed.) *Handbook of clinical and experimental hypnosis.* New York: Macmillan, 1967, Pp. 44-79.

London, P., Conant, M., and Davison, G. C. More hypnosis in the unhypnotizable: Effects of hypnosis and exhortation on rote learning. *J. Pers.,* 1966, *34,* 71-79.

London, P., Cooper, L. M., and Johnson, H. J. Subject characteristics in hypnosis research: II. Attitudes toward hypnosis, volunteer status, and personality measures. III. Some correlates of hypnotic susceptibility. *Int. J. Clin. Exp. Hypn.,* 1962, *10,* 13-21.

London, P., and Fuhrer, M. Hypnosis, motivation and performance. *J. Pers.,* 1961, *29,* 321-333.

Marx, M. H. Intervening variable or hypothetical construct? *Psychol. Rev.,* 1951, *58,* 235-247.

Marx, M. H. *Theories in contemporary psychology.* New York: Macmillan, 1963.

May, J. R., and Edmonston, W. E., Jr. Hypnosis and a plethysmographic measure of two types of situational anxiety. *Amer. J. Clin. Hypn.,* 1966, *9,* 109-113.

Melei, J. P., and Hilgard, E. R. Attitudes toward hypnosis, self-predictions, and hypnotic susceptibility. *Int. J. Clin. Exp. Hypn.,* 1964, *12,* 99-108.

Milgram, S. Behavioral study of obedience. *J. Abnorm. Soc. Psychol.,* 1963, *67,* 371-378.

Orne, M. T. The nature of hypnosis: Artifact and essence. *J. Abnorm. Soc. Psychol.,* 1959, *58,* 277-299.

Orne, M. T. On the social psychology of the psychological experiment: With particular reference to demand characteristics and their implications. *Amer. Psychol.,* 1962, *17,* 776-783.

Orne, M. T., and Evans, F. J. Social control in the psychological experiment: Antisocial behavior and hypnosis. *J. Pers. Soc. Psychol.,* 1965, *1,* 189-200.

Patten, E. F. The duration of post-hypnotic suggestion. *J. Abnorm. Soc. Psychol.,* 1930, *25,* 319-334.

Rosenhan, D. On the social psychology of hypnosis research. In J. E. Gordon (Ed.) *Handbook of clinical and experimental hypnosis.* New York: Macmillan, 1967. Pp. 481-510.

Rosenhan, D., and London, P. Hypnosis: Expectation, susceptibility, and performance. *J. Abnorm. Soc. Psychol.,* 1963, *66,* 77-81.

Rosenhan, D., and Tomkins, S. S. On preference for hypnosis and hypnotizability. *Int. J. Clin. Exp. Hypn.,* 1964, *12,* 109-114.

Rosenthal, R. Experimenter expectancy and the reassuring nature of the null hypothesis decision procedure. *Psychol. Bull., 1968, 70,* (6, Pt. 2), 30-47.

Sachs, L. B., and Anderson, W. L. Modification of hypnotic susceptibility. *Int. J. Clin. Exp. Hypn.,* 1967, *15,* 172-180.

Sarbin, T. R. Role theoretical interpretation of psychological change. In P. Worchel and D. Byrne (Ed.) *Personality change.* New York: Wiley, 1964. Pp. 176-219.

Sarbin, T. R., and Andersen, M. L. Role-theoretical analysis of hypnotic behavior. In J. E. Gordon (Ed.) *Handbook of clinical and experimental hypnosis.* New York: Macmillan, 1967. Pp. 319-344.

Sarbin, T. R., and Lim, D. T. Some evidence in support of the role-taking hypothesis in hypnosis. *Int. J. Clin. Exp. Hypn.,* 1963, *11,* 98-103.

Secter, I. I. An investigation of hypnotizability as a function of attitude toward hypnosis. *Amer. J. Clin. Hypn.,* 1960, *3,* 75-89.

Shor, R. E. Physiological effects of painful stimulation during hypnotic analgesia. In J. E. Gordon (Ed.) *Handbook of clinical and experimental hypnosis.* New York: Macmillan, 1967. Pp. 511-549.

Shor, R. E., Orne, M. T., and O'Connell, D. N. Validation and cross-validation of a scale of self-reported personal experiences which predicts hypnotizability. *J. Psychol.,* 1962, *53,* 55-57.

Shor, R. E., Orne, M. T., and O'Connell, D. N. Psychological correlates of plateau hypnotizability in a special volunteer sample. *J. Pers. Soc. Psychol.,* 1966, *3,* 80-95.

Slotnick, R., and London, P. Influence of instructions on hypnotic and nonhypnotic performance. *J. Abnorm. Psychol.*, 1965, *70*, 38-48.

Spanos, N. P., and Barber, T. X. "Hypnotic" experiences as inferred from subjective reports: Auditory and visual hallucinations. *J. Exp. Res. Pers.*, 1968, *3*, 136-150.

Spanos, N. P., and Chaves, J. F. Two hypnotic paradigms: An overview and evaluation. Dept. of Sociology, Boston University, 1968. (Mimeo)

Spielberger, C. D., and DeNike, L. D. Descriptive behaviorism versus cognitive theory in verbal operant conditioning. *Psychol. Rev.*, 1966, *73*, 306-326.

Sutcliffe, J. P. "Credulous" and "skeptical" views of hypnotic phenomena: A review of certain evidence and methodology. *Int. J. Clin. Exp. Hypn.*, 1960, *8*, 73-101.

Thorne, D. E., and Beier, E. G. Hypnotist and manner of presentation effects on a standardized hypnotic susceptibility test. *J. Cons. Clin. Psychol.*, 1968, *32*, 610-612.

Troffer, S. A. H. Hypnotic age regression and cognitive functioning. Unpublished doctoral dissertation, Stanford University, 1966.

Troffer, S. A. H., and Tart, C. T., Experimenter bias in hypnotist performance. *Science,* 1964, *145*, 1330-1331.

Weitzenhoffer, A. M. *General techniques of hypnotism.* New York: Grune & Stratton, 1957.

Weizenhoffer, A. M., and Hilgard, E. R. *Stanford hypnotic susceptibility scale: Forms A and B.* Palo Alto, California: Consulting Psychologists Press, 1959.

Weitzenhoffer, A. M., and Hilgard, E. R. *Stanford hypnotic susceptibility scale: Form C.* Palo Alto, California: Consulting Psychologists Press, 1962.

Weitzenhoffer, A. M., and Weitzenhoffer, G. B. Sex, transference, and susceptibility to hypnosis. *Amer. J. Clin. Hypn.*, 1958, *1*, 15-24.

Williamsen, J. A., Johnson, H. J., and Eriksen, C. W. Some characteristics of posthypnotic amnesia. *J. Abnorm. Psychol.*, 1965, *70*, 123-131.

Wilson, D. L. The role of confirmation of expectancies in hypnotic induction. Unpublished doctoral dissertation, University of North Carolina, 1967.

Name Index

319

Subject Index